First Edition

Handwritten notes:
week 5 ch 4 + 5
week 6 Ch 8
week 7 ch 8
week 8 ch 9
9 ch 13
10 —
11 —
12 ch 8, 10, 11
13 ch 12
14 ch. 14

PARENT EDUCATION

WORKING WITH GROUPS AND INDIVIDUALS

Handwritten: UMN internetid BITTN060

D0770263

Deborah Campbell and Glen Palm

Bassim Hamadeh, CEO and Publisher
Kassie Graves, Director of Acquisitions and Sales
Jamie Giganti, Senior Managing Editor
Jess Estrella, Senior Graphic Designer
Jim Brace-Thompson, Acquisitions Editor
Brian Fahey, Senior Licensing Specialist
Abbey Hastings, Associate Production Editor

Cover image copyright © 2015 by iStockphoto LP/svetikd.
copyright © 2015 by iStockphoto LP/pixdeluxe.
copyright © 2016 by iStockphoto LP/Petar Chernaev.

Printed in the United States of America

ISBN: 978-1-5165-1527-1 (pbk) / 978-1-5165-1528-8 (br)

cognella® | ACADEMIC PUBLISHING

ACKNOWLEDGMENTS

The authors wish to acknowledge the following programs, organizations, groups of people, and individuals who supported our work as parent educators, teacher educators, administrators, and researchers to help us understand the importance of parent education and inspire us to write about science and artistry of the field that we have witnessed in Minnesota and around the country. We want to thank and acknowledge:

- The many parents and children in Early Childhood Family Education programs who have given us the opportunity to learn from them and grow as parent educators.
- The families and staff who participated in Minnesota Family Literacy programs in St. Cloud, Sauk Rapids, Worthington, and Willmar for the pioneering work in developing successful two-generation programs.
- The parents and children in the Sauk Rapids–Rice and District 742 (St. Cloud) Early Childhood Family Education programs whose photographs appear in the text.
- The parent education students at St. Cloud State University who have participated in our classes, shared a passion for the field, and encouraged us through their questions to continue to learn and explore new ideas for improving practice.
- The professional parent educators we have observed, mentored, and learned from in our work as teacher educators and supervisors.
- The National Parenting Education Network for its continued efforts to move the field of parent education forward and colleagues Betty Cooke, Mary Kay Stranik, Dana McDermott, Harriet Heath, and Stephanie Jones for the discussion on parent educator roles and competencies.
- The National Council on Family Relations and the leadership of Dawn Cassidy in the growth and development of the Certified Family Life

Educator credential that has provided a model for a national credential for parent and family educators.

- The Minnesota Council on Family Relations and the Ethics Committee for the continued focus on ethical thinking and practice as critical to best practices in the field of parent and family education.
- The Minnesota Association for Family and Early Education for the support of the Parent Education Core Curriculum Framework as a tool for creating tailored parenting curricula.
- Minnesota Fathers and Families Network and fatherhood colleagues Rob Palkovitz, Jay Fagan, Lowell Johnson, and Adrienne Burgess who have helped keep a clear focus on the importance of fathers in families.
- Greater St. Cloud Area Thrive as an early childhood mental health initiative that has modeled collaborative work among practitioners and the Access Project that has built bridges of understanding between immigrant and refugee parents and early childhood practitioners in our community.
- Aline Auerbach, Delores Curran, Jean Illsley Clarke, Linda Braun, Jennifer Coplon, Phyllis Sonnenschein, Charles Smith, Judy Myers-Walls, Wally Goodard, Steve Duncan, Bill Doherty, and Ted Bowman whose works we have used as a foundation for teaching about group process in the field of parent education.
- Jim Brace-Thompson, Senior Specialist Acquisitions Editor at Cognella for his ongoing support and encouragement on this project.
- Our spouses Larry Campbell and Jane Ellison whose encouragement, support, and patience helped us complete this project.
- Our children who have taught us about the joys and challenges of parenting and the value of parent education and support for all parents.
- Our grandchildren who delight us with their energy, curiosity, and love.

Latin Families - Ballard

Strengths - Familismo
       Simpatías - politeness
       Religion
       Machismo / Marianismo

Concerns -
      navigating US legal + social systems
      educational success for children
      language barriers
      transportation issues
      financial support

Barriers - immigr. status, childcare, transportation
      language

Modes of learning - relaxed, inclusive, music, small group
      humor, stories

Program successes: FLAME, Chicago

CONTENTS

GROUP PARENT EDUCATION:
Rationale and Assumptions

Group parent education is alive and flourishing in thousands of programs across the United States and in other parts of the world (Carter, 1996; Bennett & Grimley, 2001; Long, 1997; NPEN, 2016; Stolz, 2011). A group of mothers of toddlers meets one morning a week in Chicago at a Family Resource Center to discuss some of the challenges of managing the energy and emerging independence of 2-year-olds. A group of fathers of Head Start children in California meets once a month to play with their children and talk about how to be involved in their children's lives in positive ways. A group of first time parents of infants meets weekly in the evening for eight weeks at a hospital in Washington, D.C, to learn more about infant development and the changing dynamics of family life. Immigrant parents of young children meet in a family literacy program twice a week to learn English, attend parent education classes, and spend time with their children in parent-child interaction time. Parents of preteens meet for four evenings at a middle school in North Carolina to learn about puberty and the physical changes that 10- to 12-year-olds experience and how to support their children's learning and social development. A group of fathers in a state prison meet once a week for three months in Minnesota to learn how to create and maintain a supportive relationship with their children. In each of these programs, a parent educator is responsible for organizing the sessions and guiding parent learning in a group context.

This book is written to examine group dynamics in parent education groups where emotions are intense and the diversity of parent experiences creates a powerful and complex learning environment. Parent educators must understand group dynamics unique to parent education as well as individual needs and personalities as they guide parents in learning to trust each other, listen to each other, and understand typical child development and family changes while addressing immediate concerns. Facilitating parent groups is challenging work. It demands parent educators who are skilled in working with diverse groups and individuals while facilitating group learning and maintaining a positive and supportive group environment where parents learn from each other and the facilitator.

This chapter will describe reasons that group parent education continues to be an effective format for supporting parent growth and development in contemporary society. The chapter's second section articulates basic assumptions about parents and group parent education that form the foundation for effective practice. The final section describes the major goals of the book and outlines the content of each chapter.

Box 1.1 Parent Education Definitions

Parent Education is the general term for providing information and support to parents to develop new understanding and skills that support the parent-child relationship and promote positive child growth and development. This can be done in a number of different formats, including small groups, individually, large group presentations, webinars, or online classes.

Group Parent Education is parent education that is provided to a small group of parents (typically 8–12) for a specified period of time, typically 4–20+ weeks, that meet on a weekly basis. This format will involve a specific focus, such as discipline issues, or a more general curriculum.

Individual Parent Education is parent education that is offered to an individual parent or co-parents that focuses on individualized parenting goals that are developed in collaboration with the parent(s). It is often conducted in the parent's home but could also be in an office or a comfortable private space.

Parents gather on a weekly basis for support and discussion

RATIONALES FOR GROUP PARENT EDUCATION

Why is group parent education an important and effective format for parent learning? This question will be addressed by looking at the changing social context for parenting and the changing needs of parents (Lerner & Nightingale, 2016). Those participating in parent education groups range from middle-income fathers of infants in Florida to low-income single mothers in South Carolina and mothers of toddlers in a suburb in Minnesota to parents of children with disabilities in Washington (Carter, 1996; Senior, 2014). Group parent education programs are located in schools, community centers, prisons, and hospitals (Carter, 1996). These classes are sponsored by a variety of health care, human services, and education agencies and address a complex array of parent needs (Smith, Cudaback, Goddard, & Myers-Wall, 1994; National Academies of of Sciences, Engineering, and Medicine, 2016). Parents come to parent education groups for many different reasons:

- To learn about child development and what to expect

- To learn how to manage toddler tantrums
- To learn how to support child self-esteem through effective communication
- To learn how to keep their infants and toddlers safe
- To develop negotiation skills around sharing child-rearing responsibilities
- To learn how to support and enhance child learning and readiness for school
- To understand new research about brain development in young children
- To learn new strategies for child guidance
- To discuss co-parenting after a divorce or separation

Parents come to parent education with many different goals and beliefs about parenting. They are looking for ideas and support to be good parents. Some people believe that parents come to parent education classes only because they have problems managing their children's behavior. There are many parent education programs that are targeted towards parents who have children with behavior problems (e.g., Webster-Stratton, 2000). There are also parent education programs for parents who are going through divorce (McKenry, Clark, & Stone, 1999) and for parents who are at risk for child abuse (Bavelok & Bavelok, 1988). The emergence of universal access programs for parents of young children in Missouri and Minnesota during the last 35 years has begun to shift this view of parent education as a solution to problems toward a more inclusive view that parent education is a preventive service that can be beneficial for all parents (Carter, 1996; MNAFEE, 2015). Parent education can support individual growth and development as parents face typical challenges in the family life cycle, in addition to assisting families who may face specific challenges.

Parents in the 21st century are more aware of the diverse resources available to them (e.g., classes, video resources, books, magazines, websites, blogs, and apps) to learn about parenting (Walker, 2015). They may also be confused by the conflicting advice of parenting experts (Simpson, 1997; National Academies of Sciences, Engineering, and Medicine, 2016). Parents realize that the way that their own parents raised them may not be the most effective way to meet their own children's needs or it doesn't address the new issues they are facing in raising their children. For example, the use of cell phones and social media by children are new concerns. Most parents today also face the task of balancing a career or work and family life in a fast-paced, information-rich society. Parents are further acutely aware of the perceived faults and failings of their own parents and how these have influenced their own lives. Parents worry about their children growing up too soon and the dangers they may face as they move into a world where the media and digital technologies (games and websites) depict violence and explicit sexuality (Walsh, 2001). Many parents are having fewer children and don't want to or don't have the time to learn by trial and error, so they look to parent education and the support of other parents in parent groups as resources for how to best raise their children. They realize that parent education can be a practical educational investment with long-term benefits for their children and family.

Group parent education remains a viable and powerful educational format to meet parent needs for support, information, a sense of community, and direct contact with other parents (Carter, 1996; Lerner & Nightengale, 2016). The proliferation of parenting books, magazines, video resources, and Internet sites has given parents greater access to information and a variety of perspectives on how to raise children (Simpson, 1997; Walker, 2015). While these resources have made information readily available, they have also created a new set of issues for parents. Which sources are the most credible and relevant to their situations or contexts and offer useful information? What happens when parents receive contradictory information about parenting practices from books, the Internet, their own parents, friends, and their family doctors? Should parents put their babies to bed and let them cry for 10 minutes before they pick them up and comfort them? Should they allow their child to sleep in the same room with them? Should they "train" babies to comfort themselves, so they can put themselves to sleep? What happens when their baby gets an ear infection and is up most of the night after they have been trying for the last 2 weeks to get the baby to learn how to sleep on his or her own? Parents find groups of other parents a valuable resource to learn about what has worked for someone else, find out about what is normal, and get support for making the right decisions for themselves and their families. Parent groups can be a valuable source of both information and support for parents, especially when a knowledgeable, sensitive, and competent parent educator can guide groups in discussing parenting issues in a safe and supportive environment. Though parents may not always have the time to commit to group parent education, it is a place where many parents are able to form new friendships and networks of support as they face both the perennial and contemporary challenges of parenthood.

Some parent education programs also provide the opportunity for parents to bring their young children to a class and spend part of the time together in an environment with other children of the same age, engaging in fun and educational activities (Kurz-Riemer, 2001; Campbell & Palm, 2004). In Minnesota where both of the authors have worked in Early Childhood Family Education (ECFE) programs for the last 30 years, parents bring their children, ages 0 through 5 to programs on a weekly basis for 1- to 2-hour sessions that include both parent-child time and parent discussion time. One advantage of this type of program is that parents are able to observe their children interacting with other same-age children. They also are able to observe other parents and early childhood educators and how they interact with young children. Parents in this context are able to see and understand typical child behavior and have a better understanding of their own children. They see that all 2-year-olds struggle with sharing toys. The parent educator also has an opportunity to observe both parent and child behavior and to better understand the dynamics and issues that a parent brings to a parent education session. A parent of a 2-1/2 year old son who is not interested in toilet training is given specific information about signs of readiness from the parent educator. Other parents in the group empathize with the frustration of trying to be patient and wait for a child to be "ready" when the parent is anxious and eager to be finished with diapers.

Parent education in groups has been an effective method for giving parents information and support in the United States for over 90 years (Auerbach, 1968; Braun, Coplon & Sonnenschien, 1984; Brim, 1959; Carter, 1996; Campbell & Palm, 2004). It continues to be an important service to parents and meets the needs of parents today by giving them information in a supportive context with face-to-face interaction with other parents. Parent education practice has evolved to include a variety of theories and perspectives on child rearing (Cowan, Powell, & Cowan, 1998; Palm, 2003). A new integration of these perspectives can guide parent educators towards skillful and reflective practice. Our understanding of parent growth, group process, family dynamics, parenting strategies, and child development has made the practice of parent education in groups more sophisticated and complex (Darling & Cassidy, 2014). The multiple perspectives from different disciplines provide a foundation for the practice of parent education. Diverse family and community settings demand new ideas and strategies that match content to family and community needs (Powell, 1986). This book will integrate these perspectives to better illustrate how one can become an effective group leader within a variety of parent groups.

Parent education in groups can be very powerful as parents learn to trust each other and to openly share feelings about parenting. Parents are exposed to different ideas about child guidance. A good parent educator helps parents explore their own goals and values, as well as individual child needs in considering how to select and use guidance and teaching strategies. Parents begin to appreciate that parenting is an important and complex set of responsibilities that deserves their best energy and efforts. Parent groups will often encounter emotional land mines when participants are trying to sort through their own emerging ideas about parenting from the legacy of their experiences as children (Gadsden & Hall, 1995). The certainty of one parent about how to handle an eating issue with a 4-year-old can make two other parents in the group doubt their own effectiveness or competence as parents. Parents may hear or observe other 3-year-olds who seem to be so well behaved, while their own 3-year-old child is demanding, is always active, and never seems to listen to them. These represent special challenges that need to be handled effectively if the group experience is to help, not harm or undermine, parents' sense of competence.

Learning child development information and learning parenting strategies are initial steps to becoming effective parents. Parents must also decide what they value in terms of child behavior (Crary, 1993). Do they want their child to be a leader, to be obedient, to be sensitive to the feelings of others, to have good manners? They must consider all of the options for guiding a child's behavior while understanding their child as an individual with unique temperamental and personality characteristics (Kurcinka, 1989). Group parent educators come into contact with strong beliefs about parenting goals and strategies, as well as raw, intense emotions related to their own childhood experiences and current feelings of success and failure. A parent educator must be prepared to guide parent learning and decision making where parents are deeply invested in doing the best they can, because they love their children.

This book is designed to build on a long tradition of group parent education as a practical way to inform and support parents. Through effective group facilitation, parents can become more confident with new skills and understanding to fully experience the joys and manage the challenges of parenting. The next section outlines important assumptions about group parent education that guide current practice.

Literacy activities help prepare children for school

ASSUMPTIONS ABOUT PARENTS AND PARENT EDUCATION

The practice of group parent education, as described in this book, rests upon a number of important assumptions about parents and the process of group parent education. The following assumptions provide a description of the beliefs and values that guide our perspective of group parent education.

1. Parents care deeply about their children and want to be good parents.

The emotional bond between parent and child is intense, deep, and complex. The literature on attachment research provides some insight into the dynamics of this bond, primarily from a child's perspective (Karen, 1998). This assumption is also based on our observations and experiences with multiple parents in different settings over the last 30 years. Parents care deeply about their children and are motivated to be good parents and do what they think is best for their children (NCOFF, 1995). At the same time, many parents struggle with knowing how to express this caring and are often uncertain about which parenting approaches and strategies will be the most effective and appropriate for their children. Parents who have experienced trauma during their childhoods may need additional help in developing a positive parent-child relationship.

2. All parents grow and learn through the challenges of parenting.

Parenthood is an important impetus for learning (Cowan & Cowan, 1988; Galinsky, 1987; McBride, 1973; Newman & Newman, 1988; Palm, 1993; Snarey, 1993). Most parents have developed some capacity for caring for their children before the children are born, and others learn it through the experience of parenting. Parenting is a challenge to most new parents. It also provides a unique opportunity for the growth and development of cognitive and emotional skills in parents (Newman & Newman, 1988; Palkovitz, 2002). Parent education in groups presents parents with information about child development and the typical issues that parents face. This provides some normalization of parent concerns and feelings. It also provides parents with new ideas about typical developmental issues. Group parent education offers a safe space to talk about parent-child relationships and honors the emotional depth of this bond. Parents, as individuals, have the potential to grow into more caring, other-directed, and empathic adults as they take on the responsibilities of child nurturance and guidance (Palkovitz & Palm, 1998). Group parent education can facilitate this growth by supporting parents through typical developmental transitions, as well as through periods of stress and crisis (Palkovitz & Palm, 2009). Parent growth is acknowledged and affirmed in a supportive group context.

3. Parents bring a unique combination of experiences and strengths to parenting.

Parents do not come as blank slates to group parent education (McGillicuddy-DeLisi, 1990). They come with their own experiences of growing up in different family settings. They have the imprints of the beliefs and practices that their parents used in raising them. They bring their own images of good parenting. These ideas may coincide with how they were raised or may be in sharp contrast to their own parents' beliefs (Galinsky, 1987). All parents bring their own unique understanding of parenting to a group parent education experience. They also bring unique strengths and perspectives that can benefit the group in exploring good parenting practices. Parent groups can be enriched by the diverse experiences and strengths of the parents in a group. The parent educator must tap into these resources by providing a safe space to explore these experiences and affirming the latent strengths that parents bring to a group (Curran, 1983; Family Resource Coalition, 1996).

4. Parenting is shaped by parent beliefs, knowledge, and skills.

In working with parents in groups, it is important to address parent beliefs, parent knowledge, and parenting behavior. For example, some parents may believe that children are born as innocent, blank slates to be inscribed with the values that parents hold most dear. Other parents may believe that children will have a natural tendency to manipulate parents and must be controlled in a strict and consistent manner so that they will not become spoiled and demanding children and adults. Parent beliefs are not always easy to understand, and parents may not hold a logically consistent set of beliefs. The parent educator must assist parents in clarifying and articulating their beliefs through clarifying questions and sometimes gentle confrontation. The knowledge that a parent brings to a parent group may consist primarily of his or her own limited experience growing up in a small family with one or two siblings. It may also be based on formal education in child development or work experience with many different children in various circumstances. In this context, parents may have developed fairly sophisticated understandings and skills for managing a child's behavior. All of these experiences must be honored in a group parent education setting, for they all make up the rich mix of resources that group members bring to the process (Curran, 1989).

5. Group parent education has a unique and enduring role to play in the evolving field of parent education.

Today, there are numerous ways for parents to receive and process new information on child rearing. Printed information in books, parenting magazines, and newspaper columns has been a common source of information during the past 100 years and continues to be popular and accessible (Simpson, 1997). The introduction of video resources (i.e., TV programs about parenting, educational video resources) and Internet resources (websites, podcasts, webinars) has brought the advice of the experts into the privacy of parents' homes, where they can access this information at their convenience. The use of social media (Facebook, Twitter, etc.) has also provided new avenues for social communication and support. Despite the increasing amount and accessibility of information and advice on parenting, the role of the parent group can still play an important role for many families. The group replaces some of the informal support systems that parents had in previous generations. Many new parents do not live close to their own parents, who may be less accessible, as grandparents continue to work and pursue their own careers and interests. Many parents are eager to hear about the challenges of parenting from peers facing similar issues unfamiliar to their own parents, who raised children in a different generation with different expectations and demands. Grandparents who, on occasion, attend parent groups with their children and grandchildren comment on new ideas and challenges that their children face as parents. They often mention the value they see in parent education groups in providing information and support that they wished they had received.

6. Parents learn from each other and help define and understand norms while adjusting their own ideals with current realities.

Group parent education provides a unique social context for helping parents define their own ideals and compare these ideals with group norms. Galinsky (1987) described a model of parent growth and development that is based upon comparing ideal images of what children and parent-child relations should be like with the realities of parenting that they experience. The group context of parent education can give a parent of a toddler new understanding of the toddler's typical push for independence when the group discusses tantrums. Parents may also raise their expectations for their children if they see that other 2-year-olds are able to sit still during a snack time. Parents often use their observations of other children as a way to adjust their own expectations and behavior toward their children (Galinsky, 1987). The parent group provides an opportunity for parents to do this in a direct and interactive manner by discussing expectations, individual differences, and the most effective ways to guide their children toward acceptable social behavior. Guided observation is a regular part of some parent education groups. Good parent educators are able to guide parent discussion and thinking toward a clear understanding of developmental norms and the application of these norms to individual children.

7. Parents represent diverse family and community contexts, beliefs about parenting, and cultural values.

Parent educators must be able to understand and appreciate this diversity in parents and adapt their approach for the needs and goals of different groups. Family diversity manifests itself in a variety of different ways that characterize family life in America today (Fine & Lee, 2000). First, family structure has been changing to include more single-parent families, cohabiting couples, gay and lesbian families, and blended families, in addition to the two-parent married family (Demo, Allen, & Fine, 2000). Another area of family diversity that has a major impact on family life is parent employment patterns. There are dual career families, the more traditional breadwinner and stay-at-home parent family, and families where one parent works full-time and the other parent works part-time. In single-parent and extended family structures, employment patterns also vary. Cultural diversity is another important area of diversity that influences family life and must be considered in group parent education (Fine & Lee, 2000). The increasing number of children of color and the dramatic increase of new immigrants from all parts of the world present additional challenges to parent educators (National Academies of Sciences, Engineering, and Medicine, 2016). Parent educators who work with parents in groups must be able to understand the potential impacts of family diversity upon parent groups. It is often easier to facilitate a group that is more homogeneous. There are limits to group heterogeneity that parent groups can accommodate and still function effectively. The parent educator must address parent differences in an open and respectful manner that helps parents to better understand both their own views and those of other parents. Diversity can be a powerful catalyst for new ways of thinking and acting as a parent. Diversity within parent groups can also be a powerful resource for new understanding and acceptance of different approaches to parenting.

8. All parents can benefit from access to parent education opportunities.

One of the tensions that has emerged in parent education is the focus on targeted parent education as the most cost-effective use of limited resources. While research supports the notion that targeted groups tend to benefit more than non-targeted groups, there are some problems with making parent education an intervention for certain groups (National Academies of Sciences, Engineering, and Medicine, 2016). This approach creates or reinforces a stigma around parent education as a service only for people with parenting deficits. In addition, it creates a practical problem of having to identify who "needs" parent education services. Universal access as an approach has unexplored potential benefits, including building the capacity of all parents to provide positive parenting to their children, preventing problems that otherwise might occur, decreasing parent and family stress, building a sense of community among new parents, and creating a belief that parenting offers an opportunity for individual growth and development.

9. Facilitating group parent education is an art that blends a parent educator's dispositions, skills, and knowledge to meet the needs of a specific parent group.

This artistry is honed through experience and reflective practice and consultation to increase the effectiveness of parent group leaders. Different professionals and paraprofessionals provide parent education in a variety of contexts (Cowan, Powell, & Cowan, 1998; Heath & Palm, 2006; Jones, Stranik, Hart, McClintic, & Wolf, 2013). An underlying premise of this book is that group parent education involves a set of complex tasks that requires specific preparation and focused development of competencies that leads to effective practice. The development of certification and licensure programs for parent educators has provided some of the important dimensions of preparation for this work. The National Council on Family Relations (NCFR) has created a framework for content areas for family life educators through the Certified Family Life Educator (CFLE) program (Darling & Cassidy, 2014). The Minnesota Board of Teaching has defined a specific set of teacher competencies for licensure in parent education. Parent group education, as an art, still needs to be more carefully explored to identify the critical characteristics, boundaries, and dimensions (Small & Kupisk, 2015). This book attempts to articulate the unique features of group parent education and to advance this artistry through a deeper understanding of parent group dynamics and effective group facilitation skills.

This book is written for professionals who deliver parent education through groups, both current practitioners and students at the undergraduate and graduate levels who are preparing to work with parents in groups. These students may be in parent and family life education, social work, early childhood education, nursing, or marriage and family therapy programs. This book is written to apply to a variety of parent groups with the major emphasis on education versus therapy or peer support groups (Braun et al., 1984; Myers-Wall et al., 2011).

GOALS FOR THE BOOK

The book will address a number of important goals in attempting to move the practice of group parent education to a new integrated level of understanding that incorporates family diversity, a variety of theoretical perspectives, and best practices derived from the literature and our own clinical experiences. These goals include:

1. Understanding how parents learn and grow through group parent education.

It is important to understand how parents learn in the context of parent education groups and how they adopt new ideas and behaviors to use as they interact with their children. The sharing and processing of new ideas and feelings with a parent group provides multiple pathways to new learning.

2. Understanding the various perspectives/theories that guide practice.

Parent education in groups has become more complex and sophisticated. It currently incorporates a number of different frameworks that must be understood at a basic level to appreciate the benefits of each perspective. Multiple conceptual frameworks provide a unique blend of insights into the complex dynamics of parent group education.

3. Understanding and managing diversity in parent groups.

The increase in diversity of family structures, cultural beliefs, and parenting practices makes the facilitation of parent groups more complex and challenging. This complexity can lead not only to more opportunities for learning, but also to more potential hazards to parents who are trying to develop parenting beliefs and practices consistent with their values and goals for their children. Cultural beliefs and values about parenting are also evolving as families adapt to social and technological changes. Many immigrant families, for example, face the challenge of adapting to United States values and laws about child-rearing and discipline practices that are confusing and often in apparent conflict with traditional values from their countries of origin and their own experiences growing up.

4. Understanding and managing the dynamic balance between education and support in parent groups.

Most parent education includes new information for parents, as well as emotional support for the difficult choices that parents make and the stressful issues that today's parents face. Education and support are approached as dynamic forces that can be carefully blended and balanced. Some parents are looking for new ideas about child rearing, whereas others are seeking support for the challenges they face in raising an active toddler or a challenging teen.

5. Understanding the important skills educators need to effectively facilitate parent groups and individual learning.

We are learning more about group process as it applies to parent groups and the emotional content that parents bring to parent education sessions. This book articulates the specific skills that parent educators need to manage group dynamics and individual learning. This focus on skills is offered to help individuals examine their current facilitation skills, to assess their strengths, and to identify areas for improvement.

6. Exploring common problems/challenges in group parent education and possible strategies for addressing these problems.

The book will address specific problems that are common in parent groups today. It is helpful for group leaders to gain insight into these behaviors to understand their possible origins and meanings. These situations will be examined along with a range of possible strategies to apply.

7. Examining parent education services and a continuum model for families, including families with complex needs, and providing some guidelines and boundaries for practice.

Parent education has been seen as an important service for families with many different needs, including families with literacy needs, families with children with disabilities, and families with parents who have been neglectful or abusive. Parent group leaders need to understand the unique challenges of this work and to develop strategies that address some of the issues they will face.

OVERVIEW OF THE CONTENTS OF THE BOOK

Chapter 2 presents an historical perspective of parent education, including recent developments and their implications for practice. Chapter 3 introduces a continuum model of parent education practice and the multi-disciplinary collaboration that can best serve parents with different needs and from different contexts. This chapter also examines the relationship patterns between parent educator and parent at different levels. Chapter 4 describes several conceptual perspectives to understand the development and dynamics of groups. Four main frameworks from related disciplines will be examined and applied to parent education groups. Chapter 5 explores four frameworks that describe the role of the leader of parent groups. It examines the function and character of the leader, the value of modeling, and the parallel process for parent group leaders. Chapter 6 describes the design process for parent education programs and curricula.

Chapter 7 focuses on the critical component of parent education—the relationship between parent educators and parents. Content examines the important interpersonal connections within professional boundaries that are imperative for parent educators to develop as part of healthy group development and the importance of understanding group members and their behaviors. Chapters 8 and 9 address specific facilitation skills for leading groups of parents. Strategies for handing difficult moments and behaviors in groups, and strategies for referrals will be addressed. Chapters 10 and 11 examine some of the special considerations, issues, and challenges of working with targeted populations, along with intervention strategies. Chapter 12 focuses on working with parents individually as a complementary role to group parent education. It includes individual consultation (coaching), individual sessions, and home visits. Chapter 13 describes the benefits of incorporating parent-child interaction time into group parent education and discusses how to design this component to provide for the practice of new skills. Chapter 14 examines the role of professionalism for parent educators, looking at the stages of growth, what knowledge and skills are necessary at different levels and what support professionals need as they grow and develop. The book ends with a Conclusion that looks ahead to the future of parent education and the need for change in the field to continue to meet the goals and needs of contemporary families.

SUMMARY

The continued importance of group parent education and the evolution and improvement of parent group education practice are the reasons for exploring the goals in this book. Our understanding of parent group dynamics and effective practices has continued to grow through increasing knowledge about family, parent-child relationships, and adult education. The artistry that Auerbach described in her 1968 book provides a useful perspective for contemporary parent educators. This book is presented as an integration of our growing understanding of both theory and practice of group parent education. Reflective practice is described as an effective approach to supporting practice and moving the field toward a better understanding of the continued need for program evaluation, experimentation, and adaptation by skilled and experienced parent education professionals.

DISCUSSION QUESTIONS

1. Why are group parent education programs an appropriate and effective format for contemporary parents in the United States?

2. Do you agree with the statement that all parents care deeply about their children? Why or why not?

3. What does parent education as artistry mean to you?

REFERENCES

Auerbach, A. (1968). *Parents learn through discussion: Principles and practices of parent group education.* New York, NY: John Wiley.

Bavelok, S., & Bavelok, J. (1988). *Nurturing program for parents and children birth to five years: Parent handbook.* Eau Claire, WI: Family Development Resources.

Bennett, J., & Grimley, L. (2001). Parenting in the global community: A cross-cultural/ international perspective. In M. Fine & S. Lee (Eds.) *Handbook of diversity in parent education* (pp. 97–133). San Diego, CA: Academic Press.

Braun, L., Coplon, J., & Sonnenschien, P. (1984). *Helping parents in groups.* Boston, MA: Wheelock Center on Parenting Studies.

Brim, O. (1959). *Education for child rearing.* New York, NY: Russell Sage Foundation.

Campbell, D., & Palm, G.F. (2004). *Group parent education: Promoting parent learning and support.* Thousand Oaks, CA: Sage Publications.

Carter, N. (1996). *See how they grow: A report on the status of parenting education in the U.S.* Philadelphia, PA: Pew Charitable Trusts.

Cowan, C.P., & Cowan, P.A. (1988). Who does what when parents become partners: Implications for men, women, and marriage. *Marriage and Family Review, 13,* 105–132.

Cowan, P.A., Powell, D., & Cowan, C.P. (1998). Parenting interventions: A family systems perspective. In I.E. Sigel & K.A. Renninger (Eds.), *Handbook of child psychology, Vol. 4: Child psychology in practice* (pp. 3–72). New York, NY: John Wiley.

Crary, E. (1993). *Without spanking or spoiling.* Seattle, WA: Parenting Press.

Curran, D. (1983). *Traits of a healthy family.* Minneapolis, MN: Winston Press.

Curran, D. (1989). *Working with parents.* Circle Pines, MN: American Guidance Service.

Darling, C., & Cassidy, D., with Powell, L. (2014). *Family life education: Working with families across the life span.* Long Grove, IL: Waveland.

Demo, D., Allen, K., & Fine, M. (2000). *Handbook of family diversity.* New York, NY: Oxford University Press.

Duncan, S.F. & Goddard, H.W. (2011). *Family Life Education: Principles and practices for effective outreach.* (2nd ed.). Thousand Oaks, CA: Sage.

Family Resource Coalition (1996). *Guidelines for family support practice.* Chicago, IL: Author.

Fine, M., & Lee, S.D. (2000). *Handbook of diversity in parent education: The changing faces of parenting and parent education.* New York, NY: Academic Press.

Gadsden, V., & Hall, M. (1995). *Intergenerational learning: A review of the litera-ture.* Philadelphia, PA: National Center on Fathers and Families, University of Pennsylvania.

Galinsky, E. (1987). *The six stages of parenthood.* Reading, MA: Addison Wesley.

Heath, H. & Palm, G. (2006). Future challenges for parenting education and support. *Child Welfare, 85*(5), 885–895.

Jones, S.T., Stranik, M.K., Hart, M.G., McClintic, S., & Wolf, J.R. (2013). A closer look at diverse roles of practitioners in parenting education: Peer educators, para-professionals and professionals. National Parenting Education Network (NPEN) retrieved at http://npen.org/wp-content/uploads/2012/03/diverse-roles-in-PE-white-paper_-12_17_13.pdf.

Karen, R. (1998). *Becoming attached.* New York, NY: Oxford University Press.

Kurcinka, M.S. (1989). *Raising your spirited child.* New York, NY: Harper Perennial.

Kurz-Riemer, K. (Ed.) (2001*) A guide for implementing early childhood education pro-grams.* Roseville, MN: Minnesota Department of Children, Families and Learning.

Lerner, C. & Nightingale, M.O. (September, 2016). Tuning in: Parents of young children speak up about what they think, know, and need. *Zero to Three, 37*(2), 42–49.

Long, N. (1997). Parent education/training in the USA: Current status and future trends. *Clinical Child Psychology and Psychiatry, 2,* 501–515.

McBride, A.B. (1973). *The growth and development of mothers.* New York, NY: Barnes & Noble.

McGillicuddy-DeLisi, A.V. (1990). Parental beliefs within the family context: Development of a research program. In I.E. Sigel & G.H. Brody (Eds.), *Methods of family research: Biographies of research projects: Vol. 1. Normal families* (pp. 53–85). Hillsdale, NJ: Lawrence Erlbaum.

McKenry, P., Clarke, K., & Stone, G. (1999). Evaluation of a parent education program for divorcing parents. *Family Relations, 48*(2), 129–137.

MNAFEE (Minnesota Association for Family and Early Educators). (2015). *Minnesota's Early Childhood Family Education: Answers to commonly asked questions.* Retrieved at http://www.mnafee.org/vertical/sites/%7B2555CA3F-B6AD-4263-9177-3B66CE5F2892%7D/uploads/ECFE_Digital_FINAL.pdf.

Myers-Walls, J., Ballard, S., Darling, C. & Myers-Bowman, K. (2011). Reconceptualizing the domain and boundaries of Family Life Education. *Family Relations, 60,* 357–372.

National Academies of Sciences, Engineering, and Medicine. (2016). *Parenting mat-ters: Supporting parents of children 0–8.* Washing, DC: The National Academies Press. doi: 10.17226/21868.

National Center on Fathers and Families, University of Pennsylvania (1995). *Core learnings.* Philadelphia, PA: Author.

Newman, P.R., & Newman, B.M. (1988). Parenthood and adult development. In R. Palkovitz & M. Sussman (Eds.) *Transitions to parenthood.* (pp. 313–338). New York, NY: Haworth.

NPEN (National Parenting Education Network), Professional Preparation and Recognition Committee. (2016). Parenting educator competencies resource document. Retrieved from: npen.org/wp-content/uploads/216/04/Competencies2.23.16pdf.

Palkovitz, R., & Palm, G. (1998). Fatherhood and faith in formation: The developmental effects of fathering on religiosity, morals and values. *Journal of Men's Studies, 7*(1), 33–52.

Palkovitz, R. (2002). *Involved fathering and men's adult development: Provisional balances.* Nahweh, NJ: Lawrence Erlbaum Associates, Inc.

Palkovitz, R., & Palm, G. (2009). Transitions within Fatherhood. *Fathering, 7*(1) 3–22.

Palm, G. (1993). Involved fatherhood: A second chance. *Journal of Men's Studies, 2*(2), 139–155.

Palm, G.F. (2003). Parent education for incarcerated parents: Understanding "what works." In V. Gadsden (Ed.) *Heading home: Offender reintegration into the Family* (pp. 89–122). Lanham, MD: American Correctional Association.

Powell, D. (1986). Matching parents and programs. In J. Parsons, J., T. Bowman, J. Comeau, R. Pitzer, & G.S. Schmitt. (Eds.), *Parent education: State of the art* (pp. 1–11) White Bear Lake, MN: Minnesota Curriculum Services Center.

Senior, J. (2014). *All joy and no fun: The paradox of modern parenthood.* New York, NY: Harper-Collins Publisher.

Simpson, R. (1997). *The role of the mass media in parenting education.* Boston, MA: Center for Health Communication, Harvard School of Public Health.

Small, S., & Kupisk, D. (2015). Family life education: Wisdom in practice. In M.J. Walcheski & J. Reinke. (Eds.), *Family life education: The practice of family science* (pp. 17–26). Minneapolis, MN: National Council on Family Relations.

Smith, C.A., Cudaback. D., Goddard, H.W., & Myers-Walls, J. (1994). *National extension parent education model.* Manhattan, NY: Kansas Cooperative Extension Services.

Snarey, J. (1993). *How fathers care for the next generation: A four-decade study.* Cambridge, MA: Harvard University Press.

Stolz, H. (2011). Parenting Education. In S.F. Duncan & H.W. Goddard (Eds.) *Family life education: Principles and practices for effective outreach* (pp. 191–210). Thousand Oaks, CA: Sage.

Walsh, D. (2001). *Dr. Dave's cyberhood.* New York, NY: Fireside.

Walker, S.K. (2015). Family life and technology: Implications for the practice of family life education. In M.J. Walcheski & J. Reinke. (Eds.), *Family life education: The practice of family science* (pp. 117–130). Minneapolis, MN: National Council on Family Relations.

Webster-Stratton, C. (2000). The incredible years training series. *Juvenile Justice Bulletin* (pp.1–23).

THE HISTORY AND EVOLUTION OF GROUP PARENT EDUCATION

"We have seen that the leader in parent group education is part of a fascinating interplay of people and events in which he plays a decisive role. In taking on this role, he assumes responsibility to see that the group sessions become the learning experience for which the program is set up. The description of the procedures that facilitate this learning have naturally included what the leader does at various steps to help the parents achieve the group's goal. Obviously, his performance is not static or fixed. He acts in certain ways at certain times, as different stages of group development are reached and specific episodes occur. He acts as the particular moment requires and fits the immediate moment into the overall plan."

Auerbach, 1968

The leader in a parent education group plays a dynamic role in the complex process of group parent education. This is a role that has evolved over time as our understanding of children, parenting, adult education, and group processes has changed. This chapter will provide a brief historical review of the evolution of parent education in groups. The changing nature of parent education and the role of the group leader will be traced from the 1880s through the present. A review of recent factors (2000–2016) that have influenced the contemporary practice and implementation of parent education in the United States will be examined. An integrative model of competencies for group leaders in parent education will be presented to reflect our current understanding of this role. This model serves as a guide for self-evaluation and reflection on developing parent group facilitation knowledge and skills. An assessment tool is provided in Appendix A as a way for individuals to identify current strengths and limitations around competencies for parent group leadership.

HISTORICAL OVERVIEW OF GROUP PARENT EDUCATION

Parent education in groups has been traced back to the early 19th century, when groups of mothers in New England formed maternal associations (Berger, 2000). These groups, composed primarily of middle-class mothers, met and discussed issues such as discipline and moral training. They might be comparable to parent support groups where parents meet and share knowledge, experiences, and feelings as part of a mutual support and learning process. Groups of parents today also share experiences and gain knowledge and support through discussions on websites or through social media like Facebook (Walker, 2015). Early forms of mass media, such as books and magazines about parenting followed from the 1820s through the 1840s (Sunley, 1955). Parenting was becoming a more defined area of study, as seen in the thoughtful reflections and writings that were being produced during this time. The information and support that parents (mothers) can share in a group setting about the joys and challenges of child rearing were experienced by parents at least 200 years ago. Though little is known about the early years of parent education in the United States, we have more extensive information about the evolution of parent group education over the last 100 years (e.g., Auerbach, 1968; Brim, 1959).

Auerbach (1968) described the early evolution of parent group education as carried on by the Child Study Association, which began in 1888, when "a small group of mothers came together to get the best information they could find to help them understand and deal with their children" (p. 14). The fields of academic psychology, child development, and psychoanalysis began to develop a knowledge base that was shared with parents to improve their understanding of child development and to suggest effective parenting techniques. This information was shared with parents through public meetings, conferences, and written materials. Many parents were eager to learn about child psychology and to use this information generated by research and clinical practice to guide and improve their child rearing practices and family lives. Professionals in child psychology and parent education often led the small discussion groups for parents that emerged in the1920s. They shared the latest theories and research about child development and parenting techniques with parents in a lecture and discussion format (Anderson, 1930).

Parent education, as a unique field of study, began developing strong roots during the 1910s in several different disciplines. Public health nurses, social workers, early childhood educators, psychologists, and home economics educators all used the emerging knowledge base about child development and effective parenting to provide parent education services to different populations of parents. Public health nurses provided information on child rearing and health-related issues through home visits to low-income families. Health-related information about issues like feeding infants was of critical importance for infant wellbeing during this time, when the infant mortality rate was very high. Social workers provided information on parenting to poor immigrant families through settlement house programs in urban areas to help parents adjust to life in the United States. Psychologists and early childhood educators were more likely to work with middle-class parents in study groups or nursery school settings, sharing the latest research and theories about child development. The 1920s was a particularly active time for parent education as a discipline, which was connected to progressive education and the recognition of the importance of parents in children's early learning (Arlitt, 1932). The development of parent education services through different formats (parent groups, correspondence courses, and individual study) and the development of academic training for parent educators took place during this time (Anderson, 1930). In fact, parent education preparation was focused on graduate studies in the physical and mental development of children, adult education, methods of conducting study groups, child training, and field work (practice). The parent educators were also expected to be *mature* individuals who had previous experience working with children.

Discussion groups led by these trained parent educators were popular in the 1920s and 1930s (Arlitt, 1932). The first groups were conducted in a didactic manner as lectures, with the leader playing the role of a teacher and using situations for discussion and the application of child rearing methods. Auerbach (1968) described the evolution from the 1920s to the 1950s of different approaches to parent group education:

> At first, groups were conducted didactically, with the leader acting as the teacher in the traditional, academic sense. They then became lecture-discussions, with the leader acting as a speaker and answering questions in a

discussion period. Subsequently, they took the form of discussion groups, in which parents learn through participation in the group process. (p. 14)

In this latter approach to group parent education, the increasing knowledge about group dynamics and effective group facilitation skills emerged as important competencies for guiding parent learning. The study of small group behavior in the 1940s and 1950s influenced the changes in our approaches to group parent education and recommended a more active role for parents in defining and discussing parenting issues (Auerbach, 1968).

The continued development of group parent education during the 1950s and 1960s built on this new understanding of group process and how learning could be facilitated in groups, rather than taught in a more traditional lecture format. Auerbach (1968) described various trainings for parent group facilitators, from social work students and early childhood educators to public health nurses and church leaders that she conducted during the 1960s. These trainings were directed at different groups of professionals who were parent education practitioners. Each group came to parent education training with a different set of skills and a unique knowledge base that reflected their professional discipline and preparation. A generic set of skills for parent group leaders emerged from these training efforts and was applied to each group in different ways to build upon their already acquired knowledge and skill base. For example, social workers might have experience with group therapy and understand group dynamics around emotional issues but might have limited information about child development and education methods to stimulate acquiring new knowledge and skills. A variety of institutions (healthcare, social service, and education) continued to sponsor group parent education during this time. The mental health of children, rather than their physical health, became an important theme in parent education during these two decades, as the knowledge base about child social and emotional development became a primary focus (Brim, 1959).

New parent education initiatives continued to emerge during the late 1960s and 1970s. These were often organized around targeted populations of parents who "needed" parent education. The Head Start program as a part of the War on Poverty focused on low-income children and their parents. Though initially the program was an early education intervention for young children, it soon became obvious that parents were essential partners in this intervention process (Bronfenbrenner, 1978). Parent education was one way to teach parents effective ways to support and reinforce early education lessons at home. Parent education services were often delivered on an individual basis through home visits. The group parent education model was included and fit well with the Head

Start philosophy of working collaboratively with parents. Parents of children with disabilities were another target population that participated in group parent education (Auerbach, 1968; Braun, Coplon, & Sonnenschien, 1984). Parent education was also developed as a primary prevention strategy to combat child abuse and neglect during the1970s and 1980s (Bavelok & Bavelok, 1988).

A renewed interest in parent education for parents of young children occurred in the 1980s and 1990s in response to dramatic family changes and a renewed focus on the importance of parent-child relationships. Systematic Training for Effective Parenting (STEP) Early Childhood (1976) and Incredible Years (1987) are examples of programs introduced during this time (National Center for Parent, Family, & Community Engagement, 2015). Both Missouri and Minnesota initiated state-level, universal access programs that used group parent education as the primary format for educating parents. There were also numerous targeted initiatives for parent and family education in other states during this time (Family Resource Coalition, 1996). Parent education for parents of young children continued to flourish in a variety of contexts, such as community family resource programs, early childhood programs, early childhood special education programs, and public health programs.

From our experience ... We've learned to be creative in offering parent education groups in settings that appeal to parents. While we are comfortable in our work setting, parents may not be. In the community where I worked, I noticed that there were many young families in low-income housing developments who were not attending the programs offered in the school. Quite a bit of outreach was done with flyers and other promotions, but we decided that the best approach was to go to the families, if they weren't coming to us. I talked to an apartment management company, and they had a number of empty apartments that they agreed to let us use for parent-child groups that included parent education sessions. It was a great success! Other sites in the community where the program was offered included mobile home park centers, the local hospital, Women, Infants, and Children (WIC) clinics, and county human service offices. Being creative and flexible allowed us to serve many more families than those who chose to attend at our center.

Thomas and Cooke (1986) examined parent education services in Minnesota during the early 1980s. They discovered that these services were offered in a variety of settings, such as hospitals, schools, early childhood programs, mental health agencies, churches, and social service agencies. This study introduced the word *embeddedness* to describe the role of parent educator in these different institutional settings. This concept acknowledged that most people who delivered parent education services at that time did so as part of a larger professional identity, such as social worker, psychologist, public health nurse, pediatrician, or early educator. Parent educator was not their primary role or identity, but it was one of the important functions that they fulfilled in their role as education, healthcare, or human service professionals. The diversity of parent education services in different settings in the 1980s and 1990s reflected the deep roots that have continued to grow from the early part of the 20th century and that have sprouted numerous new branches over the last 25 years of the 20th century. This diversity also made it difficult to develop a common understanding about what parent education was or whether it should develop its own professional identity (Carter, 1996). Consequently, parent education groups are facilitated by a wide variety of lay and professional leaders with different levels of preparation and different approaches to educating parents. The knowledge base that supports parent education practice (i.e., child development, adult education, group process and dynamics) has continued to expand, yet the development of parent education as a unique profession has been stymied by the lack of consensus on who should facilitate parent education groups and what level of preparation is needed to work with different groups of parents and families.

Programs make a variety of resources available for families

DEFINING PARENT EDUCATION

Some of the current confusion about parent education can be traced to changing families and needs, different theories of change models, and different contexts for implementing parent education. Initially, parent education had the specific focus of improving parent knowledge of child development and introducing effective techniques for child rearing. Confusion about the purpose and scope of parent education has come from conceptual models that define parent education as an approach to parent involvement in education programs or see it as one aspect of parent support services in the community (Epstein, 1995; Family Resource Coalition, 1996). Family support is defined by Dunst (1995, quoted in Carter 1996) as "a broad array of services and activities that are designed to enable and empower by enhancing and promoting individual and family capabilities that support and strengthen family functioning in general and parenting capabilities specifically" (p. 8). The National Council on Family Relations (NCFR) also included parent education as one important domain of the larger field of family life education (Darling & Cassidy, 2014). The specific meaning and role of group parent education can get lost in these broader contexts of parent involvement in education settings, family life education, and community family support.

The National Parenting Education Network (NPEN) has developed the definition of parent education that will be used in this book. Carter (1996) described NPEN as a group of parenting education leaders who work together to strengthen the field of parenting education. NPEN (2015) defined parent education as "a process that involves the expansion of insights, understanding, and

From our experience ... As a member of NPEN over the last 20 years, I have observed the careful, focused work of NPEN leaders to define the field and provide a national forum for communication among individuals who identify themselves as parent educators. This has led to the creation of state organizations in places like North Carolina, Oregon, and Connecticut that have helped move the field forward with training and support for parent educators. At the national level NPEN has helped to clarify the roles of paraprofessionals and studied the competency systems that have been developed for parent education practitioners to create a consensus about core competencies.

attitudes and the acquisition of knowledge and skills about the development of both parents and their children and the relationship between them."

This definition provides a clear focus on important goals and the process for parent growth and changes. It is a good match for understanding the diverse goals of group parent education. The parent group provides fertile ground for the parent growth described in this definition. It also provides the flexibility to address the multiple goals and needs of contemporary parents. The focus is on the educational process, which takes advantage of the strong affective component of parenting to support parent growth.

The development of specific curriculum materials (e.g., Systematic Training for Effective Parenting (STEP), Parent Effectiveness Training (PET), Active Parenting, the Nurturing Program), coupled with some skepticism about professionals and experts on parenting, led to the development of more parent education support groups and peer-led parent education groups (Hamner & Turner, 1996). The idea that the genuineness and practical knowledge of experienced parents make them the most effective parent educators appealed to parents who wanted practical advice from someone with "real experience." This is especially true given that parenting experts don't agree about the best ways to rear children, and parents are then confused about which advice to follow. Minnesota Early Learning Design (MELD, 2002) is a good example of peer-led parent education. The MELD program model recruits parents who have participated in a parent group, providing them with training on group facilitation skills and supplying curriculum materials to conduct parent education/support groups. This approach has been adopted as a model by many programs in the United States, and MELD has provided excellent training and ongoing support for these groups. There are also professionals from a variety of disciplines (social work, nursing, psychology, and early childhood) who function as parent group leaders. There has been some effort to create a defined professional identity for parent and family life educators through carefully designed preparation programs that lead to a license or certificate in parent or family life education (Darling & Cassidy, 2014; NPEN, 2015).

Minnesota is one state that has developed a Parent Educator teaching license. This license has attracted people from a variety of different disciplines and who build upon previous college coursework and work experiences. The initial license in the mid-1970s identified a specific set of course requirements that were necessary to complete a licensure program. The development of the Early Childhood Family Education (ECFE) program in Minnesota created an impetus for more detailed preparation for parent educators. A new license was created in the 1980s that required a bachelor-level degree and course work in child development, parent education, family relation, adult education, group process, and parent education methods. A student teaching experience was also required to gain practical experience leading parent groups under the supervision of a licensed parent educator. These requirements replicated teacher-training programs for K–12 teachers during this time. This licensure program went through additional revisions in the mid-1990s, as all teaching licenses moved to a competency-based model. Students were required to demonstrate the general competencies of effective teaching and specific content competencies related to parent education. Other examples of this movement toward specific professional preparation are the Certified Family Life Educator (CFLE) credential created by the NCFR in the 1980s and Family Support credential created for family support workers in New York through a program at Cornell University (Darling & Cassidy, 2014).

Braun et al. (1984) attempted to draw some important distinctions about group services for parents. They described three distinct types of parent groups: the support or self-help group, the education group, and the therapy group. These distinctions are helpful in defining some boundaries for the practice of group parent education. There is still some uncertainty about the boundaries between therapy and education. The goals for parent education are more complex, and the work is more challenging when serving parents with multiple needs (e.g., family literacy programs, incarcerated parents). The National Extension model of parent education (Smith, Cudaback, Goddard, & Myers-Wall, 1994) carefully articulates a set of interconnected goals for parent education that includes a variety of "critical parenting practices" under the general areas of guidance, nurturance, care for self, understanding, teaching, and advocacy. These goals matched a more diverse and holistic set of needs of parents in the late 1990s and continue to reflect the complexity of parenting today. With regard to goals, methods, and providers, group parent education does differ in some important ways from parent support or self-help groups and from therapy groups (Braun et al., 1984). However, each of these types of services can play an important role in supporting good parenting.

The focus on parent education as a unique professional field begins to define some boundaries that allow the field to grow in depth, not just breadth. This growth can lead to more thoughtful and more effective practice. The Braun et al. (1984) book on group parent education described practice at a very concrete level. It made a strong case for the importance of parent education as a unique discipline and defined a specific knowledge base, personal characteristics, and skills that parent educators should acquire. These are very similar to the descriptions that Auerbach (1968) presented 15 years earlier. The addition of more specific educational methods by Braun et al. (1984) provided a balanced view of the parent educator role that blends both group facilitator and educator roles and skills. Auerbach's description of parent education practice and the need for balance in a number of areas also reflected a deep understanding and appreciation for the artistry of parent education. Both Auerbach (1968) and Braun et al. (1984) understood the importance of the role of the parent group leader and contributed to our current knowledge of effective practices in group parent education. Kumpfer and Alvarado (1998) also acknowledged the critical role of the parent educator in their description of factors that influence the quality of parent education programs.

RECENT DEVELOPMENTS

A number of recent developments have influenced the practice of parent education during the last 15 years. Some of these are the continuation of long-term trends (changes in family structure), and others are new developments from research: Adverse Childhood Experiences (ACEs); early brain development; changes in Information and Communications Technology (ICT); public policy (No Child Left Behind); and the emphasis on accountability. These factors have placed new pressures on parent education as a field to address a number of different social issues, from gaps in academic achievement and decreasing family stability to early childhood trauma and family stress in culturally diverse communities with an influx of immigrants from around the world. How have each of these factors impacted the implementation and practice of group parent education?

RESEARCH ON EARLY DEVELOPMENT

Parent education has always focused on helping parents understand how children grow and develop. New insights about child development based on brain research have provided a deeper understanding and new explanations for factors that impact children's social and emotional development and early learning (Center for the Developing Child, 2016). The role of adverse childhood experiences has also been introduced into how parent and family behaviors can influence development and, later, health. Our understanding of early trauma and how to recognize and treat it through working with the parent-child relationship has influenced parent education practice. There is more definitive evidence about positive parenting practices, such as warmth, sensitivity to infant cues, contingent responsiveness, support for exploration and early language and literacy (National Academies of Sciences, Engineering, and Medicine, 2016). These are critical during the early childhood years. The field of infant mental health has also grown due to this research, and parent education plays an important role in promotion of these parenting practices and prevention of abusive and neglectful behaviors (Child Welfare Information Gateway, 2013).

CHANGES IN FAMILY LIFE

The changes in family demographics that started in the 1980s have continued through the early 2000s. There are more single-parent families, the number of births to unmarried women (40% of births in 2014) has continued to rise (Hamilton et al., 2015), and there are now more grandparents caring for their grandchildren. There are also more women with young children working full-time and using various forms of childcare (Boushey & Vaghul, 2016). These changes have impacted the nature of the audiences who may benefit from parent education and the limited times that they may be available for parent education services. Families have also continued to become more culturally diverse, with 50% of births to non-white parents starting in 2013 (Pew Research, 2016). The change in ethnic and cultural backgrounds creates new challenges for parent education where curriculum resources based on majority white families of the 1980s were developed. The diverse beliefs about parenting in minority and recent immigrant families demand a different approach and provide new opportunities for more inclusive discussions of parenting practices. Working with English language learners also makes facilitation of parent groups more complex. Changes in family life have further impacted fathers and their roles in families. In many families both the mother and father work full-time and sharing of childcare and household chores is a new area of tension. Programs report that more fathers are attending parent education sessions, sometimes with their partners and sometimes on their own. There are also more opportunities for fathers to attend programs that are specifically designed for them (Fagan & Palm, 2004; Bronte et al., 2012). Cowan et al., (2009) introduced co-parenting classes (Strengthening Father Involvement (SFI)) as a more effective way to engage fathers. This inclusion of the mother-father relationship adds another dimension and area of discussion for parent groups. While many fathers are more involved in parent education, there are a number of fathers who are not living with their children. This group is interested in being involved and is more challenging to reach and engage in parent education programs. This is a new group that needs both education and support and can benefit from participating in parent education services. Diverse family systems require more thoughtful adaptation and design of parent education curriculum materials.

From our experience ... Work with immigrant families is an important learning opportunity for parent educators. I participated in a project that focused on providing greater access for immigrant families to early childhood services in the community. It was funded for three years, and we worked with community leaders from four different immigrant groups to develop co-learning events for families and early childhood professionals. During this time, we developed co-learning cafes, which are opportunities to discuss powerful questions in small groups. These sessions addressed parenting concerns that had been identified by focus groups. We worked with community leaders from each group to design the cafes and learned that each had a different approach to creating an inviting environment for these co-learning events. Food that was familiar to each group was a universal requirement, and the use of skilled interpreters was also an essential element. These events provided both parents and practitioners an opportunity to learn from each other about topics like child development, child abuse and neglect laws, and discipline.

INCREASED FOCUS ON ACCOUNTABILITY AND RISE OF EVIDENCE-BASED PROGRAMS

The No Child Left Behind legislation created a greater emphasis on accountability in education that has trickled down to parent education with a greater emphasis on evidence-based curriculum (Small & Huser, 2015). This has led funders and state and federal agencies to limit funding to programs unless they use only evidence-based curricula. A 2015 report (National Center for Parent, Family, and Community Engagement, 2015) of evidence-based programs for early childhood (0–8) parenting programs lists more than 20 programs that have met the criteria as evidence based. These programs have been through evaluation research that provides evidence of positive outcomes for parents and children based on various goals and studied with different groups of parents. The majority of the programs were developed in the 1980s and 1990s and will have to be adapted to meet the needs of our more diverse populations of parents and families today (Center for Developing Child, 2016). This body of evidence has been an important factor in supporting the efficacy and importance of parent education as a strategy for strengthening families and having a positive impact on child outcomes. It is also a challenge to communities with diverse populations with unique needs to find existing evidence-based programs that match these needs. Comprehensive preparation of parent educators is one way to ensure that the existing evidence-based curricula can be implemented in a flexible manner and that new curriculum materials will continue to be developed to meet changing parent and family needs (Center for the Developing Child, 2016).

CREDENTIALING OF PARENT EDUCATORS

The NPEN emerged in the 1990s as an organization with the goal to advance the field of parenting education. Cooke (2006) addressed the issue of competencies that are needed for parent educators and outlined some of the efforts at national (NCFR and the CFLE) and state levels to identify competencies and create credentialing systems. There were programs in six institutions that were listed that represent six different states (Iowa, Minnesota, Illinois, North Carolina, New York, and Washington). Since that time, there have been additional efforts at the state level (beyond a single university) to create some type of recognition or credential for parent educators. The Professional Preparation and Recognition Committee of NPEN (2016a) has updated the efforts that have been made at the state level, and there are now eight states that offer some type of recognition or credential for parent educators. Some states have devised a recognition system (e.g., Texas and Oregon) and others have a credential with some specific requirements (e.g., Connecticut, New York, and North Carolina). Minnesota has a long-standing teaching license for parent educators that was instituted in the 1970s. Canada has also created a certificate program for Canadian Family Educators. Some of the state systems have identified different levels of parenting educators (e.g., Texas, Oregon, and New York) and include a range of roles and preparation requirements. The NPEN report on the value of peer and paraprofessional parent educators has helped to shine light on the broad range of individuals who are engaged in some type of parent education work (Jones et al., 2013). The task of identifying the core competencies for professional parent educators has continued as part of the NPEN committee work. It is clear that the unique contribution of parent educators has been recognized and that clarification of the competencies, roles, and boundaries of parent education as an emerging profession will continue to evolve. This should support focused preparation of parent educators and the effective delivery of services to parents and families.

CHANGES IN DELIVERY OF PARENT EDUCATION SERVICES

The introduction and use of information and communication technologies (ICT) in family life has been described as revolutionary over the past 30 years (Walker, 2015). The ubiquitous cell phone allows instantaneous communication with people around the world through a variety of apps and access to information from the Internet, in addition to being a video and photo device. This has changed family life in ways that researchers are only beginning to understand. ICT has both unique opportunities and challenges for parent education. ICT has created a need to help parents to assess and decide how to use, limit, and monitor ICT devices in the family. It also enables parents to have instant access to parenting and family life information from a variety of sources. The challenge is determining which sources are reliable and support positive parent-child relationships and research-based parenting advice. This is an important topic for parent education class discussion. It can also change the role of parent educators from spending less time providing research-based information to more time helping parents assess parenting information for their families. The integration of ICT into parent education programs can supplement parent education classes with new opportunities for communication and support among group members. How do parent educators use the potential of ICT to improve parent education programming and reach out to busy parents who may have limited time and varying schedules?

FRAMEWORK FOR CONTINUUM OF PARENT EDUCATION SERVICES

Another factor that has started to appear in parent education literature is the effort to develop a framework that identifies different levels of services based on parent and family needs (National Academies of Sciences, Engineering, and Medicine, 2016). Figure 2.1 depicts the continuum of needs from universal promotion and prevention services for all parents and targeted intervention for parents with risk factors to intervention services for parents with identified family and mental health issues (National Academies of Sciences, Engineering, and Medicine, 2016). Figure 2.1 defines each service level and gives an example of possible parent and family education services at each level. The framework begins with universal services to build the capacity of all parents and families. The model also connects healthcare, education, and human service sectors and creates opportunities for collaborative programming. The framework describes the complementary role that different sectors can play in meeting parent and family needs. It is also a model that focuses on the different needs of parents and different levels of service intensity and duration to meet these needs. It shows how professionals with different backgrounds can work together to build a comprehensive network of parenting support services. This model will be explored in greater detail in Chapter 3.

Figure 2.1 Continuum Model of Parent Education Services: Definitions and Examples

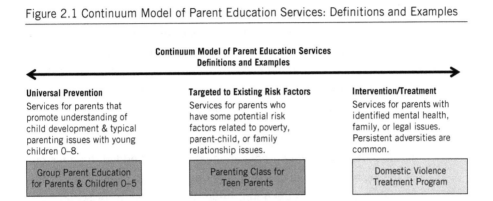

Continuum Model of Parent Education Services
Definitions and Examples

Universal Prevention
Services for parents that promote understanding of child development & typical parenting issues with young children 0–8.

Group Parent Education for Parents & Children 0–5

Targeted to Existing Risk Factors
Services for parents who have some potential risk factors related to poverty, parent-child, or family relationship issues.

Parenting Class for Teen Parents

Intervention/Treatment
Services for parents with identified mental health, family, or legal issues. Persistent adversities are common.

Domestic Violence Treatment Program

LESSONS FROM HISTORY

The evolution of group parent education over the last 100+ years illustrates a shift from an emphasis on didactic teaching about child development and child-rearing techniques to a complex interplay of sharing information, employing interactive teaching methods, and facilitating parent discussion. The art and science of group parent education has become more sophisticated. The scientific gains are reflected in the growing knowledge base about child development, family life, and parent-child relations (Center for the Developing Child, 2016). Research on program effectiveness has provided a foundational set of evidence-based programs for parent educators to use as a starting place in selecting and adapting curriculum tools (National Center for Parent, Family, and Community Engagement, 2015). Advances in artistry are seen in the growing appreciation of family diversity, where family culture and values, family structure, and socioeconomic status are all perceived as important factors in understanding families and designing engaging and effective parent education programs. The development of preparation programs for parent educators has helped to more clearly define a set of competencies (knowledge, skills, and dispositions) that support effective parent education (NPEN, 2016b). Research on the efficacy of parent education has focused primarily on parenting programs, as defined by a specific curriculum. There has been limited research on the parent educator as a variable in the effectiveness of parent education programs (Center for the Developing Child, 2016). Kumpfer and Alvarado (1998) estimated that the "quality of the trainer" accounts for between 50% and 80% of the effectiveness of the program (i.e., program outcomes for parents and children). The preparation of parent group leaders may be the most important factor in improving program quality, yet this has not been the focus of parent education research and evaluation studies (Kumpfer & Alvarado, 1998; Medway, 1989; National Academies of Sciences, Engineering, and Medicine, 2016; Todres & Bunston, 1993). This is an area where future research should be conducted to clarify the competencies that are essential to an effective parent educator.

Several important lessons can be gleaned from the following overview of the history and evolution of group parent education:

1. *Parent education has deep roots related to a variety of disciplines and professional roles.* Parent education is often embedded in and is one of the secondary functions of a larger professional role, such as nursing, early childhood education, infant mental health, or social work. No single discipline has focused on parent education practice in a holistic manner. It is clearly a multidisciplinary field. There have been a few attempts to create a separate identity for parent educators. Late 1920s and early 1930s literature indicates a strong effort to create a professional identity through the definition of specific educational requirements and the development of a professional organization with a journal (Anderson, 1930). This early initiative faltered after the Laura Spellman Rockefeller Foundation withdrew funds during the mid-1930s (Brim, 1959). More recent attempts have been made during the last 20 years through the development of recognition, licensure, and credential programs in parent and family education (Darling & Cassidy, 2014; NPEN, 2015). Parent education programs will continue to be offered in a variety of settings, and professionals will remain embedded in other disciplines. The development of a unique profession for parent educators remains uncertain despite the specific knowledge, skill, and disposition base that has been identified (NPEN, 2016b). The field could also be developed as a specialization for professionals who take on parent education as a major responsibility in their roles as education, mental health, or health care professionals.

2. *The goals of group parent education will continue to expand and to reflect the multiple roles of parents and the complexity of family*

systems today (Smith et al., 1994; National Academies of Sciences, Engineering, and Medicine, 2016). Parenting practices identified by research as important for child wellbeing provide clear goals for parent education programs (National Academies of Sciences, Engineering, and Medicine, 2016). The number of diverse groups for parents has continued to grow and become more focused on the age of the child, level of child ability, family culture, and family structure (Carter, 1996). This movement challenges parent group leaders to be even better prepared to address the diverse parent needs and to work collaboratively with parents to identify their values and goals and create effective parent education programs.

3. *The practice of group parent education will continue to evolve as the art of balancing education, support, group and individual needs, research-based information, value-based parenting practices, the needs of parents and needs of children, and the needs of mothers and fathers are all addressed* (Auerbach, 1968; Small & Kupisk, 2015; Center for the Developing Child, 2016). Facilitating parent education groups effectively is a real art requiring knowledge and skills and "wisdom in practice" (Small & Kupisk, 2015, p. 17). This added factor includes experience, the ability to reflect, and an understanding of the context, ethics, and deliberation. Parent group leaders must contend with a growing body of empirical knowledge, as well as the increasing awareness of and sensitivity to family diversity. The practice of group parent education will benefit from clearer boundaries, more research on the competencies of parent educators, and more carefully designed parent educator preparation programs. The identification of promising practices (Bronte et al., 2012) through increased research and the use of reflective consultation will also help to improve the practice of group parent education.

This historical overview provides some background for understanding the current state of group parent education. The final section of this chapter provides a detailed description of important competencies for parent group leaders. These competencies represent an integration of different ideas about effective group leaders that are organized into three categories: knowledge, skills, and dispositions. The set of competencies also serves as a framework for self-assessment and reflection for parent group leaders. It does not include the content knowledge base (e.g., child and adult development, family studies) that is also important for effective parent education practice.

Parent-child programs include time for children to explore the environment

COMPETENCIES FOR PARENT GROUP LEADERS

The competencies for parent educators are presented in three different categories: knowledge, dispositions, and skills. These three concepts are used in teacher preparation. This list of competencies represents ideas taken from previous literature on group parent education (Auerbach, 1968; Braun et al., 1984; Darling & Cassidy, 2014; NPEN, 2016b). There is an additional set of competencies that have been identified as general areas of knowledge for parent education, including child development, family dynamics, parent-child relationships, adult learning, community resources, and diverse family systems, that are not included in the list (Cooke, 2006; Kurz-Riemer, 2001; NPEN, 2016b). In the section that follows, the focus is specifically on group dynamics and group facilitation skills, which are the primary focus of this book.

KNOWLEDGE

The following are areas of knowledge specifically related to understanding group dynamics and facilitating parent learning in a group context:

- Developmental stages of group process
- Theories of group dynamics
- Roles and boundaries
- Emotional aspects of parenting
- Leadership styles

- Assessment strategies
- Learning methods
- Community resources
- Diversity issues
- Impact of childhood experiences
- Gender implications on groups

DISPOSITIONS

The category of dispositions refers to character traits and emotional attitudes that have been identified as important for parent educators (Auerbach, 1968; Braun et al., 1984; Clarke, 1984; NPEN, 2016b). These are different from general personality traits or types, such as introvert and extrovert. Each individual will have his or her own unique blend of these dispositions:

- Mature
- Caring
- Nonjudgmental
- Sensitive
- Organized
- Flexible
- Creative
- Enthusiastic/optimistic
- Honest
- Genuine
- Humorous

SKILLS

The following are facilitation skills for parent educators to successfully lead groups:

- Creates warm/welcoming environment
- Creates safe environment to share ideas and feelings
- Guides discussion, giving it form and structure
- Models acceptance of individuals
- Takes responsibility for positive learning environment
- Fosters relationships and interaction among members

The self-assessment tool in Appendix A addresses the above in more detail and provides specific examples. It is based on the knowledge-disposition-skills categorization of parent group leader competencies and should be used to identify strengths and possible areas for improvement. When using this tool for self-assessment, it is important to remember that the tool was not developed to present the profile for an ideal or perfect group parent educator. No one should expect to develop all of these competencies to their highest levels. The unique profile that is obtained from completing the tool will reflect your personality, previous preparation, and experience. Your reflection on this profile should help you as a practitioner to feel more comfortable with and appreciate your strengths, in addition to providing direction for professional development. Use it as a guide for self-understanding and improvement, not as a report card of your competencies.

SUMMARY

Chapter 2 provides an overview of the history and development of group parent education with a specific focus on the last roughly 100 years. Examining the historical roots of group parent education elucidates some of the issues that continue to challenge parent education today, including the meaning of parent education, the practice of parent education in different contexts, and the complexity of the role of parent group leader. Recent developments reveal the continued importance of parent education across different settings and at different levels of intensity. The levels of parent education intervention support the importance of competent parent educators to meet the varied needs of parents and families across the framework of parent education practice. This complexity of practice is demonstrated through the integration and description of competencies that parent group leaders need to acquire to become effective in their work with parents. This detailed description of the knowledge, skills, and dispositions for parent group leaders forms the foundation for the information presented in the remaining chapters.

DISCUSSION QUESTIONS

1. What are the major changes in the approach of professionals to group parent education over the past 100 years?

2.   Why is the role of the group parent educator more complex today than it might have been in 1930?

3.   How has embeddedness of parent education shaped our current practice? What are the advantages and disadvantages of this characteristic of the field?

4.   What recent developments have had the greatest impact on parent education practices in your community? Why?

5.   What are some possible collaborative efforts in parent education services that could improve accessibility to parents of children?

CLASS ACTIVITIES

1.   Evaluate Parenting Apps
Meet in pairs to review two different apps on phone or iPad. Begin by exploring each app to discover what it does.

   a.   What information is being presented?

   b.   How is it presented?

   c.   What do you like about the app?

   d.   Is it fun and engaging?

   e.   What might you add for parents?

   f.   Is the information useful, practical for parents?

   g.   Is the information reliable and based on current research on child development and parenting?

   h.   What populations of parents would find the information and style of presentation most appealing/the best fit?

2.   In small groups of 3–4, review a lesson plan on a topic, like discipline, from a curriculum from 30 or more years ago. (For example, a curriculum from 1934 was available from the archives of a local

university.) What concepts and advice are still relevant to parents today and what might have to be changed to be relevant to parents today and consistent with our current knowledge of child development and parent-child relations?

REFERENCES

Anderson, J. (1930). *Parent education: The first yearbook.* Washington, DC: National Congress of Parents and Teachers.

Arlitt, A. (1932). Parent education in the National Congress of Parent and Teachers. In *Parent education: The second yearbook* (pp. 1–9). Washington, DC: National Congress of Parents and Teachers.

Auerbach, A. (1968). *Parents learn through discussion: Principles and practices of parent group education.* New York, NY: John Wiley.

Bavelok, S., & Bavelok, J. (1988). *Nurturing program for parents and children birth to five years: Parent handbook.* Eau Claire, WI: Family Development Resources.

Berger, E. (2000). *Parent as partners in education* (5th ed.). Upper Saddle River, NJ: Merrill.

Boushey, H., & Vaghul, K. (2016). Working mothers with infants and toddlers and the importance of economic security. Washington Center for Equitable Growth. Retrieved from http://equitablegrowth.org/research-analysis/working-mothers-with-infants-and-toddlers-and-the-importance-of-family-economic-security/.

Braun, L., Coplon, J., & Sonnenschien, P. (1984). *Helping parents in groups.* Boston, MA: Wheelock Center on Parenting Studies.

Brim, O. (1959). *Education for child rearing.* New York, NY: Russell Sage Foundation.

Bronfenbrenner, U. (1978). Who needs parent education? *Teachers College Record, 4,* 767–787.

Bronte, J., Burkhauser, M., & Metz, A. (2012). Elements of promising practices in fatherhood programs: Evidence-based research findings on interventions for fathers. *Fathering, 10*(1), 6–30.

Carter, N. (1996). *See how they grow: A report on the status of parenting education in the U.S.* Philadelphia, PA: Pew Charitable Trusts.

Center on the Developing Child at Harvard University (2016). From best practice to breakthrough impacts: A science-based approach to building a more promising future for young children and families. Retrieved from http://www.developingchild.harvard.edu.

Child Welfare Information Gateway (2013). Parent education to strengthen families and reduce the risk of maltreatment. Retrieved from https://www.childwelfare.gov/pubs/issue_briefs/parented/.

Clarke, J.I. (1984). *Who, me a group leader?* San Francisco, CA: Harper & Row.

Cooke, B. (2006). Competencies of a parent educator: What does a parent educator need to know and do? *Child Welfare, 85*(5), 785–802.

Cowan, P.A., Cowan, C.P., Pruett, M.K., Pruett, K., & Wong, J.J. (2009). Promoting fathers' engagement with children: Preventive interventions for low-income families. *Journal of Marriage and Family, 71,* 663–679.

Darling, C., & Cassidy, D. (2014). *Family life education: Working with Families across the Lifespan.* Long Grove, IL: Waveland Press.

Epstein, J. (May, 1995). School/family/community partnerships: Caring for the children we share. *Phi Delta Kappan,* 701–712.

Fagan, J., & Palm, G. (2004). *Fathers and early childhood programs.* Clifton Heights, NY: Delmar Publishing.

Family Resource Coalition. (1996). *Guidelines for family support practice.* Chicago, IL: Author.

Hamilton, B.E., Martin, J.A., Osterman, M., Curtin, S.C., & Matthews, T.J. (2015). Births: Final Data for 2014. *National Vital Statistics Reports, 64*(12). Retrieved from http://www.cdc.gov/nchs/data/nvsr/nvsr64/nvsr64_12.pdf.

Hamner, T., & Turner, P. (1996). *Parenting in contemporary society.* Needham Heights, MA: Allyn & Bacon.

Jones, S.T., Stranik, M.K., Hart, M.G., McClintic, S. & Wolf, J.R. (2013). A Closer Look at Diverse Roles of Practitioners in Parenting Education: Peer Educators, ParaProfessionals, and Professionals. NPEN White Paper retrieved at: http://npen.org/wp-content/uploads/2012/03/diverse-roles-in-PE-white-paper_-12_17_13.pdf.

Kumpfer, K., & Alvarado, R. (1998, November). Effective family strengthening interventions. *Juvenile Justice Bulletin* (pp. 1–15).

Kurz-Riemer, K. (2001). *A guide for implementing Early Childhood Family Education programs.* St. Paul, MN: Minnesota Department of Children, Families, and Learning.

Medway, F. (1989). Measuring the effectiveness of parent education. In M. Fine (Ed.), *The second handbook on parent education* (pp. 237–256). San Diego, CA: Academic Press.

Minnesota Early Learning Design. (2002). Retrieved from www.meld.org./program.cfm?Page ID=1700, January 8, 2003.

National Academies of Sciences, Engineering, and Medicine. (2016). *Parenting matters: Supporting parents of children 0–8.* Washington, DC: The National Academies Press. Doi: 10.17226/21868.

National Center for Parent, Family and Community Engagement. (2015). *Compendium of parenting interventions.* Washington, DC: National Center on Parent, Family and Community Engagement, Office of Head Start, U.S. Department of Health and Human Services.

National Parenting Education Network. (1999). Retrieved from www.ces.ncsu.edu/depts./fcs/npen/aboutnepn.html#Definition, January 8, 2003.

National Parenting Education Network (2015). History of NPEN. Retrieved from http://npen.org/history_or_npen/.

National Parenting Education Network. (2016a). Parenting educator credentialing system matrix. Retrieved from http://npen.org/wp-content/uploads/2016/07/Matrix-Updated-2016-FINAL-20160404.pdf.

National Parenting Education Network. (2016b). *Parenting Educator Competencies Resource Document.* Retrieved from: npen.org/wp-content/uploads/216/04/Competencies2.23.16pdf.

Pew Research, (2016). It's official: Minority babies are the majority among the nation's infants, but only just. Retrieved from http://www.pewresearch.org/fact-tank/2016/06/23/its-official-minority-babies-are-the-majority-among-the-nations-infants-but-only-just/.

Small, S., & Huser, M. (2015) Principles for Improving Family Programs: An Evidence-Informed Approach. In M. Walcheski & J. Reinke (Eds.), *Family Life Education: The Practice of Family Science* (pp. 255–266). Minneapolis, MN: National Council on Family Relations.

Small, S., & Kupisk, D. (2015) Family Life Education Wisdom in Practice. In M. Walcheski & J. Reinke (Eds.), *Family Life Education: The Practice of Family Science* (pp. 217–226). Minneapolis, MN: National Council on Family Relations.

Smith, C.A., Cudaback, D., Goddard, H. W., & Myers-Wall, J. (1994). *National Extension parent education model.* Manhattan, NY: Kansas Cooperative Extension Services.

Sunley, R. (1955). Early nineteenth American literature on child rearing. In M. Mead & M. Wolfenstein (Eds.), *Childhood in contemporary cultures* (pp. 150–163). Chicago, IL: University of Chicago Press.

Thomas, R., & Cooke, B. (1986). Summary of profile of parent education study. In J. Parsons, T. Bowman, J. Comeau, & R. Pitzer (Eds.), *Parent education state of the art* (pp. 19–26). White Bear Lake, MN: Minnesota Curriculum Services Center.

Todres, R., & Bunston, T. (1993). Parent education program evaluation: A review of the literature. *Canadian Journal of Community Mental Health, 12*(1), 225–257.

Walker, S.K. (2015). Family life and technology: Implications for the practice of family life education. In M.J. Walcheski & J. Reinke. (Eds.), *Family life education: The practice of family science* (pp. 117–130). Minneapolis, MN: National Council on Family Relations.

TOWARD A CONTINUUM FRAMEWORK OF PARENT EDUCATION PRACTICE

"Society benefits socially and economically from providing current and future generations of parents with the support they need to raise healthy and thriving children" (National Academies of Sciences, Engineering, and Medicine, 2016, p. I-1)

This chapter will describe the scope and goals of parent education practice across a continuum of parent needs with an emphasis on desired coordination of services across disciplines and service institutions. As discussed in Chapter 2, parenting education has occurred in various institutions since the early 1900s and continues in various formats in healthcare, education, social service, faith-based, and criminal justice settings (Thomas & Cooke, 1986; Carter, 1996; National Academies of Sciences, Engineering, and Medicine, 2016; Shonkoff & Fisher, 2013). Programs offered in these settings tend to meet different goals that can be placed on a continuum of needs and intensity of services. A model based on a continuum of parent needs and the programs specifically designed to address them provides a useful framework for understanding the different goals and practices in parenting education. The levels model (Doherty, 1995; Doherty & Lamson, 2015) and the Domains of Family Practice model (Myers-Wall et al., 2011) are discussed in Chapter 5 and are related to the concept of a continuum but are focused on different dimensions of practice. A continuum model is introduced here with broad descriptions of different areas of practice along the continuum and examples of current programming for each area. The concepts of timing, dosage, and duration of services will also be addressed in relation to the continuum model. The relationship between the parent educator and the parent is a critical component of effective parent education practice (See Chapter 7). This relationship will be explored in some detail to distinguish its core characteristics and differences that are related to the timing, intensity, and duration of the parent education service on the continuum. The chapter creates a space through the continuum model to explore the boundary issues between different parent education services and the goals of the services providers. This continuum framework also provides a foundation for building a more coordinated network of effective parent education services.

WHY A CONTINUUM MODEL IS IMPORTANT FOR PARENT EDUCATION

Parent education services and practices encompass a wide range of activities with a common core of outcomes for parents, parent-child relationships, and children. These outcomes also have ripple effects for families and communities that are important to articulate and consider as part of program evaluation. The benefits of creating a continuum framework or model include:

- Helping to clarify different program goals around parent education and levels of program intensity (dosage and duration) to achieve these goals.
- Bringing into focus the diversity of programming that is labeled parent education and the individuals and institutions that deliver programs (National Academies of Sciences, Engineering, and Medicine, 2016).
- Helping to focus on different parent and family needs and the importance of tailoring programs to meet these needs (Minnesota Association for Family and Early Education, 2015; Center for the Developing Child, 2016).
- Providing a way to think about resources needed and cost-benefit ratios for different types of efforts, from universal prevention to intensive intervention (Prinz et al, 2009; Sanders et al., 2008; Doran, Jacobs, & Dewa, 2012).
- Providing a platform for collaboration across disciplines and institutions and the development of a common language for communicating across programs (Weatherson, Kaplan-Estrin, & Goldberg, 2009).

The continuum model is also useful for understanding the individual roles and competencies of parent education service providers that are required for different levels of service. This includes the basic core competencies required to provide parent education, as well as the impact of experience, which moves the parent education practitioner from a novice toward an expert (See Chapter 14).

CURRENT EFFORTS TO OUTLINE A CONTINUUM MODEL

Ideas for building a framework for a continuum model of parent education services have emerged from a number of different sources. The Center for the Developing Child (2016) describes a model with four levels, ranging from universal services for all children and families and targeted services for families with low levels of education and income to intensive intervention for young children with families at high risk for experiencing toxic stress. The field of infant mental health has outlined different levels of professionals who serve very young children and meet parent and family needs along a continuum of service models (Weatherson, Kaplan-Estrin, & Goldberg, 2009). The recent publication *Parenting Matters: Supporting Parents of Children Ages 0–8* (National Academies of Sciences, Engineering, and Medicine, 2016) has proposed a three-tier model for services that range from universal prevention to targeted services for populations at risk (e.g., children with special needs or behavioral problems, parents following divorce) and families that face persistent adversities (e.g., parents reported for child maltreatment or parents with mental illness, substance abuse issues, homelessness, and/or ongoing poverty). There is recognition in all of these descriptions that some level of universal parent education is important from a public health perspective. Table 3.1 provides an overview and summary of characteristics of the three different models of a continuum of services, based on parent and family needs and intensity of services.

The Triple P program (Positive Parenting Program) has been used in a number of countries and provides a framework of parenting education services along a continuum that includes 5 levels and uses a public health approach to parent education (Pickering & Sanders, 2015; Doran, Jacobs, & Dewa, 2012). This program employs electronic and print media to reach all parents with messages about common parenting issues at the first level. The second level is focused on brief parenting interventions through large group seminars or one to two brief individual consultations. Topics focus on parenting information that promotes healthy development or strategies to address a specific developmental problem. Level 3 offers two group sessions or three to four individual sessions that provide advice and skills for parents with specific needs. Level 4 meets the needs of parents who want more intensive training on parenting skills. Sessions

Table 3.1 Models for Continuum of Parent Education Services

TRIPLE P POSITIVE PARENTING PROGRAM Pickering & Sanders (2015)	FROM BEST PRACTICES TO BREAKTHROUGH IMPACTS Center for the Developing Child (2016)	PARENTING MATTERS: SUPPORTING PARENTS OF CHILDREN 0–8 National Academy of Sciences (2016)
Five Levels	Four Levels	Three Levels
1. Public health messages about parenting issues for all parents—electronic and print media	1. Universal services for all parents—e.g., prenatal care	1. Universal prevention: core aspects of parenting by age of child—varied formats, settings, and intensity
2. Brief intervention on topics—large group seminars or one to two individual consultations	2. Broad-based programs across SES spectrum—e.g., programs for children with special needs, Pre-K programs	2. Targeted for populations at risk—children with special needs or behavioral problems—parents with mental health issues
3. Advice and skills related to specific parent needs—two groups sessions or three to four individual consultations	3. Target supports for families with low levels of education and income—parent education and coaching	3. Families facing persistent adversities—multiple long-term issues—intensive, long-term, and integrated services
4. Needs of parents who want more intensive training—10 hours online or workbook with telephone consultation	4. Intensive intervention for high-risk children with chronic stress, child maltreatment, and parents with substance abuse or mental health issues	
5. Parents who have children with behavior problems—tailored programs with various modes of delivery		

cover about 10 hours and are presented either online, through an individual workbook with telephone consultation, or in five 2-hour group sessions. The final level (5) is for parents who have children with behavior problems and/or current family challenges. Families at this level receive an individually tailored program with up to eight individual sessions. There are also other focus areas at level 5 with tailored methods and modes of delivery. The Triple P program has implemented a continuum of services that is consistent with the first two levels that have been described by the *Parenting Matters* (Academies of Sciences, Engineering, and Medicine, 2016) review and the Center for the Developing Child (2016). The delineated services have been researched in a variety of settings with different populations of parents, and an extensive evidence base for the effectiveness of its services has been developed. It is not as clear how this model might address the "persistent adversities" that are described in the National Academies of Sciences, Engineering, and Medicine (2016) model. To reach all families may not be possible and there may be another set of needs and goals beyond parenting knowledge and skills that is a necessary pre-requisite for some parents. The Triple P program is a useful case study of how a parent education program conceptualizes and approaches the universal needs of parents and builds more targeted services based on expressed parent needs at different levels.

Each of these conceptual models has some common core elements that are important for creating a complete system of parent education and support services. The different proposals recognize that all parents can benefit from some parenting information and support. The level or intensity of information and support depends upon the parent's needs. There is a clear understanding that programs should be tailored to parent needs and that an array of possible services and modes of delivery can help to reach as many parents as possible. The models also acknowledge the need for more intense and longer duration programs for families with multiple needs.

PROPOSED CONTINUUM OF PARENT/FAMILY SERVICES MODEL

The continuum model goals range from promotion of positive parenting practices (National Academies of Sciences, Engineering, and Medicine, 2016) to intensive interventions with parents with clearly identified family, mental health, or legal needs. A public health perspective of parenting education has been used and is an appropriate paradigm to develop a continuum model of parent education services. The broad overarching goal is to provide parents with information about child development and parenting practices that will be beneficial for parent-child relationships and child outcomes and that can be provided either in group settings or individual consultation with parents. In moving toward a National Framework of parent education services, the National Academies of Sciences, Engineering, and Medicine (2016) model recognizes the diverse set of programs that are currently offered as parent education services and the need

From our experience ... We have had the opportunity to be involved in the universal access program Early Childhood Family Education (ECFE) in Minnesota in a variety of ways over the last 35 years. We've watched this program for parents of children aged 0–5 evolve over this time from a generic parent education program to one with different intensities of programming serving parents with varied needs.

In addition to weekly sessions, services are delivered through special events, toy lending libraries, newsletters, and home visits. ECFE parent educators are required to have a parent education license and to participate in professional development to expand their skills to serve parents and families with multiple needs. There was no model of a continuum of parent education services, yet programs evolved to serve the changing needs of families in their communities. ECFE programs grew organically around the needs of parents, children, and families without a specified curriculum and have been successful at serving all families through collaborative efforts. The continuum model, as it has evolved in ECFE, creates possibilities for building vibrant community networks of family education and support.

to move toward more coordination and quality control of programs, so that they would be both more effective for parents and children and the most efficient use of public resources. The model that is presented in this chapter is based on ideas from the other models and is offered as a combination of the conceptual ideas proposed for a framework and the concrete practices from programs like Triple P (Prinz et al., 2009). It is best characterized as a mid-level model that labels and organizes some of the current parent education services across disciplines provided through the health, education, social services, and justice systems. It is meant as a way for a community to think about the services that might be offered at different levels of parent and family needs.

This model describes three different areas of services and needs that are depicted in Figure 3.1. While this model has three unique columns of services, the dotted line between the columns denotes the permeability between services and possible overlap of parent audience needs. The shaded areas in some of the service boxes represent possible collaboration through co-facilitation or working in concert to offer complementary services to address parent needs.

Parents share their ideas and support each other

PROMOTION/UNIVERSAL PREVENTION

In the first column, the emphasis is on services for parents that promote an understanding of child development and typical parenting issues with young children ages 0–8. This model could be expanded through the teen years, but research on early family support and intervention (Center for the Developing Child, 2016) makes a strong case for the greatest impact for services occurring during early childhood. One example listed in this column is a class for parents of young children ages 0–5 that meets at the local early childhood program in a neighborhood school for 8 weeks on Tuesday evenings. There may also be less intensive services, such as a parenting seminar on toddler tantrums at a community day care center. A class for parents of newborns might meet with a parent educator and nurse at the local healthcare facility for three to four sessions focusing on the transition to parenthood. Information for parents could also be offered through a website that addresses typical parent concerns for different ages of children. Parents of three year olds might enroll in an online class that focuses on early language development and literacy. These examples and others in the boxes under Promotion/Universal Prevention all concentrate on increasing parent knowledge and skills to promote healthy child growth and development. In addition, their services can support parents through predictable transitions (e.g., transition to kindergarten). The dosage and duration of programing at this array of service varies from one-time encounters, for example, reading an article online, to parent groups

Figure 3.1 Continuum of Parent/Family Services For Parents of Children 0-8

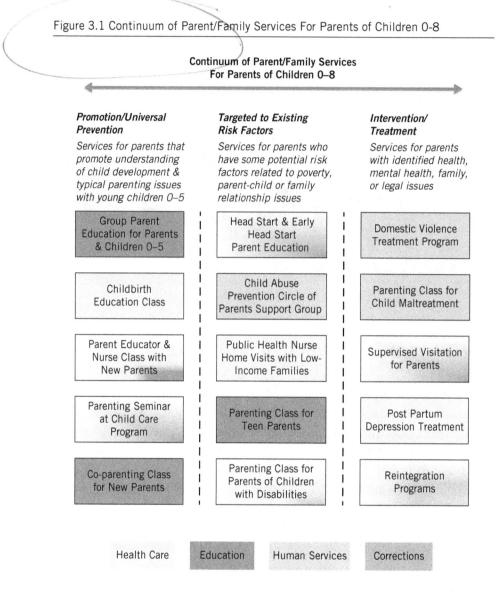

that may meet weekly for several weeks. One of the strengths of the universal prevention programming is that engaging in parenting education services is not stigmatized as only for "bad parents." All parents can benefit; parent education is not just for parents who are struggling with parenting or having problems with their children.

TARGETED TO EXISTING RISK FACTORS

The services in this column focus on parents who have potential risk factors related to poverty, parent, child, or family issues. The services still address generic parenting needs but in specific contexts where parents share some common risk factors. Programs that fit into this column reach out to parents facing specific stressors, such as teen parents or parents of young children with disabilities. Parent education programs maintain their focus on parenting knowledge and skills but also are able to examine more carefully how these impact parents and families in their shared circumstances. The purpose of parent education for targeted groups of parents with similar risk factors is to provide early intervention that identifies the potential negative impact of the risk factors on parenting and provides parents with specific information and strategies in order to strengthen their protective factors. The core of parent information and skills for the general population may also be helpful but has to be adapted to meet individual circumstances. For example, parents who have children with identified disabilities still need to know about child development and guidance skills but they have to be presented and adapted to match the children's abilities. In addition, parents of children with disabilities face unique challenges, such as finding needed resources and managing new family stresses. Parents who are meeting as a group with similar risk factors become an important support system for each other. The parent educator has to keep in mind that this support may be a more important goal for groups at this level than those at the promotion/universal prevention level.

INTERVENTION/TREATMENT

The services in the third column are for parents who have been identified as having physical or mental health, family, or legal problems. Families at this level will need more intensive services and may also be involved with more than one agency, especially if they face persistent adversities (National Academies of Sciences, Engineering, and Medicine, 2016). Parent education services would have to be integrated with other community services to be effective. Some of the parent issues that fall under this category are mental health issues, such as depression, substance abuse, or anxiety, and family issues, such as domestic violence and incarceration. These tend to be more chronic and severe conditions that interfere with parent-child relationships. Interventions may be more intense (e.g., individual or parent-child therapy) and may last longer. Parents may also require a number of different community services in order to have a long-term impact, with parent education as part of a comprehensive plan.

Practitioners working with these families should be experienced and have clear boundaries and realistic expectations about their work. They should also be aware of the impact that different conditions might have on parenting behaviors and how to adapt parent education practice to fit the family situation and parents' conditions. When parents or families have been identified at this level, there may be compounding factors (e.g., poverty, family instability, isolation) that make interventions more complex and challenge our current systems to provide consistent and effective services to address multiple family needs (National Academies of Sciences, Engineering, and Medicine, 2016).

EXAMPLES OF DIFFERENT LEVELS

PROMOTION/UNIVERSAL PREVENTION EXAMPLE

Dads and Kids Book Club—This father-child class fits under promotion with a dual purpose of supporting father-child relationships and providing fathers with information and skills to support emerging literacy skills in their young children (Palm, 2013). Fathers come with their young children ages 3–6 to a 1.5 hour session in the evening for 6 weeks. A different book with a father as the main character is introduced each week with literacy related activities for fathers and children to do together that are connected with the book. These activities include dramatic play, crafts, art, writing, and snacks with recipes. The session begins with an experienced male early childhood teacher reading the book of the week and modeling different ways to engage children in the reading experience. This is followed by a song and description of the father-child activities for the evening. The last 20–30 minutes are spent in a parent session for the fathers, while the children are with the early childhood teacher. The parents discuss the content of the book and any related parenting issues. For example, with the book Owl Moon, the fathers talk about sharing the value of nature with their children. Each father is given a copy of the book and a tip sheet that provides ideas for reading the book and promoting early literacy skills, story comprehension, and new vocabulary and having fun with children's books. While this program has a promotion focus, it is marketed to all the fathers in the community, and groups include fathers from the local Head Start program.

TARGETED SERVICES TO RISK FACTORS EXAMPLE

Early Head Start Class for Parents of Toddlers—The Early Head Start class for parents of children ages 1–3 meets one morning a week for 2 hours during the school year. The format includes parent-child interaction time. The parent educator and early childhood educator provide toys and other materials for the parents and children to enjoy playtime together. The parent educator meets with the parents for the last half of the session to discuss any immediate concerns and address specific parenting needs and typical parenting issues around toddler development, such as toilet learning, setting limits, and guidance strategies. The group members are able to share some of their common experiences being both parents in low-income families and raising toddlers. The emphasis is often on support and problem solving. Sometimes parents need assistance connecting with local resources. The parent educator works closely with the Early Head Start family advocate who helps connect parents to resources around needs like housing, food, and energy assistance. The main focus of the parenting program is on creating positive parent-child relationships through sharing information, learning new ideas about guidance, and dealing with family stresses while raising a toddler. What makes this type of parent education service different from the universal prevention level is that the parents are managing risk factors related to low income and are struggling with parenting issues, often in isolation, and lack family support systems. A parent group setting also helps parents experience positive peer relationships, which can have long-term positive effects related to increased family support and connection to the larger community.

INTERVENTION/TREATMENT EXAMPLE

First Steps Parent Education Home Visit Program—First Steps is a parent education home visiting program in a women's shelter with elements of child-parent psychotherapy. It has been adapted for mothers of children ages 0–3 (Ellison, 2014). This program addresses the mental health needs of infants and toddlers who have experienced domestic violence. The program is an 11-week program that meets for 1 hour each week and is offered to each mother of a child aged 0–3 years old when she comes to the shelter. The goal of the dyadic work in this context is to improve the quality of the parent-child relationship and to restore the child's trust in the parent's capacity to keep the child safe. The 1-hour sessions consist of playtime with mother and child and a play activity focusing on making a connection (e.g., mother blowing a cotton ball for child to catch). The content for each session centers around attachment (e.g., spoiling versus responding to your child's needs), brain development (e.g., appropriate stimulation), and health and safety (e.g., sleep). The parent also is given a board book (e.g., *My Mom, Goodnight Gorilla*) that is connected to the topic. The parent educator introduces a song (e.g., *Bumping Up and Down in Mommy's Lap, Criss Cross Applesauce*) to share with the child. Each week, the parent educator videotapes a short 5-minute clip of the session that is later made into a DVD to give the mother as a keepsake. A magnet reminder provides a short summary of the session focus. A benefit of working in the shelter is the presence of the other staff members who help connect parents with housing, legal assistance, mental and medical health resources, and other support services. The program is flexible and adapted to the individual parent and child. The parent educator may follow the parent and child into their new housing after they leave the shelter to complete the 11-week series. The program is a powerful component of a comprehensive array of services to help families by addressing the needs of the vulnerable child and stressed parent with the goal of strengthening the parent-child relationship.

SUMMARY OF THE CONTINUUM OF PARENT/ FAMILY SERVICES MODEL

The proposed continuum model shares a core of parent education and support content that centers around information on child development and developing parenting skills (e.g., communication, guidance, teaching, using community resources). The knowledge and skills base changes with the age of the child but is central for all the parent education services along the continuum. The overarching goals are to promote a positive parent-child relationship and build the capacity of parents to create and maintain basic trust by meeting a child's needs and guiding the child's behavior. The assumption is that these outcomes for parents will, in turn, lead to positive child development outcomes. At the intervention point in the continuum, the emphasis moves from one of educa- tion and support to a more specific focus on change in thinking and behavior patterns that will lead to improved child behavior. The language of education is about learning, and the language of intervention is about making a more profound change. It is expected that the duration of the services in intervention may take more time, depending upon the severity of the identified problem. The knowledge and skills required by practitioners at the intervention end of the continuum typically includes specific diagnostic and treatment approaches that address underlying issues and change behavior patterns so that parent learning can occur.

DIFFERENT ROLES OF THE PARENT EDUCATOR

The core role of parent educators in each type of parent education service along the continuum is to be a caring teacher. The parent and family educator role as a teacher is multifaceted (knowledge, skills, and dispositions from Chapter 2) and demands a commitment to continuous professional development. In the promotion/universal prevention types of services, the emphasis is on providing current knowledge about child development and parenting strategies. The teaching of practical skills is also important. This may include communication, empathy, and behavior guidance skills. The theory of change is based on parents being open to and able to learn with limited interference from other factors (e.g., poverty, their own adverse childhood experiences, physical and mental health issues). The introduction of knowledge and skills are enough to promote positive parenting behaviors and parent-child relationships.

The second type of parent education programming takes a more targeted approach on specific types of risk that may interfere with parenting practice (e.g., poverty related stresses or the parent's childhood experiences of abuse). Programs may also focus on new challenges (experiencing a divorce, having a child diagnosed with a disability, or dealing with a chronic health issue). Parent educators who are working with parents in these types of programs will encounter more challenges to achieving the goals of increasing parent knowledge, skills, and positive parenting practices. The process of change must include understanding and helping parents manage or overcome some of the barriers they face. Helping parents to discover their own strengths and motivation to change may be central to the role of the parent educator. The parent who wants to avoid abusing their child because of their own experience of abuse will need more assistance to practice new guidance skills that may be foreign to them. Parent education services that target risk factors demand that the parent educator has a deeper knowledge of the issues and barriers, increased empathy and understanding, and skills to coach parents as they learn new parenting practices. Learning to take on this role will be easier for the more experienced parent educator, and it can sometimes be an advantage if the parent educator has some personal experience with the risk factors that members in the group experience.

The third type of service for parents who have already been identified with specific problems is similar to a public health model, which focuses on a particular diagnosed health concern of the individual. A diagnosis adds clarity and direction to the type of intervention that is required. Parenting may not be the main focus of the treatment, but parenting services can serve as important adjuncts or supplemental services. Parent education services have to work in coordination with the main interventions, for example mental health or substance abuse counseling. Therefore, the needs of the parent or family will be prioritized, and the focus on parent education may be delayed or minimized until other more immediate concerns are addressed. In this category of services, it is critical that an individualized approach be utilized and that professionals work collaboratively to design strategies that are timely and appropriate for each family.

The added skills required for the parent educator in this role include working with other professionals and aligning parent education to fit with the other treatment strategies. A deeper understanding of the barriers to positive parent-child relationships and parenting practices will also be necessary. Parenting education for incarcerated parents is an example of the type of parent education service that may be offered in the last column of the continuum. Parents in this situation may encounter many barriers and need help with adult education to develop the knowledge and work skills to be successfully employed. They might also have to complete substance abuse treatment and may face legal issues around visitation, custody, and child support. Parent education services can still focus on the basic goals in the first two columns of the model, as adapted to the parent's circumstances.

Parent educators have to understand and respond to the boundaries of the work they are doing in each category of service. (See Chapter 7 for more information about professional boundaries.) They are not mental health counselors or case managers. They must have a deep understanding and appreciation of the complex barriers this group of parents has to overcome to achieve positive parenting goals.

RELATIONSHIPS AT DIFFERENT POINTS ALONG THE CONTINUUM

Chapter 7 addresses the importance of building relationships with parents in parent education and describes relationships between parents and parent educators as the heart of effective practice. There is a core set of relationship skills that a parent educator develops to build a professional, caring connection with parents. The introduction of a continuum of parent education services suggests that the nature of the relationship changes as one moves along the continuum from promotion to intervention. One of the differences is that the degree of parent need will be greater at the intervention end of the continuum. The parent educator will be required to support parents in ways that call for more effort and intentionality. Parents who have risk factors or significant identified needs are more vulnerable, and the level of emotionality will typically be higher in the interactions with the parent educator. This leads to greater depth in knowing who the parent is and a more intense and emotional relationship than one with a parent who is focused on learning more about child development and wanting to acquire some new strategies for guiding their toddler's negative behaviors. The parent educator at the promotion level may ask some basic questions about a child and how they respond to different situations. They may even delve into a more emotional area and ask how it feels when a child talks back or hits them. However, they do not probe more deeply at this end of the continuum about the parent's background or relationship history. Parent education services that focus on at-risk populations and parents with identified problems lead to a different type of relationship where the parents' needs are greater and the level of intimacy based on knowledge of the parent's vulnerabilities and strengths is also deeper. Parent educators will need to have more knowledge about early trauma and the impact of various risk factors on parenting attitudes and behavior. Parent educators who are coming from an educational perspective need to learn more about other resources and how to manage some of the deeper emotions and more complex issues they may encounter that interface with parenting practices.

The mutual expectations of the parent educator and parent also change at different places along the continuum. The emphasis on parent as learner and parent educator as guide changes to more intentional work to build protective factors that ameliorate risk factors and work toward deeper, life-altering change. This can be thought of as an unwritten "contract" that delineates the expectations of each person involved. A parent who is participating in intervention services has a different contract and expects and needs a deeper level of emotional support and understanding. This type of relationship requires the parent educator to understand and process at a deeper level the emotions of the parent while they continue to focus on parent education goals.

Parent educators, through their modeling of caring, empathy, and support for parents, provide an experience that some parents did not receive as children. This is different from modeling responses of guidance behavior (e.g., listening and reflecting a child's feelings) for parent educators to demonstrate and parents to emulate. When parent educators treat parents with respect, empathy, caring, and patience, it can help build the capacity of parents to understand, at a visceral level, how children feel and how to respond in more caring ways. This is another dimension of the relationship that may be different moving toward the intervention end of the continuum. Parents who are unfamiliar with this type of acceptance and empathy may struggle with how to transfer these qualities to their relationships with their children.

From our experience ... As a director of a parent-child program and supervisor of parent educators, I have had the opportunity to choose amazing staff and watch them grow in their skills and professional development. Some of them came directly out of licensure preparation programs, while others brought considerable experience to their positions. There were certain attributes and personal qualities that I looked for when choosing staff to work in programs that offered services to complex families, particularly in collaborative partnerships with other agencies. Some parent educators came from personal backgrounds where they could identify and empathize with the challenges of at-risk families. For some this was an asset; however, for others, it provided boundary challenges and could interfere with being objective in their relationships with parents. I found that those who did well in these programs were most open to working as a member of a team. These parent educators had a curiosity about other programs and willingness to learn from other professionals, in addition to sharing their perspectives and expertise. In their relationships with parents, they were thoughtful and intentional. They acted as advocates for parents without becoming over involved and showed genuine concern and care in their interactions. These parent educators needed a good sense of self, a clear understanding of the challenges parents face, an absence of blame or judgment regarding the parent's circumstance, and a commitment to serving families with complex needs. Having an approachable style, a sense of humor, and a calm demeanor were all qualities that helped them in this role.

NEW OPPORTUNITIES FOR COLLABORATION BETWEEN SYSTEMS

There are many opportunities for greater collaboration, as depicted in the continuum model, where parent educators can work jointly with other professionals who have a set of complementary skills. There are a number of examples of parent educators in the early education system working with nurses, mental health professionals, or caseworkers, reflected in Figure 3.1. The vision that the continuum model creates is one of building a coordinated network of community services focused on family education and support.

One of the major benefits of collaborative work is to be able to build understanding and respect for the skills of other professionals working with children and families. Appreciating the healthcare knowledge that a nurse may bring to a parenting class or knowing that a social service case manager has a solid grasp of community resources and how to access them for parents leads to more coordinated support for families. There may also be some opportunities for co-facilitation in parent groups where a parent educator and a family therapist work together to lead a co-parenting class for unmarried parents. This is a chance to experience the unique knowledge and skills of each profession and to see where they complement and perhaps overlap each other. A final benefit of improved collaboration is the likelihood that referrals will be more successful for parents when the parent educator knows both the individual professional and the services that another agency offers.

There are also many challenges that need to be acknowledged about collaborative and network building efforts. It is often hard to work with other systems based on the documentation and record-keeping requirements in each system. For example, in a collaboration between Head Start and the public schools offering a family literacy program, there were three different sets of application materials that needed to be completed by families entering the program. This created a burden for both families and staff members. Moreover, the funding streams for different systems often lead to different levels of compensation for similar types of work. When a parent educator in a public school early childhood program worked with a family therapist in a community mental health center as co-facilitators of a parenting class, the levels of pay and sources of pay were different and had to be addressed to understand the requirements of both systems. The different "languages" of mental health, education, and social services can also be a barrier. The jargon around different policies, diagnostic tools, evaluation measures, and codes of ethics can make communication difficult. Finally, an additional barrier to collaboration is the investment and commitment of time that it takes to work toward mutual goals and understanding. These difficulties are real and challenge professionals in any programs that work together to best meet the needs of parents and families. However, working together often provides the best options for parents and their children.

It takes leadership from the top of an agency or organization to initiate and support the work that is needed for successful collaboration. It also requires a belief in the value of building a coordinated network of parent education and support services and an investment of time and resources. Leaders with a vision of the long-term positive outcomes resulting from this type of investment are crucial to the success of these collaborative arrangements that provide the best services for parents, children, and families.

SUMMARY

Parent education services have continued to change and evolve based on new research, a new understanding of children's early brain development (Center for the Developing Child, 2016), and the renewed appreciation for the role of parenting practices especially during the early years (National Academies of Sciences, Engineering, and Medicine, 2016). The impetus to create a more coherent and coordinated system of parent education and support that includes all parents has gained momentum. The framework presented here is an image of the potential of such a system and one to which we can aspire. It provides a comprehensive system for parent education practitioners who specialize in providing parent education services in collaboration with other professionals as either a primary focus or an adjunct, supplementary service.

DISCUSSION QUESTIONS

1. What are the major benefits of a continuum model for the work that you see yourself doing?

2. What are some of the benefits of promotion/universal prevention in the model from a public health perspective? How will these types of services impact the community?

3. What should the role of evidence-based parent education programs/curriculums be?

4. The role of parent education practitioners changes along the continuum. How does pre-service preparation interface with previous work and personal experiences in preparing individuals to work effectively at different places along the continuum?

5. How does parent education at different points on the continuum relate to the dispositions that may be most important for the parent educator?

CLASS ACTIVITIES

1. Ask class members to look at the continuum and think about where they are currently or might be working along the continuum and which other systems/programs they might be collaborating with.

2. Ask class members to review the dispositions from Chapter 2 and discuss how important each might be at different places along the continuum?

REFERENCES

Carter, N. (1996). *See how they grow: A report on the status of parenting education in the U.S.* Philadelphia, PA: Pew Charitable Trusts.

Center on the Developing Child at Harvard University (2016). From best practice to breakthrough impacts: A science-based approach to building a more promising future for young children and families. Retrieved from http://www.developingchild.harvard.edu.

Doherty, W. (1995). Boundaries between parent and family education and family therapy. *Family Relations, 44,* 353–358.

Doherty, W.J., & Lamson, A.L. (2015). The Levels of Family Involvement Model: 20 Years Later. In M. J. Walcheski & J. S. Reinke (Eds.), *Family Life Education: The Practice of Family Science* (pp. 39–47). Minneapolis, MN: National Council on Family Relations.

Doran, C.E., Jacobs, P. & Dewa, C.S. (2012). *Return on investment for mental health promotion: Parenting programs and early childhood development.* Alberta, Canada: Institute of Health Economics.

Ellison, J.R. (2014). "I didn't think he remember": Healing the impact of domestic violence on infant and toddlers. *Zero to Three Journal, 35*(2), 49–55.

MNAFEE (Minnesota Association for Family and Early Educators). (2015). *Minnesota's Early Childhood Family Education: Answers to commonly asked questions.* Retrieved from http://www.mnafee.org/vertical/sites/%7B2555CA3F-B6AD-4263-9177-3B66CE5F2892%7D/uploads/ECFE_Digital_FINAL.pdf.

Myers-Walls, J., Ballard, S., Darling, C., & Myers-Bowman, K. (2011). Reconceptualizing the domain and boundaries of Family Life Education. *Family Relations, 60,* 357–372.

National Academies of Sciences, Engineering, and Medicine. (2016). *Parenting matters: Supporting parents of children 0–8.* Washington, DC: The National Academies Press. Doi: 10.17226/21868.

Palm, G. (2013). Fathers and Early Literacy. In Jutsna Pattnaik (Ed.) *Father Involvement in Children's Lives: An International Perspective* (pp. 13–29). New York, NY: Springer.

Pickering, J.A., & Sanders, M.R (2015). The Triple P-Positive Parenting Program: An example of a public health approach to evidence-based parenting support. *Family Matters, 96,* 53–63.

Prinz, R.J., Sanders, M.R., Shapiro, C.J., Whitaker, D.J., & Lutzker, J.R. (2009) Population-based prevention of child maltreatment: The U.S. Triple P system population trial. *Prevention Science, 10*(1) 1–12.

Sanders, M.R., Ralph, A., Sofronoff, K., Gardomer, P., Thompson, R., Dwyer, S., & Bidwell, K. (2008). Every family: A population approach to reducing behavioral and emotional problems in children making the transition to school. *Journal of Primary Prevention, 29*, 197–222.

Sanders, M.R. (2008). Triple P-Positive Parenting Program as a public health approach to strengthening parenting. *Journal of Family Psychology, 2* (3), 506–517. Doi:10.1037/0893-3200.22.3.506.

Shonkoff, J.P., & Fisher, P.A. (2013). Rethinking evidence-based practice and two-generation programs to create the future of early childhood policy. *Developmental Psychopathology, 25*, 1635–1653.

Thomas, R., & Cooke, B. (1986). Summary of profile of parent education study. In J. Parsons, T. Bowman, J. Comeau, & R. Pitzer (Eds.) *Parent education state of the art* (pp. 19–26). White Bear Lake, MN: Minnesota Curriculum Services Center.

Weatherson, D.J., Kaplan-Setric, M., & Goldberg, S. (2009). Strengthening and recognizing knowledge, skills and reflective practice: The Michigan Association for Infant Mental Health competency guidelines and endorsement process. *Infant Mental Health Journal, 30*(6), 658–663. Doi: 10.1002imhj.20234.

CONCEPTUAL FRAMEWORKS—
PART I: *Models for Understanding Group Dynamics*

Parent education groups have a variety of different purposes that range from teaching parents specific behavioral techniques to sharing stories and providing support. In order to provide a better understanding of the complex dynamics in different parent education programs, key conceptual frameworks will be outlined in this chapter. A conceptual framework is composed of a set of concepts and assumptions related to a practice that are woven together to elucidate important dynamics of parent learning and support in group parent education. These perspectives mirror the different theoretical frameworks that have been used for understanding families. The first two frameworks have been applied to group dynamics in very specific ways and parallel family processes of development and instrumental and expressive family functions. The systems theory and gender and power frameworks offer additional insights into parent group dynamics, based on concepts used to understand family dynamics. This chapter will provide an introduction to four frameworks that will be used throughout the book. It will also describe the primary contributions of each framework for understanding parent learning and parent group dynamics. Each framework or perspective makes a unique contribution to our understanding of group parent education.

Parent educators use a variety of methods to facilitate group discussions

These frameworks are not fully articulated nor tested theories about parent groups. They are carefully constructed sets of concepts based on family theories and group practice that have been applied to parent education practice. The research emphasis in parent education has been on curriculum format, content, and program outcomes, not on group dynamics. The purpose of describing different conceptual frameworks here is to acknowledge different ways of thinking about parent groups. These frameworks reflect different assumptions, goals, and strategies for facilitating parent groups. Together they represent a patchwork understanding of groups and group dynamics that can be integrated into useful guidelines and concrete suggestions for practice.

The first framework, the **developmental** perspective, describes how a group changes over time in predictable ways (stages). The **functional** approach, a second framework, examines two basic functions of groups and how these apply to group parent education. A third, **systems perspective**, utilizes systems theory concepts, such as open and closed systems, goal-generating systems, and synergy, to describe salient aspects of group dynamics in parent education. Finally, a fourth perspective, a **gender dynamics** framework (Van Nostrand, 1993), uses gender as a critical concept for understanding parent group interactions, parent roles, and power dynamics. Chapter 5 will outline four additional conceptual frameworks that focus on different perspectives for understanding the roles of parent group leaders. These two chapters introduce the theoretical foundations for group parent education. They help to describe and explain different frameworks and concepts about parent group dynamics and the roles of the parent group leader.

FRAMEWORK 1: THE DEVELOPMENTAL PERSPECTIVE—STAGES OF GROUP DEVELOPMENT

The life cycle of a group tends to progress through several predictable stages, following patterns typical of other developmental stage theories for children, adults, and families. Parent groups, like other groups, are dynamic; they possess an energy that moves them through a variety of experiences that encourage parent learning and support. The developmental perspective of groups indicates that, like other living things, groups have cyclical patterns of growth and development. This section will examine stages of group development and how these stages apply to parent group dynamics.

A commonly accepted theory of group development identifies five separate stages: forming, norming, storming, performing, and adjourning (Curran, 1989). Each stage has specific characteristics and goals that require careful attention from the group leader. Group members have particular needs, as well as tasks to accomplish, during each stage toward the common purpose of group learning and support through parent and family education. It is helpful for the parent educator to be aware of the dynamics and behaviors during each stage so that he or she can respond to them and assist the group in transitioning to the next stage.

There are, however, some limitations in applying the stages of development framework to all parent groups. Groups must be ongoing and of sufficient duration for these stages to occur. Parent groups that meet a limited number of times (fewer than six times) may exhibit some of the characteristics of individual stages. However, an ideal representation of group development will typically occur in groups that meet for longer periods of time. There is generally overlap between the stages (Corey, 1999). Groups may move back and forth between stages or move quickly through one and perhaps become stuck in another. The stages, therefore, should not be seen as absolute or as following a preordained time frame. Finally, group membership and characteristics can greatly influence the stages of development. For example, if established groups are open to new members, the developmental progress may be affected when new parents join. Members who enter an existing group have not experienced the previous stages and will need to proceed from a different point. Their presence also changes the structure of the group, and this variation may interfere with the group's progress. Past experiences of parent participants may also change the development of groups. Members who have had other experiences in groups, who know each other or the parent educator, or whose personalities make them comfortable or uncomfortable with the group experience can influence group development. The theory of group development helps parent educators understand typical stages, but each group is unique and will experience its own version of the group life cycle.

> ***From our experience …*** I was asked to co-facilitate a faith-based group of parents who wanted to explore the development of spiritual beliefs in children. The parents in the group all knew each other, so the initial stages of building trust had already occurred, and the group was able to go into the work, or performing, stage more quickly than previous groups that I had led. This was a real benefit as the sharing of ideas and feelings happened at a deeper level by the second session.

STAGE 1: FORMING

Groups begin with the forming stage. In this initial stage, the group comes together as members get to know each other and the leader. The forming stage should feel safe as parents begin the group experience, perhaps with some uncertainty about what it will be like. Parents may "be on their best behavior," and the overall atmosphere can be described as polite. Time is spent on practical matters, as well as sharing information regarding the purpose of the group and discovering the common interests of the group members. There is usually some small talk, with guarded self-disclosure, as members begin to make informal connections to other individuals in the group.

During the forming stage, parents may have questions such as:

- "Will I be accepted in this group?"
- "Do I belong here?"
- "Can I be myself?"

- "What will this experience be like? Will it be what I expected?"
- "Are there other members with whom I feel comfortable?"
- "Will I get my needs met here?"

Goals for the parent educator are to share the necessary basic information about the group, to set a positive and welcoming tone, and to help parents feel comfortable and help them get acquainted with each other. Activities, such as asking parents to share "one thing they like best about their child," encourages them to actively participate early on in the group and may provide more safety than asking members to share information about themselves. The parent educator typically provides more structure during the forming stage of the group, for the purpose of ensuring safety for members. However, maintaining too much structure early on may set a pattern for the duration of the group experience in which the group expects the leader to do all the work, thus stifling discussion. This can inhibit participation, spontaneity, and ownership. The first session is critical in setting the tone for participation and shared ownership of how the group will function.

STAGE 2: NORMING

The second stage in development is the norming stage. This stage occurs early in the life cycle of a group and is often intertwined with the forming stage. Goals are stated, expectations shared, and group rules set. The parent educator may ask the parents to spend time identifying what they want from this experience, choose particular topics or issues they want to explore, and share some of their own expectations for the group.

Parents ask:

- "What are the rules here?"
- "How should I behave?"
- "What will I get from this experience?"
- "What role will I play in this group?"

It is beneficial for ongoing groups to develop clear ground rules. This can be done in a variety of ways, including the parent educator presenting a prepared list of suggested ground rules and asking for additions or asking the group to design their own. Another way to get all members involved is to lay out suggested rules on individual note cards and ask each member to select an item that is meaningful to them and explain why. However, when setting up ground rules, it is important for group members to have some input into their development, since shared ownership of the group is a significant aspect of early group development.

Ground rules are agreed-upon rules or guidelines for the group. Group members, along with the leader, adopt the rules using a consensus model. Ideally, ground rules should be written and then posted on the wall at each session, so they can be referred to, if needed. If a ground rule is broken, the leader may need to remind the group what was agreed upon. For example, a ground rule may have been set that members avoid talking about others who are not present. If the group begins to discuss an absent parent, the leader has a responsibility to protect that person and can refer to the ground rule: "When we designed our ground rules, we agreed that we would avoid talking about members who aren't present. Let's make sure we follow that rule in our discussion."

If the group accepts new members after the group has begun, they also need to be aware of the ground rules, so posting them and reviewing them occasionally is helpful. Couples who share attendance, where one parent attends one week and the other the next, may provide a challenge for the parent educator. In this case, it is recommended that the facilitator remind parents to share information with the absent co-parent so that they will be aware of what has been discussed or decided.

Box 4.1 Sample Ground Rules

Set 1

1. Everyone participates.
2. Everyone has the right to pass.
3. Listen to each other's opinions.
4. All disclosures made in the group are confidential.
5. Limit side conversations.

Set 2

1. We are here to share our feelings and experiences about parenting, but this is not a therapy group.
2. We will respect and maintain confidentiality.
3. We will avoid interrupting each other.
4. We will all participate and avoid side conversations.
5. We will try not to discuss persons who are not present.
6. We will support each other and avoid making judgments.

Group norms are also developed during this stage. Norms tend to be subtler and are often not stated. They are standards that indicate what behaviors are expected of group members. Group norms are similar to social skills that each of us learn in order to function in society. They are a guide to behavior and offer a sense of consistency and predictability for members so that they know what to expect.

All groups have norms. There are norms for parties, parent-teacher conferences, church meetings, standing in line in the grocery store, and eating in a restaurant. People follow these social norms to conform and to fit in. Group behaviors or norms are typically modeled and often unstated. Group norms may be that parents openly share their feelings, that parents feel comfortable disagreeing with each other and/or the leader, that humor is accepted in the group, that food can be brought into the session, or that parents speak freely without waiting to be asked a question. Members quickly internalize these norms. This happens quietly and may not be verbally noted, but members quickly learn what is acceptable and what is not. Parents with limited social skills can often miss or incorrectly interpret the cues from the leader and other members that identify norms. They may behave in ways that do not match the norms of the group and, therefore, will not be accepted by others. The group leader plays a role in modeling acceptable behavior and sometimes needs to gently confront behaviors that do not match the group norms. For example, a parent who uses profanity in the group may offend others. Although most parent educators may ignore a few inappropriate words, a constant infusion of them needs to be addressed. Speaking with the parent privately after group to point out that others seem offended and asking his or her cooperation may be necessary to bring this member's behavior back into the accepted range of group norms.

The norms governing communication within a group are established quickly in the initial stages. Parents watch carefully to learn the "rules" of communication. If the parent educator speaks first and members wait until they are questioned, this will probably develop as a pattern or norm. Ideally, communication in a group will flow between members, as well as from the leader. A leader who speaks after each parent offers a thought or opinion establishes this as a norm and inhibits free discussion between members. When observing parent education groups, it is interesting to track the flow of conversation.

Parent educators have the initial responsibility to model appropriate norms in a group. Members carefully observe the leader as he or she sets an informal or formal atmosphere, welcomes or discourages questions, offers ample opportunities for parents to talk, or dominates the discussion. Parents observe the

From our experience ... Part of my responsibility as a director of a family education program was to observe and evaluate parent educators. A technique that was particularly helpful was to draw a rough sketch showing the table and a mark for each parent and the leader. Keeping a pencil on the paper, I would draw a line from each member to the next as they spoke. Ideally, the "drawing" would look much like a spider web with the flow of discussion between members. If every parent statement was followed by a comment from the group leader, it was clear that a norm had been established that the leader spoke after each member. This can be prevented by leaving a "pause of silence" after a parent speaks, giving permission for another parent to comment, rather than setting the pattern of responding to each comment.

leader's use of humor, language, and behavior to set the standards of their own behavior. Although the parent educator plays a predominant role in setting the group norms, group members also observe the behavioral cues of other parents to make decisions about their own behavior in this setting.

During the norming stage, members are beginning to feel comfortable, or perhaps uncomfortable, about the group experience. They are carefully listening to each other with a spirit of cooperation and respect. There is beginning to be an open exchange of ideas, and members tend to feel safe staying on neutral topics. Some groups may become stagnant in this stage and be reluctant to move on.

During this stage, the parent educator encourages connections between members, listens carefully to learn more about each individual, and takes advantage of members' willingness to participate in this safe environment by choosing topics and issues that encourage discussion. Though any topic can elicit controversy in a group, topics such as common characteristics of children this age, communicating with children, and fostering healthy self-esteem tend to offer enough safety for parents to participate without fear of high levels of self-disclosure or conflict.

The parent educator can use this stage to find similarities between members and build on common interests and issues. Parents have a need for inclusion and a feeling of belonging in their group. Activities that offer opportunities for noting commonalities and facilitation strategies that build on and connect parents' issues will help to lay a foundation during the norming stage where connections are made and a comfortable and safe atmosphere develops. Because the next stage of development challenges this safety, parent educators can mention that groups typically go through stages, and there will be times when we disagree. This keeps things interesting, and as long as we are respectful to each other, it is good to have a variety of opinions and ideas. This sets the tone that things may change and also gives parents permission to be honest when sharing their views.

STAGE 3: STORMING

Groups now move into the storming stage, where an established sense of trust allows members to disagree with each other or the leader. Conflicts between members may arise as different values and ideas emerge. Until now, the group has operated at a fairly safe level, where most issues were met with agreement from the group. Perhaps there were differences of opinions, but they were not generally expressed. Tension may now result from diverse opinions or from personal or relational issues. Parents can feel judged because of responses to their self-disclosures and, therefore, not accepted by certain members. Or, they may feel a need to defend their viewpoints, which might differ drastically from those of others. Members ask themselves:

- "Do I agree or disagree with this idea?"
- "What can I contribute as a group member?"
- "To whom do I feel most connected?"
- "How comfortable am I with conflict?"
- "Why do some parents have such different ideas about parenting than I have?"

The response to the storming stage is unique to each parent. Common reactions may be those of either "fight or flight." Individuals who come from families where conflict and disagreement were not allowed may have a strong negative reaction to any controversy. They might attempt to mediate the conflict and bring the group back into a safer state, or they may withdraw emotionally from the group through lack of participation. Others who have family or other life experiences where conflict was common and intense may act out aggressively in their interactions. Ideally, parents will be able to handle some conflict by respectfully agreeing to disagree and will accept the guidance and modeling of the facilitator who sets this as an acceptable norm.

During the storming stage, the parent educator acts as a moderator of conflict. The term *conflict* often arouses a negative reaction. It is the role of the facilitator to assure the group that conflict is not always negative and can be a positive way for adults to learn from each other. It can also be stressed that the parent educator's role is to ensure a sense of acceptance for all members and that the expectation for discussion is that everyone will be treated respectfully. The leader's attitude about conflict is quickly interpreted by the group. If conflict is avoided at all cost and immediately stopped by the facilitator, members will soon learn that there is no room for divergent thinking in this group. If the leader, however, models an acceptance of different ideas and at the same time maintains an expectation of respect for all members, parents will learn not only that appropriate conflict is allowed but also how to approach it. Learning how to constructively challenge the ideas of others by asking questions that show a willingness to engage and learn about their views will assist in moving the group into the next stage of development.

It is during the storming stage that the group either breaks down or moves through the tension into the next and most productive stage of development. If the storming stage is accepted by the parent educator as an expected aspect of development and as a means of moving into a more productive level, parents will be more accepting. Parent educators benefit from taking a reflective approach to understand how they personally react to conflict. Family-of-origin issues have a powerful impact on group leaders' responses to conflict. Although the setting and the participants are different, the presence of conflict can elicit an emotional reaction from a group leader who remembers conflict issues within their own family. Examining experiences of conflict in other areas of the group leader's life will give a broader understanding of these dynamics. The parent educator who can consciously avoid personalizing conflict will be able to work with this dynamic as a means of group development, rather than struggling to eliminate it. The presence of conflict and disagreement can be challenging for parent educators, especially those who are unaccustomed to it. The emotional intensity of disagreement should, of course, be monitored so that members continue to feel safe. However, when managed appropriately, it becomes a positive growth experience for a parent group.

STAGE 4: PERFORMING

Ideally, all groups will reach this stage in their developmental process. It is here that the group becomes solid; group morale and loyalty are high. Members feel an appreciation for each other and the experience. Collaborative problem solving brings support to individual members, and the focus of the group is working on issues and reaching a new understanding of self and others. There is usually a high level of honesty in the performing stage, where members are free to share ideas, opinions, and feelings. As members solidify their relationships with each other and the leader, a connection develops that is built on mutual respect and reciprocal care. The group is now characterized as having fun and working hard together. During this stage, parents are actively involved and focusing on the work of the group. There is less uncertainty than in other stages, less focus on questions of purpose or needs, and more intentional problem solving and support. It is during this stage that parents become more aware of the group identity that has evolved and on the needs of individual members, rather than focusing on their own participation. A balance between relationships and tasks has been achieved, and there is shared ownership and responsibility for all members of the group.

The topics addressed during this stage can have more depth, and the level of self-disclosure increases. Family-of-origin issues, family stresses, and co-parenting issues become safe topics to explore. Parents trust they will be able to disclose feelings and experiences to the group and the leader without judgment.

The performing stage of the group is the most productive and satisfying for both the members and leader. The parent leaves a session armed with new knowledge and a sense of accomplishment for having participated with other group members. The parent educator has accomplished a major goal of assisting members to solve problems, address issues, and collaboratively support each other in their parenting journey.

STAGE 5: ADJOURNING

The final stage of group development is the adjourning stage, where the focus is on the termination of the group. There is a sense of accomplishment that goals have been achieved and that real learning has occurred. There may also be some apprehension or sadness in anticipation of the end. Members have become close to each other and now wonder what is next. This is an important stage in the life cycle of a group, and the parent educator will need to pay close attention to the needs of members.

Parents may ask:

- "Will I miss this experience?"
- "What will happen to the relationships that have developed?"
- "How can I express my feelings about ending?"
- "What comes next?"

Just as parent educators plan for closure of each individual session, final closure to the group must also be planned. Depending on the depth of involvement, parents may need an opportunity to express their feelings about the experience. They can be asked, "What is the best thing you have gotten from this experience?" They may need an informal opportunity to plan for some kind of continuation of the experience. Although the formal group is finished, parents sometimes choose to continue to meet informally for support or socializing. The parent educator can assist in empowering members to make these arrangements but needs to be willing to abandon the role of facilitator. He or she will no longer be involved if the group continues to meet.

Table 4.1

PARENT SATISFACTION SURVEY
We would like to know how you feel about the program and how it has helped you. This information will help us to make program improvements. All of the information will be confidential and will be shared only as group information.
Program Components
Write down comments about each part of the program and then rate it, using the numbers 4 = Very Satisfied, 3 = Satisfied, 2 = Dissatisfied, and 1 = Very Dissatisfied
_____1. Home Visits
_____2. Group Discussion Time
_____3. Handouts and Articles
_____4. Parent-Child Interaction Time
Additional Comments
1. What did you like best about the parenting program?
2. What are the three most important ideas about parenting that you are taking away with you?
3. What specific ideas would you offer the teacher about how to change the program for future classes?
4. How would you describe the program to a parent who was thinking about taking the class?

Typically, agency-sponsored parent education groups ask parents to evaluate their experience in this group. This is most likely done with a written evaluation, giving feedback to both the program and the parent educator. Although adult educators may feel their performance is being judged, it is important to carefully consider the feedback from parents and adjust future groups accordingly. Table 4.1 is one example of a program evaluation form that addresses program satisfaction and assessment of different program components.

A second type of program evaluation might focus on parent self-assessment. The purpose of this type of evaluation is to better understand program outcomes for parents. Table 4.2 is an example of a program impact questionnaire.

Table 4.2

FAMILY LITERACY									
Program Impact Evaluation									
The purpose of this survey is to find out from parents how the family literacy program has changed you and your child during the past year. This information will help us to improve the program. All of the information will be confidential and will be shared only as group information.									
A. CHILD IMPACTS									
The following questions reflect the program goals for children. Think about how the class has affected your child by rating your child at the beginning of the year and again at the end of the year using the 1–10 scale to show changes in your child.									
1. My child is comfortable separating from me and staying with the teachers.									

Beginning of Program

Low									High
	1	2	3	4	5	6	7	8	9	10

End of Program

Low									High
	1	2	3	4	5	6	7	8	9	10

2. My child likes books and being read to.

Beginning of Program

Low										High
	1	2	3	4	5	6	7	8	9	10

End of Program

Low										High
	1	2	3	4	5	6	7	8	9	10

3. My child is learning new words.

Beginning of Program

Low										High
	1	2	3	4	5	6	7	8	9	10

End of Program

Low										High
	1	2	3	4	5	6	7	8	9	10

4. My child is able to calm down and talk with me when upset.

Beginning of Program

Low										High
	1	2	3	4	5	6	7	8	9	10

End of Program

Low										High
	1	2	3	4	5	6	7	8	9	10

B. PARENT IMPACTS

The following questions reflect the program goals for parents. Think about how the program has affected your parenting by rating yourself at the beginning of the year and again at the end of the year using the 1–10 scale to show changes in your parenting.

1. I understand and accept my child's emotions.

Beginning of Program

Low										High
	1	2	3	4	5	6	7	8	9	10

End of Program

Low										High
	1	2	3	4	5	6	7	8	9	10

2. I understand my child as an individual with unique needs and interests.

Beginning of Program

Low										High
	1	2	3	4	5	6	7	8	9	10

End of Program

Low										High
	1	2	3	4	5	6	7	8	9	10

3. I understand how children develop and I have realistic expectations.

Beginning of Program

Low										High
	1	2	3	4	5	6	7	8	9	10

End of Program										
Low										High
	1	2	3	4	5	6	7	8	9	10

4. I understand that there are multiple discipline methods to teach my child acceptable behaviors and set clear limits.

Beginning of Program										
Low										High
	1	2	3	4	5	6	7	8	9	10

End of Program										
Low										High
	1	2	3	4	5	6	7	8	9	10

5. I understand emotion coaching strategies and how to use them to respond to difficult feelings my child has.

Beginning of Program										
Low										High
	1	2	3	4	5	6	7	8	9	10

End of Program										
Low										High
	1	2	3	4	5	6	7	8	9	10

This type of assessment asks parents to reflect on different program goal areas and report on changes that they may have experienced as a result of participation in the program. Program outcomes may also be measured in a more formal and objective manner using self-report measures on parent attitudes before and after classes to assess parent changes.

The stages-of-development theory provides a framework for parent educators to understand and respond to the needs of the group over time. Although each group is unique and will progress in a different way, this model provides a

Table 4.3 Stages of Group Development: The Role of the Parent Educator

STAGE	GOAL	CHALLENGES	PARENT EDUCATOR STRATEGIES
Forming	Setting warm, welcoming tone Addressing specifics of group Encouraging connections between members	Addressing parents' apprehensiveness Addressing limited self-disclosure Addressing uncertainty about group experience	Building relationships Connecting parents' experiences and ideas Providing a welcoming atmosphere
Norming	Setting group ground rules Discussing goals Determining group norms	Providing meaningful discussion within a safe setting Setting appropriate behavioral norms	Modeling norm expectations Listening carefully to learn Encouraging and modeling disclosure
Storming	Allowing for divergent thinking Encouraging parents to begin to disagree respectfully	Monitoring conflict Maintaining respect Protecting parents who are vulnerable	Utilizing conflict in a constructive manner Modeling acceptance of diverse ideas
Performing	Achieving goals Achieving honest, open atmosphere Sharing group ownership Addressing topics in depth	Keeping parents focused Fostering shared decision making Managing intense feelings	Providing meaningful topics Asking powerful questions Connecting parent experiences Acknowledging strong feelings

Adjourn-ing	Realizing accom-plishment	Approaching end of group	Providing closure activity
	Providing positive ending	Dealing with unmet needs	Sharing possible resources
	Evaluating experience		Providing evalua-tion opportunities

typical, and perhaps ideal, guide for understanding the life cycle of a group. Table 4.3 summarizes the different stages with challenges and possible strategies to address these challenges. By viewing the group process through a developmental perspective, the parent educator realizes his or her responsibility to both the parent and the group.

FRAMEWORK 2: THE FUNCTIONAL PERSPECTIVE—TASK AND MAINTENANCE FUNCTIONS

Education and support in a parent group are, in many ways, analogous to the task and maintenance functions described in cooperative group learning literature (Johnson & Johnson, 1975). The word _function_ in this context refers to the basic goal orientation for parent groups in terms of accomplishing specific educational outcomes and creating and maintaining a healthy group environment. These two sets of functions complement each other in parent groups. The leader is responsible for monitoring how these functions operate and for maintaining a balance between goal orientation and group maintenance activities. Each group member, as well as the leader, brings personal characteristics, ideas about learning, and specific skills to the group context. For example, Suzanne may be very good at asking clarifying questions to keep the group focused on the goal of understanding children's emotions. Derek may bring a good sense of humor that helps relieve tension and creates a relaxed group atmosphere. Janine knows how to support and affirm a parent who is struggling with toddler tantrum behavior. The role of the parent educator is to be aware of the different functions that support building a sense of group cohesion and those functions that support the learning of new ideas, new ways of thinking, and new skills. The professional parent educator has the primary responsibility of understanding and monitoring how the two functions work in a parent group setting. The leader must be able to identify and model specific behaviors that support each function.

Box 4.2 lists some of the critical behaviors that support the maintenance function for cooperative group learning (Johnson & Johnson, 1975). These were modified to illustrate how they would create a sense of support in a parent education group. The parent educator is responsible for modeling these behaviors and encouraging and affirming parents when they exhibit them.

Box 4.2 Maintenance Functions in Parent Education Groups

1. Encouraging participation by all members

2. Keeping harmony and willingness to compromise

3. Helping to reduce stress/relieve tension

4. Clarifying content for the group when something is confusing

5. Monitoring the emotional climate of the group

6. Observing and describing group processes and dynamics

7. Explaining expectations for behavior in the group

8. Listening to and reflecting concerns of different members

9. Creating a feeling of safety and trust in the group

10. Resolving interpersonal problems in the group

Awareness of the importance of maintaining a healthy group atmosphere is essential for parent group leaders. In a group that is functioning in a positive manner, many of the behaviors that support group maintenance are shared among members. The parent educator has more responsibility and greater investment in creating a supportive group environment. An effective parent group facilitator has created a positive group atmosphere when the maintenance

Box 4.3 Task Functions in Parent Education Groups

1. Providing new ideas and perspectives for the group

2. Asking others for their ideas and opinions

3. Getting a discussion started

4. Providing clear directions to the group to complete a task or exercise

5. Summarizing major points in a discussion

6. Clearly defining a problem

7. Bringing positive energy to get a task completed

8. Evaluating what the group has done and what remains to be completed

9. Checking in with group members about the pragmatic details of ideas

10. Coordinating tasks and goals to manage time

behaviors are shared among group members according to their individual characteristics, skills, and strengths.

The particular mix of parent personalities and characteristics will influence the sense of cohesion in a group. Also the number of sessions that a group meets is an important factor influencing group cohesion and the potential sharing of behaviors to maintain a positive group environment. If the group has more time to grow and develop, it will exhibit more sharing of group maintenance behaviors as people define their roles and feel successful at contributing to a positive group atmosphere. For example, in an evening parent group of 14 mothers and fathers, Georgia has taken on the role of asking questions of a quiet group member to invite her participation in discussion. Paul is frequently an observer of the group process, noting the energy level of the group and how the group solves problems

From our experience ... In working with a project to provide access to early childhood services to new immigrant and refugee families, the Art of Hosting (INCOMMINS, 2012) was introduced as a model for group work on the project. A number of its basic concepts fit well with working with parent groups. The Access Project adopted a group model for each session that included three parts: 1) Relationships, 2) Co-Learning, and 3) Work. This model balances function and maintenance tasks in groups. The sessions began with **relationship building** that included ways for each member of the group to share something about their life in response to a simple probe. For example: "Share how your culture thinks about and celebrates the new year." The **co-learning** component was an acknowledgment that everyone in the group brings knowledge and perspectives that are important to share so the group can learn from each other. For example, two members of the group attended a conference on language development in young children who are learning two different languages and shared their insights with the group. The **work** part of the session was time for the group to focus on the specific goals that the group had agreed upon. In a parent group this might be a chance to explore strategies and practice skills around attending to a child's non-verbal cues. These simple concepts are powerful reminders of the essential components of a session.

when there is a conflict. Sometimes a group will share the responsibility of bringing a snack for the parent group time. This is a way to build group cohesion; besides providing refreshment, it can create a sense of caring for each other that comes from sharing a snack prepared by one of the group members.

Box 4.3 outlines some of the important task orientation functions. Though having fun and sharing support during challenging times is important, most parents also want to feel a sense of accomplishment through learning new ideas and strategies for effective parenting.

The parent educator takes responsibility for guiding a group toward its goals of learning, processing new ideas, and practicing new strategies. As the group evolves, these tasks also begin to be shared among parents. A parent who attended a recent workshop on car seats for infants may share this information with the group. The parent educator may know that Angela is always ready to start a discussion and may look to her when the group seems to be bogged down. The parent educator may also engage the entire group in summarizing the major points of discussion for the day. The goal of shared leadership has a very delicate balance when a paid professional parent educator is leading a group. The more a skilled leader engages the strengths of the group, the more resources can be accessed for the whole group. Parents come to most groups with an abundance of information and support resources. The parent educator monitors and orchestrates these resources so that the group experience is a positive learning opportunity. The functional perspective creates an awareness of the behaviors that support the two major functions in a successful parent education group.

The primary contribution of this model is the principle of balance and how to maintain a healthy group atmosphere while assisting the parents in defining and achieving their goals. The functional framework assists the group leader in discovering and utilizing the strengths that different members bring to the group. Some parents bring a sense of caring and concern for other group members that enhances the relationships between group members. Others may bring a good sense of humor that allows the group to laugh at some of the perils of parenthood. The group leader must recognize the contributions of each member and strive to maintain a sense of balance between education and support..

FRAMEWORK 3: A SYSTEMS PERSPECTIVE

Family systems theory is used by therapists to understand family relationship patterns, to strengthen healthy patterns of behavior within families, and to change those patterns that are not beneficial to families (Broderick, 1993). In this framework, a family is seen as a system that is made up of individuals who interact with each other as information and energy is exchanged between members and the outside environment. Internal family dynamics and relationships between the family and outside systems are both examined. Family members are connected to each other, but they still maintain their individuality; they function as members of the system and also as independent people. Some of the important concepts in the family systems theory focus on relationship and communication patterns and include:

- Open and closed systems
- Rules, roles, and communication
- Dynamic equilibrium
- Synergy

- Diversity

These concepts from family systems theory are relevant to working with therapy groups (Connors & Caple, 2005) and can be applied to understanding parent group dynamics. This section will examine how system concepts can provide important insights into relationships and communication patterns that can assist parent educators in understanding and managing internal group dynamics.

Two general goals for parent groups as systems are (a) to create supportive relationship patterns and (b) to develop open and healthy patterns of communication. Each group builds and expands on these goals by generating its own unique goals that meet the needs and interests of parents in the group. The concept of open and closed systems is used in a variety of contexts. For example, Satir (1972) described an open family system as one in which members have a high sense of self-esteem; communication is direct, clear, specific, and congruent; and rules are overt, current, and open to change. In a parent group, educators also attempt to create an open system of communication to provide a safe space for the development of caring and supportive relationships and openness to individual parent growth and learning.

Groups, just like families, develop and maintain patterns of rules, roles, and communication that keep their structures open and flexible or closed and rigid. Every group has particular rules that govern behavior and add predictability and stability for members. Rules may be explicit in that they are clearly stated, as in the case of ground rules. These rules are negotiable and can be changed through discussion and consensus. Others may be implicit; typically defined as norms, they are modeled and often unspoken. The existence of group rules is imperative for healthy functioning. Without the structure and safety that rules offer, a group could not function effectively.

Group members also have roles within the system, just as each family member has a particular role. In families, birth order, gender, and temperament often determine what role each person plays. In a group, these factors may also influence members' roles. For example, those with more parenting experience may take on a leadership role, offering advice or suggestions based on their learning through previous parenting experiences. Group members whose temperament encourages the use of humor, mediation, support, or other influential behaviors might take on a particular role in the group to support group cohesion. Roles can be positive in helping to establish a cohesive and caring group or disruptive to the group by pursuing tangents and distracting the group from its goals.

Just like families, groups develop patterns of communication, both verbal and nonverbal. Members in parent groups may communicate openly and honestly as they share their views, feelings, and experiences. In other groups where the level of trust is less developed, members may communicate only what they think is expected of them. For example, a group may develop a pattern where the parent educator initiates most of the talking by asking questions of specific group members. Another group might share only comments that show agreement with the views of the parent educator. These patterns typically develop very early as the group is establishing norms and as members unconsciously learn what patterns of communication are expected and acceptable.

Modeling by the parent educator is crucial in developing an environment of open communication. The parent educator listens carefully, uses nonverbal communication that is affirming and accepting, encourages different views, and gives clear and direct verbal messages. The process of creating an open parent group is described in detail in Chapter 7 where the focus is on developing relationships within the group. The open system concept also stresses the importance of connecting with outside resources to meet the needs of parents in groups. This may include bringing in a speaker on nutrition for parents who have expressed a need for this information or making a referral to a mental health practitioner to help a parent who is struggling with episodes of depression. Systems theory provides helpful guidelines for monitoring relationship and communication patterns that are open and that create a healthy group environment for parent growth and learning to occur.

Family systems theory also examines family behaviors that keep the family's structure open and flexible or closed and rigid. From this perspective, a group may be welcoming to new members, or it may be a closed system that works to keep "outsiders" isolated. Issues of belonging can arise in these groups when new members are added throughout the span of the group. The parent group can also function in ways that are open to new information, ideas, or strategies, or it could respond with resistance to new ideas. Parent groups that meet on a regular basis and are ongoing tend to take on one or the other of these characteristics.

Nonverbal patterns also emerge in groups that support or exclude certain members. Seating patterns, judgmental or nonjudgmental gestures or facial expressions, use of eye contact that avoids certain members, or looks for approval from the parent educator are all examples of subtle nonverbal behaviors that can easily become ingrained in the behavior patterns of group members and leaders.

Another important concept that can be derived from systems theory is synergy. Synergy is the realization of the unique energy and power that is generated when a group is able to combine the diverse resources and strengths of individual members in a positive manner to achieve group goals. Synergy is group "magic" where the whole is greater than the sum of all of the individual parts.

This principle is often experienced in a positive way and is one of the reasons that group parent education remains a unique and powerful learning experience.

For example, synergy is experienced in a group during a discussion on gender role development in children when the group knowledge and experience base comes together to create unique insights and new opportunities for learning. Both mothers and fathers talk about and share their experiences and leave with a greater appreciation for how gender roles are learned and how they as parents can limit and constrain their child's growth and development. Synergy in a parent group explains the powerful learning that goes on within a group that is open and has developed comfortable and trusting relationships.

A parent group, just like a family, may have a desire to keep things in balance. Dynamic equilibrium is another systems concept that can be useful to apply to group parent education practice. This concept conveys the importance of both stability and change in a group. The developmental perspective described earlier in this chapter charts different stages of group growth and change. The systems concept of dynamic equilibrium emphasizes the importance of group learning and of creating a sense of stability and trust that allows for critical self-reflection and potential change in individuals and for the group. This allows the group to evolve to the stage of positive "group performing." The parent educator must create the safety and stability to challenge the group to move to the next stage to meet the next set of issues.

If conflict arises, members may also work hard to keep a sense of equilibrium in the group. Often group members bring the feelings and behavior patterns of their family into the parent education group. For example, those who are uncomfortable with conflict or controversy in their families replicate these feelings and responses in the group. If a disagreement occurs, even if respectfully approached, some members might respond in ways that divert the attention of the group or discount the difference of opinion. When the atmosphere of the group changes because of conflict, members can feel a sense of being out of balance and respond by trying to bring things back into a homeostatic balance.

Diversity or differences between members are often dealt with in families by forming subgroups with those who share some similarities or commonalities. In systems theory, these are called subsystems. Similarly, group dynamics can draw parents to form smaller groups or subsystems. They can consist of members who are of similar gender, age, or race. Mothers or fathers in the group may begin to identify as a subsystem and sit together, agree with each other, and connect on a separate level from other members. Parents who have something in common that is not shared by other members may begin to form a special bond that separates them from others. These commonalities might include living in the same neighborhood, belonging to the same organizations, or having children involved in the same activities. Subsystems, similar to cliques, often begin to form when dual relationships exist for group members. Parents who socialize outside the group may feel naturally more drawn to each other in this setting. Though subsystems are typical in families and other systems and also in parent groups, ideally members of these groups will identify primarily with the group as a whole and see their main function as working as a member of the larger system or parent group. Each member needs to have a sense of belonging within the group. To be functional, both families and groups need to cherish and respect the individuality of each member, while allowing for the development of subsystems that do not threaten the larger group or individual members.

The primary contribution of systems theory is to assist the group facilitator in approaching parent groups as complex and dynamic systems that thrive on diversity, positive energy, and a clear set of goals. Though parent group facilitators are given the responsibility of making the group work, it is more of a two-way street than is often acknowledged or practiced. The systems perspective helps group leaders understand the dynamic nature of groups and the importance of developing healthy relationships with balanced, reciprocal communication patterns. Parent groups that can attain peaks of group synergy have tapped into the dynamic power of group parent education.

FRAMEWORK 4: GENDER AND POWER PERSPECTIVE

Attention to parent gender and power brings a different focus and emphasis than the previous three frameworks by directly examining the interactions in mixed-gender parent groups. There is literature that examines gender as a factor in small group dynamics and describes some typical behavior patterns that occur in mixed-gender groups (Van Nostrand, 1993). This literature, however, has not been extended to look specifically at parenting groups The general patterns of male/female communication behaviors that have been observed (Tannen, 1990) can also be applied to parent groups and may provide insight into group dynamics in mixed-gender groups. The gender dynamics in groups needs to be considered in exploring specific problems that occur in male-female interaction patterns in groups. In many parent groups, couples attend together or alternate attending sessions. This makes the gender composition of parent groups more likely to be mixed and ratios of men to women may change from session to session.

The predominance of female participants and female parent educators has limited the need to carefully review gender as a factor in parent group dynamics. The emergence of father-only groups (Johnson & Palm, 1992; McBride, 1990;

Fagan & Palm, 2004) and the recent focus on responsible fatherhood pro-grams (Bronte, Burkhauser, & Metz, 2012) have initiated discussion on mother and father differences in relation to parent education. These are reflected in Palm's (1997) description of different needs, goals, and interests that fathers and mothers may exhibit as they come to parent education groups. Tannen's (1990) discussion of male and female communication differences provides a framework for examining the influence of gender on parent group dynamics. Descriptions of gender differences in parent education should be approached with some caution about not creating stereotyped expectations. The tendency to be more inclusive and talk about generic parents instead of mothers and fathers has limited our discussion and understanding of gender as an important factor in parent education group dynamics.

A feminist perspective on mixed-gender groups and group dynamics that may be most relevant to parent educators comes from Van Nostrand (1993). She made a strong case for group leaders to increase their sensitivity and awareness of gender bias and sexism in mixed-gender groups and to take steps toward what she labeled "gender responsible leadership." Van Nostrand presented some relevant concepts that can be applied to parent education groups. Because parent groups tend to be an environment dominated by women in terms of numbers of both leaders and participants, the experience of gender bias and male privilege may be unique. Females have been socialized for parenthood more directly and tend to bring both more knowledge and experience to parenthood (Palm & Palkovitz, 1988). These factors tend to give more power to women in mixed-gender parent groups. It should not be assumed that males will automatically have more privilege or power in the typical mixed-gender group parent education setting. The concepts that will be explored here are gender-responsible leadership and male privilege through male patterns of dominance and detachment combined with female patterns of deferring to male group members and describing problems without seeking solutions. The basic assumption with this perspective is that we should strive for a balance of power and involvement between genders in mixed-gender groups.

Gender-responsible leadership (Van Nostrand, 1993) is defined as leader-ship that recognizes gender bias and sexism in the self and others, takes steps toward remediation, and creates a balance of power. The awareness of gender bias in groups that are predominantly female, such as parent education groups, needs to be carefully considered. How can there be bias against women when women appear to have control of the groups both as leaders and as the majority of participants? It becomes clearer how this can occur when one looks at what happens when an individual male joins a parent group. In these cases, women are likely to be very welcoming and pleased to see a man taking an interest in his children by attending a parent education class. They may also be likely to listen more carefully and to defer to his interests in group interactions.

How does male privilege, the assumption that male needs, opinions, and interests are more important, fit with parent education? Van Nostrand (1993) identified two common patterns in mixed-gender groups that men display that help them to maintain male privilege: dominance in the group setting and detachment from the group. Two typical female responses that also interact with these male behavior patterns and assist men in maintaining this power privilege are deferring to men in a group setting and describing imbalance problems but not acting to resolve them. Examples of these dynamics are presented in the brief examples of group interaction described in Boxes 4.4 and 4.5.

The two examples in Boxes 4.4 and 4.5 provide insight into potential gender bias and the concept of male privilege in a parent group setting. Gender power imbalance often seems to be avoided or circumvented in mixed-gender parent groups. This could be considered collusion with the members who are exhibiting biased behavior patterns. It may also be that the group has not developed to the point where challenging power issues is likely to be successful, because a trusting relationship has not been established with the fathers in these two situations The fathers are probably not aware of how this feels to the mothers in the group. There are also subtle gender-related dynamics that may work to maintain male privilege. For example, some men may use humor or sexual innuendo to distract from and even discount the parenting issues that are being discussed.

The challenge of gender-responsible leadership in parent education should be studied more carefully as fathers become more frequent members of parent groups. It is clear that strong socialization patterns continue to influence males and females to think and behave in different ways. These differences can continue to create an imbalance of power in mixed-gender parent groups. The gender-responsilbe leadership perspective reminds parent educators that gender bias and power imbalances are potent factors to consider in understanding interactions in parent groups. In a typical parent group, there may be one or more fathers who attend on a regular basis, and even more are likely to come to evening groups. Many men enjoy being part of a mostly female group and quickly adapt to the rules and take on a more cooperative style of participation, which is perceived as the group norm. It is difficult to make broad generalizations about negative gender patterns in parent groups, but gender must still be considered an important factor. Individual personality traits may also be a confounding factor in understanding group dynamics and problems that group leaders of mixed-gender groups encounter. The gender of the group leader is another area that could be examined in more detail as it affects parent learning.

Box 4.4 Example of Male Domination

A group of parents of toddlers meets once a week on Wednesday mornings. The group consists of eight parents—seven mothers and one father. The mothers attend on a regular basis, and the father comes every third or fourth week when he can take time off from his job. When the father, Jeff, does attend, he is warmly greeted by the group leader, who goes out of her way to say that she is so glad he made it today and that she wishes that more fathers would take the time to come to classes. Jeff appears very comfortable in the group and doesn't mind talking about his twin 2-year-old daughters. He likes to describe how smart they are and all the new words that they are learning. The leader has noticed that when Jeff does come, he tends to dominate a discussion, telling stories and freely giving advice to the other mothers in the group. Some of the mothers, especially Carmen and Celina, who are typically quiet, hardly say a word when Jeff is present. Carol makes a comment 1 week after Jeff has attended a group how the group is different when a dad partic- ipates. The group leader, Joyce, lets the comment go this time, because she doesn't want the group to talk about a parent who is not present. At the same time, she is aware of the difference in group dynamics and wonders what she should do as a group leader to address this issue in a positive and direct manner.

In this parent group, it appears that Jeff has a privileged position that allows him to be the center of attention and get his needs met. The mothers in the group have deferred to this privilege by not asserting their own needs. Even Carol, who "di- agnoses the dysfunction," only describes the problem, hoping someone else will take action. It is especially difficult with a father who does not attend on a regular basis to confront and or limit this privilege. The fear would be that he might not come back. Joyce, the group leader, must recognize this pattern early on and take steps to intervene to protect the quiet members of the group who may not be getting their needs met. What would a gender-responsible leader do in this situation?

Box 4.5 Example of Male Distancing From the Group

Kerry is the quiet father of 3-year-old Sam. He comes to the Tuesday evening parent group on a regular basis, as his wife Sheila is a nurse who works the evening shift at the local hospital. Kerry is often the only father in the group. Sometimes he sits back from the group with his arms folded and a look of mild boredom. In a parent discussion about discipline and bedtime, the parent educator, Joanne, trying to involve Kerry in the group, asks him how he would get Sam to stay in his room once he was put to bed. Kerry responds, "That would never happen. Once I tell him to go to bed, he knows I mean business, and he won't play games with me." The mother who has been struggling with this issue grows silent and embarrassed, and the group pauses to process Kerry's response. The group leader confers with her supervisor the next day about what is going on and asks how she can engage Kerry to participate in a positive manner. They discuss the role of gender and the pattern of maintaining male privilege by withdrawing from the group and discounting others' ideas and feelings about parenting. Men in parent groups sometimes maintain distance from the group and also maintain a mask of competence and control over difficult parenting situations. What would a gender-responsible leader do in this situation?

SUMMARY

This chapter has examined four different perspectives that are useful in examining and understanding group dynamics. The developmental perspective provides a framework that describes typical stages that group members experience as they grow together and become a cohesive, functioning support system. The functional approach examines the effects of differing behaviors and roles that support healthy group processes. The systems approach provides an understanding of the common elements that parent education groups share with families and other systems. Finally, examining gender and power in groups illuminates some of the unique dynamics that can occur related to group membership. Each of these frameworks assists parent educators in having greater insight into understanding parent education group dynamics.

DISCUSSION QUESTIONS

Developmental Perspective

1. Compare and contrast the sample ground rules in Box 4.1. How do you think each might have been developed? What kind of group does each imply to you?

2. How do you typically respond to conflict? How comfortable or uncomfortable are you when conflict affects others or yourself? How might your feelings about conflict affect your performance as a group facilitator?

3. What are the major benefits of parent assessments of program components? How can parent self-assessment of changes assist a program?

Functional Perspective

1. Consider your role as a group leader regarding task and maintenance functions. With which do you feel most comfortable? Why?

2. To facilitate a balance of task and maintenance functions, what goal(s) might you set for yourself?

Systems Perspective

1. Consider the following questions about your own family of origin:

    a. What roles did various members play?

    b. What rules did your family have? Which were stated; which were implied?

    c. Would you describe your family of origin as an open or closed system? Why?

2. How aware are you of your own nonverbal behavior? What do you notice about the nonverbal behavior of others?

3. What advantages and challenges could you anticipate as a group begins to form subgroups or subsystems?

Gender and Power Perspective

1. How important is the concept of male privilege to understanding group dynamics in mixed-gender parent groups? Why?

2. What are the sources of power that women may bring to a mixed-gender parent group?

3. How important is the gender of the parent group leader to mixed-gender parent education groups? Explain.

REFERENCES

Broderick, C.B. (1993). *Understanding family process.* Thousand Oaks, CA: Sage.

Bronte, J., Burkhauser, M., & Metz, A. (2012). Elements of promising practices in fatherhood programs: Evidence-based research findings on interventions for fathers. *Fathering, 10*(1), 6–30.

Connors, J.V., & Caple, R.B. (2005). A Review of Group Systems Theory. *The Journal For Specialists In Group Work, 30*(2), 93–110.

Corey, G. (1999). *Theory and practice of group counseling.* Pacific Grove, CA: Brooks/Cole.

Curran, D. (1989). *Working with parents.* Circle Pines, MN: American Guidance Service.

Fagan, J., & Palm, G. (2004) *Fathers and Early Childhood Programs.* Albany, NY: Delmar.

INCOMmons (2012). *Art of Hosting: Training Workbook.* InCommons.org.

Johnson, D., & Johnson, F. (1975). *Joining together: Group theory and group skills.* Englewood Cliffs, NJ: Prentice Hall.

Johnson, L., & Palm, G. (1992). *Working with fathers: Methods and perspectives.*

McBride, B.A. (1990). The effects of a parent education play group programon father involvement in childrearing. *Family Relations, 39,* 250–256.

Palm, G. (1997). Promoting generative fathering through parent and family education. In A.J. Hawkins & D.C. Dollahite (Eds.), *Generative fathering: Beyond deficit perspectives* (pp. 167–182). Thousand Oaks, CA: Sage.

Palm, G., & Palkovitz, R. (1988). The challenge of working with new fathers: Implications for support providers. In R. Palkovitz & M. Sussman (Eds.), *Transitions to parenthood* (pp. 357–376). New York, NY: Haworth.

Satir, V. (1972). *Peoplemaking.* Palo Alto, CA: Science and Behavior Books.

Tannen, D. (1990). *You just don't understand.* New York, NY: Ballantine.

Van Nostrand, C. (1993). *Gender-responsible leadership.* Newbury Park, CA: Sage.

5

CONCEPTUAL FRAMEWORKS—
PART II: *Models for Understanding*
Group Leadership Roles

Whereas the four conceptual models presented in Chapter 4 focus on group development and dynamics, this chapter will explore four additional frameworks that address the role of the group leader: (a) the levels of involvement of parent educators in a group setting, depending on the purpose and needs of the group; (b) the domains of family practice; (c) the styles of leadership that influence the group process; and (d) the moral character and virtues of parent educators that form the foundation for ethical thinking and behavior related to group leadership. Each of the frameworks can be examined within the context of the Continuum of Parent/Family Services model presented in Chapter 3. The role of the parent educator and the relationship with the parent strengthens as the connection with parents evolves, based on the needs and the type of programs provided.

FRAMEWORK #1: LEVELS OF INVOLVEMENT FOR PARENT AND FAMILY EDUCATORS

The challenge of understanding and maintaining clear boundaries between parent education and therapy was addressed by Doherty's (1995) model of levels of involvement for parent and family educators. In Doherty's original model, he developed a continuum of involvement approach to conceptualizing and defining different levels of involvement with parents, based on intensity, necessary knowledge base of the practitioner, and requisite skills for prevention, education, support, and intervention. Having initially designed the model for physicians and, later, for school psychologists, Doherty further developed it for parent and family educators as a way of encouraging the inclusion of personal experiences, emotions, and feelings in parent education. More recently, Doherty and Lamson (2015) have updated and clarified the model by further defining the levels and their implications for contemporary practice. The model provides a structure for parent educators to meet the needs of parents that includes the important affective aspects of learning without crossing into therapy in the group or individual setting.

Uncertainty about how deeply to delve into the feelings and background experiences of parents in groups challenges most parent educators. Defining parent education solely as providing information and teaching practical skills while defining therapy as dealing only with personal experiences and the feelings of parents limits both disciplines. Therapy typically involves some educational components, with parents often learning new skills or strategies, although educational instruction is not the primary focus. The therapy experience involves engaging with intense feelings, attitudes, and values of parents in therapeutic settings. In this model, parent education is not therapy, yet it includes addressing feelings and attitudes as part of the learning process that can be therapeutic. The inclusion of the parent learners' personal experiences and feelings distinguishes parent education from standard educational courses in child development. Parent education, by its nature, has more personal depth than other forms of education. Yet, there are limits to the depth that is appropriate to explore under the auspices of parent education. The levels of family involvement model allow parent educators to approach their work through a continuum model that distinguishes differences between therapy and parent education and defines varying levels of involvement to meet the diverse parenting needs of individuals and groups. The strength of the model describes the levels of intensity that are based on the severity of the families' needs. At Level 5 of the model, family therapy involves the diagnostic process for identifying underlying dynamics and treatment modalities that are delivered by licensed mental health professionals.

The five updated levels represent institution provided parenting information through family therapy intervention. It is not assumed that practitioners at each level possess all of the skills of the previous level, but it can provide a useful framework in considering appropriate professional roles and the families' needs. Professionals at multiple levels can provide a variety of educational services and interventions to benefit individual families. The model can be used either in group work with parents or in one-to-one interaction. This section will describe each level of involvement, focusing primarily on Levels 2, 3, and 4.

LEVEL 1: INSTITUTION-CENTERED

Level 1 is included, not as a recommended methodology for parent educators, but as an example of the least possible–involvement with parents. Parents are included in Level 1 experiences only for practical or legal reasons. Policies are created and implemented by professionals with little attention to the individual needs or input of parents. Information is provided in a directive or noninteractive lecture approach with communication typically being uni-directional. This may also include written information used in various media, including handouts, TV commercials, internet articles, blogs on topics, such as breast-feeding, child vacinations, or back-to-sleep campaigns.

Level 1 Example: *A school may conduct informational meetings for parents to learn about policies and procedures that have been developed. Parents are not involved in discussion but participate by receiving the necessary information from professionals. In this level, there is no partnership between parent and professional, and the main focus is on the needs of the institution to convey pertinent information to parents.*

LEVEL 2: COLLABORATIVE DISSEMINATION OF INFORMATION

Level 2 involves parents in learning activities regarding child and human development, parenting, family life, communication, positive self-esteem, and healthy interpersonal relationshiops. The parent educator is required to have good teaching and presenting skills, since the main focus is on sharing information and advice with parents. The educator engages the parents in the learning process by eliciting questions, making practical recommendations, and providing information about community resources for families. Frequently, one-time presentations regarding a particular aspect of parenting are classified as a Level 2 practice. However, ongoing parent education groups may also function at this level, with parents as recipients of the knowledge shared by the educator. An advantage of Level 2 practice is that a large number of families can be reached with important information in a didactic setting. Online parenting programs and speakers on parenting topics are examples of successful Level 2 learning opportunities. There may be some limited time for questions and answers as part of this process.

Because the teaching skills and knowledge base of Level 2 parent educators are typically addressed and emphasized through most training programs for parent educators, this level of involvement provides a high level of comfort for group leaders. Parent educators feel confident in utilizing their teaching skills to present information they understand. However, working exclusively at this level with parents does have limitations. Level 2 provides a safe environment for parents to learn new information and skills, and may elicit emotions from parents that are not directly addressed. Any interactive component at this level typically focuses on the content of the presentaiton, rather than on the personal or unique experiences of the participants. This can limit the depth to explore common feelings and apply new skills or techniques. Although parents are receptive to information about child development, without involvement in a more meaningful and personal discussion of their beliefs and feelings, the experience results in standardized assimilation of information for participants where parents have to translate the information received to their own families.

Level 2 Example: *A 3-week parent education series is offered by a family gency on the topic of using effective discipline and guidance strategies with young elementary age children. Registration is open to the public. A parent educator trained in child development presents a 1-hour session each week that includes basic developmental information about children in the elementary*

Parents gain support from sharing ideas and issues

ages, realistic expectations of parents, and examples of specific techniques that parents can use to guide their children's behavior. The group leader does most of the talking, using handouts, overheads, and short video clips to demonstrate the topic. Parents are encouraged to ask questions, and recommendations are given by the parent educator to address specific discipline challenges within the group. The series ends after 3 weeks with parents learning about appropriate expectations for children and new strategies of discipline that some parents are able to apply to the issues they encounter.

LEVEL 3: WORKING WITH FAMILY MEMBERS' FEELINGS AND NEED FOR SUPPORT

Level 3 embraces the solid knowledge base of child development, family life, and parenting that encompasses Level 2. It is in this next level that parent educators elicit the feelings and experiences of the group members and use their personal disclosures as an important part of the learning experience. In addition to being a confident teacher, the Level 3 parent educator must use more complex and nuanced communication and facilitation skills, such as:

- Listening empathetically
- Gently probing for feelings and personal stories
- Encouraging collaborative problem solving
- Creating an open and supportive climate
- Offering recommendations tailored to individual parent needs in a culturally sensitive manner
- Protecting parents from too much self-disclosure
- Knowing when to conduct a referral for other services

These skills are also foundational to the work that therapists do with clients, but at this level in parent education, the focus remains on typical parenting issues which often includes strong and ambivalent emotions. This is within the professional realm of parent education and the skills of parent educators. Most of the Level 3 skills are basic to relationship building and nurturing a trusting learning environment. The ability to recognize that the needs of a particular family go beyond this experience is a strength of parent educators who should be well trained on normal child and family development and have the ability to identify what is not within the range of healthy family dynamics. Understanding the typical development of children and family issues provides an immediate guide for parent educators to recognize behaviors or issues that cannot be universalized. Being able to identify family and/or psychological dysfunctioning does not imply that parent education can or should treat these issues. It does, however, require the parent educator to make a determination that further services may be beneficial and to be able to conduct a referral. Parent education in this context may also provide supportive services as a complementary experience to individual and/or family therapy, with the possibility of the parent educator and therapist collaborating to enhance family learning and therapeutic effectiveness.

Typical issues in Level 3 settings deal with normal stresses in family life, rather than more traumatic situations or challenges that stem from painful family-of-origin experiences. The focus remains on parenting issues, and the skillful parent educator keeps the participants grounded in issues that currently affect parenting. The perspective is generally on the here and now. Although some childhood recollection and insight into the effects of parents' backgrounds is beneficial, the primary work is done on the current challenges of parenting children.

As with each level, there are limitations to Level 3. Parent educators must feel confident in their abilities to address emotional responses in a group. They must have insight into their own emotions regarding parenting and family issues in order to keep them separate from the emotions of the parents. Common tendencies at Level 3 are to move too quickly back to Level 2 when emotions arise, to cut off a parent by turning the issue back to the group for ideas, to offer premature advice when parents may first need understanding and empathy, or to probe too deeply into the parent's emotions and thus become intrusive and make other parents uncomfortable in the group setting.

Level 3 provides a level of involvement with parents toward which all parent educators can work. By allowing and encouraging expression of the feelings and experiences of parents, the parent educator has a deeper understanding of parents and becomes both a more sensitive teacher and a supporter of parents in their learning. The expectation that a group experience at this level is optimal is supported by findings that parents want leaders who can create interactive and participative learning environments instead of a more lecture or directive approach. (Forslund Frykedal & Rosander, 2015). Ongoing parent education groups develop through relationship building that creates an atmosphere of trust. It is in this setting that parents learn to trust the leader and each other, allowing a deeper level of disclosure and investment in the learning process.

Level 3 Example: *An ongoing parent education group is addressing the issues surrounding the discipline of preschoolers. The group has met for 5 out of 15 sessions, and parents feel comfortable with each other and the leader. Time has been spent during the previous weeks getting to know each other and developing an open atmosphere where parents feel free to discuss matters openly. The topic content includes strategies for guiding children's behavior but also allows for much open discussion about issues and challenges.*

The parent educator encourages members to share some of their experiences by asking questions such as "What are you experiencing with your children around discipline issues?" Several parents express frustration over current challenges with getting children to cooperate. The parent educator gently probes to learn more about the situation with statements, such as "Tell us more about what happens" and "How do you feel when he reacts this way?" Supportive comments, such as "This can be a challenging and frustrating when children are beginning to assert themselves" reassure parents. Self-disclosure comments such as "I remember dealing with similar issues with my own daughter" can ensure that the parent feels listened to and understood. The leader then moves to the remaining group members for ideas and similar experiences. This not only provides some problem-solving opportunities but also universalizes the issue, thereby assuring the parent that they aren't the only one struggling with this concern and that their feelings are shared by others in the group. The parent educator offers some suggestions based on realistic expectations of children at this age and encourages the parent to apply some of the new strategies. Although the parent educator supports and encourages the parent, information about child guidance is also shared. In this format, the group leader teaches within the context of a group discussion and elicits and builds on members' attitudes, feelings, and experiences, rather than giving a formal presentation.

LEVEL 4: PSYCHOEDUCATIONAL INTERVENTION FOR COMPLEX OR CHRONIC FAMILY CONCERNS

Building upon some of the skills of Levels 2 and 3, Level 4 moves to a more formal intervention approach to parent education that adds the dimension of personalized problem solving for family members who need help with more complex and chronic concerns. The parent educator develops a plan of action or intervention specific to a particular family.

Parent educators who work in Level 4 must have more background and training in family systems to make an assessment of the situation and execute a planned brief effort to help the parent address these more challenging problems. Typically, the issues benefiting from a Level 4 intervention occur in groups of parents that are in higher-risk situations. These might include parents with multiple stressors, those who are chemically dependent or are living in abusive relationships, teen parents, or those who are incarcerated. Although these populations generally bring more challenging issues to a group, other more typical parent education groups may also move into Level 4 as issues arise. Level 4 situations generally go beyond typical parent-child issues and may involve co-parenting conflicts, interfering family members, or struggles with services from another family support system. Although, the couple relationship may also be of concern and might even be contributing to the problem, in this model, Level 4 parent education does not focus on changing patterns in personal relationships that are unrelated to parenting and/or family issues. If the parent begins to move into couple or relationship concerns, the parent educator may ask, "How does that affect how you are parenting?" or "How is this affecting your family life?" This keeps the focus on parenting and family relations, which is the purpose of the parent education experience. If the group leader sees that the marital or personal relationship may benefit from therapeutic services, a referral can be made privately with the parent. According to Doherty, family situations at Level 4 are often referred to mental health professionals in the community (Doherty & Lamson, 2015).

Doherty (1995) considered Level 4 parent education an elective competency level. He acknowledged that this level represents the upper boundary of parent and family education practiced by experienced parent education professionals with additional training in this area who choose to work with special populations of parents. Parent educators who work in Level 4 must be self-aware, authentic, and flexible; have good problem-solving skills; and be willing to take risks (Campbell, Kristensen, & Scott, 1997). Furthermore, Level 4 interventions require a clear contract with the parent or group of parents to engage in more intensive work than regular Level 3 information and support activities. Whereas Level 3 is presented as a level in which all parent educators should be able to function, Level 4 is typically the exception in parent education settings. With the growth of parent education programs that serve populations with more complex issues, Level 4 skills will allow meaningful experiences for diverse groups. However, the need for Level 4 intervention in every parent education setting is not warranted.

In addition to understanding family systems theory, the Level 4 parent educator needs to be able to:

- Formulate a series of questions that provide a detailed picture of the family's dynamics
- Develop a deeper understanding and hypothesis about the problem
- Work with the parent for a brief period of time on the issue either in the group or individually
- Know when to return to Level 3 support or when to refer the parent to therapy and collaborate with therapists and community support systems
- Use communication and problem-solving skills that probe, clarify, and help the parent develop a strategy for change

- Be comfortable with directly addressing issues, interpreting behavior, addressing immediate concerns, and assisting parents with setting goals

Common errors for parent educators working in Level 4 include (a) moving into this depth of interaction without realizing it and then getting stuck or overwhelmed; (b) not having an agreement or consent from the family to engage in the intervention; (c) not spending sufficient time building rapport with the family; and (d) staying at Level 4 when it is not helping (Doherty, 1995).

Doherty (1995) believes that programs that do provide Level 4 services also need to allocate time for reflective consultation with a therapist who can assist in maintaining healthy boundaries and placing firm limits that prevent the parent educator from taking on the therapy role. Providing insight into complex family dynamics and behaviors helps parent educators work interventively with parents and still stay grounded and focused on the parent education goals of the program.

A Level 4 intervention typically refers to a brief amount of time allocated to an individual parent's concern during a group session. This effort begins only after permission is given by the parent, as well as the other group members. The parent educator responds to cues from the parent that a Level 4 intervention may be appropriate. These include situations where:

- The parent keeps returning to a particular concern that goes beyond typical parent-child issues.
- The parent dominates group time with the concern.
- The parent expresses or implies an immediate desire for advice, intervention, or change.
- The parent demonstrates a higher level of emotional distress.
- The facilitator is concerned about a deeper issue, but the parent has not directly focused on it.

Level 4 also has limitations in the parent education setting. Because it is the most emotionally charged and has the need for immediate intervention, parent educators may believe that their groups are not beneficial unless Level 4 intervention occurs. In the Levels of Involvement model, Level 3 is seen as the ideal due to the blending of educational information and emotional support in a safe group setting.

Because Level 4 interventions focus primarily on an individual's issue, group time needs to be reallocated, which may be inconsistent with group ground rules that encourage equal participation. It is important to remember that if a Level 4 intervention is used, it is to be on a limited basis.

Additionally, there are characteristics of parents and their circumstances that should make the parent educator cautious about moving to a Level 4 intervention. If any of the following exist, a parent educator should not initiate a Level 4 intervention:

- The problem is not related to parenting.
- A serious mental illness or chronic family dysfunction exists.
- The parent is too emotionally dysregulated to be able to engage in the process.
- The parent is stuck or blocked in their current ways of thinking about an issue to change or has been unable to benefit from Level 3 support.
- The group is not ready for this level of depth.

Level 4 Example: *A special group has been offered for parents involved in the child protection system. Typically, parents in this group have been referred from social service agencies that work closely with the parent educator. The focus will be on providing positive discipline strategies to their children. As the parent educator begins the group, parents immediately feel comfortable and begin disclosing information about their own painful and abusive childhood experiences. The parent educator supports them with empathetic comments and keeps the group focused on how these experiences can affect parents' discipline choices for their own children.*

One parent becomes quite emotional and describes how she often loses her temper and is verbally aggressive to her child. The parent educator determines that these incidents are probably not reportable as child abuse but realizes that they are of great concern and that the parent has few resources for developing new approaches. She uses the skill of immediacy by reading the parent's emotional cues and says, "I'm concerned about some of the things you are saying. I'm wondering if you would like to spend some time working on this issue right now." The parent agrees and the parent educator asks the group for permission. "It looks like Joan is interested in focusing on this challenge here in the group. It is probably something that many of us could benefit from, but I also realize it takes time away from our agenda. We can either do this now or she and I can talk about it privately after group. How do you feel about working on her concerns here tonight?"

Requesting permission from the group helps to minimize other members' negative reactions to spending a larger amount of time than usual on one member. In this way, the parent educator uses simple, probing questions to get a picture of the real circumstances. This helps to clarify the issue for the parent educator, the other members of the group, and the parent. If the parent hasn't already had enough time to express feelings about the situation, the parent educator allows for this. The group leader then makes some interpretive, nonjudgmental comments that summarize what is happening with the parent.

A statement, such as the following, may help to universalize the issue, focus on the behavior, and offer the parent an opportunity to identify:

> *"Something we know about parents is that when they are experiencing stress, and their own childhoods were difficult, they may often choose discipline techniques that aren't very effective. They may not have the experiences of being treated respectfully as a child, and it seems natural to simply repeat their own experiences. Does this sound like what happens for you?"*

Next, the parent educator assists the parent in developing a plan of action. This discussion may include opportunities for group members to support and assist. The process begins with asking the parent to consider which strategies she would feel comfortable trying. This is followed by getting a commitment to try a few new ideas, facilitating a plan, identifying obstacles and resources, summarizing with a time frame, and empowering the parent to make the change.

This intervention may take 20 minutes of group time; then, the parent educator moves back to continue the topic with parents. In this example, the group moves from a Level 3 to a Level 4 intervention to address a particular issue and then returns to Level 3 support.

LEVEL 5: FAMILY THERAPY

Level 5 is clearly outside the boundaries of parent education. Therapy typically involves a longer process of repeated sessions that focus on treating serious psychological and family problems that encourage significant change in family interaction patterns. Although trends in therapy have changed so that brief, focused therapy is becoming more common, the intensity of involvement with a family is still of more depth than is appropriate for parent education. Therapy includes services that require assessment, diagnosis, intervention, and consent from the parent. Whereas Level 4 stays focuses on parenting issues, Level 5 includes couple relationship issues, complex family-of-origin problems, and diagnosed mental health issues of individual family members. A Level 5 therapist works comfortably with intense emotions and difficult family issues. A therapist may escalate conflict in the family in order to focus on it and assist with change or work intensively with a family during times of crises. At this level, the mental health professional specifically works to address dysfunctional behaviors through intense therapeutic interventions.

Table 5.1 Summary of Levels of Involvement

Level 1: Institution-Centered—least possible involvement with parents

Level 2: Collaborative Dissemination of Information

Knowledge base:	Child and parent development, family life, communication, community resources, parenting skills and issues, cultural awareness
Skills:	Teaching, presenting, eliciting questions, making recommendations

Level 3: Working with Family Members' Feelings and Need for Support

Knowledge base:	Same as Level 2 plus understanding stress and emotions and how to respond, awareness of own feelings/emotions, problem solving of general issues
Skills:	Listening, probing, and questioning with empathy, engaging group in problem solving, creating supportive atmosphere, modeling appropriate boundaries, conducting referrals, tailoring recommendations to individual needs

Level 4: Psychoeducational Intervention for Complex and Chronic Family Concerns

Knowledge base:	Same as previous levels plus family systems, understanding of impaired family functioning and effects of stress on families
Skills:	Assessing family challenges, guiding brief focused intervention, problem solving of deeper issues, responding to higher emotional levels, intervention skills with individuals, ability to work individually with parent

Level 5: Family Therapy—therapeutic treatment of serious and psychological/family problems outside realm of parent education

Doherty's levels of involvement model provides a useful framework through which parent educators can understand the boundaries of their work. It makes distinctions between education and support and therapeutic interventions by describing levels of parent education according to intensity of involvement based on parent or family needs. This boundary can assist parent educators who work with a variety of parents with diverse needs to determine which level is most appropriate for each group. Doherty suggests Level 3 as the ideal degree of intensity for ongoing parent education, Level 2 as appropriate for one-time information presentations, and Level 4 as appropriate for specialized work with parents with more intense needs.

Finally, Doherty stresses that professionals working at each of the levels do not necessarily have all of the skills of the previous levels. For example, a Level 5 therapist uses skills and training for intensive interventions, but may not have the knowledge or skills to deliver educational instruction regarding healthy family functioning. The model is designed to encourage professionals to (a) evaluate the intensity of the family's needs, (b) determine the kinds of services to be offered, and (c) assess whether they have the skill set and scope to deliver the appropriate service. This depends upon a clear understanding of the interdisciplinary work that other family professionals do and the knowledge and skills that they possess. The continuum model from Chapter 3 begins to define the general goals and boundaries for parent and family education practice that are a starting place for collaborative possibilities.

FRAMEWORK #2: DOMAINS OF FAMILY LIFE EDUCATION

A second framework for examining parent and family education practice is the Domains of Family Practice (DFP) introduced by Myers-Wall, Ballard, Darling, and Myers-Brown (2011). The Domains of Family Practice model is distinguished by three types of family education: (a) Family Life Education (FLE), (b) Family Therapy (FT), and (c) Family Case Management (FCM). FLE is defined by the National Council on Family Relations (NCFR) to involve preventative education for individuals and families (Darling & Cassidy, 2014). The Certified Family Life Educator credential has been developed by NCFR and addresses the following 10 content areas:

- Families and individuals in societal contexts
- Internal dynamics of families
- Human growth and development across the life span
- Human sexuality
- Interpersonal relationships
- Parenting educaiton and guidance
- Family resource management
- Family law and public policy
- Professional ethics and practice

- Family life education methodology

Myers-Wall et al. (2014) introduced this model in response to the limitations of the Doherty LFI model in describing the role of family life educators. Their concerns were the perception of the LFI model as a hierarchical view of family services that limited the goals and range of families that could be served by family life educators. They developed the DFP model to provide a clearer description of the professional involvement of different sectors with families that recognizes both the overlap and uniqueness of FLE and FT. The actual content areas covered in FLE, as listed above, are rich in family and couple relationship knowledge and similar to the knowledge base about families in the FT field, which Myers-Wall et al. assert provides a wider range of possibilities for FLEs to work beyond the narrow scope of parenting issues in the LFI model. They also feel that high-risk and high-needs families can benefit from parent and family education that focuses on some of the typical parenting challenges and family transitions that don't require therapeutic intervention with FTs. A strength of the DFP model is that it places the central focus on the shared goal of family professionals as promoting and supporting the strengths and healthy wellbeing of all families.

The model starts with defining the different purposes/goals for each group: FLEs help families by providing them with knowledge and helping them develop skills; FTs help families repair relationships and functioning; and FCM professionals help families access resources and comply with systems' laws and policies. The model also illustrates the various points of overlap of the knowledge base about parents and families. FLEs and FTs both deal with interpersonal relationship skills, a life course perspective, and healthy sexual functioning, while FLEs and FCMs share a common core of information about family resource management and family policy. This description can be helpful in understanding the needs of families and working in a collaborative manner. The model also acknowledges that there is a core of common knowledge and wisdom that is shared by all three groups of family professionals. This core is often hidden by jargon in each of the disciplines, but the model describes it in clear terms that reflect our current understanding of best practices across our work with families, including understanding family systems, being sensitive to diversity in family cultures and structures, using research to inform practice, and paying attention to socio-ecological contexts. Family professionals in all areas have also developed their own clear set of values and ethics that guide their practice.

The DFP model further distinguishes the specific techniques and specialized knowledge and skills that each group uses to accomplish their primary goals. FTs use specific diagnostic tools to help identify family and individual problems that lead to a treatment plan that is guided by a particular theory and treatment modality. This process is also funded through a mental healthcare model, and the relationships may be more long-term and involve more probing into family and individual history, reflecting the depth and intensity that Doherty refers to in Level 5 of LFI. The parent and family life educator also may be involved in assessment at a different level to help parents identify their needs and strengths and set goals for themselves and their families. This can be done in a group of parents with common concerns or with individual parents in home visits. The specific skills of FLEs include the ability to draw upon and create a variety of educational techniques and methods to help parents increase their understanding of their children, explore their own attitudes and feelings about parenting and family life, and

From our experience ... The divisions of services and real collaborative possibilities represented by the DFP model can be seen in many programs that serve at-risk populations. We were involved with a family literacy program that had multiple goals and provided services by professionals from each of the DFP domains to 10–12 families at a time. The program focused on families with young children ages 0–7 and provided early childhood education for the children, parent education for the parents (FLE domain), adult basic education, and english language instruction for adults when English was not their first language. In addition, families had access to a school social worker to help them connect with community resources (FCM) and a therapist (FT) who helped families with mental health issues. This program was successful at helping parents complete their education goals, support their families through connections to additional resources, and learn new parenting skills. The professionals who worked with the domains had different skill sets and were able to offer services that complemented each other with some collaborative overlap. For example, mental health professionals worked with small groups on common issues, such as anxiety, that impact parenting. Family educators helped parents develop positive attachment relationships by modeling parenting skills, such as sensitivity, to both parent and child cues and needs.

develop new skills related to common developmental and family transitions. The role of family case management involves a different set of assessment skills related to helping families cope with meeting legal and policy mandates and finding resources to meet basic family needs. Many contemporary families may benefit from family professional help in each of these areas. A homeless family consisting of a mother and two young children may need help with finding stable housing, food, childcare, individual therapy for anxiety and depression, and ideas and support for managing a demanding toddler and active 4-year-old.

CONTRIBUTIONS OF THE DOMAINS OF FAMILY PRACTICE MODEL

The DFP model adds to our understanding of how to best serve families by clarifying some of roles of different family professionals and defining specific areas of expertise (knowledge and skills). This is particularly helpful to the emerging field of parent and family education. The FLE knowledge base extends the educational domain into typical family life issues, such as couple relationships and transition issues around co-parenting.

This model also opens the possibilities for working with groups of high-need families that also can benefit from education and support around common parenting challenges. This requires that parent and family educators be able to gain additional training for trauma-informed practice and know when to refer individuals for trauma-focused therapy. FLE services provided to high-risk or high-need families may also take away some of the stigma and provide some contact with less stressed parents who are dealing with some of the same common, yet challenging, parenting issues. While the model does not perfectly describe clear boundaries around work with families, it helps to distinguish core goals and methods and can create better understanding and respect for the unique knowledge and skills that each group possesses.

FRAMEWORK #3: LEADERSHIP APPROACHES

Each parent educator develops a unique style that is influenced by his or her personality traits and temperament, as well as his or her perspective of the parent educator role. A parent educator whose personality is outgoing and extroverted, who uses humor easily, and who is described as a "people person" is likely to create an atmosphere in groups that reflects these qualities. On the other hand, a more quiet, introverted, and reflective facilitator will be likely to set a very different tone. It is important to realize that different styles appeal to different group members. Therefore, there is no one style of leadership that works well with all groups and all individuals.

Beyond identifying approaches that reflect the personality and style of group leaders, professionals can examine their personal philosophy as reflected in the role they choose as a parent educator. Depending on the makeup, interests, and needs of the group, along with the topic or content area, the role of the parent educator will reflect their own philosophy of their role (Dail, 1984). It is this professional philosophy that develops over time for the educator and dictates the role they assume in their work.

A variety of approaches are described by Duncan and Goddard (2017), which are detailed below. There are strengths and limitations to each of the philosophical approaches, and their successes or challenges are influenced by a match of group needs and the approach of the parent educator.

Expert Approach: This educational approach assumes the parent educator is the primary source of information and knowledge. As a teaching model, the goal is to disseminate information to the parents through the use of a structured curriculum and formal agenda (Price, 2000). In the group setting, parents are present as passive learners, while the group leader acts as the authority on the subject matter. It is assumed that the parents are not well informed on the content or motivated to learn and are seeking the expertise of the leader. In this approach, there is no discussion or sharing of experiences by group members.

Facilitator Approach: This approach to leadership is less structured than that of the expert. There is typically no specific agenda, and parents, rather than the group leader, set the direction of the group. The facilitator is viewed as an equal member of the group, and there is a strong sense of shared ownership within the group. In this setting, parents need to have a substantial knowledge base from which to draw, be motivated to participate, and possess fairly high-functioning group skills. Although the group facilitator is knowledgeable, his or her role is to draw information, ideas, and solutions from the group members and keep the momentum of the group going forward. The educator acts as a facilitator of the learning process by guiding, organizing, and evaluating the learning experience.

Collaborator Approach: This cooperative approach recognizes and values the knowledge that both parents and the group leader bring to the group. The parent educator contributes his or her specialized knowledge, and the parents contribute their own personalized experiences. The group leader prepares an agenda that specifically addresses the needs of individuals and the group as a whole, yet the agenda is flexible and can be adjusted. Group participation is encouraged by the parent educator who maintains guidance over the direction of the group. This approach is presented as falling between the expert and facilitator role (Myers-Walls, 2000).

Critical Inquirer Approach: In this approach, questions are posed to the group to initiate critical thinking and discussion of important parenting and family issues. The group leader draws upon members' experiences and beliefs as a way to encourage their responsibility to contribute in meaningful ways. This approach reflects a leader whose role is to address and evaluate policies that affect parents and families. This is done by posing questions to stimulate discussion about policies among group members.

Interventionist Approach: Through an educational process, this approach works toward assisting parents in making behavioral, attitudinal, and cognitive changes to their parenting. Behavioral and learning objectives are clearly planned, and desired behaviors are modeled through step-by-step demonstrations. Parents are given opportunities to practice new strategies, which are reinforced by the leader through affirmations and feedback. This approach typically relies on a curriculum that acts as a change agent for participants to improve their functioning as parents.

Eclectic Approach: In this final approach, parent educators use parts of each of the above approaches, depending on the situation, the type and needs of the group, and the topic. For example, an expert approach may, indeed, be appropriate and successful when working with a group that has little knowledge on a topic and is interested in learning concrete information based on current research. Another group looking for an opportunity to learn from each other and increase their knowledge from a respected and informed group leader may benefit from a collaborator approach. An astute parent educator will draw on the strengths of each approach and design sessions that combine varying approaches to group leadership to match individual circumstances.

The choice of which approach to use depends not only on the philosophical comfort level of the parent educator, but also upon the parents and the purpose or goals of the group. For example, a group of teen parents with little knowledge of practical parenting strategies may benefit most from the expert approach. The parent educator is viewed as a knowledgeable teacher who is present to impart practical parenting strategies to the group. However, there would also be times and topics for the same group that would benefit from a more collaborative approach. Addressing the topic of intergenerational family dynamics presents the opportunity for the parent educator to share information and strategies, but it also provides opportunities for teen parents to share their experiences of living in intergenerational families and provide support to each other.

An open atmosphere is critical for parents to share their concerns

Examination of these six approaches to group leadership encourages parent educators to reflect on their own beliefs about the roles they choose with parents. Developing and understanding their philosophies about group leadership and the impact on their work helps to provide a sense of professional direction and purpose and can expand their ability to adapt to different parent groups with varying needs.

In addition to understanding and developing a particular stylistic approach to group leadership, there are common characteristics and personal strengths that should be present in each of the approaches. These leadership qualities include self-understanding, confidence in being in a a position of authority, and ability to respond positively and comfortably with group members' feelings and emotions (Jacobs et al., 2006).

Facilitator Approach Example: *Matt is an experienced facilitator who leads groups of parents with teenagers. His style is very nondirective. On the first night of class, Matt states that "This is your group and you can make it whatever you want." Some of the parents look confused, but others jump right in to decide what issues they want to address. Matt has a wealth of knowledge regarding families, parenting issues, and adolescent development. He does very little formal planning for each session and tends to "let the group go their own way." He is successful at guiding the learning process for parents by allowing them to manage the direction of the group. Several parents in the group are very outgoing and immediately take charge. They rely on Matt for specific information and resources when needed, but generally, the group time is an open discussion that flows from one topic to another. At the end of the session, parents decide what topic they would like to discuss next week.*

- What are some positive aspects of the atmosphere of this group?
- What parent needs might be met in this group?
- What limitations do you see?
- How might some quieter members feel about this experience?
- At the end of 10 sessions, how do you think parents might feel?

Collaborator Approach Example: *Maria is a parent educator who is very comfortable in her role. She enjoys the parents in her groups and feels that she has a solid knowledge of child development, as well as group skills that keep parents coming back each week. During the first few weeks of the parent group, Maria spends time getting to know the group members and plans some structured activities for them to learn about each other, as well. She tells the parents that she has useful information for them about parenting issues, but they are the experts on their own children. Each session includes time for informal sharing of immediate concerns that parents bring to the group.*

Maria encourages parents to share their ideas and support each other. She also guides the group process and clearly offers purpose and direction to this learning experience. Weekly planning results in sessions that address topics chosen by the parents, and includes practical information, as well as ample time for discussion. Maria pays close attention to the cues of the group members and changes the agenda and direction of the group, as needed.

- What are Maria's strengths as a facilitator?
- How might parents respond to her leadership style?
- How does she balance teaching, time for discussion, and emotional support?
- How might these parents feel after the 10-week session ends?

Interventionist Approach Example: *Jo is new to her role as a parent educator, working with a group of parents with multiple needs whose children are in elementary school. This is her first experience leading a parent group, and she is enthusiastic and full of ideas. She has chosen a formal curriculum for which she has been trained that includes many structured activities that teach specific parenting skills. Several parents in the group clearly enjoy the hands-on and group activities and come into each session eager and curious about what is planned for this week. Others seem less involved in the activities and occasionally interrupt to bring up a related issue or idea. Jo listens to these interjections, responds or affirms, and quickly moves back to the agenda.*

Each lesson includes opportunities for Jo to demonstrate strategies and time for parents to practice these newly learned skills. Jo watches each parent as they role play and offers positive feedback and helpful suggestions. At the end of each session, parents are given an assignment to try during the week, and they are encouraged to bring their questions and updates to the next session.

- Why might Jo plan her sessions as she does?
- What type of parent would benefit from and enjoy this approach?
- What is missing in this experience for others?
- What are the strengths of this approach and its challenges?

FRAMEWORK #4: MORAL AND ETHICAL CHARACTER OF PARENT EDUCATORS

A parent educator's style of leadership is anchored by his or her moral character. There have been numerous attempts to list the important characteristics of parent educators (e.g., Braun et al., 1984; Clarke, 1984; and Campbell & Palm, 2004). These lists tend to combine technical skills, dispositions, and character. The focus in this section will be on dispositions and character. Moral character or virtue is used to refer to the moral and ethical qualities of group leaders. The major emphasis in preparing and assessing parent and family educators must focus on skills that they need to develop as group facilitators. The issue of character has been neglected but is critical for guiding ethical practice and grounding effective practice. This framework will review and examine the core character traits that are essential for parent education practice.

The first recognition of this the underlying notion of moral character comes from Anderson (1930) in using the term "maturity" as a prerequisite for the preparation of parent educators. He linked this with also having direct experience working with children to assure familiarity with child behavior. The term *mature individual* suggests moral virtues that include understanding, empathy, self-awareness, and prudence gained from experience. This was seen as a foundation for learning the knowledge and skills related to good parent education practice. Recent attempts (Braun et al., 1984; Campbell & Palm, 2004; Goddard & Marshall, 2015; MnCFR, 2016) elaborate on the core of moral and ethical character traits and provide some consensus about the importance of including this as a relevant framework for understanding parent education practice.

The various terms from different perspectives identify the core character traits (e.g.,Campbell & Palm, 2004; NPEN, 2016). Braun et al. (1984) identifies the most appreciated traits of parent educators by parents as warm, accepting, receptive, nonjudgmental, and understanding. This is a good starting point and offers more concrete detail than the older notion of maturity. The Minnesota Council on Family Relations (MnFCR) group began to examine ethics in parent and family education and surveyed parent educators in Minnesota, which led to a list of 40–50 different virtues in search of the important traits for parent educators. The list was overwhelming and contained some overlapping concepts. The group consulted with Doherty (1991) and selected three core virtues that were most salient to parent education practice in Minnesota at that time. The list has been reviewed and reaffirmed in the most recent revision of the booklet on ethical thinking and practice (MnCFR, 2016). These virtues are described in more detail as core characteristics of ethical practice in parent and family education.

The first virtue that was selected was **caring**. Caring in the context of parent and family education refers to the disposition to "enhance the welfare of family members as agents in their own lives" (MnCFR, 2016, p. 3). Caring is an essential place to start relationship building that will be supportive without being enabling. Genuine caring provides a safe place for parents to build trust and to feel comfortable growing as parents. The parent educator must develop this caring to include all parents, especially those who may have very different beliefs about child rearing or exhibit behaviors that may be potentially harmful to children. Caring is expressed through understanding and support for parents to make their own thoughtful decisions about parenting practices.

A second virtue that emerged as important was **prudence**, or **practical wisdom**. This virtue includes the ability to carefully consider different needs and make decisions based on reflection and consultation. Prudence was selected to counter the tendency to avoid or circumvent difficult decisions and accept any beliefs or behaviors around parenting as being of equal value to any other values or as good as any other set of beliefs or behaviors. This expression of relativism can get confused with acceptance of family and cultural diversity. A prudent parent educator recognizes that there are conflicts involving beliefs around issues like gender roles and discipline techniques. It takes both wisdom to see contradictions in values and courage to help parents consider what tradeoffs they are making in selecting potentially harmful parenting practices. Practical wisdom can be modeled for parents, so they may see how to make difficult decisions about child rearing. For example, a parent educator may believe in the importance of avoiding physical punishment with very young children and may also believe in respecting different cultural beliefs about child rearing. The conflict in principles can paralyze the parent educator who, through no response to a parent's description of harsh physical punishment in a group setting, appears to condone this action. Prudence will help parent educators address and manage potential conflicts like this in a thoughtful and respectful manner.

The final virtue that was selected was **hope** and the **optimism** that accompanies hope. This is defined in the context of parent education as the ability to see the strengths of family members and recognize the positive potential, even in the most difficult situations. The complexity of family life and the many difficulties that some parents may face (e.g., intergenerational poverty, physical abuse, neglect, and domestic violence) can be overwhelming to parent educators. Families may also face barriers created by program policies or public policy that increase family stress and a sense of despair. A sense of hope and the ability to see the strengths in parents and children can help maintain a positive outlook to help individual families move forward and to advocate for families in difficult situations. This virtue helps parent educators acknowledge that parents care deeply about their children and want the best for them. It also is a strong affirmation of the ability of parents to grow and change. A sense of hope and optimism is most important for parent educators working with families in difficult circumstances.

Individuals bring many different strengths and positive characteristics to the practice of parent education. There may also be specific areas, such as being judgmental of certain types of families, that parent educators will have to focus on to change their dispositions and develop new ways of thinking. The three virtues that have been described provide a strong foundation for parent educators working with families in contemporary United States society. There are many other virtues that could be added to the list, such as honesty and genuineness. The individual moral character of the parent educator is important and establishes a strong foundation for ethical practice.

Goddard and Marshall (2015) address this issue of moral character in their article "Getting Our Hearts Right," focusing on family life educators and the underlying qualities that are important for working with parents and families. They also describe three specific character traits that closely align to the MnCFR (2016) virtues. Their list begins with humility, which means an openness to the views of others and also includes a willingness to admit and take responsibility for our own mistakes. It also involves a comittment to continue to learn and grow. In parent education practice, this is critical to not playing the role of the "all knowing" expert and, instead, taking on the role of co-learner with parents. It is in this space that we can come together to explore parenting issues and problem solve together.

A second characteristic or core virtue described by Goddard and Marshall is compassion. In parent and family education, this means having the capacity to put aside our own distress and manage our emotional responses. Then, we can listen to, understand, and empathize with parents who may be in distress. This calls for self-awareness of what triggers our emotions that can make it difficult to connect with parents. Compassion involves joining with the parent in distress and serving as a strong and secure base of 'being with" the other in their emotions without judgment to help them move on with challenging issues.

The final trait that is proposed by Goddard and Marshall is positivity. This is described as the ability to see the goodness in others and to remain optimistic. At the core, this is a leap of faith, believing that all parents possess a basic goodness and that they truly care about their children even when they struggle with the capacity to express this care in positive ways. This trait is similar to the MnCFR virtue of hope/optimism in how it is expressed.

Table 5.2 Comparison of Character Traits and Virtues

MnCFR Virtues	Moral Character	Dispositions
MnCFR (2016)	Goodard & Marshall (2015)	NPEN (2016)
Caring—Understanding and support for parents	**Compassion**—Care for parents	Supports the **Well-being** of parents
Practical Wisdom—Careful consideration of needs	**Humility**—Openness to learning and admit limitations	Demonstrates **Openness to Learning**
Hope and Optimism—Sees the strengths in others	**Positivity**—Ability to see goodness in others	Believes in **Family Strengths**

Respect: An Exploration

Lawrence-Lightfoot (2000)

Respect is a verb moving towards symmetry and relationship including:

- *Curiosity* and *attention* to stories of others;
- *Empowering* others to take control;
- *Healing* and *nourishing* well-being in others;
- *Engaging* in *dialogue* and symmetry.

NPEN (2016) has also explored these core moral traits under the concepts of dispositions (habits of the mind) and attitudes. They include a longer list, including building respectful relationships with parents, believing in family strengths, honoring differences, and remaining open to learning. Table 5.2 compares the character traits, dispositions and virtues from these different sources and illustrates the similarities and the common threads that come from the different disciplinary perspectives involved in work with families that are similar across groups. The concept of respect is included as a more comprehensive and universal activity that integrates and breathes life into the abstract concepts.

This framework is essential to understanding the core virtues or dispositions that have evolved with the practice of parent and family education. Box 5.1 helps to illustrate how the basic concept of respect from Sara Lawrence-Lightfoot brings these ideas together as a bridge from moral virtues or dispositions to action. These are played out by parent educators working at the prevention and promotion levels of the continuum as models of respect that parents can apply in their relationships with their children. At the intervention end of the continuum, this might better be described as parallel processing, where the relationship is based on therapeutic processes.

Box 5.1

"RESPECT IS A VERB"

In my parent education work with incarcerated fathers over the last 20 years, I always asked during the first class about ground rules for making this a safe space to talk about being a father. The men were typically familiar with group work from other classes and interventions that they had encountered and were quick to come up with the typical ground rules for group work. The one word that always came up was "respect." I would dig deeper and ask what respect would look like in the group. It would take a while to elicit the behaviors that demonstrated respect, such as not interrupting, using a supportive tone of voice, and not putting down other people. This was helpful, and I learned that the deeper meaning of respect was really essential to building trust among the fathers in the group. They understood the visceral meaning of respect but were not always aware of the different ways that it appears in a parenting class.

I then discovered Sara Lawrence-Lightfoot's book on respect (2000) that offered a deeper understanding of both the goals and multiple dimensions of this important word that held such profound meaning to the men in the group. Respect is the direct path to developing positive personal and professional relationships. Lawrence-Lightfoot explores multiple angles on respect that involve symmetry and reciprocity as a route to respectful relationships. It is acts of respect that go beyond the disposition or inclination to value respect as an abstract quality. This expression often starts with curiosity and genuine interest to understand the other person and be able to listen to their story. The meaning of respect related to entitlement or hierarchy of position is not what she is talking about. As a teacher, I come into this situation with this privilege, but I have learned that I must earn a different sense of respect by demonstrating respectful acts, not relying on my authority as the "teacher." It is often a fine line to be responsible for setting limits and still be respectful in this deeper way.

Lawrence-Lightfoot offers concrete lessons for building respectful relationships that are relevant to parent education and that I believe are the core of the moral character that this fourth framework represents. It is a combination of a genuine commitment to the deep concept of respect and the ability to display it in our work with parents. It begins with listening with full attention and curiosity to the stories of parents to better understand their attitudes and behaviors, especially those that may distress or concern us. Understanding the context and the constraints of the setting and being sensitive to the language we use, our gestures, our tone of voice, and the subtle nuances of our responses all engender respect. We have to anticipate misunderstandings and navigate moments of dissonance. In working with parents, respect also involves understanding the sometimes harsh and traumatic experiences of parents, in addition to being fully engaged in silence to be able to think, feel, and empathize in a way that heals, not wounds. Respect is a verb, not a set of techniques or an attitude, but a living expression of creating a tapestry of connection that fits the context and the different roles that you might play as a parent and family educator.

Parallel process, typically referred to in social work and psychotherapy super-vision, is a concept that indicates that processes at one level of an organization may be expected to reflect those at another. In these professions, it is related most often to the relationship between the supervisor and helping professional being replicated between the professional and client (McNeill and Worthen, 1989; Sullivan, 2002). In other words, the supervisor mentors and supports the professional in ways that culminate in similar interactions between that professional and the client.

It seems, therefore, that a similar process could be extrapolated to the relationship between the parent educator and parent with that of the parent and child. If the parent educator models respect, openness, patience, and non-judgmental understanding with the parent, this experience could help the parent employ these behaviors in their interactions with their child. It affords a new way of being in a relationship.

Particularly for those parents who have not experienced the crucial feelings of acceptance, respect, and nurturance, a relationship with a parent educator who acts in this capacity can provide a model for a healthy, positive level of interaction for parents with their own children. These new experiences and feel-ings become integrated and can be passed along in their family interactions.

Example of parallel process: *Dennis works with a group of parents who have complex and challenging issues in their lives. This group consists of parents who have difficult upbringings, have experienced physical and/or emotional abuse in their families of origin, and struggle to break the cycle of violence in their own families. Many of them have had involvement with child protection services, and they are making efforts to improve the relationships with their children. It is clear to Dennis that it is difficult for them to pass along positive messages to their children, since they, themselves, have never received this kind of affirmation within their families of origin.*

The parents in this group have little trust in various community service systems and generally show a lack of confidence in helping professionals. The group meets once each week with child care provided during the parent discus-sion time. Dennis has worked to develop a sense of trust and rapport with the parents by connecting on common interests, affirming their parenting strengths and successes, and providing an open and nonjudgmental atmosphere for the group.

Some of the strategies he uses, such as giving positive feedback and sup-port, are starting to make a difference in the group cohesiveness. Parents are more willing to open up and honestly share some of their challenges, as well as successes. Dennis also notices that some of the interactions between parents and children mirror his strategies with the parents. For example, he hears the parents repeating the same messages to their own children that he has given them in the group.

"You're doing well!"

"Everyone makes mistakes. It's okay."

"You can decide what to do."

"Let me know if you want some help."

Parents who have not experienced positive messages from their own families of origin are now receiving them as adults from the parent educator. Whether consciously or unconsiously, this positive experience is being passed along within the interactions they have with their children. This parallel proces is not formally referred to in the group but is a subtle strategy that can have an important impact on the growth and development of parents, particularly those with multiple risk factors and less-than-optimal past experiences.

SUMMARY

Each of the four conceptual models presented in this chapter address points to consider in the actual practice of group parent educaiton and are detailed in Table 5.3. A group leader will benefit from being familiar with each framework and the concepts they present to have a more holistic understanding of the role of the parent educator and access to different strategies for guiding parent learning and support. There is great potential for cross-fertilization of different frameworks that the creative and thoughtful parent educator may discover. There are other frameworks, theories, and concepts that would also apply to the role of the group leader.

These frameworks were selected, because they provide a deeper understanding about the roles and various aspects of group leadership. They also present a basis for practical strategies and tips, which by themselves, are often taken out of context. This results in the practitioner having to experiment in a trial-and-error fashion to learn when to apply them. It is important for parent educators to begin to examine their professional role as they learn to lead groups of parents. The levels of involvement and the domains of family practice models identify boundaries, new possibilities, and the skills needed for effective parent and family education practice. Understanding the parallel process that can affect changes in parent-child interaction provides a thoughtful reminder to the parent educator of the potential for influencing family dynamics. Finally, the focus on group leadership qualities describes styles of leadership and examines the importance of moral character for ethical leadership. This set of frameworks represents a variety of perspectives drawn from family theories and practice to enrich our current understanding about parent education practice in small groups.

Table 5.3 Summary of Conceptual Frameworks for Understanding Group Leadership Role

FRAMEWORK	MAJOR FOCUS	IMPORTANT CONCEPTS	APPLICATIONS
Levels of Involvement	Focus on depth of involvement and skills of the parent educator	Levels of involvement: Institution-centered Collaborative dissemination of information Feelings and need for support Psychoeducational intervention Family therapy	Creates guidelines for boundaries for practice Clearly delineates skills at each level
Domains of Family Practice	Unique roles of FLE, FT, and FCM	Core focus of family professionals of each discipline Overlap of knowledge and skill sets Expanded roles for FLE	Assists family professional in understanding different roles Promotes collaboration
Leadership Styles	Role of leader and relationship to parent group needs	Leadership approaches: Expert Facilitator Collaborator Critical Inquirer Interventionist Eclectic	Assists parent educator in assessing and monitoring own style and philosophy
Moral Character	Moral character, virtues, and actions of leader	Virtues/character: Caring Prudence Hope/ Optimism Compassion Openness Positivity Respect	Creates virtues/ moral character to guide professional/ethical behavior Disposition: habits of mind & heart Respect as a verb

DISCUSSION QUESTIONS

Levels of Involvement Model and Domains of Family Life Education

1. In which of Levels 2, 3, or 4, do you feel most/least comfortable in your work with parents? Why?

2. What skills will you need to function at a more intense level of involvement?

3. What parent feelings are you most and least comfortable managing in a parent group situation?

4. As an FLE, what content areas are you most confident addressing with a group? Least confident? Why?

5. What are specific types of parent groups that you feel least prepared to lead? How might you build your knowledge and skills to work with this type of group?

Leadership Style

1. Which of the six approaches is most appealing to you? Why?

2. How do you see your role in the group? As that of an expert or a peer? Why?

3. How much flexibility would you allow with a planned agenda?

4. How would you modify your approach to group leadership with a group of teen parents from a different SES and cultural group?

Moral/Ethical Character/Respect

1. Of the virtues described in this section, which do you believe would be most commonly found in a beginning parent educator? Why?

2. Thinking about your views of respect, what are some new ideas you might consider in developing respectful relationships with parents?

CLASS ACTIVITIES

Observe a parent education group. Choose one of the following:

1. Which of the six leadership approaches discussed in this chapter do you see? What behaviors and characteristics of the parent educator influence your determination?

2. At which level of involvement do you believe this group is functioning? Explain your reasoning as it relates to the model.

3. What actions do you see the family educator take that will help create a respectful environment?

REFERENCES

Anderson, J. (1930). *Parent education: The first yearbook*. Washington, DC: National Congress of Parents and Teachers.

Braun, L., Coplon, J., & Sonnonschien, P. (1984). *Helping parents in groups*. Boston, MA: Resource Communication.

Campbell, D., Kristensen, N., & Scott, M. (1997). *Manual for implementing Levels 3 and 4 family involvement in early childhood family education*. Roseville, MN: Minnesota Department of Children, Families, and Learning.

Campbell, D. & Palm, G. (2004). *Group Parent Education*. Thousand Oaks, CA: Sage.

Clarke, J.I. (1984). *Who, me lead a group?* San Francisco, CA: Harper and Row.

Dail, P.W. (1984). Constructing a philosophy of family life education: educating the educators. *Family Perspective, 18*(4), 145–149.

Darling, C.A. & Cassidy, D. (with Powell, L.) (2014). *Family life education: Working with families across the lifespan*. Long Grove, IL: Waveland Press.

Doherty, W.J. (1991, Winter). Virtue ethics: The person of the therapist. AFTA Newsletter (pp. 19–21).

Doherty, W. (1995). Boundaries between parent and family education and family therapy. *Family Relations, 44,* 353–358.

Doherty, W.J., & Lamson, A.L. (2015). The levels of family involvement model: 20 years later. In M.J. Walcheski & J.S. Reinke (Eds.), *Family life education: The practice of family science* (pp. 39–47). Minneapolis, MN: National Council on Family Relations.

Duncan, S.F., & Goddard, H.N. (2017). *Family life education: Principles and practices for effective outreach* (3rd Ed.). Thousand Oaks, CA: Sage.

Forslund Frykedal, K., & Rosander, M. (2015). The role as moderator and mediator in parent education groups—a leadership and teaching approach model from a parent perspective. *Journal of Clinical Nursing, 24,*1966–1974.

Goddard, W. & Marshall, J.P. (2015). The art of family life education: Getting our hearts right. In M.J. Walcheski & J.S. Reinke (Eds.), *Family life education: The practice of family science* (pp. 9–17). Minneapolis, MN: National Council on Family Relations.

Jacobs, E.E., Masson, R.L., Harvill, R.L. (2006*). Group counseling strategies and skills*. Pacific Grove, CA: Thomson Brooks/Cole.

Lawrence-Lightfoot, S. (2000). *Respect: An exploration.* Cambridge, MA: Perseus Books.

McNeill, B.W. & Worthen, V. (1989). The parallel process in psychotherapy supervision. Professional Psychology, Research and Practice, 20(5), 329–333.

Minnesota Council on Family Relations (2016). Ethical thinking and practice for parent and family educators. St. Paul, MN: MnCFR.

Myers-Walls, J.A. (2000). Familly diversity and family life educaiton. In D.H. Demon, K.R. Allen, & M.A. Fine (Eds.), *Handbook of family diversity* (pp. 359–379). New York, NY: Oxford University Press.

Myers-Walls, J.A., Ballard, S.M., Darling, C.A., Myers-Bowman, K.S., (2011) Reconceptualizing the Domain and Boundaries of Family Life Education. *Family Relations, 60,* 357–372.

Myers-Walls, J.A., Ballard, S.M., Darling, C.A., Myers-Bowman, K.S. (2014). Reconceptualizing the domains and boundaries of family life education. In M.J. Walcheski & J. S. Reinke (Eds.), *Family life education:The practice of family science* (pp. 49–60). Minneapolis., MN: National Council on Family Relations.

NPEN (National Parenting Education Network). (2016). Parenting educator competencies resource document (draft). Retreived from; npen.org/wp/content/uploads/2016/04/Competenies2.23.16.pdf.

Price, D.W. (2000). Philosophy and the adult educator. Adult Learning, 11, 3–5.

Sullivan, C., (2002). Finding the thou in the I: Countertransference and parallel process analysis in organizational research and consultation. *Journal of Applied Behavioral Science, 38*(3), 375–392.

6

EDUCATIONAL CONTENT AND METHODS

The purpose of this chapter is to shed some light on the educational function of parent education and to examine how this focus complements providing parents with emotional support. The dynamic and creative balance between education and support in parent education has often been an area of tension. The background discipline and preparation of parent educators often influence which role a particular parent educator prefers and knows how to implement. Education and educators are value-laden words that conjure up different images and connotations about parents as learners (Canning & Fatuzzo, 2000). The negative stereotypes of parent education depict parent educators as "narrow-minded experts" who tell parents how to raise their children with little understanding and respect for diverse family and cultural values. This chapter will introduce two approaches to selecting educational content and methods for parent education and will outline a comprehensive process for creating curricula based on current research, theory, and practice (National Academies of Sciences, Engineering, and Medicine, 2016).

The design process for educational curricula for parent education has continued to evolve over the last 20 years. This chapter begins by describing two different paradigms for thinking about and implementing parent education curricula (Center for the Developing Child, 2016). There is a strong emphasis on using evidence-based curricula, and yet, there are also compelling reasons for carefully defining a theory of change and designing new curriculum materials (content and methods) to match identified parent needs and cultural contexts. These are two different paradigms for addressing parent needs through parent education curriculum. The first paradigm is to select an evidence-based curriculum that matches the identified needs of a group of parents. There are a number of different sources of identified evidence-based curricula (e.g., National Center for Parent, Family, & Community Engagement, 2015). This source is very helpful in describing the measured outcomes for parents and children, as well as the requirements and cost for training. One limitation of the lists of evidence-based curriculums is that most (70%) of the 20 listed by the National Center for Parent, Family, and Community Engagement (2015) were developed more than 20 years ago. Advances in research on child development and changes in the complexity of family life today require continued efforts to develop new curriculum materials.

Some of the factors to consider in deciding if an evidence-based program will be the best choice include (National Center for Parent, Family, & Community Engagement, 2015):

- What programs are currently being used, and how effective are they?
- Does the program address the child outcomes that are important in your community?
- Does the program match the identified needs of parents, families, and children in your community?
- Does the format and length of the program fit with parent and family time and availability?
- What kinds of adaptations would have to be made to be consistent with cultural and family values?
- Do staff members have the backgrounds to benefit from the training, and will they stay in the community to make the investment of training funds worthwhile?

Evidence-based curricula are great tools to have available and should be carefully considered as one way to establish and deliver quality parenting education services. The rest of this chapter will focus on the process for developing a parent education curriculum and materials that are tailored to parent and child needs and community context. The Center for the Developing Child (2016) recommends that our early childhood programs, which include parent education, need to engage in ongoing research and development and learn from developing new approaches for programming for parents.

From our experience ... Implementing a packaged curriculum can be challenging for a number of reasons. I was asked to be part of a field test for a new curriculum focused on parents of young children (ages 0–5). It was a great learning experience. I was exposed to the thoughtful evaluation process that goes into developing a packaged parent education curriculum. In preparation each week, I would review the plan, read the background material, and gather the materials for the session. At times, I found myself unsure of the content and concepts that were used and felt like I needed a deeper knowledge base to feel confident that I could answer questions from the parents. There were also times that I didn't agree with some of the concepts that I was supposed to present and discuss with parents. Because this was a field test, I was able to send in my comments along with group evaluations after each session. The current focus on evidence-based curricula and fidelity to content and process is important to replicate a successful program. My insight from this experience was in understanding the importance of a deep knowledge of a program's conceptual framework to be able to present the content with confidence. In reality, one should fully embrace the curriculum and become a "true believer" in the underlying framework to present the program with the needed fidelity. This becomes a limitation to the scaling of evidence-based curricula. The background knowledge and skills of the parent educator are essential components of program effectiveness that must be considered in successful implementation of parent education curricula. The parent educator also has to have a strong belief that the evidence-based program will work.

The second paradigm for addressing parent needs is to create a curriculum that uses current research, theory, and best practices to tailor content and methods for a specific group of parents. The process for creating a curriculum will be presented in this chapter, using the Core Curriculum model for parent education programs as a resource (MNAFEE, 2011). Table 6.1 depicts an adapted version of the Core Curriculum domains that outline important content areas covered in parent education programs. This list of content areas and the underlying goals and indicators of parent learning are based on current research

Table 6.1 Parent Education Core Curriculum Framework

PARENT DEVELOPMENT	PARENT-CHILD RELATIONSHIPS	CHILD DEVELOPMENT	FAMILY DEVELOPMENT	CULTURE AND COMMUNITY
Role of Parent	Attachment	General Principles	Family Values	Family Support Networks
Changing Parent Role	Relationship Skills	Emotional Development	Family Traditions and Rituals	Community Environment
Parenting Philosophy	Nurturing	Social Development	Family Dynamics	School and Community
Gender and Parent Roles	Guidance	Approaches to Learning	Family Communication	Community Diversity
		Language and Literacy Development	Family Relationships	Community Resources
		Artistic and Creative Development		Societal and Global Forces
		Cognitive Development		
		Physical Development and Health		

Adapted from Minnesota Association for Family and Early Education, "Table Form: Parent Education Core Curriculum Framework," *Parent Education Core Curriculum Framework: A Comprehensive Guide to Planning Curriculum for Parent Education Programs*, p. 6. Copyright © 2011 by Minnesota Association for Family and Early Education.

and theory on child development, parenting, and family life topic areas. The framework can be used as a starting point for identifying core content and creating tailored curricula for different groups of parents with young children. This framework recognizes the central importance of child development and parent-child relationship information as strong elements of the core content. In addition, it also includes a focus on parent and family development as essential elements and adds culture and community as important contextual elements. The framework provides a comprehensive model for understanding parent-child relationships and the role of parenting in different family and cultural contexts.

The Core Curriculum framework (MNAFEE, 2011) is a good starting point for identifying content and goals. This publication also describes a careful process for three phases of curriculum development. Phase I includes a preliminary assessment of needs and review of current research related to the specific group of parents that the curriculum will serve. Phase II begins initial curriculum planning by reviewing the different domains and specific indicators of parent learning goals that match the perceived needs of the parent group. Phase III describes the creation of integrated lesson plans identifying instructional activities that match the learning goals, sequence, dosage, and evaluation of the curriculum. The process for creating parent education curricula should also be guided by evidence-informed practice (Small & Husar, 2015) that identifies important principles for guiding the development of parent and family life curriculum. The specific principles from Small and Husar that will be used to guide the curriculum design process are:

- Define clear learning goals for the program
- Use theory-driven and research-based concepts and knowledge
- Use a variety of learning approaches and instructional methods
- Ensure that content is socio-culturally relevant
- Support relationships among parents in a group
- Employ well-trained and committed staff
- Implement program assessment strategies for continuous improvement

The Core Curriculum process and the practice-based principles will be used to inform the curriculum design process that is presented later in this chapter.

Table 6.2 summarizes the main benefits and limitations of the two different approaches to curriculum implementation: 1) implementing an evidence-based curriculum or 2) designing a tailored curriculum. The summary lists the important differences in the two approaches and can help a parent educator or program decide which pathway best fits their needs. There are other parent education curricula that have not been systematically evaluated and designated as evidence-based that could be also be good choices in searching for the best match for a community or specific group of parents. The major advantage of selecting an evidence-based program is the intentional design of materials and the research results demonstrating positive parent outcomes. The creation of a new curriculum takes more time and effort. There are additional economic factors that should be considered in determining how much each approach might cost.

Table 6.2 Benefits and Limitations of Different Approaches to Curriculum Development

EVIDENCE-BASED CURRICULA APPROACH	
BENEFITS	**LIMITATIONS**
1. Positive outcomes are documented by previous research	1. Parent population may differ from original groups and outcomes may not be similar
2. Evidence-based curricula require minimal training to implement	
3. Focused goals and clear sequence	2. Cost of the materials, training, and ongoing supervision and evaluation may not match available resources
4. Guidance for fidelity of implementation	3. Person who delivers the curriculum may need additional training and preparation to match the skills of the educators used in the research
5. Evaluation tools have been established to use for ongoing evaluation	
6. Funders may require that only evidence-based programs are used	4. Fidelity to program may limit the ability to adapt to fit the parent needs
CORE CURRICULUM APPROACH	
1. Core Curriculum provides a research base for important topics	1. Takes time to create needs assessment and to develop content and materials
2. Tailored for diverse audiences based on assessment of needs	2. Cost of development
3. Can integrate latest research and theory into content	3. Evaluation process can be costly and it may be difficult to provide evidence of effectiveness
4. Can incorporate best practice ideas	4. Assumes that the parent educator has the knowledge and skills to create curriculum materials
5. Can incorporate new information technology more quickly	

6. Responsive to changing needs of participants

7. Educator is more familiar with and connected to the materials

5. Some potential funders may not be willing to provide resources for a curriculum that does not have an established evidence-base

CURRICULUM DESIGN PROCESS

The design process consists of six stages that follow a clear sequence, from the initial stage of understanding parent needs and interests to the final stage of putting it all together in a logic model to guide curriculum evaluation. The curriculum process is a creative and dynamic endeavor. It is structured to be responsive to parent needs and to use current theory, research, and practice to carefully construct integrated lesson plans to guide parent learning. The six stages are:

1. Understanding parent needs and interests

2. Articulating a theory of change model and defining relevant learning goals for the curriculum

3. Creating a logical sequence of content/topics

4. Selecting methods to match learning goals and stages of group development

5. Constructing lesson plans for individual sessions

6. Using a logic model to guide program evaluation

STAGE 1: UNDERSTANDING PARENT NEEDS AND INTERESTS

Understanding parent needs and interests is an ongoing process in parent education programs. Parent needs are not always self-evident or easy for parents to articulate. Parenting is a developmental process where parents grow and change through interactions with their children. The growth through experience is not always smooth or positive. Parent education should guide parents through typical transitions and support understanding and skill development to enhance individual growth and change. The parent educator can work with parents to discover and understand their values and goals, as well as their uncertainties about parenting. This is a lively, interactive process where a skillful parent educator listens to parents in many different ways. Not all communication about parents' needs and goals comes in the form of their spoken words about values, goals, or needs. The processes for discovering and clarifying needs and interests can be seen as a complex dance. The skillful parent educator engages parents in defining and reflecting upon their own goals for parenting in light of different family values, contexts, and understanding of development and parenting.

Who should make decisions about what parents need, parents as consumers or parent educators as experts (Powell, 1986)? There are many possible points along the continuum, from parent-directed to educator-directed. This way of thinking about parent needs suggests that a balance between parent and educator influence is optimal. The actual process of creating this balance is more complex than the continuum model suggests. It makes sense to think about what parents bring to this process and what we might expect a professional parent educator to bring. Parents bring their values and images of good parenting. These reflect their current family situation, community, and cultural contexts. The parent educator brings a general understanding of child development, parent-child relations, family dynamics, and the ways culture and social class influence family life. He or she also brings skills to design educational programs and lead parent groups in clarifying values, needs, and interests. The parent educator has the responsibility to create a balance along this continuum and to work at discovering and understanding parent values and needs.

The following strategies for discovering parent needs can be used to design and make ongoing adaptations to a parent education program. The ability of parent educators to implement these strategies will maintain a healthy balance between parent and educator influence on program design and implementation.

STRATEGIES FOR IDENTIFYING PARENT NEEDS AND INTERESTS

1. **Interest Checklist.** Typically introduced at a first session, checklists can be generated by parents with the educator adding core items, or it can be prepared by the parent educator, who then invites parents to add topics to the list. It can be helpful for parents to see a list of topics to stimulate their thinking about important topics. The checklist gives a parent educator clear indicators of expressed parent needs and interests at the beginning of a new group. The results are useful to design a sequence of topics that can be revisited as the group

develops. Table 6.3 is a sample checklist for parents of infants that includes some typical topics of interest for this age group.

2. **Icebreakers.** These can help parent educators learn about the parents in their group. They are short and nonthreatening ways to begin a session: for example, "Share a funny incident that recently happened with your child" or "What parenting advice would you give to your sister who is having her first child?" Responses to these types of questions can help the educator understand parent beliefs and values. They can energize the group by inviting the participation of all members at the beginning of a session. Icebreakers should be connected to the topic or issue that is the class focus for the day, which provides a smooth transition to the topic. An effective icebreaker activity engages and energizes parents to get them ready to examine and discuss a topic. It also helps to build familiarity and relationships among participants.

Table 6.3 Parent Discussion Topic Survey: Infant Class

Check the topics that are of most important to you as a parent

_____ Child development (physical, cognitive, language, social, emotional)

_____ Temperament and individual differences

_____ Soothing a crying infant and spoiling

_____ Sleep patterns and issues

_____ Play and learning

_____ Nutrition and feeding concerns and mealtimes

_____ Nurse practitioner (available to answer questions)

_____ Babysitters and child care

_____ Adjusting to parenthood

_____ Brain development and attachment

_____ Child proofing your home and other safety issues

_____ Communication and infant cues

_____ Comfort items (bottle, pacifier, blankets)

_____ Breastfeeding and weaning

_____ Discipline (limit setting)

_____ Sharing parenting responsibilities

_____ Changes in family systems (siblings, grandparents)

_____ Infant health concerns

_____ Balancing work and family

_____ Infant massage

---

3. **Joys and Concerns.** This common practice provides a chance to check in at the beginning of a class to find out about recent events, successes, and challenges that parents may want to share with the group. Joys and concerns help to update changing parent and family circumstances and give parents the opportunity to share immediate concerns that may need to be addressed before planned topics. This type of activity demonstrates the parent educator's flexibility and willingness to listen to new issues as a parent group evolves. It also opens up the possibility that parents may spend most of the group time bringing up immediate concerns and never get to planned topics and general information on parenting that some groups members want and need. Parent educators have to recognize the importance of parents expressing immediate concerns and sharing family crises as part of developing group trust and providing support. They also have a responsibility to address the topics that the group expects for the class. Some ways that facilitators create this balance is to set a time limit for joys and concerns or to address immediate concerns during the last 10 minutes of a class. Joys and concerns help parent educators better understand parent needs and stresses and to consider these as they plan future sessions.

4. **Class Exercises.** There are many exercises in parent education that involve parents sharing their experiences from growing up or current beliefs about parenting that help the parent educator understand them. Early recollections, sharing of experiences from childhood, and checklists of values are some common exercises that reveal parents' expectations for their children and beliefs about child development.

An agenda is posted, yet the parent educator is flexible to meet parents' needs

For example, in a parent group for fathers of young children, participants were asked to reflect on their childhood and remember a time when their own fathers or grandfathers had read or told a story to them. Their recollections, or lack of recollections, provided insights into male models of early literacy activities and served as a springboard for the discussion of fathers and their influence on early literacy development in young children. This information helped the parent educator understand parent beliefs and attitudes about fathers and literacy. A simple checklist on desirable child characteristics (e.g., Crary, 1993) is another activity that can provide some concrete information on parents' values and expectations for their children. The use of class exercises is a critical part of effective lesson plans in raising awareness and assisting parents in shaping their own parenting beliefs and behaviors. Parent responses help the parent educator better understand their needs and interests and use this information to adapt future sessions.

5. **Class Discussions.** Parent sharing of beliefs and attitudes about child development and parenting practices often occurs in the context of class discussions. The more comfortable and safe parents feel, the more they reveal about their own needs, concerns, and dreams for their children. A variety of methods can provide different opportunities for both involvement and sharing of beliefs and values. Clear, focused discussion questions assist parents in expressing ideas and feelings during discussion time. The parent educator can use discussion as a time to listen carefully to parents and gently probe for parents' beliefs and attitudes. A basic discussion question, such as "What discipline techniques did your parents use with you?" with a follow-up question of "What did you learn from these experiences?" reveals a great deal regarding parent attitudes about discipline techniques. This provides the parent educator with practical information for planning later lessons about discipline strategies.

6. **Observations of Parent-Child Interaction Time.** The strengths of both parents and children can be gleaned from observations of their interactions. These interactions may also reveal some of the challenges parents experience. Parenting programs that include this option provide a window through which the parent-child and family dynamics can be viewed. Not all parents are comfortable in the program environment, and most will be on their best behavior. It is the responsibility of the educators to create a comfortable and supportive environment. Non-obtrusive observation can lead to insights about needs that may never be verbally expressed by parents. The parent educator role is not to judge and focus on problems but to understand and appreciate the child's unique characteristics and to note parent strengths and better understand their challenges. For example, observing a father-child dyad experience difficulty with separation helps the parent educator empathize and better understand that this father does not feel comfortable with leaving his child with the early childhood teacher. There will be further discussion of parent-child interaction time in Chapter 13. This is another opportunity to informally learn about parent needs, interests, and challenges.

These informal strategies identify important sources of information about parent needs, values, and interests. Identifying parent needs is an ongoing process of listening and observing with the goal of better understanding parents. In some groups where more intense parent services are provided, there may be additional paths for learning about parent needs. In a family literacy program, initial interviews allow the parent educator to meet individually with parents and learn more about their family situation and their reasons for wanting to participate in the program. Sometimes information about parents is passed along from a referral source with a release of information. Home visits are also used in some programs and provide a time and space to learn about parents and their family lives. Learning about parent needs occurs in the context of developing relationships between parents and parent educators in the evolving group context. Though understanding parent needs is presented as a first step in designing educational sessions, it is clearly an ongoing task that should continue to shape the content and design of parent group sessions. The process for discovering parent needs will vary depending upon the length of the group, the intensity of the program, the parents' personality characteristics, and the investment of parents.

STAGE 2: ARTICULATING A THEORY OF CHANGE MODEL AND IDENTIFYING LEARNING GOALS

One of the challenges of parent education curriculum development is to clearly describe from research and theory what changes in parent knowledge, attitudes, and skills are the major focus of the curriculum. How do proposed learning goals fit together in a logical model of change? What are the long-term impacts on parenting behavior, parent-child relationships, and child outcomes? Parent education curricula often focus primarily on outcomes that are related to specific theories about parent growth and development. Palm (2003) delineates five different conceptual frameworks that are the driving theories behind parent education curricula for incarcerated parents.

- Attachment theory that focuses on parent-child relationships
- Parenting skills that emphasize communication and discipline
- Self-development that depends upon building parent self-esteem and self-confidence as a starting point in changing behavior
- Social support and empowerment
- Parenting beliefs and attitudes that are the underlying foundation for changing behavior

Each of these frameworks has a basic set of assumptions about the important dynamics of parenting behavior and how to best influence these behaviors. In some cases, a curriculum may combine different frameworks to be more comprehensive. It is critical to articulate a theory of change that underlies and connects curriculum goals.

Defining learning goals is a critical step in any educational process. The educator has the major responsibility for defining clear, pragmatic, and relevant goals for parent education sessions. Working with adults in parent education involves sharing this responsibility with parents. The possible goals for parent education encompass a number of different content areas. Defining parent education goals is not a simple task due to a number of factors. Parenting is a complex enterprise that includes multiple roles and tasks. Table 6.4 outlines six general areas that have been identified in the National Extension model of parenting practices (Smith et al., 1994). The examples listed are adapted from the National Extension model and define the various parent roles and functions that parents are expected to perform.

Table 6.4 can be used as a starting point for identifying learning goals or outcomes for parent education. It provides a generic list of the knowledge and skills base for contemporary parenting. The actual learning goals for each session will be more specific and will describe what the parent educator hopes parents will take away from a specific session. For example, in a session on discipline, the outcomes might be:

- Parents will examine their attitudes about physical punishment.
- Parents will understand the long and short-term consequences of using physical punishment on children and also its effects on the parent-child relationship.
- Parents will develop an expanded set of guidance and intervention tools.

The main benefit of the model in Table 6.4 is that it provides a holistic view of parenting and the varied and interrelated functions that form the basis for creating specific learning goals for parents. This broad set of parenting practices and research on parenting practices (National Academies of Sciences, Engineering, and Medicine, 2016) should guide the development of specific learning goals.

AREAS OF LEARNING/CHANGE

Three areas of potential learning/change for parents are new knowledge, skills, and attitudes. In addition to understanding domains of parenting practices, parent educators must consider these different types of change as they design learning goals. These three distinct but interrelated areas of change are discussed below.

1. **Knowledge.** In parent education, knowledge refers to our understanding of specific content areas, such as typical child development. For

Table 6.4 Important Domains of Parenting Practices

1. UNDERSTANDING

- Observe and understand how children grow, learn, and develop.
- Understand how children interact with and influence their environment.
- Understand a child's individuality and unique strengths.

2. NURTURE

- Provide warmth and affection to children.
- Display sensitivity and responsiveness to a child's feelings and thoughts.
- Provide for basic needs.
- Teach self-respect.
- Provide a connection to family and cultural roots.

3. ADVOCACY

- Understand and access community resources for children.
- Help create healthy communities for children.
- Build healthy relationships within family and community.

4. GUIDANCE

- Model desirable values and behaviors.
- Set clear limits for children.
- Teach and foster responsibility and problem solving.
- Monitor activities and relationships with peers and other adults.

5. MOTIVATION

- Encourage curiosity and imagination in child.
- Help child develop understanding of self and others.
- Provide supportive learning conditions.

6. CARE FOR SELF

- Manage personal and family stress.
- Develop respectful and cooperative relationship with child-rearing partner.
- Identify family values and goals.
- Be aware of own strengths as a parent.
- Give and ask for support as needed.

SOURCE: Adapted from Charles A. Smith, et al., *National Extension Parent Education Model of Critical Parenting Practices*, p. 14. Copyright © 1994 by Kansas Cooperative Extension Service.

The educator connects with the child, modeling positive interactions

example, understanding children's typical developmental patterns for expressing anger from ages 2–5 is important and practical information for parents of preschool children. This type of knowledge can lead to understanding children's behavior and tempers a parent's response to what otherwise might be considered "willful" misbehavior. Child development knowledge helps parents develop appropriate and realistic expectations for child behavior. Though child development information may be clearly presented to parents, they must still incorporate this knowledge into their own mental models of development. Helping parents to process new information and understand the application to child-rearing practices is a challenge.

2. **Skills.** Skill development in parent education includes a wide range of parenting behaviors that cluster around guidance and communication. Skills involve learning specific strategies for confident and effective parenting. Setting clear limits on a 2-year-old's safe exploration of a home environment by carefully arranging the environment is a skill.

Observing and distinguishing different infant cues for hunger and tiredness is a skill. Clearly communicating empathy for a child who is losing a best friend, because the friend's family is moving to a new state is a parenting skill. Monitoring an adolescent's peer relationships in a supportive manner is a parenting skill. Helping parents develop practical skills is the major focus of parent education programs. Skills involve the appropriate application of strategies to guide and manage child behavior. Skills are the next step after knowledge and understanding; they are knowledge in action. What makes skill development challenging is that parents may have grown up with poor or no role models and thus have developed habits that are not effective and compromise parent-child relationships. Old habits must be discarded to make room for new skills. Learning a new skill also takes time for practice, coaching, and encouragement. Parents must be convinced that the new skill is worthwhile and matches their beliefs about children and parenting. Skills must also fit the family and community context to be practical. The presentation and modeling of new skills may be easy for the educator, but parent integration and practice of new skills is not always a smooth or simple learning process.

3. **Attitudes.** In parent education, attitudes refer to beliefs parents hold that involve a strong emotional component. For example, parents may believe that young children are intrinsically strong-willed and manipulative and need to be punished so that they will learn to respect adult rules. The diversity of attitudes and beliefs about good parenting make it difficult to clearly define which attitudes or beliefs to target for change. The parent educator's role is to help parents carefully examine their attitudes and, when appropriate, consider alternative beliefs and practices. This is the most difficult area to change, but it is critical to address in parenting programs. It may be futile to teach new discipline skills or strategies if a parent strongly believes that children must learn respect for parents and other adults through physical discipline and intimidation.

These three areas of change must all be addressed in a careful and systematic manner. Sensitivity to group process is one important consideration for how to approach each area of change. Sometimes it can be safer in a group to address and discuss knowledge of development before moving into attitudes that evoke strong feelings—although most child-rearing issues can trigger strong feelings in parents. The learning goals must be carefully defined with regard to content, change areas, and stages of group development. Lesson plans can address all three areas of change in one session or provide some time to focus on attitudes in one session before moving into specific strategies and skills in the next session. For example, with topics like spanking or sexuality, it helps to elicit parent attitudes and have parents consider their goals for children before the group moves into learning specific strategies. All three areas of change fit together and need to be examined in designing effective sessions for promoting parent growth and development. This conceptual model for educational change is both simple in defining three specific areas of change and complex in how these areas interact and influence each other.

Stage 2 includes identifying theories that form a foundation for approaching parenting practices in the curriculum. This includes listing assumptions from different theoretical frameworks that explain the focus on specific learning goals. These theoretically based assumptions and goals form the basis for developing a logic model that depicts the underlying theory of change.

STAGE 3: CREATING A LOGICAL SEQUENCE OF CONTENT/TOPICS

The creation of a logical sequence of topics is a third step in creating a curriculum. The sequence should consider the development of the group, as well as the flow of topics that would build upon each other. In the Core Curriculum process this is Phase II, which considers how the different learning goals fit together and determines a logical sequence and dosage, or number of sessions, that are needed to meet the goals. The theory of change developed in Stage 2 and identified parent needs from Stage 1 also need to be considered when creating the sequence. The curriculum should be focused on clear long-term outcomes that are guided by the theory and research. A curriculum that covers too many topics that are not connected in a logical sequence is likely to have limited impacts (National Academies of Sciences, Engineering, and Medicine, 2016).

Table 6.5 is an example of a sequence used in a curriculum for incarcerated fathers developed by one of the authors. The sequence begins with identifying the importance of fathers as a basic assumption and starting place for the class. The first two classes also address the different parenting, family, and cultural values that participants bring to the class. This is important to build acceptance of different views since the class typically includes a variety of different cultural groups. Building trust among the participants is essential in this group. The next part of the class addresses understanding child development, child expression of emotions, and child needs. This is meant to build understanding and empathy for the child's perspective. The middle section is devoted to development of communication and guidance skills. The final sessions focus

From our experience ... Creating a logical sequence for the content and learning goals is essential for an effective curriculum. I use interest surveys in my groups and consider two factors in designing the sequence: 1) group process and building trust and 2) building on early content as a foundation for later content. For example, in my work with incarcerated fathers, I quickly learned that the topic of relationships with the children's mothers was an immediate concern that had strong negative emotional reactions, and the group was easily side-tracked before it had developed a sense of trust. The emphasis on the importance of fathers and an understanding of children and their needs in the beginning sessions provided a strong foundation for later discussion about father-mother relationship issues. A sequence that connects topics through ongoing sessions helps piece together content in a coherent manner. Giving attention to the development of the group helps parents learn to trust each other before learning from each other.

on the relationship with mothers and co-parenting. The class concludes with a session on rupture/repair of relationships and reconnection with children. The different goals and content areas build on each other to address the more emotional issues after building trust in the group and providing content to support the parent-child relationship as a central theme. This class is based on attachment theory as a motivating force that is reinforced with communication and guidance skills to support the father-child relationship.

STAGE 4: SELECTING METHODS TO MATCH LEARNING GOALS AND THE GROUP PROCESS

The use of a variety of methods has been a hallmark of best practices in parent education (Braun et al., 1984; Kurz-Riemer, 2001; Small & Husar, 2015). It is assumed that a variety of methods is the best strategy to meet different learning styles and, thus, engage everyone in the group. Variety also keeps the attention of participants who might become bored with a limited number of teaching methods. Methods like an occasional game or more interactive exercise bring a different level of energy to a group, as well as a different kind of engagement. Though variety of methods in and of itself has some merit, matching of methods to areas of change and to group development is a critical consideration in designing effective parent education sessions.

Table 6.5 Incarcerated Fathers Class Outline

1. Introduction to Circle of Security (COS) concepts and Paths to Good Fathering

2. Defining Cultural/Spiritual Traditions and Family Values: Lessons from Dad

3. Understanding Children: Realistic Expectations and Individual Differences and Needs

4. Understanding Feelings in Children and Promoting Emotional Intelligence: COS "Being With" Children

5. Communicating with Children from a Distance: COS Reading Cues and Miscues

6. Supporting Children's Self-Esteem and School Success

7. Discipline: Exploring Attitudes, Values, and Behaviors

8. Discipline Game: Finding Strategies That Work for You

9. Male Socialization and Fatherhood: COS Being Bigger, Stronger, Wiser, and Kind

10. Overcoming Negative and Missing Role Models: COS Understanding "Shark Music"

11. Developing Respectful Relationships with Your Child's Mother:

    Co-parenting Models

12. Parenting as Partners: Communication Skills Practice

13. Legal Issues: Paternity, Child Support, and Parenting Time

14. Reconnecting and Repairing Relationships and Finding Support

Table 6.6 is presented as a practical guide for thinking about different areas of change and which specific methods may be most effective in promoting change in these areas. It also illustrates the wide variety of methods that can be used in parent education. Videos have become a popular tool for bringing real life examples to a session. Video clips can be used in different ways, depending upon the learning goal. For instance, if the goal is to give parents information about different types of social play, an instructional video with clear examples of child play behavior is an appropriate choice. Alternately, a short video clip from a popular movie or TV show can be used to trigger discussion on male and female communication styles. Incredible Years (Webster-Stratton, 1998) uses video clips of specific parent-child situations for practicing the application of new skills. Table 6.6 can be used as a general guide to help parent educators think about their intended outcomes by asking, "What educational change areas am I targeting?" and "What methods are best suited for facilitating these learning goals?" In effective planning, it is essential to ask what are the learning goals for this session and what types of change the parent educator wants to address. Table 6.6 reminds parent educators that a variety of methods can be used and that methods should be carefully selected to promote the intended outcomes.

Another important factor to consider in selecting appropriate educational methods is the stage of group development. In Chapter 4, the stages of group development were outlined as a way to understand how groups typically cycle through different stages. The first stage of forming and last stage of adjourning are more focused on building relationships and bringing closure to a group and are less focused on new content and on processing ideas, attitudes, and feelings. The middle three stages of group development provide space for new learning. At each phase of group development, different instructional methods might be a better match with the group development process. While the group is "norming," it is important to use methods that help group members share basic values and goals and develop common ground. Information can be provided about less controversial topics through videos on development or short interactive mini-lectures on topics, such as typical sequences of language development. More controversial topics and interactive methods can be most effective during the performing stage.

Several other important factors should be considered in selecting instructional methods. One factor that is mentioned most frequently is different learning styles (e.g., visual, auditory, and kinesthetic). Awareness of these different styles reminds parent educators that each parent may process information differently. Visual learners process information by seeing, so visual aids, such as videotapes, whiteboards, and cartoons, are effective ways to convey information and ideas. Auditory learners learn through listening, indicating the use of mini-lectures and discussion as appropriate techniques. Kinesthetic learners learn best by doing and need to be more actively engaged through methods, such as role-playing and games. In most parent groups, there will be a range of learning styles, and the parent educator should carefully observe which methods are most effective at engaging different members. Learning style surveys can also be used to identify parents' preferences. This activity can be integrated into the topic of understanding children's learning styles. Using a variety of methods and considering which methods address different learning styles is a key to keeping parents engaged. Parent educators also need to be aware of their own learning style in order to avoid slipping into their own comfort zone and avoiding those methods they don't like or are not comfortable using. The parent

Table 6.6 Methods of Promoting Change in Knowledge, Attitudes, and Skills

KNOWLEDGE	ATTITUDES	SKILLS
Lecture/Mini-lecture	Stories	Demonstration/Modeling
Reading Materials Parenting books Popular press articles Website articles	**Structured Exercises** Checklists Early Recollections Quiz-myths about . . .	**Guided Observation** Learn child cues Child development
Visual Pictures Posters Infographics Cartoons	**Trigger Video** Discussion starter	**Role Playing and Games** Practice new skills and Apply new stratgies
Video Lecture, e.g., Ted Talk YouTube video	**Case Study** Parenting situations	**Video Clips** Parenting situtations
	Role Play Child's perspective	**Video Feedback** Parent-child interactions
	Panel Presentation Different perspectives	**Homework** Practice new strategies Journal of quality time

educator's observations of parent responses to different methods can be used to assure a high level of parent engagement.

Other factors that must be considered are cultural backgrounds, literacy levels, learning disabilities, and gender. Each of these areas can pose significant challenges for selecting and using different educational methods. Different cultural norms may exist for sharing feelings and discussing problems, even after a group has built a sense of trust, and a genuine sharing of differences has begun. It can be helpful to acknowledge both differences and similarities in a group early in the group process. Sensitivity to cultural differences is essential for parent educators. Selecting methods that build a common understanding and establish an ethic of respect for differences can help diverse parent groups function effectively and learn from each other.

Literacy is also an issue that has received attention in parent education during the last two decades (Brizius & Foster, 1993). The issues around parent or family literacy come from two different directions. First, the family literacy programs established in the early 1990s have sensitized parent educators to the fact that many parents may have limited literacy skills. The initial response to this awareness was to simplify language and limit the use of written material or rewrite materials at a lower reading level. Family literacy programs have provided an alternative to this approach by directly focusing on improving parent literacy skills as a way to help both parents and children. Sensitivity to literacy levels is still important in groups, and written materials should match the reading levels of the group. A common myth about illiteracy is that parents who struggle with reading have limited cognitive abilities. Many parents with literacy issues have a deep understanding of parenting issues. Parents with low literacy skills have usually developed coping skills that can initially hide their limitations. They often feel embarrassed to have others recognize their challenges and have experienced the stigma that accompanies difficulties with literacy. Asking to take forms home to be completed later, "passing" when asked to respond to a written statement, avoiding writing activities where parents jot down a question are all examples that can alert parent educators to lower literacy skills.

A group of families that raise a different set of questions about parent literacy are English as a Second Language and English Language Learners (ESL/ELL) families. For this population, the use of English is a major barrier to parent education. This affects the choice of methods in ways that are very similar to working with parents with limited literacy skills. Parenting issues are complex and emotional, and limited language skills pose a major barrier in the sharing of ideas, discussion, and processing new information. It is important not to oversimplify parent feelings and knowledge in these types of parenting groups. It may be better to use an interpreter with ESL/ELL parent groups than to oversimplify concepts. This is one way to respect parent understanding and to facilitate a deeper level of discussion. The development of programs like Even Start Family Literacy has helped to advance our understanding of parent education with these two populations. Parents in these programs also have diverse learning styles and will benefit from a careful selection of methods to match group learning goals and group development.

Ground rules are developed for each group

The final factor that should be considered is the gender of the parent groups or the gender mix of the group. Parent groups have tended to serve mothers (Palm & Palkovitz, 1988), and most parent educators are women. The development of groups for fathers (Johnson & Palm, 1992; McBride, 1989; Palm, 1997; Fagan & Palm, 2004) has generated some insights into the educational methods for parent education. Men, in general, may not be as direct in expressing feelings and may be more reluctant to share problems. Some activities (methods) that may be very comfortable and effective for most mothers may not be comfortable for many fathers. In a recent parent session observed by one of the authors, the topic for the day was "Taking Care of Ourselves" and addressed managing stress. One of the closing activities was to pass around hand lotion to use as an example of taking care of yourself. Because the parent group consisted of only mothers, this was an effective method. However if a father had come to the class that morning, this activity may have been uncomfortable for him. Gender composition of a group should be considered when deciding which activities and methods to introduce to a group.

This section on selecting methods has outlined a number of specific factors to consider in designing effective parent education sessions. The goals of the session and the stage of group development are major areas to address, but other factors may also influence the selection and use of methods. It is evident that the selection of methods is a critical stage for designing effective parent education sessions.

STAGE 5: CONSTRUCTING LESSON PLANS FOR INDIVIDUAL SESSIONS

The lesson plan is a blueprint for organizing a session. It is the integration of information from the steps outlined in the previous sections. There are a number of reasons for investing time in creating lesson plans. A well-designed lesson plan ensures that the session will have a clear focus by articulating specific learning goals. It also helps the parent educator think carefully about matching methods to goals and think about how to present new information in interesting ways while meeting the needs of different learning styles. Careful lesson planning also can help avoid or prevent common group process problems, such as a quiet or tired group or individuals who tend to dominate parent discussion time.

LESSON PLAN FORMAT

There are different ways to organize or structure lesson plans. The following format is simple and has six basic components that should be included in planning parent education sessions. It incorporates the same basic ideas that are included in the Core Curriculum framework planning process, which involves six different components (MNAFEE, 2011).

1. **Learner Outcomes.** A clear description of two to four different learning goals provides the major focus for the session.

2. **Introductory Activity.** The introductory activity engages the group in the topic and encourages active participation at the beginning of a session. In the Core Curriculum process, there is a section on guided check-in and review of goals from the last session that could be part of the introduction activity.

3. **Session Activities with Discussion Questions.** This section includes a clear outline of the sequence of activities to be used in a class session. Related discussion questions should be included to help initiate and guide the processing of major ideas and related feelings.

4. **Closure.** There are many different ways to end a session, from summarizing discussion points to encouraging parents to try out new strategies from the session. This component ensures that closure will be considered an essential part of the class, and some specific strategies for closure should be included in a lesson plan.

5. **Resources.** A list of resources used to prepare the content should be included, e.g., articles, books, websites.

6. **Materials list.** This is useful to remember what is needed to conduct the class, including handouts, video or other technology, markers, etc.

The Core Curriculum includes two additional sections. One addresses home application, which is an effective way to explicitly focus on how to extend new skills into home life. The other focuses on reflection and evaluation of the plan.

These six components allow parent educators to outline a clear plan starting with the description of learning goals. The format also includes the opening activity and closure, because both are essential to an effective session. The session activities should be carefully outlined using the planning principles that have been described earlier in the chapter. This format is not as detailed as some lesson plans in a published curriculum, which may include a more complete script, resources for background information, and a list of materials. It is presented here as a basic guide to assist parent educators in outlining and designing their own sessions. The addition of resources and list of materials are good reminders to be fully prepared.

Table 6.7 provides a list of practical tips to use in planning effective and engaging parent education sessions. The tips stress the major points from the chapter in simple terms and strive to balance education and support. They are

Table 6.7 Lesson Planning Tips

1. Give parents information and ideas that are new for them.

2. Clarify issues that parents have about a topic before creating a plan.

3. Stay focused on two or three important points for parents to take away.

4. Adapt topics for different ages of children.

5. Provide information that will reassure parents.

6. Present something that interests you.

7. Don't try to discuss and cover everything you know.

8. Clear up misconceptions that parents bring to the group.

9. Adapt materials to different learning styles.

also reminders of ways to use parent input to ensure the information presented is relevant and interesting. Two different lesson plan outlines are presented as examples of how to use the lesson plan format. Table 6.8 outlines a lesson plan for an initial session with a group of parents of young children. This session emphasizes the initial goals of helping parents get to know each other, to understand the program, and to set up ground rules for discussion. This beginning session is for a 45 to 60 minute time period in a program where parents and children come together for a 2-hour session and spend the first hour together in parent-child interaction time. In longer initial sessions of 1½ to 2 hours with parents alone, some initial content would also be included.

Table 6.8 Lesson Plan for Parents of Young Children: Program Orientation

I. LEARNER OUTCOMES

A. The parents will get to know each other and the children.

B. The parents will know program philosophy and goals.

C. The parents will help develop guidelines for discussion.

II. OPENING ACTIVITY

Have a variety of items on the table. Ask parents to share their names, their children's names and ages, and whether they have been in a group before. Also ask them to choose one item on the table that in some way represents their child and ask them to explain why.

III. SESSION ACTIVITIES

A. Have schedule on board. Describe different components of the schedule, pointing out "who's in charge" during different components of the program.

B. Group discussion guidelines:

1. Introduce bright-colored card activity with statements that will help parents feel comfortable sharing. Ask parents to choose the statement that "speaks to them" and share why.

2. Mention important group guidelines, if not mentioned (right to pass).

C. Program philosophy and goals:

1. Review program goals and basic beliefs of the program about importance of parent education and support.

2. Time for any questions about the program.

IV. CLOSURE

A. Ask parents to comment on their child's reactions or feelings about coming to the program.

B. Remind them that next time the group will be choosing topics.

V. RESOURCES

Program philosophy – Booklet from program about program policies and philosophy.

Sample Ground Rules – Campbell, D. & Palm, G. (2004). *Group Parent Education*. Sage.

VI. MATERIALS

A. Set of 10 common items for opening exercise (pen, toy car, book, etc.)

B. Set of cards that represent typical ground rules.

C. Handout on program philosophy.

The final lesson plan in Table 6.9 is for a parent group comprised of couples that is meeting for the second of 10 sessions. The plan focuses on helping couples understand some of the typical tensions they may experience, based on the differences between mothers and fathers. The plan incorporates an exercise using cartoons to identify some common gender tensions as a way to explore some of the underlying feelings. It also uses a game format to help parents see different responses and perspectives about common parenting issues. The closure is a way for parents to reflect on the session and bring a reminder of a new lesson home in the form of a postcard to put on a refrigerator.

These lesson plans were chosen to provide examples from different groups at different points in group development in order to demonstrate how some of the principles outlined in the chapter are practiced. All of the sessions were planned for parents of young children where parents and children come together for a parent education program that has an early childhood component, as well as parent-child interaction time. Lesson planning demands an investment of time using the matching process that has been discussed. It is assumed that parent educators can creatively blend their knowledge of group process with content and use a variety of methods to help parents grow and develop their skills and confidence.

Table 6.9 Lesson Plan for Parenting Together Session 2: Gender Tensions as Normal

I. LEARNER OUTCOME

A. Parents will continue to learn about each other and build group trust.

B. Parents will understand tensions around sharing household responsibilities and the feelings that these create for men and women.

C. Parents will understand different perspectives about parenting together.

II. OPENING ACTIVITY

Ask each parent to finish the following sentences:

The thing that made it most difficult to get here today was . . .

Something we both enjoy doing together is . . .

III. ACTIVITIES

A. Gender Tensions Around Household and Child Care Responsibilities

1. Ask parents to select a cartoon that speaks to them out of 10–15 cartoons placed on a table and read it to the group and share why it is relevant to them.

Summarize some of the main themes from the cartoons:

a) Different expectations—Mother knows best

b) Women's endless list—never enough time or help

c) Men don't listen/don't show feelings

d) Disagreements about who is on duty

e) Fathers feeling left out—don't take time for kids/family

Discussion:

a) What are the feelings that come up for these men? For these women?

Examples:

Men	**Women**
Left out	Angry, unfair
Defensive	Unsupported
Guilty	Overwhelmed
Inadequate	Inadequate, unorganized

b) How do these feelings get in the way of working together as parents?

c) How can these feelings be managed in a constructive manner?

2. Couples Scrupples

a) Explain the rules of game (Three response cards; Yes, Maybe, and No).

b) Split the group into two groups by gender.

c) Read a situation and ask each person to select a response card and explain to the group why they chose that card.

d) Debrief the game, e.g., lessons, different persepctives of child impacts.

IV. CLOSURE

Ask each member to share one lesson that they are taking away from the session and then write it down on the postcard reminder to bring home and think about during the next week.

V. RESOURCES

Pruett, K., & Pruett, M. (2009) *Partnership Parenting: How Men and Women Parent Differently*. Cambridge, MA: Da Capo.

VI. MATERIALS LIST

Cartoons of situations that depict mother-father differences (10–15 cartoons)

Set of Response Cards for each member (10–12 sets)

Parenting situations that may elicit different responses/persectives (5–8 situations)

Adapted from a lesson plan developed by Jane Ellison and Glen Palm, Sauk Rapids ECFE, for a couples class, the third of four sessions.

STAGE 6: ONGOING PROGRAM EVALUATION

Stage 6 of curriculum development focuses on evaluation and the ongoing process of program improvement. The creation of a logic model guides the evaluation process by articulating a theory of change and a set of short- and long-term curriculum learning goals for parents. Figure 6.1 depicts an example of a logic model for a curriculum developed for incarcerated fathers. The model connects program assumptions (research and theory base) with program activities that are designed to lead to short-term outcomes (learning goals) and long-term outcomes. This model outlines the learning goals for parents and the expected long-term outcomes for fathers and families that come from the different program activities.

The program evaluation process can utilize a variety of strategies. The first set of strategies is the ongoing monitoring of parent responses to individual sessions. Some of the ideas in Stage 1 addressing parent needs and interests, such as responses to exercises and reporting on the progress of using new skills are informal indicators of parent engagement and changes in understanding and skills. The Core Curriculum process (MNAFEE, 2011) recommends a time for reflection and session evaluation after each class. Three questions help to guide this reflective process:

1. How do I know the lesson objectives were met?

2. How did the learning activities work?

3. What should be followed up in the next session?

This type of process helps refine a curriculum while in process and allows a parent educator to make adjustments to both content and methods that match the parent needs and interests.

The final evaluation at the end of the program is an important opportunity to assess both parent satisfaction and learning. Parents can respond to a series of questions about the program format. These might include feedback on the number of sessions, the time of day sessions were offered, and the length of sessions. Questions could also focus on the content of the curriculum. What content was most useful? What instructional methods were most helpful? When were parents most engaged in the session? Parent responses to these types of questions can be useful in making changes to the curriculum.

In addition to process questions, parent outcomes should also be assessed. Parents can be asked to reflect on and report their level of change regarding

Figure 6.1 Parenting Program Correctional Facility

ASSUMPTIONS	ACTIVITIES	SHORT-TERM OUTCOMES	LONG-TERM OUTCOMES
1. Fathers care deeply about their children and their future.	**Individual Interviews**—Initial interview conducted to understand family situation, needs, and interests	1. Build relationship with group members	**Increase in Protective Factors**
2. Fathers are motivated to examine parenting attitudes and behaviors to help guide their children to not follow in their footsteps.	**Parenting Class**—12 sessions focused on building and maintaining positive connections with children and families	2. Understand unique situations and needs	1. Increase in responsible fatherhood behavior
3. Incarcerated fathers are capable of positive relationships with their children.	• Understand child feelings and behaviors	1. Understanding the importance of fatherhood	• Positive relationship with child
4. Fathers benefit from connection and regular communication with children and other family members.	• Importance of fathers to children	2. Understanding and accepting child's emotions	• Able to meet provider role
5. Fathers benefit from the support and understanding of other incarcerated fathers.	• Communicating from a distance	3. Increase own emotional awareness and regulation	• Role model for child
6. A key to the father-child relationship is developing a positive co-parenting relationship.	• New ideas about guiding child behavior	4. Increased level and quality of communication with child	2. Develop positive guidance skills
7. Fathers can benefit from research-based information about child development and family relations.	• Clarifying family values and goals for children	5. Able to express support to other fathers	3. Improve relationship with co-parent
	Building/maintaining respectful relationships with co-parents	6. Decrease in problem behaviors	4. Increase in empathy
		7. Change in attitudes about discipline	5. Increase in emotional regulation (patience)
		8. Understand child's mother's feelings/thinking	6. Break family cycle of negative parenting
		9. Increase in number of ways to teach, guide, discipline child	7. Reduce parenting/family stress
		10. Improve communication skills with child's mother	

ASSUMPTIONS	ACTIVITIES	SHORT-TERM OUTCOMES	LONG-TERM OUTCOMES
	Daily Fathering Journal Creating habits of good fathering behaviors	Increase in sense of efficacy and self-esteem around fathering	**Decrease in Risk Factors** • Change in beliefs about physical punishment • Realistic expectations for children • Feeling of isolation around parenting • Decrease in conflict with child's mother
	DVD Stories • Read story to child on video and share feelings	Positive connection with child Role model importance of literacy	**Decrease in recidivism rate**

selected learning goals from the program. This gives parents an opportunity to reflect on their own learning and provides evidence of parent progress regarding different goals areas. It also informs changes that need to be made in program content and methods to strengthen parent learning. These are all practices that parent educators can implement to support continuous curriculum development. Most programs are not able to implement pre- and post-test assessments using more formal measures of parent changes or use a random control trial design to test for program effectiveness. Implementing ongoing monitoring of parent responses to lesson plans and providing a format for parent feedback at the end of a program is most appropriate and will inform ongoing program effectiveness.

PHYSICAL ENVIRONMENT/ARRANGEMENTS

Parent education groups are held in a variety of settings: schools, hospitals, community centers, church basements, prisons, apartment buildings, mobile home parks, cultural centers, and anywhere else parents gather. Often parent educators work in settings that are not designed specifically for their work, but are merely available for their use. While the environment can make a significant difference in the quality of the group experience, it is often beyond the control of the parent educator. This section will address characteristics of a physical environment that are conducive to a positive group experience, as well as practical ideas for making parents feel welcome.

There are a number of things parent educators can do to make parents feel comfortable in the group environment, regardless of how optimal the facility is.

- Posting welcome signs
- Greeting parents as they arrive
- Connecting with each parent before the group begins
- Playing music as parents enter
- Conducting an icebreaker at the beginning
- Posting a "question of the day" as a discussion starter
- Displaying an agenda, so parent know what to expect
- Making simple refreshments available for parents

The design and use of the physical space are important considerations. The following ideas reflect ideal settings that are not always possible but provide suggestions for group settings:

From our experience ... As I observed parent educator teacher candidates leading groups during their field experiences, I saw a wide variety of settings in which they worked. All of the teacher candidates were placed in school settings. Some parent discussion rooms were designed specifically for this purpose and not shared with other programs or used for other purposes. These facilities often had intercom systems linked to the rooms next door with large one-way glass windows where parent educators practiced guiding observations of the children in the adjoining room. Adult-size tables and chairs, whiteboards, and mounted television screens were strategically placed in each room. On the other end of the continuum, I visited placements where parent education took place in empty offices, libraries, open areas with room dividers, and even storage rooms. The parent educators did the best they could within these confines, and the overall experience for parents and children was positive. Yet the value that school boards and administration placed on these programs was reflected in the environments provided for parent education.

1. Rooms need to be of adequate size to accommodate some movement for small group activities and discussion. If brainstorming or other activities are planned, group members need to be able to easily move between various locations. On the other hand, rooms that are too large can have a feeling of disconnection for group members (Eller, 2004).

2. The group leader should be in a physical place where he/she can see all group members. A round table is ideal, since everyone is visible to each other.

3. Different types of groups and different facilitators have varying preferences for whether to place parents around a table or form an open circle of chairs. One perspective is that the table provides a barrier between people, and many enjoy a more open atmosphere that promotes discussion and sharing without a barrier. Another way of thinking is that sitting at a table is more comfortable; provides a buffer, rather than a barrier; and keeps group members from feeling too exposed or vulnerable. Depending on the style of the facilitator and the type of group, consideration should be given to which arrangement might work best.

4. The room should contain equipment that supports the goals of the program. Observation windows, intercom systems, whiteboards, and necessary technology equipment should be easily accessible.

5. Adult-size tables and chairs need to be available to accommodate adult learners. Too often, particularly in school settings, parents are expected to sit in small chairs designed for children. This sends a strong message that the parents' needs and comfort are not important.

6. Practical considerations can make a big difference. Can the parent educator see the clock? Is the temperature of the room comfortable? Does the décor of the room reflect cultural diversity that sets an inclusive atmosphere? Are posted items written in easy-to-understand language that is void of jargon?

Many times the above suggestions are not possible due to parent education groups sharing space with other programs. Respecting each other's space is key to developing positive relationships with other professionals. If a facility is used by multiple programs and staff, there should be conversations and agreements about how the rooms will be left after the use of each program. Checklists are helpful to make sure items are returned to their original positions. Care needs to be taken to respect materials and equipment in each setting. Additionally, professionals need to be understanding of different uses of space and keep communication open regarding any concerns.

SUMMARY

Designing parent education curricula and effective parent education sessions to guide parents toward learning new ideas and skills and clarifying their beliefs and goals around child rearing is a complex process. This chapter was included to emphasize the importance of integrating educational content and goals into parent group sessions. The process for implementing parent education programs and designing curricula, when appropriate, was described. This process delineated six stages that started with understanding parent needs and interests and translating them into concrete educational goals for parent groups. The next steps included reviewing research and theory to begin building a logic model as a foundation for the curriculum process. The careful design of lesson plans using a variety of methods was another stage. The final stage involved implementation of evaluation strategies to assess program effectiveness. The final section described the importance of the design and preparation of the physical space for parent education programs.

DISCUSSION QUESTIONS

1. What are the advantages of implementing an evidence-based curriculum in your community for a group of parents of infants?

2. Examine the domains and components of the Core Curriculum model and select content areas for a group of parents of typically developing children ages 3–5 to include in an 8-week parent program.

3. Which strategies for identifying parent needs and interests are most useful for planning and adapting content for parent education sessions? Why?

4. Why is it useful to identify areas of parent change when designing parent sessions?

5. What strategies would you use to evaluate a new curriculum that you have developed for couples that are going through the transition to parenthood?

CLASS ACTIVITIES

1. Create a simple logic model for a group of parents in your community for whom you would like to develop a curriculum.

2. Have a small group of students (four to five) define a parent population and design an 8–10 week parenting curriculum, selecting a logical sequence of topics and three learning goals for each session. Explain the logic behind the sequence of topics.

3. In small groups, design an ideal parent education setting. What elements of the physical environment would you include? Where would it be located? What would make it welcoming and appealing to parents? How does it reflect your philosophy and style as a parent educator? Did your group have different ideas about the design? If so, what were they?

REFERENCES

Braun, L., Coplon, J., & Sonnenschien, P. (1984). *Helping parents in groups.* Boston, MA: Resource communications Inc.

Brizius, J., & Foster, S. (1993). *Generation to generation: Realizing the promise of family literacy.* Ypsilanti, MI: High Scope.

Canning, S., & Fantuzzo, J. (2000). Competent families, collaborative professionals: Empowered parent education for low-income African American families. In J. Gillespie & J. Primavera (Eds.), *Diverse families, competent families* (pp. 179–197). Binghamton, NY: Haworth.

Center on the Developing Child at Harvard University (2016). From best practice to breakthrough impacts: A science-based approach to building a more promising future for young children and families. Retrieved from http://46y5eh11fhgw3ve3ytpwxt9r. wpengine.netdna-cdn.com/wp-content/uploads/2016/05/From_Best_Practices_to_ Breakthrough_Impacts-3.pdf.

Crary, E. (1993). *Without spanking or spoiling.* Seattle, WA: Parenting Press.

Eller, J. (2004). *Effective group facilitation in education—How to energize meetings and manage difficult groups.* Thousand Oaks, CA: Corwin Press.

Fagan, J., & Palm, G. (2004). *Fathers and Early Childhood Programs.* Albany, NY: Delmar.

Johnson, L., & Palm, G. (1992). *Working with fathers: Methods and perspectives.* Stillwater, MN: nu ink.

Kurz-Reimer, K. (2001). *A guide for implementing early childhood family education programs.* Roseville, MN: Minnesota Department of Children, Families, and Learning.

McBride, B. (1989). Stress and fathers' parental competence: Implications for family life and parent educators. *Family Relations, 38,* 385–389.

Minnesota Association of Family and Early Educators (2011). Parent Education Core Curriculum Framework. Retrieved from http://www.mnafee.org/ vertical/sites/{2555CA3F-B6AD-4263-9177-3B66CE5F2892}/uploads/ {FCA74A96-BD5E-4572-.

National Academies of Sciences, Engineering, and Medicine. (2016). *Parenting matters: Supporting parents of children 0–8.* Washington, DC: The National Academies Press. doi: 10.17226/21868

National Center on Parent, Family and Community Engagement. (2015). Compendium of parenting interventions. Washington, DC: National Center on Parent, Family and Community Engagement, Office of Head Start, U.S. Department of Health and Human Services.

Palm, G. & Palkovitz, R. (1988). The challenge of working with new fathers: Implications for support providers. In R. Palkovitz & M. Sussman (Eds.), *Transitions to parenthood* (pp. 357–376). New York, NY: Haworth.

Palm, G. (1997). Promoting Generative Fathering Through Parent and Family Education. In A. Hawkins & D. Dollahite (Eds.), *Generative Fathering: Beyond Deficit Perspectives* (pp. 167–182). Thousand Oaks, CA: Sage.

Palm, G.F., (2003). Parent Education for Incarcerated Parents: Understanding "What Works". In V. Gadsden (Ed.) *Heading Home: Offender Reintegration into the Family* (pp. 89–122). Lanham, MD: American Correctional Association.

Powell, D. (1986). Matching parents and programs. In J. Parsons, T. Bowman, J. Comeau, R. Pitzer, & G.S. Schmitt (Eds.), *Parent education: State of the art* (pp. 1–11). White Bear Lake, MN: Minnesota Curriculum Services Center.

Small, S., & Husar, M. (2015). Principles for improving family programs: An evidence-informed approach. In M. Walcheski & J. Reinke (Eds.) *Family life education:*

The practice of family science (pp. 255–266. Minneapolis, MN: National Council on Family Relations.

Smith, C.A., Cudaback, D., Goddard, H.W., & Myers-Walls, J. (1994). *National Extension parent education model.* Manhattan, NY: Kansas Cooperative Extension Services.

Webster-Stratton, C. (1998). Preventing conduct problems in Head Start children: Strengthening parenting competencies. *Journal of Consulting and Clinical Psychology, 66*(5), 715–730.

7

RELATIONSHIP BUILDING:
The Heart of Group Parent Education

The relationship between parent educator and parent is difficult to define. It is unlike traditional teacher-student relationships involving professionals sharing knowledge with learners. It is not a friendship with reciprocal feelings of closeness and intimate connections. For the educator, it is based on a unique blend of roles within a context of mutual respect, exploration, and affective learning. For the parent, the relationship provides mentoring and guidance from a supportive leader.

To further understand this relationship, an examination of the role of the parent educator may be beneficial. The parent educator functions on a cognitive level when teaching skills and sharing information. However, the role, and thus the relationship, expands at deeper levels of interaction. A parent educator who focuses on relationship building enhances the professional role to include support, guidance, advocacy, encouragement, and affirmation. This redefines the relationship in a broader and more meaningful way. Perhaps what makes this relationship unique is that it develops from a learning experience that focuses on some of the most challenging and rewarding aspects of life—parenting and family relations—where the content is not merely learned but lived.

This chapter will examine the importance of building relationships in successful group parent education settings. Strategies that encourage the critical development of trust, caring, rapport, and empathy will be addressed as ways of enhancing the experience for both the parents and leader. Attending skills that convey genuine concern through a strength-based approach that help to build relationships will also be addressed, along with challenging issues, such as confidentiality and self-disclosure. Finally, the importance of understanding group members' behaviors and their origins will be examined.

The success of ongoing parent education groups depends greatly on the foundation of a strong, supportive relationship between the parent educator and the participants. If the group is to move through the expected stages of development and arrive at a point of genuine learning and new insights, a positive relationship must be nurtured. If we assume that the group experience has the potential to provide parents with an opportunity for growth beyond learning new skills and information, attention to this very important connection is vital. The relationships among parents can also be supported by the group leader. These relationships lay the foundation for trust and growth within the group setting.

TRUST

Trust in the leader is imperative for healthy group functioning. It is a primary focus for the group leader in the early stages of group development. The parent educator must present him or herself professionally as someone whose expertise and leadership abilities are trustworthy. The group leader is seen as a guide who is reliable, knowledgeable, and sensitive in directing the group process and group learning. More important, the parents must feel a sense of trust in the group and environment, where it is safe for them to learn, grow, and share a part of themselves. A parent educator needs to focus more on developing a sense of trust within the group experience than a trust in their own abilities. A leader who is seen as having a quiet sense of competence in this role sets a foundation for a positive group experience.

How do group leaders provide an atmosphere of trust? Generally, this happens in the same way that trust is developed in any relationship. Group leaders model respect for members and provide an open and accepting atmosphere where parents feel free to share concerns and learn from others. Maintaining a sense of trust is a continual process. Changes in group dynamics, in levels of self-disclosure, and in types of responses from other members or the facilitator can influence the stability of trust. Continual attention to these issues is necessary throughout the life of the group.

Additionally, a variety of methods can be used early on in the development of the group that will promote trust. A beginning activity that allows parents to choose and reflect on statements that speak to what is important to them as group members will promote an atmosphere of trust. For example, the parent educator might post specific statements regarding what group members need to feel comfortable in this setting and ask parents to choose those that are most meaningful to them. Statements such as "I need to be able say what I think without being judged," "I can take the time I need to feel comfortable here," or "I can always choose to 'pass' if I do not want to respond" can generate an open discussion that enhances the level of trust and allows parents to get their needs met early on in the group experience.

Activities that give parents an opportunity to gradually share information about themselves and their children also encourage the development of trust. An ice-breaker that asks parents to "share one characteristic they have in common with their child" is a fairly safe way for parents to disclose something about themselves and their children and, at the same time, learn about others in the group.

The parent educator takes time to informally connect with parents and build relationships

CARING

Although group leaders can learn and use a variety of facilitation skills and may understand concepts of group process and have expertise in the areas of family and parenting information, without a genuine sense of caring for members, the group experience will not be successful. Genuine caring is giving sincere attention to someone by using verbal and nonverbal skills that convey attentive concern. When a parent shares his problems or experiences within the group, a caring leader will maintain eye contact, give empathetic responses, and listen intently to demonstrate a genuine sense of caring. Giving adequate time to a parent's concern, holding off on the planned agenda, and focusing on the parent's content, as well as feelings, demonstrate care.

Parent educators also demonstrate a caring attitude by following through with assisting a parent and following up on progress. If a parent shares a particularly difficult challenge in a group, the parent educator shows caring by checking on the situation at the following session or perhaps through a quick phone call during the week. A comment such as "I've been thinking about your situation and wonder how things are going" tells a parent that he or she has been heard and someone cares. Paying attention to individual issues and noting details of the parents' stories will assist leaders in demonstrating a genuine concern for each group member. This extra attention is critical in developing a trusting relationship.

RAPPORT

Rapport is a healthy connection that is based on similarities between people. Rapport seems to occur most quickly between people with more similarities than differences. Through appropriate self-disclosure, a parent educator makes a connection with members that shows they share some qualities and experiences. It is necessary, however, that the parent educator remains genuine in this process and not attempt to "be" like group members. Although there may be many differences between the leader and the parents, time spent focusing on similarities will enhance the level of trust between them. Parent educators and group members may differ in gender, class, or culture, but the most obvious similarity is their interest in the wellbeing of families and children. Group leaders can focus on more personal similarities that support common experiences, such as number of children, family-of-origin experiences, hobbies, or other fairly safe examples. Focusing on similarities that elevate the parent educator with the status of particular members should be avoided. For example, noting that the group leader lives in the same neighborhood as one or more of the group members may connect him or her with those parents but also identifies a difference from others.

Finding similarities between group members is also an important aspect of developing group member rapport. A skilled facilitator will connect parents' ideas and experiences to foster a sense that group members have critical issues in common. Universalizing concerns about safety, bedtime, and discipline in a group of parents of toddlers will strengthen connections between members. Forming a general sense of what is similar across all group members is critical for everyone to be able to recognize themselves as belonging with this group.

From our experience ... Parents bring many past experiences that affect the quality of their participation in a parent education group. For example, while many of us are comfortable and even enjoy being in the school setting, many parents remember painful experiences during their own school years. Coming into a school building for parent education can trigger unpleasant memories and past experiences. Some parents will share these feelings and concerns, while others will choose not to. It is helpful for parent educators to consider how they can develop rapport with a parent to create a new and positive experience.

EMPATHY

Empathy is the ability of the leader to understand others from the others' frame of reference, rather than from their own. An empathetic parent educator is able to think and feel with, rather than for or about, group members. He or she is able to offer empathetic responses that demonstrate genuine listening and understanding.

Each of us sees a separate reality in that we look at the world through our own "lens," which is made up of a variety of experiences, values, attitudes, and personal attributes that shape our views. Parent educators benefit from examining their own lens, so they understand why they see things a certain way. An understanding of how family experiences affect their view of parenting and family issues is critical. By carefully examining what makes up their lens, group leaders can gain an understanding of the biases and beliefs that they bring to this role. By acknowledging these beliefs and understanding their origin, parent educators can become aware of their influence as they strive to understand and respond sensitively to group members' perspectives.

A variety of factors influence our perceptions. Our own family of origin and its dynamics, values, experiences, socioeconomic status, ethnicity, and culture influence our understanding of others. For example, a parent educator whose family background has included an affluent and protected lifestyle will bring assumptions, values, and experiences that may influence perceptions of particular parents in groups. Limited experiences with people living in poverty may inhibit understanding of group members whose life experiences are different from their own. Though it is not possible or recommended to require a match for each parent with a group leader of similar background, it is important for parent educators to realize how these experiences can influence our perception of others.

Additionally, parent educators become empathetic to group members when they can see what comprises the lens of each parent. They can then understand why each parent holds particular beliefs and makes specific parenting choices. By incorporating this perspective into their work, parent educators will be able to develop an empathetic and nonjudgmental relationship with each parent and, thus, create an atmosphere of trust.

When working with particular groups of parents, such as those who have been abusive to their children, it can be very difficult for a parent educator to find common ground or acceptance of a parent. Our own experiences, values, and judgments can make it challenging to work with those we feel little empathy toward. Although parent educators do not need to condone the behaviors of others, they do need to find some level of understanding, so they can work together for the benefit of children and families.

The responses of the parent educator to individual parents and also to the group are critical in the development of a healthy relationship. These behaviors, both verbal and nonverbal, can either support or impede the establishment of the type of caring relationship needed for successful parent education to occur.

ENCOURAGING HEALTHY RELATIONSHIPS BETWEEN GROUP MEMBERS

While parent educators focus on being caring and empathetic as they develop a sense of rapport with members, they also need to focus on the relationships between parents in the group. It is difficult for parent educators to directly teach group members to be caring and empathetic, but modeling these qualities can create an atmosphere of respectful expectations and reinforce desired behaviors.

Statements that affirm positive supportive behaviors or comments between parents, such as the following, will assist in nurturing connections:

> "It helps to know others have gone through this."
> "Thank you for describing your similar experiences."
> "One of the good things about being in a group is that we can support each other."

Linking ideas of one parent to another not only keeps the group process moving, but it also links members together. By pointing out common themes and issues shared by parents in groups, the facilitator can help make important connections between individual members. Group members may rely on support from each other outside the group experience as their relationships move to another level.

Dyad or small group work within a session can also assist in building relationships between parents in groups. Many parents feel more comfortable talking in a smaller group and will freely bring up issues and ideas. Quiet members or those with limited social skills may feel even more comfortable discussing in groups of three where there is less pressure to speak. In this setting, the responsibility of discussion is divided by one more person and may provide another layer of safety for a quiet group member. In addition to encouraging more discussion, small group work links parents to others and strengthens relationships. It encourages personal sharing and helps individual members develop rapport with each other, in addition to allowing for more active participation and disclosure.

An astute facilitator will balance dyad, small group, and large group work. If a pattern is established where each session relies heavily on opportunities to talk in small groups, parents will quickly learn that they don't need to participate in the large group, because they know that time will be provided for small group discussion. This arrangement may seem safe, but it can lack depth. Additionally, it limits the group facilitator's opportunity to learn more about individual group members, because meaningful discussion happens between two or three parents. To miss the opportunity of learning from a larger number of parents and the facilitator is to miss the power of the group experience. Parent educators who believe in a dual responsibility to each individual member and also to the group can see that this pattern jeopardizes the potential richness of the group experience.

From our experience ... We've seen parents develop lasting friendships after attending parent education groups together. Programs can play a part in supporting the development of these relationships in simple ways. One program offered a room where parents could gather after class and have lunch together. Programs are often asked, with parent permission, to share contact information of members at the last class, so parents can contact each other outside of class. Friendships are made that can last a lifetime as families continue to support each other outside of the group setting.

STRENGTH-BASED APPROACH

In any relationship, people appreciate affirmation of their strengths. Parents learn early on that, if they focus on the positive behaviors of their children, those behaviors will typically increase. This same strategy works well for group leaders. Parent educators who look for strengths in each parent, as well as assisting parents in finding their own strengths, will develop more rapport and build a strong connection with each member.

Unlike some other helping professions, where a deficit model is typically used, and the professional's role is to fix a problem, parent education encompasses a broader scope. Parent education can be preventive, supportive, educational, and/or interventive. The type of group and the needs of the members will determine which leadership role is necessary. However, in each of these levels, a strength-based approach is desirable.

A major assumption about the strength-based approach is that all parents have strengths and that focusing and building on them provides a positive foundation for growth. Parent educators need to believe, with few exceptions, that all parents have some attributes that are positive. Occasionally, when working with parents who have multiple needs and risk factors, group leaders may find it difficult to identify a particular parent's strengths. The parent may also feel unable to articulate personal strengths. However, strengths may be identified as simply being willing to participate in a parent group, being able to get one's children dressed and to school each morning, finding services one's child needs, or being a good listener.

Identifying strengths may require both the group leader and parent to reframe a particular skill or quality. For example, a parent who seems to be constantly calling on professionals for assistance may be seen as a parent who puts the needs of their child above all else. If we can reframe what may seem like a negative behavior, we are able to see that within that behavior there may be a strength. This parent could be described in a deficit approach as overinvolved or demanding. However in a strength-based approach, the parent is also seen as a tireless advocate for his or her child. A parent educator who is able to identify strengths, even those that may be hidden, may find it easier to relate to and work with a particularly challenging parent. Additionally, helping parents focus on the positive aspects of their parenting can promote growth in their role with their child. By encouraging these positive aspects, parent educators can help parents appreciate and build on their strengths.

Parents can also benefit from learning to identify their own strengths. However, they may be reluctant to verbalize their strong points. They may feel uncomfortable speaking positively about themselves or may truly be able to see only their challenges. Parents may even say, "I don't know" or "I don't have any." Facilitators can remind group members that everyone has strengths and might say, "we'll come back to you in a minute after you have time to think of one of your strengths/" The group leader may even point out a strength they have noticed. Typically, parents are more comfortable identifying the positive qualities or strengths of their children, rather than their own. Group leaders may need to begin with exercises that provide parents an opportunity to focus on their children before they are able to focus on themselves. A variety of methods can be used to help parents adopt a strengths perspective. These questions may facilitate an open discussion on strengths:

- "What do you think you're best at in parenting?"
- "What are your strengths, and where did you get them?"
- "What would your kids say they like about you?"
- "Share one compliment you have received about your parenting."
- "What strength do you see in someone else that you also have?"

If these questions are asked, the parent educator might begin by sharing their own strengths. Through this modeling, parents may feel more willing to participate. Parents often appreciate being asked to write their responses first and then share. Finally, as the group progresses, activities that encourage parents to share their impressions of the strengths of others in the group may be used. This can also foster a high level of trust in the group and build connections between members. However, it is important to note that issues of gender, culture, and class may affect the appropriateness of using such techniques. Particular group members may not have been socialized to feel comfortable affirming others in face-to-face settings. This seemingly positive experience may not feel genuine to all members. Additionally, not all group facilitators are comfortable using this strategy. For an activity where parents verbally affirm each other to be successful, the parent educator must feel confident modeling the approach within a group that has demonstrated a readiness for this level of genuine interaction.

Being cautious in finding a realistic balance in a strength-based approach is helpful. If parent educators only focus on strengths and ignore parents' challenges, they negate the need for change and discount parents' issues or concerns. This may feel good for a while, but real issues may never be addressed and growth cannot occur. A strength-based approach lays a solid foundation for relationship building and skill development. However, the larger goal is to keep a strengths perspective while addressing challenges and encouraging opportunities for change.

SPECIAL CONSIDERATIONS IN BUILDING RELATIONSHIPS

NONVERBAL BEHAVIOR

Observers of human behavior and communication are aware that nonverbal behavior plays a significant role in relationships. Typically, we are very aware of others' gestures, facial expressions, and use of body to communicate, but we are often unaware of the impact of our own. Group leaders need to be aware of their own nonverbal expressive and receptive behaviors and must also be able to interpret and respond to the nonverbal expression of group members. Videotaping themselves leading groups can provide a valuable learning opportunity for parent educators. Asking a trusted peer to observe and give constructive feedback may also assist group leaders in learning more about the impact of their own behaviors.

Facial nonverbal expression has a huge influence on our communication. Eye contact, subtle expressions that convey understanding, smiling, or frowning can all influence how our message is received. Each of these behaviors, along with the use of our body, makes up our attending skills. Along with our words, they tell group members we are paying attention, that we care, and that we are nonjudgmental in our responses. Nonverbal behaviors that help connect us to group members are important. Actively listening by leaning in when someone is speaking, focusing on his or her face, and nodding and gesturing in agreement or understanding give clues to the speaker that he or she is being heard and understood. These nonverbal gestures assist in building a trusting relationship.

Cultural distinctions, however, must also be considered. Each culture has different rules about physical space, gestures, and other behaviors. Although parent educators cannot be experts on the nonverbal norms of every culture, it is beneficial to be aware that differences exist and to learn as much as possible about them. Group leaders will benefit from understanding their own nonverbal behaviors and recognizing that they are not universal.

We can also learn to interpret the nonverbal behaviors of group members for insight into their group participation and level of satisfaction with the experience. Parents who separate themselves physically from the group by choosing a chair near the back and moving slightly away from the group may be telling us they don't feel connected or that they lack a sense of belonging—or they may need more leg room to feel comfortable in this setting. Parents who cross their arms during the entire group session may be shutting everyone else out—or they may be physically cold. Parents who avoid eye contact with others, particularly the leader, may not be paying attention to what is being said or may disagree with the ideas of others—or they may have a cultural influence that teaches that eye contact is disrespectful. Misinterpretation of nonverbal expression can easily occur if our assessment of particular behaviors is not kept tentative. Parent educators can assess nonverbal behavior and speculate on possible interpretations but must be open to the possibility that they may not be accurate.

SELF-DISCLOSURE

For a sense of trust to develop in a parent education group, members and the leader need to feel free to reveal and also not to reveal information about themselves. Appropriate self-disclosure tends to bring the group to another level of healthy development where members openly share parts of themselves with others. Inappropriate self-disclosure can weaken the group and shake the sense of trust that has developed. Self-disclosure issues of both the parent educator and the group members provide areas of consideration for the leader.

It is important for the parent educator to use self-disclosure appropriately in a group. Parents need to understand who the leader is, know something about what experiences he or she has had, and have a sense of what makes this person a trustworthy group leader. This can be accomplished through thoughtful self-disclosure. A parent educator will typically share information about background, experience as a group leader, and personal information that relates to this role. This type of information is important for the parents to hear and also sets the expectation that parents will feel safe sharing some information about themselves. Parent educators also model that sharing personal details of their lives is not appropriate. Although it is typical for group members to self-disclose at a deeper level than the facilitator, this modeling sets the norm for what is acceptable.

The amount of self-disclosure should be monitored carefully by the parent educator. Sharing too many examples of his or her own children may be interesting initially but soon becomes tedious and distracting for group members. Each time a parent educator chooses to use self-disclosure, there should be careful consideration of its purpose, along with a realization that the disclosure is taking time from other members. A moderate amount of self-disclosure by a group leader is more effective than too little or too much (Cormier & Cormier, 1998).

In deciding whether to self-disclose, it is helpful to consider the goals of such a strategy. Self-disclosure may be used to develop rapport. This is accomplished as parent educators share about themselves to set an open atmosphere, demonstrate empathy, encourage trust, enrich communication, and show humanism. These behaviors build healthy connections with parents.

Self-disclosure by the group leader may also encourage self-understanding by the parent. Sharing a common experience helps to universalize an issue and can be seen as a teaching tool. It may allow a parent to understand their own experience by identifying with the experiences of the group leader.

Self-disclosure occurs on several levels. Informational self-disclosure holds more safety for the parent educator. Common experiences and situations are shared to encourage an empathetic response from the group members. This type of self-disclosure represents a lower level of sharing and is used most often. Statements like "I went through a similar experience when my child was that age" assist in building a healthy and trusting relationship with parents.

Self-disclosure may also occur on a deeper level through sharing feelings along with information. In addition to sharing a common experience, the facilitator includes reactions, feelings, and responses to this personal sharing. Statements like "I remember struggling with this as a parent and really wondering if I was doing the right thing" move the level of disclosure to more depth. This type of self-disclosure is used less frequently, has more emotional connotation and exposes the vulnerability of the facilitator in a more meaningful and human way. Parents, especially those who are experiencing frustration or other emotional reactions to parenting challenges, will appreciate feeling that others truly know what they are going through at an emotional level.

The second and deeper level of disclosure does not come without risk, however, and should be used selectively. Otherwise, the group leader may be seen as too needy or taking too much time from the group for their own issues. Parent educators who have children of similar ages to the group members'

From our experience ... Over the years, I have learned many lessons about when and how to share personal information in a way that can be effective and when not to tell a personal story just because I enjoy it. One example of this is learning how to talk about the topic of spanking. The groups of incarcerated fathers that I teach have frequently asked me if I have spanked my children. I tell them that I have not, but I need to tell them the story behind this decision. It is not that I am such a good parent or that I have children who have always behaved. I tell them that I was spanked with a belt by my father when I was growing up in the 1950s. I go on to tell them that my father was also spanked by his father with a thick leather strap for sharpening his straight razor. When I heard this from my father as an adult, I was glad that he had an electric razor.

I also go on to tell them that I would have followed in my father's footsteps and spanked my children. However, before becoming a parent I had about 10 years of experience working with children of different ages in various programs (schools, child care centers, a children's hospital, and residential treatment programs) where corporal punishment was not allowed. I had to learn other ways of responding to children when they misbehaved. I assure them that it took lots of patience and practice to learn other strategies.

Sharing this story gives me a chance to talk about child abuse and changes over the years in laws about physical abuse and how it takes two to three generations for behaviors like this to begin to change. Most of the fathers in my groups have grown up with corporal punishment that has often been abusive. Most don't want to hit or hurt their child in the same ways they were treated by their parents. They also typically don't know about other ways to respond to their children so find that it is easy to fall back on what they learned growing up.

The second point I want to stress from this story is that it will take time and real effort to learn new ways to respond to their children. It is not easy to learn new parenting behaviors, and they are likely to fall back on physical punishment, especially during times of stress.

It is important when sharing this type of personal experience not to make myself the center of the story but to use the story as an opening to talk about the topic of spanking, the boundaries of physical abuse, and the history of child abuse laws to provide some perspective. I always follow-up by providing a number of alternatives to physical punishment, along with opportunities to practice by responding to difficult situations and discussing which new strategies might work best in each situation.

children will often deal with some of the same issues. Though it is healthy to make this connection through disclosure, it can be unproductive for the group to focus too much on the parent educator's issues. Although offering an opportunity for empathy, the parent educator's personal emotions and beliefs may interfere with understanding others' perspectives.

Group leaders who, as parents themselves, have already experienced some of the challenges others bring to sessions are often reminded of stories and examples from their own families. Though sharing examples may occasionally help to support parents in the group, they should be used on a limited basis. Parent educators may find that they, like all parents, enjoy recalling a special memory or experience involving their own children. They can allow themselves the pleasure of silently recalling the example without sharing it verbally with the group. By doing this, the parent educator makes a clear distinction in this relationship between what one would share with friends and what one shares as a group leader. For example, during a discussion on temperament, a parent educator may be reminded of her own children whose temperaments are drastically different. When visiting with a friend, it would be appropriate to share a story about these differences in some detail. However, in the role of the parent educator, either a general comment or no comment about their children's different temperaments would be appropriate choices. This takes self-discipline, is more respectful to the group, and allows for the privacy of the leader's own children, who may not appreciate being discussed.

Another responsibility of the parent educator is to encourage and monitor the self-disclosure of group members. Without some level of self-disclosure from parent participants, the group may feel very safe but will have little depth. It is the role of the facilitator to model and provide a trusting environment where self-disclosure is accepted and also to protect parents and others from too much or inappropriate self-disclosure.

It is helpful to consider why parents would under- or over-self-disclose. Parents who are reluctant to disclose information or experiences typically have a lack of trust in this setting. This may be the result of unhealthy dynamics in the group, behaviors of other members, or a lack of connection with the group leader.

It may also be related to past negative experiences when they shared information and later felt regret. Negative experiences with other family support agencies may need to be overcome before a parent feels free to self-disclose in this setting. Unwillingness to disclose may also result from a family background that taught members not to trust others, especially those perceived to be authority figures.

The parent educator's responsibility to this group member is to be patient and respectful of his or her choice. Providing a safe and emotionally nurturing environment may eventually allow members to take small risks in self-disclosure. Modeling a respectful and nonjudgmental attitude should provide some assurance of safety. It's possible that some parents may not share in a group, but may be silently processing information and feelings. This may come out later through evaluation responses or from talking privately with the group leader.

Conversely, there are parents in groups who will over–self-disclose. They may begin sharing detailed personal information during first sessions. This can make other group members feel uncomfortable and perhaps question if this is the experience they were seeking and if they, too, will be expected to share on such a personal level. Each group experience has an unwritten contract or expectation of the group leader and also of the members as to what this experience will be, what depth of participation is expected, and what norms will be observed. Excessive self-disclosure early on in a group's development may provide uncertainty for other members as they observe the leader's reaction.

Parents who over–self-disclose do so for a variety of reasons. They may have poor social skills and not realize that this behavior makes others uncomfortable. They may like to dominate or monopolize the group and enjoy the attention it brings. They may be very needy and looking for sympathy from other members. They may enjoy shocking other people and watching their reactions. They may have had a previous experience in another type of group, perhaps a therapy group, that had different norms for individual sharing. Or, they may be testing the trust level, skills, and response of the parent educator to see how he or she will handle this shift in group atmosphere.

The parent educator has a responsibility to keep self-disclosure at an appropriate level. Determining the appropriateness of the self-disclosure will require assessing the developmental stage and expectations of the group. Sharing in a parent education group is different than in a therapy or counseling setting, where individuals may be encouraged to open up deeply and express their emotional responses to particular life experiences. Although parents often self-disclose complex feelings and emotions in parent education settings, it is the responsibility of the group leader to keep the focus on parenting issues. Occasionally, a parent may begin to share detailed personal information about their family of origin or intimate stresses in their present family. The parent educator can offer a supportive comment and pull the focus back to how this relates to parenting. Comments like "That must have been very difficult for you. How do you think it has affected how you parent your own children?" offer acknowledgment and keep the parent and the group focused on the purpose of the group experience.

A parent may also share information that is clearly not a topic of discussion for the parent education setting. For example, during a first session a parent may begin disclosing very personal and painful stories of childhood sexual abuse. Reading the nonverbal behaviors of the group may provide clues to the facilitator that they are uncomfortable and looking for the parent educator to provide leadership. When parents share on such a deep level, it is important that a facilitator does not minimize their experience by cutting them off by asking if others have had similar experiences or by moving too quickly back to the agenda. Whether appropriate or not, it was most likely very difficult to self-disclose at this level. A strategy that can be helpful is to focus less on the content of the self-disclosure and more on the difficulty of bringing it up in the group. Stating, "That is a hard way to grow up. I know it must be difficult for you to bring this up in group, and I hope you know that we all support you" takes the focus away from the content to acknowledging and supporting the parent in the difficulty of sharing this information. A sincere acknowledgment of understanding and an offer to connect privately after the group, when a referral for more intense services may be offered, will allow the parent to remain in a position of respect in the group.

Parents sometimes feel embarrassed after leaving a group when they have over–self-disclosed. They may worry about how they will be perceived with the recognition that they went beyond the expected norm for this setting. It is, therefore, important for the parent educator to practice the art of caring that has been identified as part of developing and maintaining a trusting relationship. If the parent does not return to the next session, a follow-up phone call or note to reassure them that they are welcome to return can be helpful.

Parents may also begin to self-disclose personal information and suddenly sense that they are going too far. They may look to the leader for guidance and an opportunity to move in another direction. The group leader can offer the parent permission to stop: "You can decide how much you want to share." This allows the parent to make a shift in self-disclosure and may subtly refocus him or her on group norms.

By protecting a parent from too much self-disclosure, group leaders are not showing disrespect. They are not setting strict limits that keep the group at a preventive or purely educational level. A parent educator who takes responsibility for keeping all members in a position of respect for themselves and each other provides a setting where issues can be raised, emotions and feelings shared, and problems solved, all within the boundaries of the parent education setting.

The parent educator may encounter a parent who has revealed too much, and others in the group may judge them. The parent educator can see it in their faces and body language. One example is a mother who has talked about her relationship issues with her child's father and how she recently refused to let her son go on a scheduled visitation with him. She was upset that the father's new girlfriend was going to be at his house, and she was concerned about this woman's use of drugs. This is a case where the parent educator can acknowledge the mother's concern and desire to protect her son as important. This can help the mother save face with the group and the parent educator can follow-up with the mother later and talk about ways to address this concern.

Expectations for self-disclosure will also vary with the developmental stage at which the group is functioning. Self-disclosure that is seen as very personal in the early stages of group development may make others feel uncomfortable and perhaps apprehensive about what is in store for them. This same disclosure shared at a later stage of group development may be acceptable. Groups that meet only a few times will probably have limited self-disclosure, because a mutual trust level has not developed. Ongoing groups that meet for longer periods of time typically become settings where members get to know each other and feel comfortable sharing information and feelings about themselves and their children at a deeper level.

Depth of self-disclosure will also vary depending on the composition and purpose of the group. A parent educator working in Level 4 with parents who have multiple stressors and needs can expect a deeper level and more frequent disclosure from members. Parents in these settings have more complex issues that affect their family lives, and including them in discussion is appropriate and helpful in making positive changes. For example, the topic of discipline in a Level 2 setting may elicit self-disclosure about trying different methods and determining what works best. Level 3 settings may include self-disclosure that focuses on the parent's frustration at not being able to guide his or her child's behavior and feelings of being a failure. Level 4 settings dealing with the topic of discipline may include the previous examples and also self-disclosures about painful memories of childhood abuse as a means of discipline. It is the role of the group leader to allow what is appropriate for the group, keep the focus on how issues affect parenting, and protect parents from exposing too much in this setting.

CONFIDENTIALITY

Confidentiality is an important ground rule for most groups. Parents need to trust that what is said in the group is not shared outside the group. Though this is often a stated ground rule, it is not possible for the parent educator to ensure that it will be followed. The complexity of confidentiality issues is magnified in group settings when compared to individual work with parents. The group leader can assure members that he or she will uphold confidentifilaity and that group members are expected to do the same. However, there is no guarantee that fellow participants will do so. Parents may indicate a willingness to adhere to confidentiality and yet leave the group and share information with others in their social or family groups. In smaller community settings where there are more connections between members, this may be a greater challenge than in other more anonymous settings. The parent educator has a responsibility to make sure the group is in verbal agreement about confidentiality and to model appropriate confidentiality in conversations. It may be necessary to remind the group of this expectation, especially after a session where personal issues and challenges were shared. A statement such as the following restates the ground rule in a respectful and clear way: "We've heard a lot of difficult and personal things today about our challenges with parenting and families. This makes our group stronger, and we all learn more from each other. I do want to remind you of our rule of confidentiality. What we talked about here today needs to stay within the group. Are we all in agreement?"

Parents also need to know that this level of confidentiality doesn't mean that they can never talk about the parent group or what was discussed. It is very worthwhile for a parent in a group to take the information back to a spouse, partner, or friend for further discussion. What needs to be clarified regarding confidentiality is that sharing personal information that might be hurtful to someone or retelling of painful self-disclosures that identify particular members needs to be held in confidence.

Parents also need to know early on in a group that confidentiality does not apply to mandated reporting laws. Professionals who work with children and families are required to report suspected child abuse to authorities. This requirement needs to be shared with each group member through written program guidelines and referenced verbally so that parents are aware of the exception. (See Chapter 9 for more information about mandated reporting.)

Confidentiality considerations also affect the parent educator when he or she is sharing information about families with other professionals. In parent-child settings, the parent educator typically teams with a children's teacher. Keeping a clear distinction between what others *need* to know and what they *want* to know is helpful. If a parent educator plans to share information from a session that would be helpful for the children's teacher to understand and better serve the child, parents need to be aware of this. For example, if a parent shares information in the group about a marital separation and the stresses of adjustment for their child, it would be beneficial for the child's teacher to understand how this might be affecting the child's behavior. When ground rules are developed, getting the parent's permission to share only information that would be helpful in working with the child can be requested. Typically, parents are supportive of this arrangement.

When staff members work together with families, clear and distinct roles emerge. One of the challenges of teaming in our work with families is that certain information may not be appropriate to share with all staff who interact with the family. For example, support staff who play an integral role in programs may not need to know certain details about a family's situation of which other staff are aware. A particular family may be involved in a custody determination, a domestic abuse investigation, or some type of law enforcement intervention. Professional staff will often be aware of details and must determine how much others actually need to know. Respect for the family is always a critical factor in making this determination.

Staff who are given some of the information may feel left out or disrespected in this process. However, supervision that supports their role and encourages them to understand the boundaries of confidentiality is critical. Not everyone involved with a family needs to have all the details about a family's circumstances. Along with knowledge or information about families comes more responsibility. The most informed staff may need to collaborate with other professionals, follow up on progress, or be involved in other systems that affect the family. Providing this perspective may help staff sort out what they really need to know about the families with whom they work.

Parent educators who work with helping professionals from other agencies regarding a common family will need to have a signed permission for release of information from a parent before any discussion occurs to assist in coordination of services. This keeps the degree of sharing at a respectful level while maintaining the privacy rights of the parent. By strictly adhering to these guidelines, parent educators model behavior that promotes a healthy and trusting relationship between professional and parent.

Parent educators who receive consultation services regarding group challenges can share general information and group dynamic issues for feedback and suggestions without divulging names and personal information. Other helping professionals often work within systems that provide regular ongoing reflective consultation and support. Many educational programs are also realizing the value of this model and incorporating it into their structure, especially in family support and education programs. Staff time is allowed for peer consultation when parent educators are able to bring challenging group situations to a supportive setting for help with problem solving. Supervisors may also offer this type of consultation to keep parent educators grounded in their work. Additionally, success is seen in ongoing consultation with helping professionals who serve in technical support positions, offering guidance and suggestions to parent educators. (See Chapter 14 for more information about reflective consultation.) In all of these models, confidentiality needs to be held to protect the privacy of parents and children.

PROFESSIONAL BOUNDARIES

Boundaries are limits that both connect us to other people and separate us. They ensure a connection without enmeshment. A boundary is different from a barrier, which keeps the relationship professional but offers no connection to a parent. Parent educators are often challenged with finding this balance in their interactions with parents. The challenge is to be involved professionally in order to make an impact with parents and yet not become overinvolved.

Typical boundary concerns for parent educators include:

- Doing things for parents that the parents could do themselves
- Self-disclosing too much or too little
- Making decisions for a parent
- Becoming overinvolved with a parent's issues
- Excessively worrying about a parent's choices
- Developing a dual relationship with one or more parents
- Doing favors for parents that are outside the realm of the role
- Discussing information about a parent with others
- Accepting gifts
- Providing services to a parent that are more appropriate from another professional
- Relentlessly asking questions of a parent
- Physically touching parents too soon or too much
- Giving unwanted advice
- Not accepting supervision
- Believing they are the only one who really understands the parent's needs

Working with special populations of parents with multiple risk factors tends to generate more complex boundary challenges for parent educators than experiences with more typical groups (Peterson, 1992). If parents have poor boundaries, they often bring special considerations to groups that make it necessary for parent educators to respond with caution.

Other helping professions, such as social work, psychology, mental health, and nursing, all routinely deal with boundaries as they develop relationships that allow them to connect with clients without overconnecting. In a study of social work and boundaries, Parker (2009) indicates that professionalism is related to behaviors, such as style of dress, tone of voice, structure of relationship, choice of vocabulary, relevant questioning, settings for interactions, and confidentiality. Attention to these issues, among others, constitutes a level of professionalism that will assist helping professionals in adhering to boundaries appropriate to their role.

To understand boundary challenges and violations, it is helpful to consider where we learn about boundaries. Although peers, media, and other sources influence our attitudes about boundaries, the most important influence comes from our families of origin. As children, we observe and practice behaviors that our families model about how connected or disconnected we are with the outside world and with each other. Every family has different boundaries related to how connected they are with others, how much nonfamily members are included or invited into their lives, and how much they trust and share with others. Additionally, families set standards for their children as to how connected individual family members are with each other. Unwritten rules govern what topics can be discussed, how much privacy individuals have, whether personal opinions are allowed, whether secrets are kept, or if outside help is accepted. All of these experiences influence our connections with other people. Adults who grow up with healthy boundaries are typically able to develop relationships in groups that respect differences and yet maintain a connection. Those who grow up with an experience at either extreme, with either very rigid controlling boundaries or a lack of appropriate boundaries, may bring many challenges to the parent educator-parent relationship.

Just as each parent brings their own unique experiences and family training with regard to boundaries, so do parent educators. It is important, therefore, for professionals to understand the dynamics of their own families and the impact they may have on their leadership role with groups. Suggestions for parent educators to maintain healthy boundaries with parents include:

- Setting professional limits on behavior
- Being a good role model for parents regarding boundaries

- Getting one's own needs met in other places than at work
- Utilizing support and supervision to keep boundary issues in check
- Knowing when to provide a referral
- Accepting one's limitations and those of the parent educator role

Box 7.1 What Has Influenced Your Boundaries?

Think about your family of origin and what kind of connections and limits were set with others. Boundaries were modeled to you regarding behaviors with the outside world and those within your family. These questions will help you identify what kinds of messages you received about healthy boundaries.

Boundaries to the "outside world":

- Were you allowed to share information with friends, neighbors, or others about problems your family was having?
- When someone came to your home, were they welcomed in or discouraged from entering?
- Were you able to keep confidential conversations with friends, or did other family members need to know?
- Did you feel obligated to have the same opinions as your parents?

Boundaries within your family:

- Was someone in your family chemically dependent or mentally ill?
- Did you feel that your behavior "made" your parents' lives good or bad?
- Did your parents ever talk to you about their personal problems?
- Were you allowed to express anger?
- Did family members talk directly with each other, or did you sometimes say things to one member, knowing they would pass your message along?
- Did you feel like you were in charge of when and how you were touched?

- Were you allowed adequate privacy when dressing or using the bathroom?
- Were you encouraged to think for yourself?
- Were your individual interests suported by your family?
- Did you feel like someone else often spoke for you?
- Did you feel like you had choices?

After reflecting on these questions, what have you learned about your own issues with boundaries?

SOURCE: Questions adapted from McGuire (1994)

Box 7.2 Boundary Challenges: What Would You Do?

Consider the following six questions to determine how you would respond to each boundary challenge below.

1. Whose needs will be met?

2. Are you worried you won't be liked?

3. How might this affect the parent educator–parent relationship?

4. How might this affect others in the group or other members of the professional team?

5. Can you identify the emotions you are feeling?

6. Is there someone you can consult with regarding this issue?

a. *Mary is one of the parents in your weekly parent education group. She is very friendly and spends a few minutes chatting before and after class with you each week. You soon realize that you have much in common. Your backgrounds are similar, her children are close in age to yours, and she enjoys the same hobbies as you do. As you get to know her more, you feel a connection and enjoy the interaction. Mary calls you at home one day and invites you to her home for the afternoon. She suggests you bring your children, so they can play with hers and also get to know each other. You know that you'd like her as a friend and think your children would get along well also.*

b. *Antoine is a new parent in one of your groups who was referred by another agency. He struggles with parenting his three young boys while his wife works long hours. Antoine is sincere and open in the group about how overwhelming parenting is for him and yet how he wants to be the best parent possible. As part of your job, you have also been home visiting him and the boys to work on specific issues of parenting. One night after class Antoine stays a few minutes and seems almost frantic about a situation the next day that requires him to be gone for a few hours to attend to important business while he has no one to watch the children. You have a home visit scheduled with him for tomorrow, and he asks if you could please use the time instead to stay with the boys, so he can conduct his business.*

c. *Malika struggles with her role as a parent. She is 18 and a single mother of two children. She attends a parenting program for young parents with a variety of risk factors. Malika feels cheated out of her youth and often takes her resentment out on her children by yelling at them. Although the children are physically well cared for, they seem to lack the nurturing and emotional support they need. You have worked with Malika in the parent group, as well as individually on her parenting issues. You find yourself worrying about her for long periods of time. You call her home frequently to see if everthing is okay and have even found yourself driving past her home after work. You have made numerous phone calls and contacts for*

Malika to enroll in a college program and continue her education, but she is not following through. You've called her extended family members to talk about how she is doing and whether they feel the children are all right. You are losing sleep over this family and find yourself thinking that if only Malika would follow your suggestions, everything would be fine.

Dual relationships can be particularly devastating to the parent group. If a prior relationship exists between a parent educator and a group member and an alternative placement in another group is not possible, the parent educator has a responsibility to separate the connections related to the parent group from those in his or her personal life. In other words, the prior relationship can stay intact but will need to exclude conversations about the group experience or other members. Additionally, information about the friendship will not be brought to the discussion of the parent group.

There should be a clear distinction between friendship and friendliness with parents in groups. The leader is friendly to all members of the group but should not develop friendships. Behaviors that are more likely to be found in a friendship need to be kept out of this professional relationship. If a parent educator becomes involved on a personal basis with one or more parents, a different kind of relationship develops with that person. A feeling of being special, of knowing certain things about each other, and of sharing outside experiences will cause an inner circle to form that excludes others. Group leaders have an obligation to make all members feel equally valued. This is not possible if a special relationship develops with a particular parent. Parent educators may feel a stronger bond with a parent who has participated in a previous class with them. Though it is natural for this to occur, it should not interfere with the group experience. This special bond tends to diminish as the facilitator builds helping relationships with new members.

When faced with a boundary issue, group leaders need to carefully consider the impact of their decision. Parent educators can ask themselves the following questions that assist in making decisions that stay within the role of a helping professional and outside the role of a friend:

1. *Whose needs will be met?* Occasionally helping professionals become overinvolved with a parent, because they feel needed. It may feel satisfying to know that another person needs them, but this puts the professional's needs above those of the group member.

2. *Are you worried you won't be liked?* Most helping professionals want to be liked. A parent educator may violate a boundary to avoid having a parent reject them or become angry. For example, because a parent educator is concerned about not being liked, he or she may agree to watch a parent's child during non-work time.

3. *How might this affect the parent educator–parent relationship?* Actions outside the realm of a professional relationship may establish a special quality. Frequently, expectations continue to increase, escalating the relationship to resemble a friendship.

4. *How might this action affect others in the group or other members of the professional team?* Other group members may feel left out or feel that they are less significant to the leader. Other team members who uphold professional boundaries may feel undermined in their efforts to maintain appropriate boundaries.

5. *What feelings can you identify that you are feeling?* Parent educators should recognize warning signs, such as frustration, guilt, confusion, or feelings of importance, that they associate with this boundary challenge.

6. *Is there someone you can consult with regarding this issue?* Team members, other professionals, consultants, and supervisors may all provide objective perspectives to assist parent educators with their boundary challenges.

Though it is probably more typical for parent educators to struggle with boundary issues that relate to overinvolvement with parents, it is also possible for professionals to err by having a lack of connection. Unwillingness to go beyond teaching content, absence of any self-disclosure, lack of interest toward the parents, and a relationship void of any caring or genuine concern are examples of boundary violations at the other end of the continuum. Each boundary challenge occurs within a unique context and must be considered carefully. Parent educators who attempt to maintain strict professional boundaries without using common sense may, in fact, develop rigid barriers between themselves and parents.

From our experience ... Parent educators who have poor boundaries with parents often do so with good intentions. They want to show their genuine concern, but do so in ways that are beyond their professional role. Often, they become more entangled in the parent's life than they intended and have difficulty reversing what they've done. This can negatively affect the reputation of the educator, their co-workers, and the program in which they work. Time can be allotted during staff or small group meetings where parent educators bring their boundary challenge examples to the group for a sharing of perspectives and guidance from peers, supervisors, or consultants. Ongoing training on professional boundaries will also keep parent educators aware of potential conflicts and how to address them. Supervisors play an important role in providing an atmosphere where boundary challenges can be openly discussed and used as part of professional development.

Parent educators have a responsibility to understand and be aware of professional expectations regarding boundaries. Codes of ethics for education and other helping professions typically address boundaries in general ways. Agencies and programs must be willing to discuss policies and expectations regarding boundaries with parent educators. Careful examination of the potential results of boundary decisions, along with consultation and supervision, should assist parent educators in maintaining healthy boundaries with parents.

UNDERSTANDING GROUP MEMBERS AND THEIR BEHAVIORS

Every parent educator experiences members in their groups whose behaviors can challenge, and often puzzle, them. Each group is comprised of a variety of diverse personalities, temperaments, and resulting behaviors that can either positively or negatively affect group process. If these factors are concerning to the group leader, the initial reaction should be to examine the relationship between themself and the parent to determine if there might be facilitation and/or relationship-building strategies that could help. Questions to consider from the perspective of the parent educator:

- What is my comfort level with this person?
- What feelings can I identify in myself when working with this person?
- How do these feelings get in the way of building a relationship?
- How have I/how can I connect in a positive way?
- Are there strengths of the parent that I can nurture and affirm?

However, sometimes the challenges of having this person in a group have little relation to the parent educator. Past experiences, personality and temperament, current and past stresses, and cultural influences all affect group members' behaviors, which then affects the entire group process.

Additionally, as parent education continues to reach more diverse groups of parents who represent a cross section of the population, it can be expected that group leaders will encounter more parents who have experienced various types of trauma in their lives. These individuals are at an elevated risk for substance use disorders; mental health problems, such as anxiety or depression; impairment in relational and social areas; and physical disorders (Substance Abuse and Mental Health Services Administration, 2014). The sources of trauma may be either from childhood or current circumstances, yet can affect adults' ability to function at any time during their lifespans. Growing numbers of parent education programs serve immigrant and refugee populations that have been exposed to war, violence, natural disasters, or other traumas and bring their own mental health challenges that affect relational and social life areas. This population also has unique cultural attitudes about parenting that may not mesh with other group members. Utilizing a trauma-informed approach will require the parent educator to have the recognition that trauma can affect adults and can also extend to significant others, family members, children, and even the community. Understanding the power of these experiences can alleviate the burden of sole responsibility educators may put on themselves and also allow for better responses to, and understanding of, group members.

FAMILY OF ORIGIN ISSUES, TEMPERAMENT, AND BIRTH ORDER

Systems theory and its relation to the parent education group is discussed in Chapter 4. In some ways, the group functions similarly to the ways in which a family operates. Individual experiences and roles a group member may have had in their family of origin can influence how that person functions in a group setting. Gender attitudes ingrained from early experiences can influence the comfort level of some members, where deference may be given to one gender or another. Behaviors that may have been productive, or even self-protective, in a family of origin can easily re-emerge in the group experience.

For example, a group member who monopolizes group time may feel more secure, because they fear what happens when they are not in control. This could have been learned early on within the family of origin, where drawing attention to themself provided a needed sense of safety during times of uncertainty. A silent member has learned in their first family that their opinion was not valued and now is reluctant to participate in a group discussion. A jokester in the group grew up bringing humor into the family to distract from addressing important issues, so they respond with humor routinely in the group. Each of these examples provide challenging behaviors for the group leader. It is important, therefore, to realize that parent educators don't always know what kinds of experiences and backgrounds members bring to the group and that many of these challenges have little to do with this parent education experience.

Temperament and personality of group members also play important roles in a group setting. Some members will be more easy going and open to new experiences and ideas. Others will show more resistance or challenge the group leader's or other members' suggestions and information. A wide diversity of personalities and temperaments can be expected in any group. A successful group leader will view these differences as normal with the potential of providing a wide variety of interesting perspectives that enrich the group experience.

Birth order is another factor that can affect the behaviors of group members. Alfred Adler was one of the earliest researchers to make a connection between birth order and personality. Adler believed that birth order influences personality and behavior and that it leaves an impression on each person's style of dealing with friendships, love, and work as they mature through life (Ansbacher & Ansbacher, 1956). Since that time, there have been a variety of studies that have addressed the validity of the theory, with many of them noting some common personality characteristics related to the order of one's birth (Eckstein, 2010).

- First born: more serious, conscientious, goal oriented
- Middle: natural mediators, compromisers, flexible, may struggle with sense of not belonging
- Youngest: outgoing, charming, control seeking, challenging, and attention seeking

In order to more fully understand the behaviors, perspectives, and personalities of group members, birth order is one more lens from which a parent educator can view group dynamics. However, there is not necessarily a definitive correlation. Birth order implications are not a one-size-fits-all framework. It is merely one more tool in understanding human behavior, but needs to be combined with gender, values, ethnicity, and cultural factors (Ansbacher & Ansbacher, 1956)).

A group activity that identifies birth order of the parents and their children, along with a discussion of common characteristics, would provide insightful information to parents about their children, families, and themselves. It can also provide valuable understanding for group leaders regarding the perspectives and behaviors of the adults in their groups.

LIFE LOSSES AND STRESSES

When parents enter a group setting, the educator may know little or nothing about what stresses or experiences of loss they bring with them. Parents may be distracted by recent difficulties, such as lack of child care, financial worries, a recent argument with a partner, a demanding day at work, or a breakdown of a vehicle. More serious challenges may also be consuming the parent's attention, such as a loss of a job or important relationship, a serious diagnosis or illness of a family member, concerns with housing, financial insecurity, legal issues, or a myriad of other life struggles. These more serious challenges of loss are described as shattered dreams that destroy the image previously held by the parent of how their life will be (Bowman, 1999).

These distractions can result in behaviors that affect the atmosphere and progress of the entire group. Taking a systems perspective, it is believed that what affects one member can have an effect on all members of a group. It is difficult to anticipate exactly how these experiences of stress might affect a group member. A parent may be withdrawn as they focus internally on their problems. Conversely, they may be irritable and unusually critical of others and express intense emotions that make others uncomfortable.

Common responses to stress include lack of focus, feeling overwhelmed, showing outbursts of anger, withdrawal, irritability, or anger (CDC, 2015). The parent educator will need to guide the group so that these behaviors don't consume and dominate the group dynamics; keep focused, yet be respectful to the parent; and decide if a private conversation would be helpful after the session. By individually approaching the parent to learn more about what is causing their difficulty, the parent educator can offer empathetic responses and provide possible options for further services.

When a parent educator understands that the parent group experience is only one small part of each member's life, it provides a more holistic perspective on what happens in the group. Realizing the potential impact of outside experiences on behaviors will benefit the parent educator in their approach and understanding of group dynamics.

BUILDING BRIDGES OF UNDERSTANDING

An important aspect of building relationships with parents in the role of parent educator is becoming aware of our own backgrounds. Understanding the values and beliefs that come from growing up in a family and in a community during a specific historical time is a starting place. Parent education students in a foundations class have been given an assignment adopted from Pipher (2006) to write a poem entitled "I Come from ..." that allows them to explore their family, culture, ethnic background, religious beliefs, and community (See Box 7.3). Our core values spring from these experiences, and once we can acknowledge where we have come from and how we have embraced or rejected these values, it gives us the chance to better understand ourselves and biases (about gender, race, social class, and religion) that we bring to our work with parents. This awareness helps us take responsibility for building bridges of understanding across areas where we may have developed blind spots. Parent educators will encounter families who are different from themselves, and this self-awareness provides a starting place for understanding the histories of those different from ourselves.

This is an exercise to think about the influences of family, culture, and environment on who we are and the rich mix of these factors that make up our roots. Following the basic style of Mary Pipher (2006) in *Writing to Change the World*, students are asked to write a short piece that describes where they come from by addressing the following:

1. Cultural background as reflected in countries of origin, food, traditions

2. Family background as reflected in family activities, rituals, values

3. Class background as reflected in places your family has lived, jobs/occupations, and experiences

4. Religious/spiritual background as reflected in beliefs, morals, and community identity

5. Geography as reflected in places your family has lived and you have lived

6. Importance of children reflected in how they are viewed/treated

Box 7.3 I am From

I am from working class Chicago, rural Missouri, and small-city Minnesota

From Downsville, Wisconsin to a fruit farm on the east side of Lake Michigan

I am from devout Catholics, close-knit families, and family reunions in the summer

I am from hard work, creativity-electric erasers and ink recyclers, and factory grime that settles in your nose

I am from large churches, teachers in black robes, dark confessional stalls, and the joy and commitment of caring about others

I am from caring for young children, supporting families, and advocating for gender equity

I am from folk music, beautiful female voices, guitar strumming, and meaningful music

I am from 8th grade education to PhDs and MD, CFLE and LMFTs, CPAs and CPDs

I am from Catholic monasticism to Unitarian Circle Dinners

THE EFFECTS OF ADVERSE CHILDHOOD EXPERIENCES STUDY

A major national study conducted by Kaiser Permanente, in collaboration with the Centers for Disease Control and Prevention (CDC, 2015) addressing the effects of adverse childhood experiences has implications for parent educators.

Over 17,000 members voluntarily participated in this study to determine how stressful or traumatic experiences during childhood affect adult health. The Adverse Childhood Experiences (ACEs) study found that more than half of the participants experienced at least one of the following, and over 20% experienced three or more:

- Emotional abuse
- Physical abuse
- Sexual abuse
- Emotional neglect
- Physical neglect
- Domestic violence, family alcohol, or drug use
- Mentally ill person in the household
- Loss of a parent due to separation or divorce
- Incarceration of family member
  (Middlebrooks & Audage, 2008)

Furthermore, the study found that participants who experienced these negative familial occurences as children had a higher rate of negative health and wellbeing as adults with issues of alcoholism, depression, poorer health–related quality of life, drug use, intimate partner violence, sexually transmitted diseases, smoking , suicide, and unintended pregnancies (Felitti et al., 1998). It is

From our experience ... It is often difficult for parent educators to watch the interactions between parents and children that reflect a lack of understanding and nurturing toward the child. One particular parent in our program had a difficult time showing affection for her infant. She held her at arms' length, seemed oblivious to her cries to be comforted, and seldom talked or interacted with her. The staff tried to model nurturing behaviors in nonjudgmental ways, gently pointing out what the child was trying to communicate. Learning more about this parent, who had been abandoned as an infant, spent much time in the foster care system, struggled with substance abuse, and had attachment issues with adoptive parents helped the parent educator be more understanding of the reasons behind her struggles with nurturing her child.

notable, that these outcomes are the very ones that expose their own children to adverse experiences and maintain the cycle for their current family.

Parent educators should realize the likelihood that some of the parents with whom they are working will have experienced adverse childhood experiences and are affected by them now as adults. These effects will, almost certainly, affect their approaches to parenting, their interactions within the group, and their relationships within their families.

SUMMARY

Each parent brings their own experiences and challenges to the parent group. These are often unknown to the group leader but can greatly affect group process, often in difficult ways. Building strong relationships with and between group members is the heart of group parent education and is done through careful interactions and strategies that demonstrate genuine caring and support. While the quality of the relationship between educator and parent should always be considered, there are influences outside of that relationship that offer clues to the behaviors of group members. Family of origin experiences, birth order, personality and temperament, stresses and losses, and cultural implications all influence the behaviors of the parent, both in the group and with their children. Instead of asking, "what's wrong with that parent?" a parent educator should ask "what happened to that parent?" This encourages an openness without judgment to gaining more insight into each individual's behaviors, perspectives, and attitudes.

DISCUSSION QUESTIONS

1. As a parent educator, how would you respond to a parent who approaches you privately regarding concerns about another parent in the group and how she treats her children? They are neighbors and this parent thinks you should know "what kind of parent she really is."

2. How comfortable do you feel about your own self-disclosure as a group leader? How could you find a balance of connection without over connecting?

3. Think, pair, share. Write down the self disclosure ground rules you would set for yourself as a group leader. Pair with another person and discuss your ground rules. Share with the class to compile a list.

CLASS ACTIVITIES

1. In pairs, list three things each of you have in common. (For example, you are each from large families, have brown hair, and drive red cars.) Then, for each of those items, determine how they are different (one has 5 siblings, the other 10; one's hair is long and straight while the other has curly short hair; one drives a compact car and the other a van).

   a. How does this activity encourage rapport among group members?

   b. Why might a parent educator include it in the beginning stages of a group?

2. In pairs, stand shoulder to shoulder, facing opposite directions, so you are unable to see your partner's face. One person is the speaker and the other listener. For three minutes, the speaker should talk about their career goals, what they find most interesting in their chosen field, and what challenges they anticipate. The listener is to remain quiet and use no nonverbal gestures to show a response. After three minutes, reverse roles.

   a. Debrief the activity, with each person describing what it was like to be a listening and a speaker.

   b. What was hard about this activity? What was missing?

   c. What insight have you gained about the power of nonverbal behaviors and gestures?

   d. What implications are there for phone conversations, email, and other communications that are not face-to-face?

3. Observe a parent group, describe the group, and note the relationship-building strategies that the parent educator used.

REFERENCES

Ansbacher, H.L., & Ansbacher, R.R. (Eds.) (1956). *The Individual Psychology of Alfred Adler*. New York, NY: Basic Books.

Bowman, T. (1999). Shattered dreams, resiliency and hope: Restorying after loss. *Journal of Personal and Interpersonal Loss*, *4*, 179–193.

CDC (Center for Disease Control Prevention) *Coping with Stress*, October 2015. Atlanta, GA: CDC, Division of Violence Prevention, National Center for Injury Prevention and Control, Division of Violence Prevention.

Cormier, W., & Cormier, S. (1998). *Interviewing strategies for helpers*. Monterey, CA: Brooks/Cole.

Eckstein, D., Aycock, K.J., Sperber, M. A., McDonald, J., VanWiesner III, V., Watts, R.E., Ginsburg, P. (2010). A review of 200 birth-order studies: Lifestyle characterisitcs, *The Journal of Individual Psychology*, *66*(4), 408–434.

Felitti, V.J., Anda, R.F., Nordenberg, D., Williamson, D.F., Spritz, A.M., & Edwards, V. (1998). Relationship of childhood abuse and household dysfunction to many of the leading causes of death in adults: The adverse childhood experiences (ACE) Study. *American Journal of Preventive Medicine*, *14*, 245–258.

McGuire, S. (1994) *Professional boundaries: Keeping clients' needs first*. Center City, MN: Hazelden.

Middlebrooks J.S., & Audage N.C. (2008) The Effects of Childhood Stress on Health Across the Lifespan. Atlanta, GA: CDC, National Center for Injury Prevention and Control.

Pipher, M. (2006). *Writing to change the world: An inspiring guide for transforming the world with words*. New York, NY: Riverhead Books.

Substance Abuse and Mental Health Services Administration (2014). Trauma-Informed Care in Behavioral Health Services. Treatment Improvement Protocol (TIP) Series 57. HHS Publication No. (SMA) 13-4801. Rockville, MD: Substance Abuse and Mental Health Services Administration.

FACILITATION SKILLS

Though parent educators need general facilitation skills for working with any group, a different set of competencies is required as groups move from sharing information to education and support to brief intervention. As the needs of the group increase, the necessary skills of the parent educator become more complex. According to the levels of involvement model discussed in Chapter 5, groups at Level 2 require solid teaching and presenting skills that share information with parents in a clear and understandable manner. Level 3 experiences require more involved relational skills that elicit and respond to feelings and emotions in a supportive atmosphere. Finally, Level 4 groups require interventive skills that assist parents with addressing challenging issues and formulating a plan for change. This chapter will deal specifically with the skills and strategies required in Level 3 settings that aid leaders in providing a meaningful experience for participants.

GROUP LEADERSHIP SKILLS

In addition to the many personal and professional qualities and characteristics that parent educators must have, a variety of specific leadership skills are needed. These skills can be classified into two categories. One set can be described as external and active; these skills are obvious to the group and are related to content and goals. They are practical and necessary for the successful

The physical setting varies according to the group and the style of the parent educator

functioning of the group. The other set of skills are more subtle and are internal and reflective. They require insight, evaluation, and internal direction, of which group members are not always aware. The challenge to parent educators is that they need to function within the two categories simultaneously.

The external/active leadership skills include:

- Leading the discussion
- Keeping the group focused and engaged
- Posing questions that generate dialogue
- Moving toward a goal
- Sharing information drawn from a solid knowledge base
- Teaching and engaging with a variety of methods to meet the needs of varying adult learning styles
- Guiding the group or individual members with problem solving

The internal/reflective leadership skills include:

- Assessing progress of the group and/or an individual
- Observing, interpreting, and reacting to nonverbal signals
- Choosing appropriate communication strategies

- Encouraging member-to-member interaction
- Leading indirectly by providing time and space for self-exploration and discovery
- Assessing parents' responses and level of understanding
- Adjusting the direction of the session in response to the group or individual needs

EXTERNAL/ACTIVE SKILLS

Foundational to the external/active skills is a solid knowledge base in order to develop sessions based on current information and research. Beginning parent educators often feel as if they must know everything about parenting, children, and families to lead groups. In reality, group leaders can give themselves permission to say, "I'm not sure about that, but I can check on it and get back to you." As parent educators grow into their professional role, they become more confident and continue to be exposed to new information on a variety of topics that increases their knowledge level, as well as their self-confidence. There are, however, particular content areas in which it is necessary to be well versed. Parent educators need to know about child and adult development, family life cycles, family system dynamics and diverse family structures, parenting strategies, cultural diversity, social issues affecting families, and community resources. Information and trends change rapidly, new parenting approaches are recommended, and research influences current thinking. Therefore, it is critical for parent educators to keep themselves informed on new research and emerging issues.

The role of the parent educator has also been affected by the influence of the internet. Today's parents are comfortable seeking out information online when they need guidance on raising their children. They often bring information to the group and the parent educator to get an opinion on whether what they've found is accurate, reliable, and advisable. This provides an opportunity for other parents to weigh in, but also for the parent educator to provide support for the information or another perspective that may be more appropriate.

The parent educator may also make note of internet resources for parents to encourage and instruct them on how to access reliable information. Helping parents know where to look on the internet, what criteria to use in evaluating the resources, and what to avoid are all helpful points a parent educator can cover in the group. Questions to encourage parents to consider the validity and relevance of online resources:

- Is the material current, reflecting the latest research?
- Is the promoted approach respectful to children and families?

- Does the information fit with the overall values of the parent?
- Are there any obvious biases reflected in the information?
- What are the qualifications of the authors?
- Do the authors have professional preparation in areas related to parenting?
- Is the information linked to promotions to sell products?
- Are there reviews of the site and parent responses to the information?

From our experience ... We have seen parents bring unreliable information to parent groups from the internet that clearly reflect opinions, rather than facts. A parent in one of our groups shared information about sleeping positions and co-sleeping arrangements that are not encouraged for infants. Her sources were found on blogs and included opinions of other parents online. She believed that because it was on the internet it was accurate. The parent educator gently challenged the source without judgment of the parent, talked about how to find updated and current recommendations on the topic, and demonstrated how to access the latest information.

Parent educators are group leaders and facilitators, but they are also teachers. Leading parent groups involves sharing some content in a clear and concise way so that parents understand. Additionally, group process skills are required that encourage dialogue and discussion to guide the group toward growth and learning. Group leaders, therefore, need organizational and presenting skills. The skill of cognitive organization helps parent educators design sessions that are productive and have purpose (Clarke, 1984). Clarke's steps in cognitive organization for parent educators are:

- Having clear objectives
- Dividing learning into orderly steps
- Having knowledge categorized to be able to respond to questions
- Being clear and willing to admit what one knows and doesn't know

INTERNAL/REFLECTIVE SKILLS

The other set of leadership skills, internal/reflective skills, are those that often go unnoticed by group members. These skills help maintain the group cohesiveness and include observation, interpersonal communication, and group process skills that guide the group toward growth and learning. These skills allow the facilitator to influence the direction of the group in order to encourage optimal functioning.

Parent educators typically teach parents to observe their children's behavior as a means of understanding and responding to them better. A parallel can be made to the group setting. Observational skills that allow a facilitator to note behaviors, both verbal and nonverbal, help group leaders form appropriate responses to individual members and to the group as a whole. Observational skills, combined with the ability to interpret behavior on the basis of knowledge of human development, assist the facilitator in guiding the group process.

It is this set of internal skills that allows parent educators to assess what is currently happening as the group progresses and to redirect, if needed. The skills involved in reflection and insight blend to assist the facilitator in taking action. On one hand, the group leader is guiding the discussion in a leadership role. At the same time, he or she is evaluating the progress of the group and making decisions about what happens next.

The skill of indirectness is also one of the internal skills of a group leader. With this skill, a confident group leader allows members to discover things for themselves (Clarke, 1984). Adult learners prefer to explore options, consider resources, and make their own decisions, rather than being told what to do or given "the answers." A parent educator demonstrates professionalism by including indirectness in his or her work with parents. Although it may be easier to teach content to interested learners, it is more meaningful to provide a guided experience of growth and learning.

Strategies that utilize indirectness include giving a variety of parenting methods and facilitating a discussion that allows parents to choose those that fit best with their values, family, individual child, and parenting style. Statements such as "Consider which methods you feel most comfortable using" or "Think about what strategy would work best with your child" encourage parents to make their own decisions about how they will parent. Questioning techniques that gently probe to get more information and guide a parent to formulate a desired model of parenting also allow the facilitator to function indirectly and help parents make changes. Questions that invite self-exploration, such as "What kind of parent would you like to be?," "What is most important to you in your relationship with this child?," or "What values do you want to pass on to your child?" encourage parents to examine their behavior and values in order to determine what parenting approaches are most compatible.

Box 8.1 Just Like a Duck

Watching a skilled parent educator is much like watching a duck swimming effortlessly down the river. Barely a ripple appears as the duck serenely floats along. He moves his head from side to side occasionally but has a clear vision of where he is going. The part of the duck that we see hardly shows any effort at all. In fact, as we watch, we assume that this effortless act uses little or no energy or thought.

What we don't see is that under the water, the duck's webbed feet are moving furiously through the water to propel him to where he wants to go. These bright orange feet are hidden under the surface, but their quick movements not only keep the duck afloat but steer him in the right direction. The duck is aware of everything around him and ready to change directions in a moment.

An experienced and skilled parent educator is much like the duck. They make their work look easy as they lead the discussion, keep the group focused, respond to difficult situations, and meet the individual needs of everyone in the group. This parent educator appears calm, relaxed, and very self-assured. What we don't see is that they are "paddling furiously." They are assessing the group's progress, gauging individual needs and reactions, determining what direction to go, choosing strategies to address challenging behaviors, and deciding how much to deviate form the careful plan they have prepared for the session.

Parents and observers may believe leading a parent group is an easy task. Until they take on the role of the parent educator and understand the complex skills involved, they may believe it is as easy as a duck swimming quietly downstream.

ACTIVE LISTENING SKILLS

Parent education groups require active listening skills from the facilitator. Parent educators must learn to listen empathetically, attend with their whole body, and respond with statements that support and encourage group members to openly explore their parenting issues. These responses also require a parent educator to universalize normal experiences, engage parents in problem-solving discussions, and refer the parent to another source beyond the scope of parent education, when appropriate.

Listening skills require more than hearing what someone is saying. By actively listening, parent educators listen to the words, observe nonverbal cues, attend and focus, and respond in a reflective and supportive manner. Considering all of the expressive language styles of participants, along with the differences of ethnicity, class, and gender that make up a group, it is understandable that active listening on the part of the group leader requires a great deal of energy and concentration (Brookfield & Preskill, 2005). Group members have a greater tendency to discuss their issues when the facilitator practices active listening skills. In the field of counseling, listening skills are seen as prerequisite in the client-professional relationship (Cormier & Cormier, 1998). If enough active listening is not done with the client, and the professional moves too quickly to find solutions, it is likely that resistance will occur. Individuals need to feel heard before they can truly move forward with self-exploration. The same concept applies to parent education. When leading groups, it is necessary for the parent educator to listen first and then assist the parent in finding solutions for change.

ATTENDING BEHAVIORS

For group leaders to truly listen, they must use attending skills that convey a message of full attention and care to individuals. Group leaders attend to parents by maintaining eye contact, leaning in toward the speaker, and using facial and other gestures that communicate understanding and generate trust. These attending behaviors tell group members, "I am being heard. This person is giving me his or her full attention." Without the connection that attending behaviors make, it is unlikely that parents will fully participate in the parent education and support experience.

Eye contact is an important attending behavior. When a listener looks away from a speaker, the connection is broken. When the leader avoids eye contact or is distracted by notes or other things in the room, the speaker begins to wonder if he or she is being heard or being dismissed as unimportant. Because cultures vary in their practice of nonverbal behaviors, such as eye contact, it is an important factor to consider for group leaders. Typically, group members feel a connection to a leader who maintains eye contact with them and makes them feel they are being listened to.

The use of the body can be very influential in using attending skills. We listen not just with our ears, but with our whole body. The acronym SOLER refers to physical attending skills that remind facilitators to communicate an empathetic connection as they listen to others. Face individuals SQUARELY. Adopt an OPEN posture. LEAN toward the speaker. Maintain good EYE contact without staring. Remain RELAXED as you interact (Egan, 1994). Although it is not helpful for facilitators to focus too intently on orchestrating the use of their body and, therefore, appear unnatural, attention to the power of attending behaviors assists in building relationships and facilitating discussion.

Just as using helpful nonverbal attending skills can help parent educators make a connection with parents, the wrong ones can easily show judgment and interrupt the parent's involvement in learning. Group leaders whose nonverbal and verbal messages are not in agreement with each other may confuse parents. Delivering supportive or affirming comments when facial gestures or body language show negative judgment typically stops the parent from communicating openly. Keeping verbal and nonverbal messages congruent is essential in healthy communication.

ACTIVE LISTENING RESPONSES

After group leaders listen to parents, they need to respond verbally in ways that confirm that they have understood the message and are supportive. Several communication strategies are used by facilitators as active listening responses. They are reflecting, clarifying, paraphrasing, and summarizing (Cormier et al., 2013), and they precede problem solving. A common error that parent group leaders make is to move too quickly to problem solving. Parents need time to express their concerns and feel they are understood and supported before they are ready to look for solutions. In addition to these active listening responses, parent educators also use universalizing as a skill in interactions that involve feelings and support.

Group leaders listen for feelings and reflect them back to the parent. A parent may not name the feeling he or she has, but it is often clear to the listener. A reflecting statement rephrases the affective part of the message. "You sound frustrated about how your child responds to discipline." This statement tells parents that you have heard what they have said, and you understand how they feel. Reflection of feelings should not be stated definitively, as in the statement "You feel frustrated ... ," but, rather, more tentatively. No one knows exactly how another person feels, but careful listening allows facilitators to identify and name the feeling they believe is present, while allowing the parent to agree or clarify.

Clarifying statements are phrased in the form of questions and are often used following an ambiguous message. "Do you mean ... ?" or "Is what you're saying ... ?" or "Could you tell me what you mean by ... ?" are all ways to begin a clarification. These statements encourage elaboration, check for accuracy, and may clear up confusing messages. Using clarification also tells the parent that the facilitator is listening carefully and values the information enough to ask for a clearer picture. Group leaders often use clarification to make things clear not only for themselves but for the other group members and for the individual parent, as well.

Group leaders paraphrase as they rephrase the content part of the message. This may help the parent focus on the content of the message and allow him or her to hear the message in someone else's words. By paraphrasing, parent educators show that they are being attentive and genuine while listening. "So, it sounds like single parenting leaves you little time for yourself, and you need a break." This statement paraphrases what the parent has been saying and focuses on content, not feelings.

Summarizing statements are also helpful to group leaders as they tie together multiple ideas expressed by a parent. A group member may ramble about a particularly challenging parenting issue. The parent educator listens for a common theme or pattern and forms a statement or two that pulls the message together in a condensed way. Summarizing can refocus the parent, who may feel overwhelmed after speaking in detail about a concern. It can assist the parent in seeing the issue more clearly and prepare him or her to move to action. Summarizing statements are typically two or more paraphrases or reflections and are used toward the end of a parent's disclosure. Additionally, the facilitator may engage the group in summarizing the material at the end of a session or ask an individual to summarize what he or she has just said. A statement such as "If you could put that into one or two sentences, what would you say?" invites the parent to condense his or her thoughts into a short focused statement or two.

A final strategy that conveys support to the parent is universalizing. This technique helps parents see that some of their problems are common to all parents. Many times, parents have unrealistic expectations of their children and of themselves as parents. They may describe behaviors of their children that are fairly typical of a particular developmental stage. For example, they may share feelings about being overwhelmed by the parenting role or incompetent in their skills as they describe a struggle with bedtime issues. A parent educator can build relationships and also encourage and affirm a group member by pointing out the universal qualities of this issue with other parents. This needs to be done without minimizing the parent's concern, so it is often combined with a reflection-of-feelings statement. "You sound very frustrated with how things are going at bedtime. It may help you to know that what you are experiencing is fairly common in households with 2-year-olds." This acknowledges the group leader's attention and caring regarding the parent's feeling about the issue and also affirms the parent in recognizing that he or she is not alone. Frequently, in a supportive group setting, other members will affirm a parent by making statements that universalize the experience. "I know what you mean. We went through the same thing at our house." This not only builds rapport between members but promotes an environment where members trust that they will be supported.

Although universalizing is an important skill for parent educators to use and one that affirms and reassures parents, it is important not to ignore a problem that really isn't common or developmentally appropriate. While parent educators have the desire to put the parent's mind at rest, they do a disservice by universalizing a behavior that is outside the norm.

All of these active listening responses are examples of ways that parent educators show their genuine care for parents as they share their struggles. Hearing what a parent is saying isn't enough. Listening closely is only the beginning. It is through verbal active listening responses that the parent feels that he or she has been heard and understood. Only then will the parent feel ready to move toward finding new solutions.

PROBLEM SOLVING

Parents in group settings present issues of concern. Though support, empathy, understanding, and universalization are helpful strategies, parents also are looking for solutions. Problem-solving skills assist parent educators in working with the individual and the group to generate possible solutions.

FOUR-STEP PROBLEM-SOLVING PROCESS

A structured four-step problem-solving process described by Dr. William Doherty of the University of Minnesota (Minnesota Department of Education, 1995) can be utlizied in the parent education group or in individual consultation with a parent.

1. Clarify the problem or situation.

2. Elicit and acknowledge the parent's feelings.

3. Discuss the child's feelings.

4. Generate solutions.

Note that generating solutions is the last step in the process. Frequently, as mentioned, group leaders move too quickly to this step, while parents are not yet ready. The first three steps involve active listening and responses that are supportive and encouraging to the parent.

Example of Four-Step Problem Solving: A group of parents with 4-year-olds has been meeting for the past several months. This week's topic is kindergarten readiness, which was identified by the parents as a common concern. The group has received information on the developmental characteristics of children ready to enter school and helpful skills and ideas for activities to assist with the transition. As the discussion evolves, Marta begins to voice ambivalence about sending her son, whose fifth birthday is this coming summer, to school. "He has no interest in anything related to school, he's small for his age, and all he wants to do is run and play with his toys." Other parents join in the discussion and describe concerns they also have, but Marta seems "stuck" and keeps coming back to her dilemma of sending her child or waiting another year. She acknowledges that it would be easier for her and her family if this child started school, because child care costs would be eliminated, and it would allow her to return to work full time. She is, however, concerned about her child succeeding in school.

The parent educator begins by clarifying the problem and asking for more information. "Tell me more about what you are seeing." "What happens when he does try some of the table activities?" "How do others in your family feel about this issue?" These clarifying questions provide a more detailed description of the concern for the leader, as well as the other group members and the parent herself.

Next, the parent educator elicits and acknowledges the parent's feelings. "It sounds like you are very unsure of which choice to make. I understand that you want your child to succeed, and yet, you aren't certain if he is really ready." There is a tendency for both parent and group leader to become stuck in this stage. It feels good for the parent to be affirmed and understood, so she may keep the focus here. The facilitator may also believe that support is enough. However, in this situation, there is a clear challenge for the parent to address and a need for a solution.

The group leader then encourages the parent to consider the child's feelings. "How do you think your child might be feeling?" What do you think your child is telling you with his behavior?" Empathy building for parents allows them to see things from their child's perspective and may assist them in making difficult decisions that are in the best interest of the child.

Finally, the parent is ready for solutions. "Would you like some ideas?" It is advisable for the parent educator not to move into solutions until he or she believes the parent is ready. Asking permission not only is respectful but also subtly signals the parent that you are moving into the action phase of the process. "What have others done with their older children?" "Some people suggest ... " "There are some alternative experiences for children before kindergarten that might be helpful. They are ... ." Now the parent feels she has been heard and is ready to consider alternatives and make a decision.

SUGGESTION CIRCLE

Another common facilitation technique that guides a process of problem solving is the suggestion circle. This fairly structured method, described by Jean Illsley Clarke (1984), is useful when a group member repeatedly returns to a particular issue, does not respond to ideas or support from the leader or other group members, and appears to be stuck. Verbal or nonverbal behaviors of the group members may indicate to the leader that they are ready to move on. The parent with a concern typically appears frustrated, and the direction of the group becomes stagnant. In this situation, the parent educator becomes fairly directive, refocuses the group, leads a process of problem solving, and then moves the group along with its agenda.

Steps in leading a suggestion circle are:

1. Acknowledge the feeling of being stuck.

2. Clarify the situation.

3. Briefly describe the process and ask for permission.

4. Designate a note taker and set ground rules.

5. Facilitate, keeping the process focused and moving forward.

6. Give closure.

7. Offer to check in next time on progress.

Example of a Suggestion Circle: *The topic of the parent education group is sleep issues and toddlers. The facilitator presents some information and then asks what group members are experiencing in their homes regarding sleep. Amira, one of the parents, describes her struggles and frustration with her toddler regarding bedtime. Other members join the discussion with supportive comments and several ideas of strategies they have tried. Amira repeatedly returns to her concerns and responds to any new ideas with resistance.*

The parent educator soon recognizes that the frustration level is rising in the group, both from Amira and the other parents. She says, "Amira, it's clear to me that you are very discouraged with how things are going. I can understand how you might feel, since it seems like many parents of toddlers go through this." She then quickly clarifies the situation. "What I'm hearing is that your child's bedtime is becoming very stressful for everyone in your house, and I think there may be some useful ideas from the group that could be helpful." The facilitator waits for acknowledgment from Amira and then asks for permission. "Would you like to try something that often works in groups that's called a suggestion circle? It's another way of generating solutions, and there may be a few ideas that could work well for you." After Amira agrees, the parent educator gives the group the ground rules for the process. "We are going to go around our circle, and each of you can give your best idea to Amira. You'll need to say it in one sentence, and she will say, 'Thank you,' after each idea. We won't discuss the ideas or decide if they would or wouldn't work, and we will make sure everyone has a chance to give their best idea." The parent educator reminds the group members that they always have the option to pass and asks for a volunteer to record the ideas on paper that will be given to Amira at the end of the process.

The suggestion circle begins in a structured format that gives each parent an opportunity to give a suggestion. If someone passes, he or she will have another opportunity at the end. Typically, the parent with a concern, in this case Amira, will attempt to pull the group back into a discussion about her concerns and try to evaluate each idea by sharing why this would not work. The facilitator's role during a suggestion circle is to demonstrate more control and direction, keeping the process moving. Helpful statements are "Remember just one sentence, describing your best idea," or "Amira, I need to remind you that you can only thank each person for their idea. We won't take the time now to discuss them." These statements keep the suggestion circle from breaking down and the group from returning to the feeling of being stuck.

At the end of the process, the facilitator thanks everyone for his or her helpful suggestions, encourages Amira to take the written list and decide which ones would be most helpful, and invites her to try those that fit for her. An offer to check in next time on how it went lets the parent know that both the facilitator and the other members are genuinely concerned. The parent educator, however, must be very cautious that the same issue does not dominate the next session. A check-in must be quick, and it needs to be made clear that the group will move on with the designated topic.

Suggestion circles are helpful when a parent appears to be stuck on an issue and is resistant to ideas that are offered. Group members immediately notice the change in tone when the facilitator firmly takes control of the group's direction. This strategy is respectful to all members. The parent with a concern gets the suggestions they need, other group members appreciate that one individual's needs do not impede the progress of the session, and the group facilitator demonstrates leadership in a challenging situation.

QUESTIONING FORMATS

Parents' self reflection is key to a successful parent group experience. Group leaders need to think carefully about what questions they ask of parents and what types of responses they might elicit. It is often helpful for beginning parent educators to write out their discussion questions beforehand until they are more experienced in questioning formats. Asking good discussion questions has a number of important functions in the group setting. They can:

- Energize the thoughts of the group or group member
- Move the parent(s) to a deeper level of self-understanding
- Clarify to avoid misunderstanding
- Link group members' ideas
- Redirect or refocus the discussion
- Encourage expression of feelings
- Encourage participation of members who have not shared
- Build relationships

The two main types of questions a group leader will ask are either closed or open ended. Closed questions are those that can be answered with either a single word or a short phrase. "How many children do you have?" is an example of a closed question. These types of questions provide information, are easy and quick for the parent to answer, and keep the control of the conversation with the facilitator. While closed questions do not encourage discussion, they are useful in certain circumstances. They may allow a group leader to step in when someone is rambling, or they may be used as a way of providing closure to a topic or group session. Additionally, they can be used at the beginning of a session, since parents who may be reluctant to open up and share their opinions will be more likely to provide a simple answer to a closed question.

By contrast, an open-ended question is likely to receive a longer answer. These questions ask the parent to reflect, think, and share their feelings and opinions. When a parent educator asks an open-ended question, he or she is handing control of the group to the parents within a shared ownership arrangement. An example of an open-ended question is "What has becoming a parent been like for you?" This question asks parents to share not only information, but a part of themselves with the group. It presents an opportunity for the group leader and members to learn more about each other and provides an atmosphere for them to share their own thoughts and feelings.

Beyond closed and open-ended questions, there are a variety of questioning formats that parent educators can effectively use as they lead a group. Utilizing an assortment of formats will keep the group interesting and interactive, without becoming repetitive or too predictable.

The technique of funnel questions starts with more general, broad questions and proceeds with those involving more detail. For example, "How would you describe your parenting style?" is a broad question that can get parents to express their philosophy of parenting in a holistic way. Following that question with those that focus on specifics gives more details to back up what they've expressed. "How do you handle discipline?" and "What specific ways do you deal with setting limits?" will zero in on details that support the original response about philosophy. In contrast, an "inverted" funnel format will begin with very specific, detailed questions and move toward broad, general questions.

Questions that ask for feelings and opinions demonstrate interest in, and respect for, group members. If shared ownership of the group is desired, then these types of questions are critical. "What is your reaction to ... " "How do you feel about ... " "What has been your experience with ... " are all examples of questions that encourage parents to open up and share their perspectives.

Prediction questions are those that ask, "What do you think would happen if you ... " Using this type of question can encourage the parent to consider a new way of thinking or contemplate a strategy that might be helpful. Parents who are resistant to change often respond more favorably to a prediction question, while they may object to a practical parenting suggestion.

Clarifying questions are useful to make sure everyone is understanding what is being said. These questions are most helpful when a parent is rambling or when a message is unclear. "Are you saying ... ?" "Before you go on, do you mean ... " "I'm not sure I'm following. Can you explain ... ?" are all examples that can refocus the speaker to ensure everyone understands what is being said.

Questions requesting information, feelings, or opinions can also be perceived as threatening to some parents who may feel they are being quizzed or put on the spot by the group leader. The same request can be asked in a "non-question" format that will garner the desired response. For example, "Tell us about … " "Say more about … " "We'd like to hear … " are all examples that encourage discussion without making the parent feel there is a "right" answer or that they are being tested.

Processing questions are asked after an activity or at the end of a session and are used to guide group members to consider what has just taken place and what they might take from it (Jacobs, 2006). Their purpose is to encourage reflection on the experience, elicit members' impressions, ask what may have had meaning for them, and encourage parents to consider how they might integrate the experience as they move forward.

Just as there are recommended questioning formats, there are also those to avoid. Questions that are leading and promote a particular response are not respectful to adult learners. "You don't punish your child by hitting, do you?" won't get an honest answer. Questions that show bias such as "Many of us don't believe in spanking, but how do you feel about it?" express our feelings and beliefs as the accepted standard. Lastly, overloaded questions that include a number of questions strung together are complicated and can confuse the group member.

Finally, while asking questions is an important facilitation skill for any group leader, the main purpose of questioning is to elicit a reply. A mistake that many facilitators make is not waiting long enough for the parent to answer. Group members need time to formulate a response, and too often, a group leader will move on to the next question or piece of information without allowing time for answers. Watching for nonverbals and allowing some silent time can be helpful in providing opportunities for meaningful discussion, based on the questions of the group leader.

From our experience … Supervising parent educators required that I observe each individual several times during the school year. I always felt as if I learned a great deal from watching them facilitate parent groups, while I also had an opportunity to provide some suggestions. I noticed that beginning parent educators often struggled with forming discussion questions that really engaged parents. Too often, they used closed questions and were met with short answers or silence from the group. Consciously formulating the questions and writing them out was helpful until they became more comfortable in asking open ended questions that encouraged parents to reflect and share their opinions and ideas.

BRAINSTORMING STRATEGIES

Brainstorming activities are another strategy that parent educators find beneficial for working with groups of parents. This activity encourages divergent thinking and production of many different ideas in a short period of time. Brainstorming is often used when a group or individual gets "stuck."

Parent educators elicit ideas through brainstorming activities

Generally, in a brainstorming activity, all ideas are accepted without criticism or evaluation. However, depending on the functional level of the group, some ground rules may be necessary before a brainstorming activity begins. For example, if the parent educator chooses to conduct a brainstorming session on discipline strategies with a high-risk group of parents and anticipates that some members may share punitive and even abusive ideas, a simple ground rule may be indicated that ideas need to be respectful to children.

Guidelines for brainstorming include:

- Evaluation or criticism is ruled out until the discussion phase.
- Quantity of ideas counts, not quality.
- Members are encouraged to build on others' ideas.
- A single issue is the focus.
- All members' ideas are important.
- All ideas are recorded.
- A defined timeframe is set for the activity.

Rules [handwritten marginal note]

There are a number of brainstorming methods described below that have been taken from a variety of sources, as well as from the experience of the authors.

Freewheeling: In this most basic brainstroming activity, group members call out their ideas, and the parent educator or another group member records them on the board. It is important for everyone to have an opportunity to participate so that a number of ideas are encouraged in a short period of time.. Discussion or evaluation is not allowed at this stage but is facilitated after all ideas have been presented.

all inclusive [handwritten marginal note]

Carousel: Several sheets of paper are placed around the room with a different question on each that relates to a common issue. Participants are divided into small groups (two to five members) and each group moves from station to station, recording ideas on the paper with a different colored marker. The facilitator can call out the time or use music to start and stop the group work. When each group has been at all locations, members take a gallery walk to read all posted ideas. Discussion follows with the large group. Ideas written in different colors identify each group and encourage opportunities for explanations and clarifications during the discussion phase.

rotational [handwritten marginal note]

1-2-3: This brainstorming strategy works well when parent groups need to make a decision. For example, they may need to decide where to go on a fieldtrip, which speaker they want to invite or topic they want to explore, where the next meeting should be held, or how the group might allocate some funds that have been designated for their use. Group members are asked to write down one idea regarding a common issue. Participants pair off to share their ideas and agree on which one they feel is the best. Members then join into larger groups (three or more), bringing their chosen best idea and are again asked to discuss and choose that group's best idea. Finally, each group joins the entire group and decides on the best strategy. The discussion around the emerging ideas is important, and in the end, all ideas have been shared, with one chosen as the very best.

Building consensus [handwritten marginal note]

The discussion phase is the most important segment of any brainstorming activity. It is not enough to generate a multitude of ideas if there is no opportunity for group members to critique and respond to suggestions. After the ideas are recorded, there is a structured time allotted for group members to clarify, evaluate, and respond. If narrowing down or prioritizing the list is the goal, voting on the ideas can be done in a number of ways. One popular method is to give each member two or three stickers, and after all ideas are recorded, participants place stickers on their top three choices. Discussion follows. Voting in this example doesn't necessarily designate the "best" idea but allows group members to see what is most important to others in the group, and this can stimulate discussion.

Brainstorming activities are used for problem solving or for identifying a variety of possible solutions or ideas. These activities can energize a group by adding a physical component to the group that moves them beyond discussion (Eller, 2004). They can also help build rapport between members as they learn more about the opinions of others.

REFERRALS

Most parent educators find making referrals for further services challenging. Deciding if the issue is of great enough concern, anticipating the parent's response, and finding the right words require many skills. In this section, we will examine the issues involved in referrals, look at possible reactions from parents, and provide a process for parent-related, family related, and child-related referrals.

Parent education cannot meet every need of every family. There will be times when a parent educator must accept the limitations of their role and recognize that a parent and/or child may require services beyond what can be offered in this setting. Mental health counseling for a child or parent, special education or speech services, domestic abuse protection, and family or marriage counseling are examples of possible referrals.

When deciding whether to refer, parent educators must rely on the information they gather from parents in the group setting or from observations of children in programs that combine services for both children and adults. Parent educators need to be trained to identify both the developmental concerns of children and family and parenting dysfunctions. Typically, universalizing the concerns of parents is a supportive and affirming method of interaction. When the issue is beyond the realm of healthy functioning or development, however, it can be inappropriate to universalize and even detrimental to the parent and/or child. When parent educators use their solid knowledge of normal family interactions and typical child development to identify a concern outside the realm of their expertise, it is their responsibility to approach the parent to offer information about further services. <u>Referrals are not done within the group</u> setting but, rather, privately with the parent.

The following questions can help a parent educator make decisions about referrals:

Assessment for referrals (handwritten note in margin)

- Is this issue of enough concern and likely to be a problem?
- Do I have enough information? What else do I need to know?
- Do I know what services are available in my community?
- Do I feel confident in the ability, approach, and reputation of the service and/or individual to whom I am referring the parent?
- What is my relationship with this parent? Is there a level of trust present?
- Am I the best person to approach him or her regarding this issue?
- What might the parent's reaction be? How will I respond?
- Am I aware of my own feelings about this issue and able to keep them separate?
- How can I approach this parent privately, and what words will I use?
- How would I want to be treated if this were me?

Different types of referrals present the need for varying skills and considerations. Initially, some referrals may seem easier for a parent educator to make than others. For example, approaching a parent about concerns of domestic abuse and possible community interventions appears much more difficult than suggesting speech services for a child who has articulation problems. However, any referral can be difficult. Though a speech concern may seem uncomplicated, it can be traumatic for the parent to address. Being approached regarding any type of developmental concern or delay that shatters the parent's dream of his or her child can be challenging (Bowman, 1994).

For example, Carol, an elementary teacher, enjoyed watching her toddler grow and develop into a happy healthy preschooler. Carol had a vision of what this child would be like as an older child and adult, the success he would have in school, and the social and developmental milestones he would achieve. As her son reached the age of 3½ years, she noticed that other people often commented that his speech was difficult to understand. Carol, however, had no problem understanding him.

At his first preschool experience, both the early childhood teacher and the parent educator had concerns about his speech development. When the parent educator approached her and asked if she had any concerns about her son's speech, Carol immediately began crying. Intellectually, Carol knew that a delay in language development could most likely be helped by speech therapy. Emotionally, she felt devastated as the perfect image of her child was shattered. Bowman (1994) referred to this as "loss of dreams." Parents who are approached about a referral for what may seem like a nontraumatic issue may experience great anxiety and distress.

In this situation, it is important for a parent educator to be supportive in acknowledging the parent's feelings. At the same time, it is helpful to be positive and realistic about the likely outcome of the suggested services.

Depending on the issue of concern and the type of referral, there are a number of possible reactions from the parent. When parent educators approach a parent about a referral for his or her child, the parent may be relieved that someone has finally acknowledged the problem and opened the door for help. Or the parent may not be ready to consider the referral and become defensive or evasive. When referrals are made for parents to access counseling or address domestic violence issues, they may suddenly appear uncomfortable with the facilitator. It feels as if the relationship with the parent educator has now changed, and the parent has been exposed and identified as someone with a complex problem. The parent may feel embarrassed and withdraw from the group. He or she may respond in a defensive way and become resistant. Or, hopefully, the parent will listen and accept the suggestion of the parent educator.

If a parent becomes defensive or resistant to the concerns of the professional, the parent educator needs to stop the referral. Continuing creates a power struggle, which typically guarantees that the parent will not cooperate. It is difficult when a professional firmly believes there is a problem and a referral to another service is in the best interest of the child or parent, yet the parent is the only one who can make the decision to accept help. Statements like "It sounds like you don't feel there is a problem. I'm still concerned, but let's give it a little more time, and I'll check back with you" give the parent time to take in the information, reconsider, and perhaps be more receptive at a later time. When parents do not see a need for change or services, attempts by the parent educator to "assist" will not be productive and can, ultimately, damage the relationship between parent and professional (Dunst et al., 1988).

When approaching a parent for a referral, several strategies should be considered. As the educator considers whether a referral is warranted, he or she can involve a trusted colleague or supervisor, depending on the program procedures. This additional perspective is helpful in determining the next steps.

Approaching the parent in a face-to-face conversation is critical, rather than relying on a phone call or other communications. This allows the parent educator to observe nonverbal responses that provide clues as to how to proceed, in addition to offering an opportunity to express their support through facial nonverbals and gestures. There may be practical challenges with this approach, however. If the child is present, it will be necessary to have someone else care for the child, so he or she does not overhear this conversation.

Referrals are conducted individually to address parents' needs that may not be met in the group setting

The concern should be stated from the perspective of the parent educator. "I'm noticing that it is hard for me and the other children to understand Marie's speech. Have you had any concerns about this?" This approach is less threatening than language that states, "There is a problem with your child's speech." It also clearly conveys concern and asks for the parent's reaction. It is important for the parent educator to use positive attending skills and also read the nonverbal language of the parent at this time. Do they take a step back? Sigh in relief? Look confused? By assessing where the parent is at that moment, the parent educator can decide how to proceed.

It is also critical for parent educators to keep their own values and experiences out of the referral process. A professional who has a child with attentional difficulties and has had a positive experience with medications and medical interventions needs to keep that bias out of the referral. Each parent and child situation is unique, and parents need to make their own decisions. Though it is appropriate to use self-disclosure to assure the parent that you may have gone through a similar experience, it is not acceptable to try to influence others' decisions on the basis of your own situation. The values, beliefs, and experiences of the professional should not be used to sway parents in their decision making.

Finally, the referral and outcome should be carefully documented. This is important for future concerns. For example, if a parent refuses a referral, and the concern surfaces again later, it will be important to document that an attempt was made by the professional, what the concerns were at that point, and what recommendations, if any, were taken.

Box 8.2 How To Make A Referral

1. Determine if a referral is warranted.

2. Involve a colleague or supervisor.

3. Meet face to face with parent.

4. Share descriptive/objective observations.

5. Describe possible next steps.

6. Be supportive, listen, and reflect feelings.

7. Present yourself as working together with the parent.

8. Be aware of your own feelings and biases.

9. Document the referral and outcome.

10. Follow up with parent later.

Example of Referral for a Child's Concern: *Eduardo's son is 4 years old and is having difficulties in the preschool program. The parents of the children meet weekly and discuss parenting challenges and strategies with the parent educator. The early childhood teacher has noticed delays in development, both physical and cognitive, and is beginning to become concerned about this child. The parent educator has a good relationship with Eduardo, and there is a high level of trust between them. She approaches him after the group one day and states, "Eduardo, we are really enjoying having Matthew in our program. We're noticing a few areas where things seem to be somewhat difficult for him. When he runs, he often trips and falls. He also has trouble with many of the table activities, like putting the puzzles together and matching games. Have you noticed any of these things?"*

Eduardo responds by saying that he, too, had noticed his son seems slower than the other children and was beginning to wonder if there were problems. The parent educator says, "Would you be interested in having someone meet with you to see if there are any areas of concern? Many times there are things early intervention teachers can do for young children to help before they start school. We have teachers who can work with your son, if you think that would help."

Eduardo seems relieved that help is available and readily agrees to having someone contact him with more information. The parent educator affirms his decision to check out the referral and stays in touch by checking in from time to time on Matthew's progress.

Example of Referral for a Parent Concern: *Shelly is a young mother of two little girls. She has been attending parent education classes, and the facilitator has noticed bruises on her arms and face several times. Shelly has confided to the group that her relationship with the children's father is violent and that they often fight. She arrives at class one night with fresh bruises on her face. She keeps covering her face with her hand during the class and afterward stays late to help the parent educator clean up the room.*

The parent educator, approaches her and says, "Shelly, I'm concerned about you. I know that things have been difficult for you at home lately. Would you like to talk about what is happening?"

At first, Shelly seems embarrassed and makes excuses for the bruises. But as they begin to talk, she opens up and admits she is being abused. She indicates that the children are present during these outbursts but are never physically abused by their father.

The parent educator focuses on Shelly's wellbeing but also asks, "Are you worried about your children watching this happen? It can be pretty devastating for children to be present and watch one of their parents being hurt by the other."

Shelly and the parent educator continue the conversation, and Shelly admits she doesn't want to live this way any longer and is concerned about her daughters growing up in this environment.

"There are people in the community who can help you. Would you like some information about where you might go?"

Shelly agrees and makes the phone call to a women's shelter from the classroom. The parent educator assists her, as needed, and supports her in her decision.

These referrals demonstrate situations where services are needed beyond what traditional parent education has to offer. The relationship between educator and parent is strong, and the parents trust the educator and are responsive to suggestions.

Approaching a parent for a referral for either the child or the parent can be very challenging. Consideration must be given to whether a referral is warranted, what the most appropriate services are, how the parent may respond, and what the best way to bring up the concern is. Parent educators rely on their observation and listening skills as they assess developmental issues of the child, family functioning, or personal or marital issues that affect family life or parenting. Referrals are made when the parent educator believes that additional services beyond the scope of parent education are warranted, are available, and would benefit the parent and/or child. Parent educators can ask themselves, "How would I want to be treated in this situation?" to maintain a professional and supportive approach.

From our experience ... Referrals can be successful but sometimes are not. A parent educator must establish a trusting relationship with the parent before an attempt is made at a referral. Even with the best intentions on the part of the parent educator, a parent may respond in a defensive manner. He or she may feel threatened and offended that someone would suggest something may be "wrong" with the child and may even exit the program. Although this happens infrequently, parent educators cannot keep the possibility of losing a parent from conducting a necessary referral.

SUMMARY

In summary, a variety of leadership and facilitation skills are necessary for the parent educator to be successful. Skills that focus on presenting content and leading discussion are important competencies that help make group sessions productive. Additionally, parent educators need to utilize higher-level skills that are more reflective, deal with the affective aspects of group process, and focus on the interconnectedness of parents as they share in the group learning experience. It is by blending these two skill areas that parent educators are able to provide quality opportunities that allow parents to benefit from the parent education experience. Finally, parent educators integrate all of these skills when they approach parents to refer them on to further services. By utilizing these specific facilitation skills within the realm of a trusting relationship, parent educators can teach, support, and intervene with parents in ways that are positive and productive.

DISCUSSION QUESTIONS

1. Discuss with another person two specific facilitation skills you have developed or would like to develop. How have you, or will you, do this?

2. Choose a reason for a referral that you think might be easiest to conduct with a parent. What issues might make it more complicated than seem obvious?

3. Create three to four discussion questions for a session on child tantrums in 2-year-olds that help parents see their child's perspective and understand their own feelings.

CLASS ACTIVITIES

1. Choose a challenging parenting situation. Role-play the four-step problem solving process to assist the parent.

2. Role-play a referral situation where the parent is not receptive. How would you respond? What feelings can you identify for yourself and for the parent?

REFERENCES

Bowman, T. (1994, February). Loss of dreams: A special kind of grief. In Comean, J.K. (Ed.), *Family Information Services professional resource materials.* Minneapolis, MN: Family Information Services.

Brookfield, S.D., & Preskill, S. (2005). *Discussion as a way of teaching.* San Francisco, CA: Jossey-Bass.

Clarke, J.I. (1984). *Who, me lead a group?* Seattle, WA: Parenting Press.

Cormier, S., Nurius, P., & Osborn, C. (2013). *Interviewing and change strategies for helpers.* Belmont, CA: Brooks/Cole.

Cormier, W.H., & Cormier, S. (1998). *Interviewing strategies for helpers.* Monterey, CA: Brooks/Cole.

Dunst, C., Trivette, C., & Deal, A. (1988). *Enabling and empowering families.* Cambridge, MA: Brookline.

Egan, G. (1994). *Exercises in helping skills.* Pacific Grove, CA: Brooks/Cole.

Eller, J. (2004). *Effective Group Facilitation in Education.* Thousand Oaks, CA: Sage Publications.

Jacobs, E.E., Masson R.L., & Harvill, R.L.(2006*). Group counseling strategies and skills.* Pacific Grove, CA: Thomson Brooks/Cole.

Minnesota Department of Education (1995). *Level three skills and common mistakes: A training tape for parent and family educators* [Video]. Crystal, MN: Robbinsdale Early Childhood Family Education.

Parker, P.J. (2009). Professional Boundaries in Social Work: A Qualitative Study. London, UK: *WITNESS.*

Peterson, M.R. (1992). *At personal risk: Boundary violations in professional client relationships.* New York, NY: Norton.

9

MANAGING DIFFICULT MOMENTS IN PARENT GROUPS

Parents exhibit a variety of behaviors in groups that create challenges for group facilitators. Disruptive behaviors can impair group process, cause conflict between members, and make other parents feel resentful and dissatisfied with the group experience. The parent educator has an obligation to monitor the disruptive behaviors and respond to them, depending on the impact on the group. Group members quickly lose respect for parent educators who ignore their duty to address disruptive behaviors (Curran, 1989). As groups progress beyond the beginning stages of development (See Chapter 4), it is common for some challenging behaviors to occur. Groups that function beyond Level 2, as described in the levels of involvement model (Chapter 5), and in targeted and intervention/treatment programs, as described in the continuum model (Chapter 3), also tend to have more of these challenges. In these programs, parents feel comfortable discussing and sharing their views and experiences. Group topics typically cover more personal and intense issues that allow members to share feelings and emotions related to the parenting experience. It is expected, then, that within this atmosphere of sharing and discussion with parents with complex needs, group behaviors can escalate and become disruptive to the group process, causing challenges for the group leader.

This chapter will identify common challenging behaviors in groups, propose possible explanations of why they occur, and suggest helpful responses from the group leader. It is beneficial for facilitators to understand likely dynamics that often cause these behaviors. However, it is also important to note that each parent is unique and that the reasons behind behaviors are speculations based on analysis of typical human behavior. Although disruptive behaviors of group members may be directly related to lack of skills in the leader or deficits in the relationship between leader and parent, these behaviors are frequently ingrained in a parent's style of interactions in multiple settings.

There has been little examination of disruptive behaviors that occur in parent education settings. However, some attention has been given to the presence and challenge of those behaviors in other professional settings serving adults. Dobmeier and Moran (2008) describe a conceptual framework to understand disruptive behaviors in adult education settings. They cite three types of disruptive behaviors: inattention, acting out, and threatening/harmful/violent behavior. In the field of parent education, it would be rare to deal with the third type of behavior. However, as programs reach out to parents involved with more complex challenges, and particularly in intervention and treatment programs, dealing with issues of inattention and acting out are not uncommon.

From our perspective, four categories of disruptive behaviors that can occur in parent education groups include:

1. **Inattention and Distraction:** yawning, lack of eye contact, side conversations, dozing, texting, phone use, checking time, distraction with other things in the room

2. **Attention-Seeking:** constant joking, involved story telling, boasting, sharing unrelated information, sighing loudly, wild gesturing, sitting near/far from the leader

3. **Distruptions to Group Process:** interrupting, monopolizing, resistance, refusing to participate, engaging others in side conversations

4. **Aggression/Confrontation:** Inciting conflict, criticizing leader or group members, complaining, judging others' views, swearing, expressing strong emotions (anger), using a loud or disrespectful tone of voice

Each of these categories is presented in a progression of how disruptive the behaviors are to the group process and require differing levels of intervention and response by the parent educator. However, there is no "correct" response or right answers to any of the behaviors, since much depends on the makeup of the group, the relationship between the leader and the group members, the personal history and mental health of the disruptive parent, and the type of group.

Parent educators who observe disruptive behaviors in their groups must decide if and when to intervene. Responding to every behavior that is not deemed acceptable will cause other parents in a group to feel uncomfortable, unwilling to share, and fearful that they too will be "corrected." Waiting too long or not responding at all sends the message that this behavior is acceptable, or at the least, tolerable. The group leader has a responsibility to maintain group process that is productive, functional, and positive for all members. Deciding when and how to intervene is a very challenging group leadership task.

Confronting disruptive behaviors is not an easy choice. Most often, group leaders have a negative connotation of confrontation. Yet, it is helpful to reframe confrontation in a positive way. It demonstrates that we care enough about the the group and the parent to address the problem. When group leaders gently but firmly confront a disruptive behavior, they show respect for themselves and the group.

These questions may help a parent educator determine a response to a disruptive behavior:

- At what developmental stage is this group?
- What are the norms for this particular group?
- Does the behavior seem to be affecting other group members? What nonverbal or verbal responses do I see?
- What is my relationship with this particular parent?
- Is this something I need to respond to immediately?
- Can I intervene in the group or should I approach the parent individually?

In a continuum model of disruptive behaviors, Dobmeier and Moran (2008) attribute the source of most disruptive behaviors to:

- Mental disability (traumatic brain injury, learning disabilities, attention deficit hyperactivity disorder, etc.)
- Substance abuse
- Poorly developed social skills
- Lack of empathy
- Life stresses of managing multiple roles
- Social anxiety issues, perceived irrelevancy of activities, or learning environment

The next section of this chapter will provide examples of various disruptive behaviors found in parent education groups. Definitions will be provided, along with an examination of why they occur and suggestions for group leaders for dealing with each behavior.

MONOPOLIZING

What Is It?

A parent dominates the group with his or her issues, provides unnecessary comments on what is being said, shares personal experiences at length, and talks significantly more than others in the group. This parent moves from one issue to the next and gives little opportunity for others to step into the conversation. The monopolizer will often respond to what someone else has said, then quickly turn the focus to their own personal experiences or ideas.

Why Does It Occur?

A monopolizing group member may actually be very insecure and need to feel in control of the group situation. By monopolizing, this parent feels a sense of security in that he or she knows what is happening in the group. Allowing the facilitator to lead or other parents to participate makes the parent uncertain of what may happen next. A monopolizing parent may also have an unfulfilled need for attention and validation (Rothenberg, 1992) or may lack opportunities in his or her life for interactions with other adults. It is also possible that an overly talkative group member has a personality type that is more verbal and outgoing than that of others in the group.

Suggestions for Leaders

- Avoid or limit eye contact with a monopolizer.
- Increase your awareness of your own body language to be less open to that parent.
- Add more structure to the group session.
- Avoid open-ended questions for this person.
- Post an agenda, and refer to the progress of the session.
- Read nonverbal behaviors of others to invite their ideas.
- Use a structured suggestion circle if this parent gets stuck on a particular issue. Each member quickly contributes an idea, and then the group moves on without further discussion (See Chapter 8).
- Consider whether this parent may benefit from one-on-one support rather than, or in addition to, the group experience.

Helpful Comments

"Excuse me. I wonder if anyone else would like to comment on that."

"Could you finish that thought, and then, we'll move on?"

"What you are saying fits well with something we heard
earlier." (Ask another member to comment.)
"If you could put all those thoughts into just one sentence,
what would you say?"

INTERRUPTING

What Is It?
Interrupting is similar to monopolizing behavior, except that the parent repeatedly cuts off the leader or other parents during discussion.

Why Does It Occur?
An interrupter may be self-centered or have poor social skills. He or she may
also be an eager parent who is excited about participating and enjoys being an
active group member. Someone who repeatedly interrupts may have problems
following a discussion or challenges with staying attentive.

Suggestions for Leaders
Gently, but firmly, interrupt the parent and give the other parent permission to
continue to finish their thought. This can also be combined with a hand gesture
that indicates you are stopping the interrupter and refocusing the discussion on
the person who was speaking first. As with a monopolizer, referring to a posted
agenda can encourage an interrupter to recognize the desire of the group leader
to stay on track.

Helpful Comments
"Could you hold on to that thought for just a minute? I'm
not sure Tom was finished."
"I'm feeling like Mary still wants to hear more from the
group. Let's back up a minute."
"I'd like to get back to Elizabeth's comment. Elizabeth,
did you have anything else to add?"

ENGAGING IN SIDE CONVERSATIONS

What Is It?
Typically, side conversations involve two group members sitting near each other
who engage in a quiet exchange of conversation while the leader or others in the

group are talking. Their discussion may or may not be related to the topic. Side conversations are distracting to the leader and other members and undermine the cooperative spirit of a group.

Why Does It Occur?

Parents who engage in side conversations may not realize that their behavior is disrespectful to the rest of the group. Like other parents who exhibit disruptive behaviors, they may lack social skills. They may be bored or feel they are above the others in the group. By engaging in this type of interaction, parents separate themselves from the rest of the group, a course of action that often stems from a feeling of not belonging. Side conversations may also be a learned behavior from being a student in a traditional school setting earlier in their lives. Parents who are reluctant or uncomfortable sharing in the larger group may feel it is safer to share their experience quietly with someone near them. Groups where some members know each other well or have developed close relationships within the group are particularly prone to side conversations. Additionally, parents whose primary language is different than that spoken in the group may align themselves with each other in side conversations.

Suggestions for Leaders

- Address side conversations during the early stages of group development when ground rules are set.
- Consider activities at the beginning of a group that divide members (use the age or gender of child) into other seating arrangements.
- Use a pause of silence to get everyone's attention.
- Gently confront with an "I message"—that is, a statement from your own frame of reference.

Helpful Comments

"Excuse me, I'm having trouble hearing Michael."

"I'm feeling distracted. Can everyone hear what is being said?"

"It sounds like you have a good example. Would you be willing to share with all of us?"

"Let's try to stay focused on one person at a time."

"Let's wait until everyone is ready."

SILENCE OF MEMBERS

What Is It?

Silent members are either unable to participate verbally in a group, unwilling to participate, or uncomfortable about participating. A distinction is made between active quietness and passive quietness (Bowman, 1987). Actively quiet members follow the conversation and are nonverbally responsive. They attend with eye contact, facial expressions, and gestures that indicate that they are actively listening. Passively quiet members, on the other hand, show few clues as to their level of connection and appear preoccupied and disengaged.

Why Does It Occur?

Parents who are silent may have a temperament that makes them shy or naturally quiet. They may be participating by listening intently and learning in their own way. They may lack the social skills that enable adults to speak comfortably in group settings. Or, they may have low self-esteem and be fearful of saying something wrong or being judged. Silent group members may also have limited cognitive abilities and find it difficult to understand the discussion. By reading nonverbal behavior and getting to know parents well, facilitators may also surmise that parents are silent, because they are not comfortable in the group, are reluctant participants, or are being mandated to attend. Court-ordered parents may initially begin a group with a negative attitude and unwillingness to participate. Crossing arms, physically sitting back from the rest of the group, and using facial expressions that imply annoyance are strong cues that this parent does not want to participate and does not feel a sense of belonging. "Spouse-ordered" parents may also feel resentful for being made to attend parent education groups and can sabotage the group process (Curran, 1989). Other parents need more time to process information and formulate their thoughts into words. They may feel left behind in fast-paced groups where others share quickly. English language learners (ELL) with limited English skills may be silent as they struggle to comprehend what is being said. Other quiet members may have an idea to share but may wait to be asked. Finally, some group members may be distracted and consumed by other issues in their lives and unable to participate beyond being present. This may be a chronic condition or simply a stressful time when one withdraws from group participation.

Suggestions for Leaders

- Consider whether full participation is a realistic goal for all groups (Bowman, 1987).

- Ask parents to write down their thoughts, or give them a short time to consider their ideas before asking for responses.
- Watch for nonverbal behaviors of members who are quiet to determine why.
- Allow for small group or dyad work where a quiet member may feel more relaxed.
- Connect with silent members before and after the parent session to strengthen the relationship.
- Accept quiet learning as a style.
- Help group members get acquainted through activities that strengthen the bonds of the group.
- Model that differences of opinions are valued.
- Ask a quiet member to help you with simple tasks, such as preparing refreshments, listing items on a board, or setting up a display.

Helpful Comments

"There are a few of you we haven't heard from yet tonight. What would you like to add?"

"I know this is something Ben has dealt with successfully with his children. Would you be willing to tell us how you've handled this issue?"

"It looks like you have something to add about this. Would you care to comment?"

SILENCE OF THE GROUP

What Is It?

Another issue related to silence involves a group that is generally quiet and relies heavily on the parent educator. When a question is asked, no one responds. This type of group is especially challenging for a group leader who relies on active participation, especially in Level 3 and 4 groups.

Why Does It Occur?

Quiet groups may be tired groups. Parent groups that meet in the evenings, especially later in the week, may be made up of parents who have low energy. They may expect to sit back and absorb information, whereas the parent educator has planned an interactive session. Quiet groups might be unclear about the norms and expectations of this particular experience. Often, a pattern has been established where the parent educator does the majority of the talking in early sessions. Quiet groups may consist of people who have not had enough time to get to know each other and feel rushed with a premature expectation of self-disclosure or sharing of ideas. It is also possible that a particular group is made up of quiet personalities.

Suggestions for Leaders

- Plan for active participation early on in the group to set an expectation of meaningful involvement by the parents.
- Ask parents to jot down their reactions; then ask, "What did you write?"
- Use open-ended questions to encourage verbal responses, such as "Tell us how you deal with this."
- Include dyad or small group work.
- Allow for some open, free conversation before beginning the topic.
- Consider leaving the group alone for a few minutes before beginning as you tend to other tasks. This often encourages members to connect with each other.
- Avoid "yes/no" questions.
- Model respect and nonjudgmental attitudes when members share their ideas.
- Avoid talking every time a group member finishes speaking. This encourages member-to-member discussion.
- Allow for some silence; do not fill in the silence with your own voice.
- Use humor.
- Use energizing activities or icebreakers that get members talking and laughing early in the session.
- Offer refreshments at each session.

Helpful Comments

"There is a lot of thinking going on in here right now. Let's hear your thoughts."

"I'd like to hear what you think about this."

"Who has experienced this? Tell us about it."

"Who will share?" rather than "Does someone have a comment?"

RESISTANCE

What Is It?

Resistance is a defensive reaction a parent may exhibit to the group that indicates an unwillingness to fully participate. It may be reflected in nonverbal behavior that resists listening to or considering the leader's or other members' ideas. Resistance may also occur when parents refuse to accept assistance or try new strategies, even when asking for help. Although resistance may exist within a person as a learned means of coping, it is often something that occurs between people. Therefore, it is important for the parent educator to examine his or her relationship with the parent to determine if a power struggle exists and if nurturing the relationship might diffuse any tension.

Why Does It Occur?

Parents who are resistant may see themselves as holding onto a self-image that says, "There is nothing wrong with me!" By accepting an idea or buying into the concept of parent education and support, the parent may feel an admission of personal limitations and vulnerabilities. This view of the parent education experience originates from a deficit model. It is important, therefore, for the group leader to reframe the meaning and purpose of parent education as a positive and supportive experience. Group members are often resistant in order to avoid change. As systems theory states, individuals have a need to keep their lives in balance, and possible changes coming from the group experience threaten that equilibrium (Cormier & Cormier, 1998). Resistant parents may also feel resentful toward a spouse, friend, or relative who is pressuring them to attend parent education classes. Or they may have personality traits or learned behaviors that make them respond quickly to anything new in a negative way.

Suggestions for Leaders

- Nurture your relationship with this parent.
- Reframe ideas to which you feel they are resistant.
- Use storytelling and metaphors in your teaching.
- Use humor to build rapport and energize the relationship.
- Give more control and choices to this person.
- Acknowledge resistance to defuse it.
- Challenge "always/never" statements.
- Suggest small changes that offer less to resist.
- Use kinesthetic activities that divert attention from the resistance.
- Avoid personalizing the resistance; this only encourages a power struggle.
- Spend time talking about the purpose and meaning of the group to eliminate a deficit model impression.
- Allow adequate time to listen before moving to problem solving. Parents need to feel heard before they can abandon resistance and take the next steps.
- Find a way to affirm an idea that was shared by the resistant member.

Helpful Comments

"Let's look at this in another way."

"I can tell you just aren't buying this."

"We've talked about several different ideas tonight. Which one could you try?"

"If you tried this, what is the worst that could happen?"

"As the parent you get to decide what is best for your child."

CONFLICT

What Is It?

Conflict typically occurs in the storming stage of group development. It is a common component of most active, productive groups and is frequently seen as differences of opinions emerge among and/or between members and the parent educator. Family-of-origin issues seem to influence how adults handle conflict, a factor that is important for parent educators to consider. Each of us has a different threshold for conflict; some group leaders are comfortable with its presence, and others avoid it at all costs. Conflict in itself is not necessarily negative. In fact, it can energize a discussion and bring it to a deeper level of understanding. However, when it is accompanied by anger, judgmental comments, sarcasm, or other negative behaviors, it can be damaging to the group process.

Why Does It Occur?

Certain behaviors or comments of members tend to elicit negative feelings from others that may result in conflict (Corey, 2000). They include remaining aloof, observing the group experience rather than participating, talking too much, constantly questioning, giving abundant advice, dominating the group, using sarcasm, or demanding attention. When parents have differing opinions, they may feel attacked by others who disagree in a judgmental way.

Suggestions for Leaders

- Adhere to ground rules regarding respect.
- Agree to disagree.
- Promote an atmosphere where differences of opinions are accepted.
- Use group activities that allow members to know each other and build on similarities.
- Acknowledge differences in backgrounds, beliefs, values, and perspectives.
- Don't always align yourself with the values of the majority group.

- Keep conflict focused on issues, not people.
- Recognize your own issues with conflict.
- Emphasize the insights and important points from differing perspectives and invite parents to make their choices about what fits for their situation and values.

Helpful Comments

"Differences of opinions make our group interesting, and yet I want everyone to feel respected."
"That's one way to look at it. Others may not agree."
"It's my job to make sure all members are respected, so I need to remind everyone about our ground rules."

From our experience ... Addressing difficult behaviors in groups often concerns students preparing for a career in parent education. We cover this material in our classes in an attempt to prepare students to be ready to handle these challenging behaviors, yet we also stress that they don't occur all of the time. Undoubtedly, there will be difficult moments in parent education groups, and it is important to have skills and strategies to address them. However, we want students to know that, in most cases, these behaviors are not a routine occurrence.

BRINGING COUPLE RELATIONSHIP DIFFICULTIES INTO THE GROUP

What Is It?

One or both parents may attend a parent education group. Occasionally, when both parents attend the group together, they bring their own relationship issues to the group in a more intimate way. Though the focus is on parenting, a couple that is in need of therapeutic intervention may use the group as an opportunity to vent or explore issues that are beyond the scope of parent education.

Why Does It Occur?

Couples who may need therapy to address difficulties in their relationship may be avoiding their perceived stigma of seeking the help of a therapist. Though couple relationships are definitely affected by the parenting experience, a parenting group may seem like a safer place to start. The couple's intention may be to address challenging parenting issues with the hope that this will help their relationship with each other.

Couples who share personal challenges of their relationship within the context of a parent education group can make other participants uncomfortable and change the dynamics and process of the group. Though they might be unaware of the inappropriateness of their disclosures, others may choose not to continue attending, because the experience is not providing what they need.

Suggestions for Leaders

- Keep the focus on issues of parenting and family life.
- Gently challenge the parents to consider how their relationship issues are affecting their parenting.
- Clarify the purpose of this particular group—what it is and what it is not.
- Privately refer the couple to counseling or to another more intensive intervention.

Helpful Comments

"How does your relationship as partners affect your parenting?"

"While the relationship between the adults in a family is crucial to the children, we want to make sure our focus in the group stays on parenting issues."

"Some of the issues you are raising, while they are very important, are beyond what we can address in this group. If you are interested, I can give you some suggestions for other programs that might be of help to your family."

MAKING POLITICALLY CHARGED STATEMENTS

What Is It?

Parents make strong statements in a group that the leader and others would judge to be inappropriate. They may be sexist, racist, or political and may cause offense to others. For example, a mother in the group may make a derogatory comment about men and their inherent inability to care for children. Another parent may use an offensive slang term to refer to an ethnic or racial group. A negative comment may be made about a particular group of immigrant families in the community. Or, a parent may speak disparagingly about a particular candidate or political party close to an election.

Additionally, statements are sometimes made that touch areas of personal sensitivity of the leader. For example, a parent may make a negative and judgmental comment about the Lesbian, Gay, Bisexual, Transgender Community, and the facilitator may have a close relative who is gay. Though the leader has a responsibility to respond, he or she must also deal with personal, and often intense, feelings of anger, hurt, or being judged by the person speaking.

A judgmental statement about particular group members is a common source of conflict. A person who makes negative statements that disrespect the views or behaviors of others can cause great conflict in groups. Others in the group may challenge those judgmental comments, or they may internalize them, which creates an uncomfortable tension in the group atmosphere. The presence of these types of statements should send a signal to the parent educator that the atmosphere in the group has suddenly changed and that group members are carefully watching and waiting for a response.

Why Does It Occur?

Group members who make strong politically charged statements do so either intentionally or unintentionally. They may enjoy making outrageous statements to spark a response from others. Their social interaction style may be that they "say what they think" and relish the attention it brings. Their statements can also be made without the intention of offense. These parents may have been raised in a racist or homophobic environment, and they believe that making offensive comments reflects their value system. They may assume that everyone in this setting agrees with them, just as others in their social group appear to.

Suggestions for Leaders

- Separate yourself emotionally from the comments being made.
- Pay attention to the reactions of others in the group.
- Use a moment of silence to bring stability to the group and give other members a chance to respond.
- Remind the group of ground rules that support respect for everyone.
- Gently challenge the group members to consider what they want their children to learn about accepting others and how this thinking affects that goal.

- Make a statement that does not place judgment on the speaker but expresses the opposing personal values you have.
- Give a sense of immediacy to what is happening in the group right now.
- Provide an objective statement of research or fact that challenges this view.
- Depending on the relationship with the group and stage of development, use a comment of self-disclosure that expresses your own experience and challenges the other.

Helpful Comments

"How are others of you feeling right now?"

"I'm sensing that not everyone agrees."

"We've enjoyed an atmosphere in our group where we can agree to disagree. I have to say that my views are very different on this issue."

"Does anyone have other ideas or thoughts about this?"

"We've talked before about helping our children be accepting of others. I'm wondering how these statements would fit with that goal."

"My family is biracial, and what you are describing hasn't been my experience at all."

EXPRESSING INTENSE EMOTIONS

What Is It?

In any parent education group, intense emotions may surface. Parents may cry, become extremely angry, express great sorrow or regret, or display other feelings that change the emotional tone and level of the group.

Why Does It Occur?

A parent may begin to cry when the content triggers an emotional connection. For example, the topic of explaining and helping children cope with the death of a loved one is often a session when parent educators can expect someone to cry. This topic can easily elicit feelings from parents who are dealing with or have dealt with the death of someone close to them. Childhood memories also can result in emotional intensity for parents. An unsuspecting parent educator might ask parents to recall holiday traditions when they were growing up. For some parents these memories are painful, and it is not uncommon for someone in a group to respond strongly in recalling memories of his or her childhood.

Suggestions for Leaders

- Be prepared for the possibility of strong emotions, particularly with certain topics.
- Acknowledge the pain or sorrow being expressed.
- Focus on giving the parent your support.
- Read the body language of other group members to determine their level of comfort.
- Focus on the difficulty of remembering and sharing these feelings and less on the content of what is being shared.
- Refocus the parent on the present and how these experiences affect how he or she parents.
- Universalize the emotion without minimizing the experience.

Helpful Comments

"It must be very difficult for you to share some of these experiences."

"This sounds as if it has been a significant part of your growing up. How do you think it affects how you parent your own children?"

"These are difficult feelings that many parents struggle with."

BRINGING TECHNOLOGY DEVICES INTO THE GROUP SETTING

What Is It?

Parents may bring various technology devices with them into the parent education group and/or parent-child interaction setting. They might make calls, check messages, and text during class. Some parents may leave the room to answer or make a call, while others will do so in the presence of other group members and the parent educator in a session.

Why Does It Occur?

Technology plays a constant role in most adults' lives. Parents are connected to their phones and other devices wherever they go. They are often in constant contact with family members, friends, or coworkers, as they use various devices to communicate. While, in the past, it would be seen as socially inappropriate to use these types of communication devices in the presence of others, today's parents may not recognize this multi-tasking behavior as being disruptive.

Suggestions for Leaders

- Address your expectations and concerns about the distraction of devices when ground rules are set.
- Consider a "break time" when parents can check messages or make calls.
- Facilitate a discussion about how this environment can be a place free from distractions.
- Ask the group to observe the children's responses when parents are engaged with their technology devices.
- Consider whether your group could be a "phone-free zone."

Helpful Comments

"Let's enjoy this time together without the usual distractions in our lives. Would you be willing to turn off your phones while we're together?"

"How would you feel if we designated this as a "phone-free zone" so that you can really focus on the discussion (or on your time with your child)?"

"It looks like your child is telling you that he needs you right now."

From our experience ... As cell phones became a part of everyone's lives, we noticed a marked change in the atmosphere during parent-child groups. Parents were taking and making phone calls during groups, stepping out in the hallway, or speaking loudly in the classroom as others played with their children. Occasionally, a parent would clearly be conducting business during class time while their child played alone or clambered for their attention. Some parent educators addressed this concern during the formation of ground rules. Others posted signs on the entrance, indicating the group was a "phone-free zone." Parents were asked to either put their phones on vibrate if they were concerned about being reached for an emergency or to turn them off during class. All of these solutions were met with varying degrees of success. Most parents, however, did recognize that the quality of this experience could be enhanced without the distraction of their devices.

REFERRING A PARENT OUT OF A GROUP

Some parents who attend parent education groups may, because of their mental health issues, current life challenges, or styles of interaction, be contraindicated for continued participation. If a parent is suffering from a major mental illness that manifests itself in disruptive behavior in the group, it is in the best interest of that parent, the other participants, and the leader to find an alternative experience. A parent who is belligerent or confrontational to the leader and others in the group does not belong in this setting. In these cases, it is the responsibility of the parent educator to guide that parent toward getting his or her needs met in another way. A referral to a mental health center and a targeted parent group for those with mental health issues would be an appropriate option. A parent who disrupts the parent education group experience for others with aggressive and negative behaviors may need to be asked to leave the group. These are exceptional circumstances and occur infrequently, but if typical strategies to address difficult behaviors in parent education groups fail, the leader must take responsibility for the wellbeing of the entire group of participants.

The previous examples of addressing difficult moments in groups have focused primarily on disruptive behaviors of group members. The following sections will address varying dimensions of group membership that can cause difficult moments.

DEALING WITH EXTENDED FAMILY MEMBERS AND OTHERS IN GROUPS

Today family structures are often fairly complicated with multiple family members and significant others involved in parenting children. Therefore, it is common that extended "family" members are included in parent education programs. Having these adults attend and participate in parent education groups creates some challenges for the parent educator, but their involvement is the reality of modern family life. This section will examine who might participate, what dynamics they often bring, and helpful considerations for the parent educator.

Extended family members can include a variety of adults involved in a child's life. Grandparents, step-parents, live-in significant others, nannies or other caregivers, and separated or divorced parents might all attend groups, either with a primary parent or separately. It is important for the parent educator to verify with the parent who is enrolled whether others might be attending, connect with these individuals to develop rapport, and attempt to learn what their caregiving role is with the child.

Remarriage, separation or divorce, extended family parenting practices and roles, incarceration of parents, or other family dynamics all result in a growing number of children having multiple adults in their lives in a caregiving role. These adults either choose to participate in parent education programs or are sometimes mandated to attend sessions. Including a wider circle of adults in parent groups creates unique group dynamics.

Difficulties can arise when the relationships between these adults are strained, yet a need exists to function cooperatively in their shared parenting experience. Parents who are divorced or separated but parenting together may bring their own relationship issues to the group, requiring the parent educator to set firm boundaries around what is appropriate to share in this setting.

Another common scenario is when grandparents attend a parent group either in place of, or along with, the parent. While Chapter 10 addresses working with grandparents who are actively parenting their grandchildren, there is another group of grandparents who are not primary caregivers, but who might occasionally attend a group.

This type of intergenerational parent education can bring an interesting perspective and positive energy to groups. Grandparents who play active, but not primary, roles in their grandchildren's lives are often interested in current strategies and approaches for taking care of children. Their participation can be enlightening for other participants and generate lively discussions. At the same time, depending on their experience and level of sharing, some of the advice might seem out of date or unrelated to current issues faced by today's parents. The parent educator will need to determine the relevance of grandparents' contributions to the group, welcome their experience and perspectives, and yet respect and keep the focus on the changing world of today's parents.

Including extended family members in the parent group will continue to be a common occurance with varying family structures. Parent educators will need to pay close attention to the relationships between family members and maintain healthy boundaries within the group. In addition to the challenges that extended family members bring to the group experience, there are many positive aspects of more adults learning together for the benefit of their common child.

From our experience ... We have seen the positive outcomes from having extended family members attend parent education groups in our programs. In these families, parents and other family members are learning the same information and often talk about how they've tried new strategies together and discussed how they worked with their child. Elders in some cultural groups have a great influence on the younger generation of parents and are frequently involved in helping care for children on a daily basis. Some groups have shown an openness to new information and great respect for parent educators, who are viewed as valued teachers. Depending on the caregiving role of the extended family member and the relationship with the parent, including them in groups can have a positive effect on the family, as well as the group.

MANDATED REPORTING

All parent educators are mandated reporters, requiring them to report any suspected child abuse and/or neglect to the proper authorities. State laws vary on the procedures and requirements, and laws can change frequently, making it necessary for all mandated reporters to receive ongoing and updated traininig in this area. Most human service or law enforcement agencies who oversee child maltreatment reporting will offer training to mandated reporters.

It is important for parents who participate in group parent education to know that any staff involved in the program (early childhood educator, paraprofessionals, parent educator, and others) are all required by law to report if they suspect abuse or neglect. It is not their responsibility to investigate or substantiate if abuse or neglect has occurred. They are only required to report to the proper authorities, who will follow up with a determination. Having this information in a parent handbook provided to each parent can be referred to quickly at an orientation session, so parents understand the legal requirement of those working with children and families.

Most parent education groups will set up ground rules, as discussed in Chapter 4, that include a statement concerning confidentiality. While the group leader does not need to dwell on the subject, it is advisable that he or she clarify that this does not include mandated reporting.

These reports are typically done anonymously, and parents are not informed who has submitted the report. A relationship of trust between human service agencies and parent education programs is critical. Parent educators need to know that their names will not be shared with the parent as the source of the report. They need to understand both the legal reporting requirements and the process of determination that is used. Therefore, parent education programs should be in contact with reporting agencies to ensure staff are using current procedures and understand the reporting system in their community.

SUMMARY

As parent education becomes more commonplace in our society, it attracts participants from a variety of backgrounds. Not only do parents bring their values, beliefs, and parenting experiences to the group but also their insecurities, past relationships with authority figures, varying levels of social skills, and their own personal and mental health issues. Though parent educators must always examine the role they play in the expression of disruptive behaviors and their relationships with parents, they may also assume that frequently these behaviors stem from the parent's issues outside the group. Parent educators must be willing to evaluate their role but also acknowledge that they cannot be responsible for each individual's behavior choices. Though it is difficult not to take some behaviors personally, they are often not intended that way.

Disruptive behaviors in parent education groups can have devastating effects on the morale and success of the group. Application of family systems theory to parent groups suggests that the behaviors of one member can drastically affect everyone else in the group, as well. Members who are invested in the experience may bring conflict to the group as they confront the offending member, or they may decide to exit the group in search of another, more rewarding learning opportunity. By setting a positive tone in the beginning and developing ground rules that support functional roles for all members, one can prevent many disruptive behaviors (Braun et al., 1984). However, when these behaviors do occur and threaten the cohesiveness of the group, the role of the facilitator is to monitor and intervene in order to maintain an atmosphere of respect for individual members and the group as a whole. When a parent educator is able to successfully guide the group through a difficult moment, group members may develop a stronger sense of trust and greater connection with each other.

This enables the group and the facilitator to address other emotional issues with more confidence.

Finally, it can be helpful for a group leader to reframe difficult behaviors and dynamics as having some positive potential for greater insight. Smith, (2009) reframes disruptive behaviors of group members as a gift. It can tell us a great deal about the relationships in the group; the personality and temperament of individual members; how group leaders are being perceived; and how members are feeling about the content, topics, and general progress of the group experience.

DISCUSSION QUESTIONS

For each situation below, consider the following two questions:

1.   What questions do you need to ask yourself before responding?

2.   How might you address this behavior?

A. Marietta and Tina are recent immigrants and have enrolled in a family literacy program, which includes a parent education group component. Both of them have good English skills, but when they are in the group, they frequently visit quietly in their primary language. You notice that other members of the group are distracted by their conversations.

B. Carlos faithfully attends a parent group each week. He is pleasant and seems interested in the topics that are covered. During the group, he appears to be listening intently, but he never volunteers his opinion or verbally joins into the discussion. You have noticed that if the group is divided into dyads, Carlos participates and freely shares his experiences.

C. Elaina is a court-ordered parent in one of your groups. Currently, her children are placed in foster care, and she is required to attend parent education classes each week. Elaina attends, but her nonverbal behavior indicates that she is bored and annoyed with having to be in the group. She often argues and disagrees with the information that is being presented. Her favorite response is "That wouldn't work for me."

D. Marie is an enthusiastic and outgoing member of your parent group. She often comments on how important this group is to her and how much she enjoys coming each week. Marie likes to talk and is the first to volunteer her opinion or bring up a challenging parenting issue. You have noticed that, each week, she seems to dominate the class, leaving little time for other parents to discuss their issues.

CLASS ACTIVITY

Role play a parent education session about a topic of interest to you. Assign three group members a different "disruptive behavior" from those discussed in this chapter. The group leader will practice responding to each of these behaviors as they occur. Debrief afterward by considering these questions:

1. How did it feel to address the behaviors?

2. What was it like for those playing the role of "disrupter?"

3. What physiological feelings can you identify in yourself in the various roles?

REFERENCES

Bowman, T. (1987). Musings about group leadership: The quiet member. *FRC Report,* No. 2 (pp. 16).

Braun, L., Coplon, J., & Sonnenschien, P. (1984). *Helping parents in groups.* Boston, MA: Wheelock College, Center for Parenting Studies.

Corey, G. (2000). *Theory and practice of group counseling.* Pacific Grove, CA: Brooks/ Cole.

Cormier, W.H., & Cormier, S. (1998). *Interviewing strategies for helpers.* Pacific Grove, CA: Brooks/Cole.

Curran, D. (1989). *Working with parents.* Circle Pines, MN: American Guidance Service.

Dobmeier, R. & Moran, J. (2008). Dealing with disruptive behaviors of adult learners. *New Horizons in Adult Education and Human Development, 22*(2), Spring.

Rothenberg, A.. (1992). *Parentmaking educator training program.* Menlo Park, CA: Banster.

Smith, M.K. (2009), Facilitating learning and change in groups, *The encyclopedia of informal education.* Retrieved November 13, 2016, from www.infed.org/mobi/ facilitating-learning-and-change-in-groups-and-group-sessions/.

10

TARGETED GROUPS WITH COMMON CHALLENGES

Parents develop relationships with each other during discussion time

Many general parent education programs are offered for universal access to all interested parents and serve the primary purpose of promoting positive parenting practices that have a preventative function. The philosophy for these programs is that healthy families, as well as those with challenges, can benefit from participation and learn from each other and the parent educator. This model works well in many cases. However, for some parents who share particular characteristics and unique common challenges, a more focused parenting program is warranted (Stolz & Sizemore, 2017). These types of parent programs fit into the middle category (Targeted Programs) in the continuum introduced in Chapter 3.

They are designed to address unique issues and challenges more directly. This chapter will explore some of the specialized targeted parenting programs and describe specific goals, related topics, unique situations, and practice issues parent educators may face in leading these groups.

There are a number of different ways to organize groups: age of child, ability of child, family structure, family ethnic or cultural background, or parent characteristics (age, gender, ability, sexual orientation, income). The specific groups and programs selected for this chapter are among the most common targeted groups that are currently offered (National Academies of Sciences, Engineering, and Medicine, 2016; Stolz & Sizemore, 2017). There have been some programs designed for specific cultural groups, such as African American, Latino, and Native American parents (Cheng-Gorman & Balter, 1997). These have addressed unique issues that each group faces (e.g., racism, language differences) and reflect specific cultural values and practices related to parenting. The research on culture-specific groups has been limited and is not conclusive about the effectiveness of culturally specific programs (National Academies of Sciences, Engineering, and Medicine, 2016). Specific cultural-focused groups are not included in this review of targeted parent groups. This is an area where further development is needed around adaptations of evidence-based parenting programs and how to assess effectiveness (Baumann et al., 2015). The deeper issues around historical trauma should be considered with Native American and African American parents to understand how this is transmitted across generations for these two groups and how it relates to parenting beliefs and practices. The targeted groups that are addressed are:

- Immigrant and Refugee Parents
- Incarcerated Parents
- Mandated Parents
- Parents with Intellectual Disabilities
- Parents of Children with Disabilities
- Teen Parents
- Grandparents Raising their Grandchildren
- Couples

IMMIGRANT AND REFUGEE PARENTS

This group of parents with young children has grown over the last two decades so that currently one in four children ages 0–8 have parents who are immigrants or refugees (Park & McHugh, 2014). One of the most significant challenges this group faces is adapting to United States culture. Almost half of the parents (47%) have limited English Proficiency (LEP), and 45% have less than a high school diploma or equivalent. A large percentage of these families (42%) are also "low-income" (200% or less of poverty level in the United States equals $24,120 for one person and $49,200 for a family of four (United States Department of Human Services, 2017)). Parenting practices and parents' engagement in schools are two important factors that impact child school success. Effective programs for immigrant families are two-generation programs (Mosle & Patel, 2012) that include adult education and workforce development, English as a second language/English language learner (ESL/ELL) instruction for parents, parent education, and early childhood education. Even Start was a template for two-generation programs that focused on family literacy for parents and their young children ages 0–8. It included adult education, early childhood education, parent-child interaction time, and parent education (groups and home visits) (St. Pierre et al., 1995).

From our experience ... I worked as a local program evaluator for Even Start programs that served immigrant families in two different communities. I watched each program evolve in its understanding of families and designing programs to meet immigrant family needs. Parents worked in shifts in a meat processing plant and would attend the program with their children three times a week for 4 hours, often after working a full day or evening shift. They were dedicated to improving their own education and learning new ways to support early learning and literacy in their young children. Through the parenting education part of the program, I witnessed success in parents who learned to create routines in their homes, enjoy reading to their children, and engage with the school. I frequently heard a parent who had been in the program for 2–3 years say that they were more self-confident and reported that they now were able to help other immigrant families in the community find resources. This ripple effect of the program out into the community was a major positive, but unmeasured, program outcome.

Immigrant adult learners tend to be conscientious about their education and committed to succeed. They are also interested in helping their children succeed in school. In addition to the adult education component, programs are designed to include group parent education. A variety of challenges exist for the parent educator of immigrant ESL/ELL families. Language and cultural barriers present hurdles for even the most seasoned parent educator.

ESL/ELL parent groups in larger communities may consist of families with the same language and culture. For example, a community may have an influx of Hmong families who are interested in participating in classes. If Hmong educators are not available, interpreters can be utilized for group discussion. The parent educator in this group becomes immersed in the Hmong culture, learning from the students while teaching and supporting positive parenting skills that are consistent with their cultural values.

In smaller communities, ESL/ELL parent education groups may include a variety of different cultures and languages. Hispanic, Vietnamese, Somali, Russian, and other parents may participate in the same sessions. This presents unique challenges for parent educators. A greater focus lies on language acquisition and basic parent and family needs (housing, food, and jobs). Since there are many cultural differences in this type of group, a wide variety of parenting practices and values will exist. The parent educator must respect and learn as much as possible about each cultural perspective while sharing the relevant parenting information and philosophy of the program. In this setting, parent educators must be willing to learn as much from the participants as parents are learning from the group experience. A cross-cultural perspective will assist the leader in remaining nonjudgmental in viewing parenting as a cultural phenomenon (Bennett & Grimley, 2000). Since most of the research on children and parents has been dominated by studies within Western culture, it is important for group leaders to avoid interpreting results as universally applicable to all cultures. One of the primary challenges in working with parents of varying cultures is to help them learn new patterns of parenting that do not violate the principles of their culture (Bavolek, 1997). ESL/ELL parents also must learn about the culture of the school system to support their children, who face the challenges of learning another language and the new culture of American schools.

Because the focus of ESL/ELL groups is often on sharing information, the primary methods used by the parent educator may be related more to teaching and less to facilitating. Parent educators who work with ESL/ELL parents often include hands-on experiences and share practical content about parenting and family life. These methods, rather than facilitating discussions about the emotional challenges and varied strategies of parenting, are often more meaningful and relevant to the ESL/ELL parent. Though group discussions may occur on some level, language differences often limit the depth of sharing that occurs in groups where most participants and the facilitator share the same language and culture. The parent educator may find that the initial trade-off for limited depth in discussion is the provision of practical information on safety, school rules, and practice of learning English. As ESL/ELL parents become more proficient in English and parent educators learn more about cultural values and parenting practices, the depth of discussion may increase. The use of interpreters and the hiring of paraprofessionals and tutors from specific cultural groups can be effective strategies for improving communication with ESL/ELL families. A skilled interpreter can help to enrich and deepen the discussion as the parent educator learns to both watch the body language of the parent and listen to the words of the interpreter. Hiring a parent educator from the specific cultural group who speaks the language would be ideal, and this should be a long-term goal for programs.

The following list identifies some of the practical topics that are relevant to immigrant families. The generic parenting topics around development, communication, understanding emotions, and strategies for promoting early literacy are still important and should also be addressed. Parent educators need to take time to learn from parents about the beliefs and parenting practices in their families of origin and culture to better understand their backgrounds. Some of the most pressing practical issues that should be addressed are listed below.

- Securing medical services
- Preparing children for school
- Navigating the school system
- Ensuring home safety
- Procuring services for young children with special needs
- Learning laws related to child abuse and neglect
- Developing parenting practices around discipline
- Accessing community resources
- Ensuring proper health and nutrition

INCARCERATED PARENTS

There is a growing population of parents in state and federal prisons and local county jails that impact 5 million children in the United States (Murphey & Cooper, 2015). The percentage of inmates who are parents has been underestimated in past research and a recent study of Minnesota correctional facilities revealed that 66% of male inmates were fathers and 77% of female inmates were mothers (Schlafer, 2015). Parent education programs for both incarcerated mothers and fathers have been developed and demonstrate effectiveness in changing parenting attitudes and behaviors (Palm, 2003). Maintaining contact between the child and parent can lower the likelihood of recidivism and support a positive parent-child relationship (LaVigne, 2005). One of the advantages of delivering parent education to incarcerated parents is that the group members all live in the same facility, making access to programs easy. This section will describe the unique goals and topics for this group of parents, including specific issues and recommendations for working with groups in correctional facilities.

The primary goal for parent education of incarcerated parents is to assist parents in building and maintaining a positive parent-child relationship. Parents who are incarcerated may have had different levels and quality of relationships with their children, depending on the ages of the children and how much time they had spent living with their children. A recent study in Minnesota reported that 66% of mothers and 56% of fathers lived with their children prior to arrest (Schlafer, 2015). It is not unusual for a father who had been unemployed to function as the primary caretaker for his young children before being arrested. Other parents may have had very limited contact with their children. Therefore, parents in a parenting class will have had very different starting points to meet the goal of having a strong parent-child relationship. They may face different barriers in creating and maintaining a positive relationship with their children. Developing an understanding of children, their emotions and behavior, and supporting parenting communication skills is a starting place. Parents who are incarcerated care deeply about their children but may not know the best ways to show this and may never have experienced positive parenting practices growing up. Parents do not want their children to follow in their footsteps by going to prison and see their children as a strong motivating force for changing their own lives. Schlafer (2015) reported that 75% of incarcerated parents are interested in taking a parenting class.

In addition to some of the typical parenting topics, such as child development, individual differences, and discipline and behavior management, there are some unique topics or adaptations for this group. The list below identifies some of the important areas to explore with incarcerated parents.

- Understanding the impact of incarceration on children
- Communicating from a distance—e.g., phone, letters
- Respectful co-parenting relationships
- Repair of parent-child and family relationships
- Reconnecting with children and family
- Making the most of visits
- Understanding their role models for parenting from their family of origin
- Attitudes and practices around discipline

These topics can raise different perspectives and strong feelings, as occurs in any parent group. Topics such as the impact of incarceration on children may create feelings of guilt and shame. Discipline is another topic that takes extra time to explore the origins of parenting practices and the changing norms and laws around child protection. Parents have to see that they have options for guiding children's behavior and responding to misbehavior without being mean. Reconnecting with children and family in a careful and sensitive manner is a critical topic for parents who are anxious to be with their children after a long period of separation.

There are a number of challenges and related considerations for working with incarcerated parents that are outlined below.

- **Be aware that the parent-child bond is deep and fragile**. Help parents to see their children's thinking and feelings and their role as parents to be the adult, not the victim.
- **Recognize strengths in parents** by identifying things that individual parents are doing that are positive or insights that they have into their role as parents during class discussions.
- **Realize that parenthood is part of a search for meaning** and different life choices and is an opportunity for personal growth. Emphasize the importance of parents in their children's lives.
- **Understand that family structures are complex** and embedded in different cultures and community environments. Parents may have complex and difficult choices to make about how to reconnect with different family members.
- **Develop understanding and respect for the correctional facility guards** and issues of security. Their roles and responsibilities are different from those of the parent educator. Parent educators are in a privileged role and often see the best of inmates as individuals who are striving to be good parents under difficult circumstances.
- **Be sensitive to cultural values and beliefs.** A typical class may include members from different cultural backgrounds. This can lead to tensions around racial stereotypes. It is essential early in the class to talk openly about parents having different values based on culture and religion or spiritual beliefs and to respect the different choices people make as parents. It is also critical to ask questions about the consequences of some choices that may be harmful to children.
- **Consider the role of parent educator in the larger context** of other services. Find ways to collaborate with adult education, case management, substance abuse treatment, and other services.

One dimension of punishment for incarcerated parents is the separation from their children and the discounting of their role as parents. A parenting class becomes an important setting to be affirmed as a parent and encouraged to be a good parent, even behind bars. One father in a parent class stated, "Fatherhood has brought maturity, more value to life. Kids are before you. It has brought me away from things like drugs, and my number one priority is my family." This is an example of the transformative potential of parenthood and the role of parent education for incarcerated parents to help create a pathway for change.

MANDATED PARENTS

While the vast majority of parents who participate in education groups do so voluntarily, there are some instances where attendance is required. Possible reasons include those who are court ordered, residents of a group home or other supervised living facility, pregnant or parenting teens, incarcerated individuals, divorcing couples, or those involved in custody determinations. This section will focus on two of these groups: 1) divorcing parents and those with custody issues who are mandated to attend parent education classes and 2) parents who are court ordered to participate due to concerns with child abuse and neglect or other serious issues affecting their parenting.

PARENTS EXPERIENCING DIVORCE AND/OR CUSTODY ISSUES

A growing number of states require parent education for contested custody and parenting issues for divorcing couples (Hughes, 2011). Along with others in similar circumstances, these parents attend specialized programs designed to address their particular issues. These programs have been developed in order to address disruption of the family unit experiencing separation or divorce and are mandated by the courts. Usually offered either online or in-person, they typically cover topics such as:

- Community resources
- Overview of legal issues
- Developmental stages of childhood
- Impact of divorce or separation on children
- Co-parenting strategies
- Conflict resolution

- Visitation issues
- Emotional and financial parental responsibilities
- Positive communication

Some parents participating in mandated programs for families experiencing divorce may feel somewhat resistant. However, since the programs are typically time-limited, include others with similar issues, and focus on the wellbeing of their children, most view it as an expectation of the legal process that they must fulfill. Shelton (2006) describes a study of participants in a Vermont Family Court–mandated program for separating and divorcing parents, who were initially resentful of being required to attend. After completion of the program, more than half reported satisfaction with the experience and indicated that it had been beneficial.

PARENTS MANDATED BY THE COURT REGARDING CONCERNS OF COMPETENCY

In contrast to divorcing parents, a smaller number of parents are mandated to attend parent education due to child abuse or neglect or other concerns regarding their competency to positively parent their children. These parents may have a history of chemical abuse, mental health challenges, incarceration, or maltreatment of their children. In these situations, the courts can order the parent to attend parent education in order to maintain or regain custody of their children or to have formal visitation rights.

Since parents in these situations have more complex needs, it is challenging for parent educators to have them enroll in typical groups. Yet, this is often the case. Due to the complexities of these families' needs and the past experiences that have resulted in a court order, it is not uncommon for these parents to be resistant to the experience, particularly as they begin the program. While some mandated parents view the parent group as an opportunity to learn and grow in their parenting, others may continue to be hostile, angry, or determined to express their dissatisfaction within the group. This level of resistance provides a major challenge to the parent educator, particularly in a general group. In addition, mandated parents who are resistant to participating affect group cohesiveness and the quality of the experience for other parents.

Resistant group members may exhibit one of two types of disengagement (Brown, 2011). Mental disengagement is expressed by daydreaming, thinking about concerns outside of the group, or planning what to say or do. These are difficult for the parent educator to determine, since they are mostly internal processes. The other type of disengagement is referred to as emotional disengagement and is usually easier to observe, since it presents along with a number of verbal and nonverbal behaviors, such as avoiding eye contact, turning away from the leader, changing the topic, starting side conversations, asking rhetorical questions, or monopolizing. The purpose of both of these types of disengagement is to protect the person from uncomfortable feelings that may arise from being in the group setting where they feel a lack of power or control.

Working with resistant group members can challenge the most skilled and experienced group leader. Having a resistant parent who is mandated in a group affects the other members' positive expectations of this experience. Generally, the parent educator will need to work on developing a trusting relationship with mandated parents, in order to move them from resistance to positive participation in the group experience. Additional information on resistance is addressed in Chapter 9.

PARENTS WITH INTELLECTUAL DISABILITIES

Parent education programs serve parents with varying abilities and disabilities, both through individual and group experiences. Depending on the needs of the parent, it is important for programs to provide any necessary accommodations. For example, an interpreter may be needed for a parent who is deaf. Adapted written materials may be required for a parent who has a visual impairment. Parents with physical disabilities may need accessible equipment in order to successfully participate in a group. Although parent educators will encounter a variety of parent needs, this section will focus on parent education strategies for working with parents with intellectual disabilities.

Historically, there has been a conflict between the child welfare system and the disability culture, one focusing on the protection of children and the other advocating for disability rights (Getz, 2011). Until recently, research has focused on a pathological bias against parents with both intellectual and developmental disabilities (National Council on Disability, 2012). Over time, attitudes have changed regarding the ability of parents with intellectual disabilities to parent children. A more current attitude reflects a different approach where parents with cognitive challenges are believed to be able to raise their children successfully with ongoing support that includes parent education services.

Parents with cognitive challenges come to parent education programs in a variety of ways. A parent may enroll in a group made up of more typical parents who are higher functioning. Another parent might join a group specifically designed for those with intellectual disabilities. Or, they may self-enroll or be referred to an individual parent education experience through a home visiting program. Cognitive challenges can result from a variety of sources, including cognitive delays, traumatic brain injury, stroke, or other medical factors affecting cognition. Parent educators may or may not know the extent of a parent's cognitive difficulties before they begin attending.

Having one parent with intellectual disabilities in a group of more typical parents provides unique challenges for the parent educator. Giving this parent adequate attention can take time away from other group members, may require the parent educator to present information multiple times on different levels, and may not meet the needs of the parent with the disability. In these cases, participation in the group may not be the best fit for this person or it may need to be supplemented with home visits or individual consultations, which is recommended by The Arc (2011). However, another possibility, which the authors have experienced, is that the other parents in the group will show patience and support for this parent and their unique needs. (See Box 10.2)

Leading a group that is designed specifically for those with intellectual disabilities presents other challenges. Although leading an entire group of parents with cognitive disabilities takes careful consideration and planning, it may be somewhat easier than having one parent in a group who is intellectually disabled. Some success has been noted with using generic parenting education curricula adapted for parents with intellectual disabilities that result in high satisfaction, ongoing participation, and the development of parenting skills (Glazemakers & Deboutte, 2013).

Suggestions for professionals from the "Family and Disability Studies Initiative" (Parent Education and Training, 2016) include the following:

- Speak slowly
- Check frequently for comprehension
- Use concrete examples and language
- Present information in small steps
- Model and demonstrate suggested strategies
- Give feedback and positive affirmations
- Allow for practice
- Build on strengths
- Use short videos and visual illustrations

Working with parents with cognitive disabilities requires thoughtful planning and execution. Many of the skills and strategies for developing trust, caring, rapport, and empathy are the same as with any group. However, the practical teaching skills, noted above, are important for the parent educator to keep in mind.

PARENTS OF CHILDREN WITH DISABILITIES

Parent education groups also exist for those whose children have special needs. This can include physical disabilities, cognitive challenges, social/emotional issues, or developmental delays. These parents are welcome in any parent education program and often enroll with other families whose children have typical development. However, for some, a group that is designed specifically for parents who share their common challenges is preferable (Ellison, 1997).

Participating in a typical parent-child program can be a wonderful experience both for the family of the child with disabilities, as well as other children and parents who are exposed to children with diverse developmental or physical challenges. Some parents whose children are typically developing may even prefer this experience to help their own children learn to be accepting of differences. It can be a time for families to enjoy time together without the constant focus on their child's disability. However, for others, it can be a painful reminder of how different their parenting experience really is and may accentuate the developmental delays of their children.

Targeted groups for parents of children with special needs provide support from others who truly understand and can empathize. In these programs, parents learn from each other about what resources are available and how to access them. Long-term friendships and social connections are created and maintained long after the group ends. Typical topics in these groups include dealing with questions about your child's differences, guiding the behavior of a child with special needs, supporting the sibling relationship, accessing community resources, and advocating for your child. Parent educators may work collaboratively with special education teachers and others with expertise to inform parents about their child's school experience. Guest speakers including those from public health, early intervention, human services, the medical profession, legal services, and others who are often called upon to share information, answer questions, and offer support to these parents. Welcoming parents whose children have disabilities into any program is critical. Additionally, offering them the option of a targeted group is respectful of their unique needs.

> ***From our experience ...*** A group of parents whose children have disabilities met weekly with a parent educator. Several in the group had attended mainstream groups but requested a separate group be offered where they could bring up issues that pertained specifically to their families. A new couple joined the group with their child who had a developmental delay. What was unique about this family was that both parents also had cognitive disabilities. The other parents in the group welcomed them, supported them, and did whatever they could to help them participate fully in the parent group. One of the parents told the parent educator, "We want to treat them just as we want everyone to treat our child when he is an adult."

TEEN PARENTS

Leading teen parent groups can be very rewarding for a parent educator. Young parents tend to have a high level of energy and unique perspectives about themselves, their children, and their lives. This section will address the relationship between the parent educator and teen parents, look at common issues, and examine the role of the parent educator who works with this population. Additionally, the inclusion of teen and young fathers will be considered.

Teen parents typically need to have a targeted parent education group designed specifically for young parents. A teen parent who enrolls, or is enrolled by their parent or caseworker, in a typical parent education group with older parents will probably feel out of place and uncomfortable. It would not be uncommon for the young parent to attend once and not return to the group. On the other hand, a group comprised of others who are of similar age and circumstances would feel safer and be more likely to retain the interest and participation of the teenage parent.

The quality of the relationship between parent educator and teen parents is critical to the success of the parent education experience. Teen parents need to feel respected as parents, that their opinions matter, and that they have the ability to be good parents. Teen parents want the same level of respect that all parents want. Ideally, when a relationship is established of mutual trust and respect, young parents will rely on the parent educator to support and guide them in their developing new role. The nurturing of this relationship, however, takes time.

The matching of a younger parent educator with teens is less important than utilizing a parent educator with an open and accepting attitude. Teens are astute at recognizing when an adult is judgmental toward them. They need to feel listened to and affirmed for their strengths. While lack of maturity can affect their ability to provide optimal emotional and physical care for their children, virtually all parenting teens love their babies and want to be the best parent they can be. Parent educators can act in the role of mentor, supporter, guide, and advocate when working with this population. A parallel process is evident as the parent educator relates to the teens in a caring and nurturing manner and, at the same time, is modeling a way for them to relate to their own children.

Practical topics include child development, basic care for your child, realistic expectations, breast feeding/bottle feeding, nutrition, positive discipline, sleep issues, community resources, doctor visits, financial assistance, housing, and continuing education options.

There are also a number of more supportive topics that offer young parents an opportunity to explore deeper elements of parenting. Examples include:

- Adjusting to parenthood
- Intergenerational living
- The role of grandparents
- Healthy partner relationships
- Positive co-parenting
- Finding time for yourself
- Changing friendships
- Depression and mental health
- Family planning
- Nurturing your child
- Career goals and planning for the future

Collaboration with other professionals and services in the community is particularly important when working with teen parents. Given the complex needs of young parents, parent educators need to work in cooperation with other educators, public health nurses, mental health providers, domestic abuse prevention staff, early intervention teachers, and representatives from other community programs that can provide guidance and assistance.

Teen parenting programs often include group participation, referrals to online information and support, and face-to-face home visits. Groups provide peer and professional support and camaraderie for young parents; online access to resources dispenses immediate information; and face-to-face home visits reinforce what has been covered in the group, allowing individual issues to be addressed. Since many teen parents live with their own parents, it can be helpful, depending on the role and relationship, to include grandparents in parts of the programming. However, this would need to be determined on an individual basis.

While the focus on teen parent education is primarily related to young mothers, teenage fathers play an important role in their children's lives, as well. (Deslauriers et al., 2012; Devault et al., 2008). Each teen father, just as the teen mother, is a unique individual with varying attitudes, perspectives, and past experiences. Therefore, it is important to determine the best approach to providing parent education to young fathers. Would the teen father feel comfortable in the group setting? How many dads are in attendance? Would a home visit better meet his needs? Would a male parent educator connect better with teen fathers? What kind of topics and activities would appeal to young men? How would the presence of teen fathers affect young moms attending a group alone? The relationship between teen mothers and their partners is typically fragile, and complex issues are often brought into the group. Depending on the current level of involvement with the mother and child, teen dads may feel more comfortable in the home visiting setting or in a group designed specifically for young fathers. The parent educator will be able to work more successfully with teen dads when their unique needs, abilities, and parenting responsibilities are considered. Deslauriers et al. (2012) advise that programs for teen and young fathers need to:

- Use flexible scheduling
- Be informative, yet informal
- Include activities like sports or outdoor events
- Link young fathers to other services (e.g., legal, financial, mental health, and job services)
- Address concrete needs first
- Develop a relationship of trust before moving to more personal issues
- Incorporate humor into meetings

Jaffee et al. (2001) warn that parent education and support programs need to go beyond encouraging teenage fathers to be involved and to learn parenting skills. Programs need to understand young fathers' developmental histories and appreciate their unique challenges in becoming responsive and responsible parents as they design support services that include teenage fathers. When parent educators make genuine connections with teen dads and spend time getting to know them, learning about their goals and hearing their histories, deeper issues can be addressed. In addition to learning about the basic developmental needs of their children, young dads will then be ready to explore the relationship they want with their children, the important role they will play in their lives, and how to ensure healthy social emotional development for their children.

From our experience ... During the time I was leading a group for teen mothers, it was clear that there was a sense of status with some of the young moms who had maintained relationships with their babies' fathers. These young women talked openly about their relationships in positive ways. There was an attitude that their lives were better than the young moms who were parenting alone. The teens who were not connected to the fathers looked uncomfortable during these conversations and said little. Inviting the teen's partners to the group proved to be too difficult for a couple of the mothers who did not attend after the males joined the group. This is a dilemma for parent educators who want to reach out to the young men but don't want to alienate the young women who are parenting alone. Looking back, it may have been a better option to have some sessions where couples attended together that were separate from the regular group of young women.

GRANDPARENTS RAISING THEIR GRANDCHILDREN

According to the United States Census Bureau (Ellis & Simmons, 2014), 3% of households contain both grandparents and grandchildren, and more than 60% of these were maintained by a grandparent. That number indicates that 2.7 million grandparents were primary caregivers for their grandchildren under 18 who were living with them. About 10% of all children in the United States live with a grandparent. This report also cites data that grandparents who live with their grandchildren, when compared with non-resident grandparents, are younger, less educated, more likely to be widowed or divorced, and more likely to live in poverty. This data reflects a group of older individuals with complex needs who can benefit from the support of a grandparent education group experience. This section will examine the changing role of those grandparents who become primary caregivers for their grandchildren and consider how a grandparent education group could address their common issues.

Why do grandparents take on the parenting role with their grandchildren? There are a variety of reasons this occurs in our society, most related to keeping children out of the foster care system. This is often due to challenges with the children's parents such as:

- Incarceration
- Death
- Abandonment of children
- Mental illness or other long-term health problems
- Substance abuse
- Military deployment
- Lack of financial resources
- Youth or inexperience of parents
- Unstable home life/homelessness

causes

When any of these issues arise for a parent, the grandparent often assumes the primary caregiver role. Taking on this responsibility can present an unexpected and drastic change in the grandparent's life.

Groups for grandparents can provide much-needed support for the overwhelming feelings they may have after such a life-altering change. A group experience can link them to other grandparents in similar situations, provide developmental and behavioral information on children, and connect them to community and other resources. Typical topics covered in such groups include:

- Understanding a changing role
- Practicing self-care
- Updating parenting skills
- Maintaining a healthy relationship with children
- Supporting the parent-child relationship
- Working with the school and community
- Managing finances
- Addressing legal issues
- Finding community resources
- Balancing work and new family responsibilities

topics

There are a number of curricula designed for groups working with kinship caregiving situations. One example is "Second Time Around: Grandparents Raising Grandchildren: A Curriculum Guide for Group Leaders" (Dannison & Nieuwenbuis, 1994). The goals of this guide and others are to provide information and resources to grandparents, along with a forum of peer support for the exchange of ideas and information.

A parent educator who leads a group of caregiving grandparents can expect intense emotions to surface. While grandparents love their grandchildren and have chosen to assume the caregiving role, the responsibility at this stage in their lives can be daunting. Both practical information and emotional support are needed. It is advisable, therefore, for the parent educator to work collaboratively with other professionals in the community to address multiple needs. Guest speakers and/or co-facilitators can be utilized to bring pertinent information to the group. The role of the parent educator may move in the direction of assisting grandparents with making connections with the children's teachers and schools, connecting them to social service programs for financial assistance, or linking them to mental health professionals who can help with the adjustment to their new life. The parent educator will need to know what community services are available and how to conduct referrals for group members. Providing linkages to community resources is particularly important when working with grandparents who have the role of primary caregiver to their grandchildren.

> ***From our experience ...*** In addition to the unique circumstances of grandparents who are primary caregivers to their grandchildren, there are many other dynamics that make a grandparent group appealing. We have learned that some grandparents may be looking for general information on grandparenting, along with a review of basic child development and childcare procedures. Others may be grandparenting from a distance and need ideas and resources to maintain a positive relationship. Estranged grandparents may seek a support and educational group to share their feelings and difficulties with a severed relationship. All of these issues can be addressed in a general grandparenting group. However, due to their unique issues, a specialized group is warranted for those who are primary caregivers to their grandchildren.

PARENT EDUCATION FOR COUPLES

Parent education designed specifically for couples is an emerging area of practice and research (Pinquart & Teubert, 2010; Cowan et al., 2009). The focus is on parenting together as partners and is different from couples' relationship education that focuses primarily on the couple relationship. This focus is also different from divorce education that emphasizes parenting issues that arise from the family separation to two households. Cowan and Cowan (1995) are pioneers in this work that initially focused around parents during the transition to parenthood. Parent groups for couples blend typical parenting issues that couples encounter, as well as content on communication and working as a team. This parent education format provides a space for couples to address parenting beliefs and practices, differences and tensions that may arise between parenting partners, and communication skills related to conflict resolution and problem-solving. It would be ideal to have male and female co-facilitators lead this type of group for the purposes of modeling healthy interaction, as well as presenting gender-specific perspectives. This type of class can serve parents who live together and are parenting as partners.

Some of the unique topics that are found in parenting as partners programs are listed below. These reflect the blending of parenting and couple issues and related skills.

- Sharing household and child-rearing tasks
- Gender tensions around child-rearing values and discipline
- Understanding different perspectives of family stress
- Boundaries and relationships with extended family
- Involved fathering and gatekeeping
- Nurturing the couple connections
- Couple communication and problem-solving
- Identifying and getting support

These topics might emerge in a general parenting education class but are not the main focus, and they may be uncomfortable to address when only one parent of the couple is present. These are topic areas that are not relevant to parents who are raising their child alone. These programs are typically designed for heterosexual couples. While gender and gender socialization are important factors, many of these issues could be reframed and used with same-sex couples. Parent educators should be knowledgeable about family system dynamics, have the necessary skills, and be comfortable working with couples and the typical tensions that arise when discussing these topics. These groups can be very rewarding when they move couples towards greater understanding, empathy and the satisfaction of being an effective parenting team.

Pinquart and Teubert (2010) describe some key findings from their meta-analysis of couples' groups during the transition to parenthood. The factors that were most important in leading to improved couples' communication, psychological wellbeing, and parenting can be useful for improving practice. The dosage of the program was important, and more than six sessions was recommended. Since the focus in most programs is on the couple relationship, as well as parenting practices, it would take more time to address both of these areas and provide adequate time to practice new skills. It is also important to include a combination of couple and parenting-focused components. The meta-analysis presented evidence for using professionals to serve as program facilitators. Because this study focused on the transition to parenthood, the recommendation was to combine some prenatal and some postnatal sessions. Programs for couples who are parenting together are more complex to lead and might be an opportunity for a mental health professional (Marriage and Family Therapist) and a parent educator or Certified Family Life Educator to work together as a team.

SUMMARY

While it is not possible to address every special population, the above groups are commonly found as targeted parent groups that may benefit from addressing common issues. They are examples that parent educators are most likely to encounter in their work and reflect the wide diversity of parents and families who participate in programs. While each parent is an individual with their own unique needs and issues, there are commonalities within the groups that can best be addressed in targeted groups. Successful parent educators will approach each parent as a distinct individual and learn as much as possible about prevalent characteristics of special populations. There may also be parents who face persistent adversities related to poverty, mental health, or substance abuse issues that require more intense services coordinated by case managers (National Academies of Sciences, Engineering, and Medicine, 2016).

DISCUSSION QUESTIONS

1. How would you respond to a parent with intellectual disabilities in your group who is clearly struggling to understand the information?

2. Do you believe a parent educator should be informed that a parent is mandated before the first class? What are the advantages and disadvantages of knowing this information about a parent before the class begins?

3. Do you believe that matching a parent educator to the group of parents is important? For example, is it more desirable for a younger parent educator or one who has been a teen parent to lead a group of young parents? What advantages and possible challenges can you identify?

CLASS ACTIVITY

1. Divide into small groups, with each group choosing one of the following to address: incarcerated parents, mandated parents who have been abusive to their children, parents with intellectual disabilities, parents whose children have disabilities, immigrant parents, teen parents, or caregiving grandparents.

    a. Describe how you would develop rapport and a healthy relationship with this group of parents.
    b. What challenges might they bring to the parent education experience?
    c. What issues would be most important to address?
    d. What would you find most challenging in working with this group of parents?

Each group will summarize their answers to the rest of the class.

REFERENCES

Baumann, A.A., Powell, B.J., Kohl, P.L., Tabak, R.G., Penalba, V., Proctor, E.K., et al. (2015). Cultural adaptation and implementation of evidence-based parent-training: A systematic review and critique of guiding evidence. *Children and Youth Service Review, 53*, 113–120.

Bavelok, S. (1997). *Multicultural parenting*. Park City, UT: Family Development Resources.

Bennett, J., & Grimley L.K. (2001). Parenting in the global community: A cross-cultural international perspective. In M.J. Fine & W. Lee (Eds.), *Handbook of diversity in parent education* (pp. 97–132). San Diego, CA: Academic Press.

Brown, N. (2011). *Psychoeducational group process & practice (3rd Ed.)*. New York, NY: Routledge, Taylor and Francis Group.

Cheng Gorman, J. & Baltar, L. (1997). Culturally sensitive parent education: A critical review of quantitative research. *Review of Educational Research, 67*(3), 339–369.

Cowan, C.P., & Cowan, P.A. (1995). Interventions to ease the transition to parenthood: Why they are needed and what they can do. *Family Relations, 44*, 412–423.

Cowan, P.A., Cowan, C.P., Pruett, M.K., Pruett, K., & Wong, J.J. (2009). Promoting fathers' engagement with children: Preventive interventions for low-income families. *Journal of Marriage and Family, 71*, 663–679.

Dannison, L., & Nieuwenhuis, A. (1994). *Second Time Around—Grandparents raising Grandchildren: A curriculum guide for group leaders* (Curriculum). Kalamazoo, MI: Western Michigan University, College of Education.

Deslauriers, J.M., Devault, A., Groulx, A.P., & Sevigny, R. (2012). Rethinking Services for Young Fathers. *Fathering: A Journal of Theory, Research, and Practice about Men as Fathers, 10*(1), 66–90.

Devault, A., Milicent, M.P., Quellet, F., Fairin, I., Jauron, M., & Lacharite, C. (2008). Life Stories of Young Fathers in Context of Vulnerability. *Fathering: A Journal of Theory, Research, and Practice about Men as Fathers, 6*(3), 226–248.

Ellis, R.R., & Simmons, T. (2014). *Coresident Grandparents and Their Grandchildren: 2012.* Washington, DC: U.S. Census Bureau.

Ellison, J.R., (1997). Parent education: Models of inclusion. *Views, 22,* 14–15.

Getz, L. (2011). Parenting with Intellectual Disabilities-Changing Times. *Social Work Today, 11*(6), 14.

Glazemakers, I., & Deboutte, D. (2013). Modifying the Positive Parenting Program for parents with intellectual disabilities. *Journal of Intellectual Disability Research, 57*(7), 616–626.

Hughes, R. (2011). Do Mandated Divorce Education Programs Make a Difference [Web blog post]. Retrieved 2016 from http://www.huffingtonpost.com/robert-hughes/do-mandated-divorce-educa_b_900800.html.

Jaffee, S.R., Caspi, A., Moffitt, T.E., Taylor, A., & Dickson, N. (2001, September). Predicting early fatherhood and whether young fathers live with their children: Prospective findings and policy considerations. *Journal of Child Psychology & Psychiatry, 42*(6), 803–815.

La Vinge, N.G. (2005). Examining the effect of incarceration and in-prison contact on prisoner's family relationships. *Journal of Contemporary Criminal Justice, 21*(4).

Mosle, A., & Patel, N. (2012). *Two generations, one future: Moving parents and children beyond poverty together.* Retrieved from http://b.3cdn.net/ascend/f52f62b126af-c10fd6_2rnm60p51.pdf.

Murphey, D., & Cooper, P.M. (2015). *Parent behind bars: What happens to their children.* Retrieved from https://childtrends.org/wp-content/uploads/2015/10/2015-42ParentsBehindBars.pdf.

National Academies of Sciences, Engineering, and Medicine. (2016). *Parenting matters: Supporting parents of children 0–8.* Washington, DC: The National Academies Press. Doi: 10.17226/21868

National Council on Disabilities. (2012). *Rocking the Cradle: Ensuring the Rights of Parents with Disabilities and Their Children.* Retrieved from www.ncd.gov/publications/2012/Sept272012.

Palm, G.F., (2003). Parent Education for Incarcerated Parents: Understanding "What Works". In V. Gadsden (Ed.) *Heading Home: Offender Reintegration into the Family* (pp. 89–122). Lanham, MD: American Correctional Association.

Park, M., & McHugh, M. (2014). *Immigrant Parents and Early Childhood Programs: Addressing Barriers of Literacy, Culture, and Systems Knowledge.* Washington, DC: Migration Policy Institute.

Parent Education and Training. (2016). Retrieved November 1, 2016, from http://www.fdsa.ualberta.ca/AboutUs/SupportingParentswithIntellectualDisabilities/PracticePoints/Training.aspx.

Pinquart, M., & Teubert, D. (2010). A meta-analytic study of couple interventions during the transition to parenthood. *Family Relations, 59*, 221–231.

Schlafer, R. (2015). Parents in Minnesota's prisons and their children. Retrieved from http://www.rebeccashlafer.com/wp-content/uploads/2015/10/MNPrisonersMinorChildren.pdf.

Shelton, L.G. (2006). *Research Lessons from a Mandated Parent Education Program.* Unpublished manuscript. Burlington, VT: University of Vermont.

St. Pierre, R.G., Swartz, J.P., Gamse, B., Murray, S., Deck, D., & Nickel, P. (1995). *National evaluation of Even Start family literacy program: Final Report.* Cambridge, MA: Abt Associates.

Stolz, H.E., & Sizemore, K.M. (2017). Parenting Education. In S.F. Duncan & H.W. Goddard, (Eds.) *Family Life Education: Principles and Practices of Effective Outreach* (3rd Edition) (pp. 186–206). Los Angeles, CA: Sage

The Arc. (2011) *Parents with Intellectual Disabilities.* Retrieved January 12, 2017, from www.thearc.org/document.doc?id=3659.

United States Department of Health and Human Services (2017). Poverty guidelines. Retrieved from https://aspe.hhs.gov/poverty-guidelines.

Week 14

Ballard - Rural Families 17-49% of US population
  defined by: administrative
                land use patterns
                economic
  "rural" is 90% of US land but only 10-25% of population
      communities are diverse
                      aging population
                      limited economic base
                      poverty
                      mental + behavioral health issues
        pluses - safe
              community is close
              less stressful pace of life
              high grad levels for H.S. low teacher/st. ratio
              "learning to get along" community

      assistance often collaborative

      9 Stressors - financial, illness, inadequate social
       institutions, generational family pressures,
       occupational unpredictability, Mayberry Syndrome
       lack health insurance, medical support systems
       occupational hazzards
Barriers to PE-
          PE - outsider
              Too small a town - no privacy
          lack of child care
          cultural bias
   increasingly aging + military populations, immigrants

11

UNDERSTANDING PARENTS WITH MULTIPLE CHALLENGES:
Intervention Skills and Strategies

Parent education programs frequently reach out to diverse populations that include parents with multiple challenges by forming collaborative relationships with other family support agencies. Chapter 3 provides a continuum model identifying the different levels of parent needs and examples of programs that serve them. Either in partnerships or in programs that serve targeted populations, parent educators find themselves working with parents who have more complex issues. Trained to facilitate general parent groups, parent education professionals are often challenged by the intense emotional issues and needs that these families face. This chapter will explore the family issues and challenges of high-need parents and how those influence the group experience. It will also present strategies for brief interventions within these groups and specific skills that parent educators can use to address parent needs. The chapter concludes with a section on the benefits and challenges of collaboration. The recommendation for more integrated services, including parent education could lead to an increase in parent educators working with other healthcare and social service providers to meet the needs of families with multiple challenges (National Academies of Sciences, Engineering, and Medicine, 2016).

UNDERSTANDING FAMILIES WITH MULTIPLE CHALLENGES

Participants in parent education groups, particularly those in settings designed for families with higher needs and multiple stresses, tend to share a variety of familial experiences that can have negative effects on a group. Chapter 7 describes Adverse Childhood Experiences that affect adults throughout their lives. All parents face the challenge of looking back on their family of origin and its impact on their current relationships and parenting behaviors. However, parents with a history of adverse childhood experiences bring patterns of family interactions to the group, resulting in challenges for the group leader.

First, the parent educator encounters parents' attitudes and behaviors that may have a negative impact on the group process. Understanding the origin of these attitudes and behaviors provides insight and enables the facilitator to manage and when necessary and appropriate, address them. Second, parent educators need to have a broad understanding of healthy family functioning in different family contexts (family structure, culture, socioeconomic status) in order to identify generational patterns that may interfere with healthy parent-child relationships and impair family relations. Ethnicity and culture greatly influence family dynamics, behavior patterns, values, and perspectives (Goldenberg & Goldenberg, 2000). It is important, therefore, for group facilitators to consider the possible impact of these factors on family functioning, rather than to prematurely interpret them as problematic. In addition, understanding trauma and the impact on children and parents helps to focus on what has happened to individuals, not what is wrong with them. A trauma-informed approach is necessay for parent educators to consider when working with families facing multiple challenges.

Box 11.1

Trauma-Informed Approach in Parent Education
According to SAMHSA (2017) a trauma-informed approach is a program, organization, or system that:

- Realizes the widespread impact of trauma and understands potential paths for recovery;

- Recognizes the signs and symptoms of trauma in parents, children, families, staff, and others in the system;
- Responds by integrating knowledge about trauma into policies, procedures, and practices; and
- Seeks to actively resist re-traumatization.

Parent education programs are, by their nature, two-generation programs and have to pay attention to both children and parents and to the developing parent-child relationship. Parent education with parents of children ages 0–8 focuses on a critical time for both prevention and early intervention related to trauma (National Academies of Sciences, Engineering, and Medicine, 2016). The roles of parent educators in implementing a trauma-informed approach include:

- Understanding the role of trauma in the parents and children that they are serving.
- Recognizing the signs of trauma in young children and their parents and making referrals to appropriate professionals, infant mental health specialists, and individual services for parents as necessary.
- Working collaboratively with other professionals to provide parent education services using evidence-based programs.
- Recognizing the boundaries of their skills and seeking additional training when necessary.
- Using mental health professionals for reflective consultation when working with parents and children experiencing trauma.

A resource for working with families of infants and toddlers experiencing trauma comes from Harden (2015), who defines trauma for very young children as "witnessing or experiencing an event that poses a real or perceived threat." This is a time of vulnerability for infants and toddlers exposed to trauma and also an opportunity for early intervention work with both parent and child.

HISTORICAL TRAUMA AND PARENT EDUCATION

Cultural experiences, values, and parenting practices add another context for understanding family patterns that may influence parent group dynamics. The concept of historical trauma (University of Minnesota Extension, 2014) adds another layer to understanding families with multiple challenges. Families may enter into parent education services with complex trauma histories related to colonization, slavery, wars, and genocide. It is important to be aware of the larger social and historical trauma context to understand how this may impact parenting practices. This source of trauma is often in addition to trauma related to generational poverty and accompanied by other adverse childhood experiences, such as substance abuse and mental health issues of parents.

Chapter 7 addresses some of the sources of challenging behaviors of group members. This section will examine, in more detail, the recurrent patterns of behavior, attitudes, and values typical of parents with multiple challenges in order to provide insight and strategies for understanding and addressing these patterns within the group context. The focus, therefore, will remain primarily on how these common issues affect group dynamics.

COMMON CHARACTERISTICS

Parents with multiple stressors and challenges have diverse early experiences that impact behaviors that can disrupt group dynamics. Parents who attend parent education groups for parents with complex challenges tend to share commonalities in their backgrounds and experiences. For example, parents in family literacy programs who have low levels of education and are working on high school diplomas tend to have higher rates of teen pregnancies, low income levels, stresses of single-parent family structures, and struggles with family violence and chemical abuse (St. Pierre et al., 1995). Parents in programs serving low-income families with multiple challenges share experiences and characteristics that reflect generational family behavior patterns. Exposure to chemical dependency, family violence, mental health issues, poverty, homelessness, child abuse, and neglect are all experiences common in their families of origin. The effects of these experiences resurface in adulthood. A family system that exhibits negative behaviors and fosters unhealthy parent-child relationships has been described as a multicar pileup on the freeway, causing damage generation after generation. It results from accumulated feelings, rules, interactions, and beliefs that have been passed along for generations (Forward, 1989). The information included in this section is presented as common behavior patterns, but is not intended to stereotype all families with multiple challenges.

Families of different cultures approach and define stress in different ways. For example, the state separating children from Native American parents for foster care or adoption has a different meaning, because of the historical trauma related to Native children being sent to boarding schools. However, according to Olson and DeFrain (2000), certain characteristics of stress and family responses are common across cultural groups:

- Families from all cultural groups experience stress.
- All stressors either begin or end up in the family.
- All families must find resources, either internal or external, to help them cope with stress.
- All families have some internal strengths for managing stress in their family system.
- Families tend to use internal resources before seeking external resources.

Adults who grew up under adverse conditions share many characteristics that affect the way they participate in group education experiences and the way they parent their children (Kristensen, 1991). According to Kristensen, there are a number of common issues that affect these parents. They can be clustered into the following four categories:

1. **Protecting an image of themselves and their family**
   - Distorted view of what is normal
   - Denial of family problems
   - Difficulties learning to trust and share struggles
2. **Boundary issues**
   - Unclear family boundaries
   - Difficulties setting limits on their own and their children's behavior
   - Resistance to seeking help
3. **Interactions and relationships**
   - Right or wrong thinking
   - Avoidance of confrontation
   - First reaction to blame others/avoid responsibility
   - Crisis orientation
4. **Parenting behaviors**
   - Over- or under-parenting
   - Unreasonable expectations of children
   - Hyper-vigilant parenting

EFFECTS OF CHALLENGING FAMILY PATTERNS ON PARTICIPATION IN GROUPS

Because parents may have learned adaptive patterns of behaviors that protected them in their family of origin (which may include adverse childhood experiences), it is helpful for the parent educator to be sensitive to possible trauma responses and know how to respond to the individual and to protect the group. In a group process approach, the group is a system, much like a family. It is natural, therefore, for group members to replicate some of the adaptive behaviors related to early family experiences. It is within the family context that they were socialized how to behave as part of a group.

Though the parenting issues noted by Kristensen, (1991) for adults with multiple challenges can affect group process, there are some that are most likely to disrupt healthy group dynamics and challenge the facilitator. Issues of control, isolation, fear of conflict, right or wrong thinking, boundary problems, protecting the self with lies and denial, and being crisis-oriented are of primary concern to the parent educator in the group context. Recognizing these behaviors is not just about managing disruptive behaviors but having a deeper understanding of parents to be able to guide the development of trust and positive interactions within the group. Table 11.1 provides a description of using a different lens (trauma) to understand parents (Ellison, 2016).

Table 11.1 Using a Different Lens

DEFICIT LENS: WHAT IS WRONG WITH THIS PARENT?	TRAUMA LENS: WHAT HAPPENED TO THIS PARENT?
How can I make this parent understand?	Recognize that behavior may be from a trauma history.
Why is this parent angry with me?	Trauma can make people misread emotions.
Why did this parent suddenly lose it with me?	Consider the possibility of trauma triggers.
How do I convince this parent to . . .	Remember, the parent used to be the child.

Adapted from Ellison, 2016

CONTROL ISSUES

Parents who struggle with control issues can require careful attention from the parent educator. Often without a conscious awareness, they become anxious in the group and want to know exactly what will happen next. These parents often grew up in homes where adults were unreliable; they learned that if they surrendered control, they were not safe. In their adult lives, if they show vulnerability, others will see them in a negative light. Control provides a buffer of safety in the group setting. A parent who needs to feel in control may monopolize, insisting on addressing personal issues, even if it is not what other members want. He or she may be resistant to the educator's suggestions or may use passive methods of control, like emotionally withdrawing from the group. These behaviors provide a shield of protection against being exposed. Parent educators can help parents with control issues learn to let go of having to be in control at all times. Modeling spontaneity as a positive approach to relationship building may help parents take small steps toward eliminating their need for control. Parent educators can also wean controlling members by offering choices that still allow parents some sense of control, rather than expecting immediate change. For example, a parent may be given a task in the group, such as choosing refreshments, deciding on the topic, or acting as a small group leader. Additionally, it is helpful for the parent educator to let parents know what will happen next by posting agendas and sharing topic lists. If parents with control issues feel safe, because they know what to expect, their negative group behaviors may decrease.

ISOLATION

Not being able to ask for help and feeling alone are other issues that can affect the group dynamics. Children who grow up in families with multiple challenges often become adults who have learned that asking for help indicates weakness. They may have been shamed by their families if they admitted feeling vulnerable or needing help from others. They struggle with trusting others, especially professionals who can seem threatening and may expose them. These parents often have difficulty opening up in discussion and have learned that sharing vulnerabilities is not safe. They may struggle with issues of intimacy (Blume, 1989) and can bring that fear into the group setting. Parent educators can focus on issues of trust with these parents. Helping them feel safe, modeling appropriate self-disclosure of shortcomings, helping them connect with other parents through small group work, and teaching the value of interdependence may help these parents see value in both giving and receiving support from others in the group.

FEAR OF CONFLICT

One of the primary goals of the parent educator is to engage parents not only cognitively, but also emotionally. Adults learn best when they participate on a feelings level. Parents with multiple challenges may have come from families where no one was allowed to express negative feelings (fear, anger, disappointment). As a coping mechanism, they have learned to deny and avoid anything that brings up strong negative emotions. These parents become uncomfortable when strong feelings come up in the group. Some have learned to deny the existence of feelings, others have learned that feelings like fear and anger lead to loss of self-control and can result in violence and abuse.

It is not surprising that, in the group context, these parents feel extremely anxious when conflict or difference of opinion occurs. Yet disagreement and conflict over different parenting views is part of healthy parent group development. Parent educators should welcome divergent thinking and, at the same time, guide respectful discussion around differences as part of the group process. Teaching the difference between expressing anger in appropriate ways versus loss of control leading to rage and violence offers a new perspective to these parents.. Modeling that disagreement is healthy and even interesting in the group setting may allow them a new way of learning that includes a new depth of experiencing feelings in a safe environment. From this experience, parents can learn to survive and grow from an exposure to conflict without fear of violence or damaging relationships.

RIGHT OR WRONG THINKING

Another common issue of parents with challenges that affects group dynamics is right or wrong thinking or believing there is only one right answer. Their experience may have taught them that people are either all good or all bad, that an idea is either good or bad, and that there is only one right way to handle a situation. As a professional, the parent educator may feel accepted by this parent one day and an enemy the next. This can be particularly confusing for group facilitators, who feel as if they never know what to expect. These parents also have a need to find "the answer" and seem frustrated with choices and alternatives that parent educators present. In their families of origin, parents made decisions for them, and they had little practice considering options. Facilitators can help parents see that there can be more ways than one to address parenting issues, depending upon the situation and the family values they want to teach. As parents, they get to make the choices for their children and their families, and being open to options gives them more choices.

BOUNDARY PROBLEMS

Boundary problems occur more frequently for parents with multiple challenges. These parents either have few boundaries or many barriers in their interactions with others. They can have difficulties showing empathy or compassion for other parents in the group. These behaviors, when applied to their children, can be linked to abusive parenting behavior. These parents are often unable to empathize with others, seem to have no understanding of other parents, and typically blame others for their problems. Parent educators can teach about the need for clear boundaries, in addition to modeling empathy within appropriate boundaries in the context of the group. Protecting members from too much self-disclosure and limiting personal sharing within a balanced approach will help parents learn acceptable social boundaries.

PROTECTING SELF WITH LIES AND DENIAL

Parents in families with multiple challenges may also use lies and denial to protect themselves. This becomes problematic in the parent group, because it erodes the atmosphere of trust that is crucial to a healthy adult learning environment. These parents use pretense to present themselves. They pretend that everything is fine. They say and do the right thing in front of others, but in fact, their lives are often unhappy. Shame has been a major emotion in their families of origin, and the family rule has been that lies are the only way to protect family secrets. Parent educators and other group members may not recognize this behavior immediately. These parents have spent a lifetime presenting themselves in a deceitful manner. However, given time, the facilitator and the other parents begin to realize that something doesn't add up. Other group members may begin to challenge the inconsistencies, and as a result, there is often conflict ending with the parent in question withdrawing from the group. It is important for the parent educator to realize the stress under which these parents operate and the enormous need for self-protection. Gentle and private confrontation may be necessary in some circumstances. Modeling honesty and affirming members who share their problems can expose this parent to another way of being.

CRISIS ORIENTATION

A parent whose life revolves around the latest crisis can be problematic for the entire group. Someone who comes from a family where one crisis quickly follows another learns to thrive on the energy and chaos of crises. Attention from others, the separation from other aspects of life, and the distraction from what is really important can all provide a way of living that revolves around a continuing list of challenges. Within the group, this parent may quickly emerge as someone in need of constant attention and assistance. The parent educator often moves quickly to involve the group in offering suggestions for this very overwhelmed parent. Initially, other members show true concern and are willing to forgo their own issues to help. However, very quickly, everyone realizes there is no resolution that will really make a difference. This parent moves from one crisis to the next and is in constant need of support and guidance, which often goes unheeded. In this situation, the parent educator will need to balance the needs of the entire group with the needs of one parent. On a one-to-one basis, it may be advisable to help the parent identify the pattern that has been established. Furthermore, constant crises are indicative of a need for a referral to other services within the community. These parents may be in need of basic resources, such as housing, food, or transportation, or there may be more complex family or personal issues that need to be addressed.

In summary, it is helpful for parent educators to understand how the past experiences, attitudes, and behaviors of parents can affect the group experience. Though insight into the origin and purpose of each behavior can give greater understanding, it is also important to assess what responsibility the parent educator has in addressing negative behavior patterns of parents with challenges. Many of the behaviors described in this chapter can be better and more comprehensively addressed through therapy with a mental health professional. However, parents may choose not to utilize individual or family therapy and yet continue to participate in group parent education. It is not the role of the parent educator to address personality issues of parent participants in a group. Nor is it appropriate to delve deeply into painful family-of-origin issues. This role is reserved for the therapist. However, understanding the probable origins of certain behaviors that affect group process can provide helpful insight for the group leader. At times, disruptive behaviors can have very little to do with the parent educator's skills in group facilitation and more to do with the experiences and patterns of behavior that a parent brings from his or her past.

Parents with multiple challenges are like all parents in that they struggle with the day-to-day issues of raising children. They often bring adverse experiences from their childhood and adaptive behaviors that can affect their full participation in group learning. Understanding these complex behaviors and their origins can assist parent educators in working with the most challenging parents in groups and offer these parents the emotional support and the experience of learning new patterns of behavior that group parent education can provide.

INTERVENTION SKILLS

Leading parent groups for families with multiple challenges typically requires advanced skills associated with Level 4 brief focused intervention (Doherty, 1995). (See Chapter 5.) Within these groups, there is usually a heightened intensity of emotions, issues are more serious, and there is a need for intervention. Child abuse or neglect, chemical dependency, incarceration of family members, grief and loss, lack of adequate food or housing, and concerns about developmental delays of children are typical issues that arise in these groups. Although these parents still deal with universal parenting issues, each challenge can be made more complex and magnified by the lack of understanding, and frequent lack of empathy, demonstrated by the parents for their children. Often, these parents did not receive the positive parenting they needed as children and may be unable to meet the emotional and physical needs of their own children. It is as if they are "parenting in the dark" (Kristensen, 1990). Although many of these parents have the potential and desire to make positive changes, without the experience of being nurtured, it is very difficult for them to provide what is needed for their own children. Therefore, the job of the parent educator is more complex than in other group settings. Additional challenges arise when unhealthy generational parenting patterns, lack of self-esteem and confidence, unrealistic expectations, and unmet personal needs are brought to the group setting.

The skills necessary to work with higher-need families are more complex and involved. Utilizing opportunities for consultation and support, parent educators must move beyond teaching, demonstrating, and leading group discussion to be successful with this population. In the Level 4 setting parent educators need to use advanced facilitation and intervention skills to guide parents on their journey. Instead of providing an opportunity for parents to learn and enhance skills, these groups address more serious situations that are likely to result in physical or emotional harm to children. This section will address specific intervention skills necessary in working with families with multiple and complex needs, in addition to describing a step-by-step process for intervention.

Building on active listening and support skills, such as paraphrasing, reflection of feelings, clarification, and summarizing, intervention skills move the interaction to another level. No longer does the parent educator support by listening and guiding the parent in finding his or her own answers. In an interventive approach, the group facilitator plays a more active role in helping the parent gain insight and develop a specific plan. Level 3 active listening skills of the parent educator assist the parent with insight and self-understanding. Level 4 interventive response skills reflect the parent educator's role to understand the parent in order to act in a guiding capacity. The parent continues to be the decision maker about what strategies he or she is willing to try and what direction he or she will take to make a change. However, the process of intervention signals a shift in the group's dynamics that requires a more directive role from the parent educator.

Parents learn new information from the educator and each other

The term *intervention* may have a confrontational connotation for some who associate it with chemical dependency or other interventions. In the context of the levels of involvement model for parent education, this association is not accurate. Intervention, in this sense, is a brief, focused process of assisting a parent in addressing a particularly complex parenting challenge and developing a plan of action for change. Although intervention occurs within the group setting, the focus is typically on one parent's issue. This type of intervention can also be used when working individually with a parent.

There are several advanced facilitation skills used within the intervention process that are necessary to delve more deeply into the issue presented by a parent. There needs to be a clear purpose in using these skills that reflect a willingness from the parent to address a particular parenting concern that will benefit from a brief focused intervention. The specific skills addressed within this section are probing, confrontation, interpretation, and immediacy.

PROBING

A parent who is under stress often brings a complex issue to the group but may be unable to present it clearly. The interventive skill of probing can be used by the parent educator to clarify and focus the parent to clearly describe the issue. Probing typically utilizes either open or closed questions to encourage a parent to:

- Elaborate: "Can you tell us more?"
- Obtain more information: "What happens then?"
- Refocus: "Which one of these issues is of most concern?"

Probing questions can be combined with a reflection-of-feelings statement to acknowledge understanding. For example, "You sound pretty overwhelmed right now (reflection of feelings). Which challenge would you like to address first?" combines statements that acknowledge, affirm, and help the parent focus on what is most important.

CONFRONTATION

The word *confrontation* tends to have a negative connotation. We can reframe confrontation in a positive way, so it becomes a matter of respect for the group and the group leader. It provides an opportunity for appropriate modeling, and it maintains group morale (Bowman, 1982). Confrontation need not be done in a negative or aggressive manner. In fact, confrontation can be presented in a very gentle way, if an adequate level of trust between the group leader and the parents exists. Parents with multiple and complex needs often have past negative experiences of being corrected by authority figures. Without a high level of trust and rapport, confrontation may feel punitive.

Two types of situations in which parent educators might use confrontation skills are (a) to address disruptive behavior in the group or (b) to point out a mixed message or discrepancy of a parent's behavior or attitude. The second situation is done on a more limited basis but can be an effective part of intervention. If disruptive behavior is not confronted in a group, it may be assumed that this behavior is acceptable. Talking about others who are not present, using inappropriate language, monopolizing, or putting other group members down are all examples of disruptive behavior. Although many of these behaviors are typically addressed in the forming stages of group development by setting ground rules, parent educators may neglect the enforcement of these rules. A parent educator will need to decide if the behavior is worthy of confrontation, if it is one-time occurrence, and how it needs to be addressed. Depending on the relationship with the parent, the severity of the behavior, and the context of the group, confrontation could occur immediately within the group or individually with the parent after the session ends.

Confrontation of a person's behavior or attitude that shows a discrepancy is more difficult to do. Presuming adequate trust and rapport, the parent educator needs to consider whether confrontation could lead to better self-understanding for the parent and, ultimately, to change. This type of confrontation is typically done one-on-one with the parent, not in the group setting. Parent educators need to use confrontation sparingly, always in the best interest of the parent, and never to prove a point or vent frustration.

Box 11.2

Considerations for Confronting

1. Make sure rapport and trust exist before attempting confrontation.

2. Check the emotional state of the parent.

3. Encourage the parent to focus on their behavior, not defend their actions.

4. Be aware of your own motives in confronting.

5. Consider the timing of confrontation and allow enough time for a response.

6. Choose an appropriate setting, whether private or within the group.

7. Structure the confrontation statement to avoid the word *but.* Use "and yet ... " instead. (For example: "You say your first priority is your child, *and yet* you admit that you spend very little of your free time with him.")

INTERPRETATION

One of the goals of intervention is to provide insight for the parent to enhance self-understanding. It is appropriate, therefore, for the parent educator to interpret or give a possible explanation of a behavior in more depth than paraphrasing. Interpretation should be based on concrete knowledge of child development, family functioning, or parenting skills, rather than on personal biases and experiences. For example, interpreting a parent's choices based on the parent educator's personal values is not appropriate. Encouraging mothers to leave their careers, because the parent educator believes that all children must have full-time care by a parent and because this is the choice they have made is not an appropriate interpretation.

Interpretations should also be phrased tentatively. Beginning the interpretation with phrases such as "Perhaps ... ," "I wonder if ... ," "It's possible that ... ," or "It appears as though ... ," or universalizing by saying, "One of the things we know about families is ... " helps to avoid defensiveness and resistance from the parent.

Finally, parent educators can assess the accuracy of their interpretation by asking if it "fits." This demonstrates openness to the possibility that the interpretation is not accurate and allows the parent to clarify its relevance.

IMMEDIACY

Immediacy is a skill used in counseling settings to draw attention to the "here and now" regarding observations or feelings of what is happening in the moment (Wheeler & D'Andrea, 2004). While typically used to point out something as it occurs or immediately after, it is a strategy that focuses the individual or entire group on what is presently occurring. It can be a way to affirm the group, to express concern, or to point out a shift in the group's direction. Forming statements of immediacy follows a few common rules (Cormier & Cormier, 1998):

- Describe it as it is happening or immediately after.
- Use the present tense.
- Use "I" statements when referring to your own feelings or observations.
- Consider the timing and trust level of the group—using an immediacy comment too soon in the development of a group may make group members feel uncomfortable and too much like a therapy experience.

There are several purposes of immediacy:

- To bring out in the open something that hasn't been stated directly ("As I'm listening, I realize that this is a serious issue for you.")
- To generate discussion or provide feedback about some aspect of the group ("I'm feeling uncomfortable when people are discussed who aren't here.")
- To maintain a focus on the "work" of the group ("It feels like there is a lot of support for each other here today. We're really coming together as a group.")
- To regroup, focus, and move in another direction ("I'm noticing we are really getting stuck. Let's move on.")

Statements of immediacy are often used to begin the process of a brief focused intervention. The parent educator states what they are feeling or observing and asks the parent if they have an interest in spending some time examining this issue in more depth within the group.

PROCESS OF INTERVENTION

When a parent educator decides that there is an issue raised either in a group or within an individual consultation that warrants a more interventive approach, it is helpful to have a process available to follow. The following five-step process outlines a series of questions and considerations that challenges the parent to address a particular problem. This is always done with permission from the parent in an attempt to process the concern and find a solution.

Doherty (1995) indicates that a Level 4 intervention is appropriate only for more complex parenting issues and those that are particularly problematic to the healthy functioning of the family system. The same interventive skills could, however, be used in a similar process of identifying an issue and working together on a plan of action for a less serious concern. The intervention process can be broken down into a step-by-step process.

1. ***Begin with immediacy.*** "I'm hearing lots of frustration from you right now. It sounds like you are wanting to spend some time really working on this issue. Would you say that's right?" This statement focuses the parent away from remaining stuck and offers the opportunity to work constructively.

2. ***Ask for the group's permission.*** "What I would suggest is that we can either look at this as a group and spend some time on it here or Anna and I can talk about it more privately at another time, and we can continue with tonight's topic. Either way would be fine." Check in with both the parent and the group, and if there is mutual agreement, continue the process.

3. ***Ask a series of questions that probe and clarify.***

    "Tell us what happened."
    "What happened then?"
    "How did you respond?"
    "So what do you mean when you say ... ?"
    These questions give a clearer picture of the issue to the parent educator, to the group, and to the parent.

4. ***Use a short interpretation of what the problem is.*** "Something we know about families is that ... . Does this sound like what happens for you?" This summarizes what is happening without judgment; interprets behavior; universalizes the issue, if appropriate; and offers an opportunity to either acknowledge or deny the "fit."

5. ***Develop a plan of action with the parent.***

   a. Imaging: "How would you like to be when you're with your child?" Concentrate on the parent's behavior and desire for change; avoid focusing on what the child should be like.

   b. Get a commitment. "Would you be willing to try a few things this week?"

   c. Facilitate a plan of alternative action to address the issue with the parent playing an active part.

   d. Identify obstacles and resources. "What would make it difficult for you to do this? "What would you need to help you?"

   e. Ask for group input. "What would anyone else like to add?"

   f. Summarize with a time frame. "So this week what you're willing to try is ... , and next week, would it be okay if we take just a few minutes to see how things went?"

   g. Restate commitment. "Are you willing to give this a try?"

   h. Empower and support the parent. "I hope some of this will work for you. Feel free to try the parts that feel most comfortable. Good luck with it!"

Interventions need to be brief in order to respect all group members. Spending too much time with one parent ignores the needs of others. It is also important to be selective in deciding to intervene. Interventions are not a strategy that would typically be used in each session. Watching for the cues of the parent that indicate a higher emotional level regarding a complex issue, along with the willingness of the group to allocate time for one member, will assist the parent educator in deciding whether to initiate an intervention.

Parent educators lead groups following a continuum of education to support to intervention. The needs of the group will dictate which skills are most appropriate for the parent educator to utilize. Interventive skills allow parent educators to move beyond teaching to assisting parents in developing a plan for change regarding significantly complex issues in their roles as parents.

BENEFITS AND CHALLENGES OF COLLABORATIONS FOR PARENT EDUCATORS

Collaborative family support programs are often formed to increase the efficiency of services, to eliminate duplication of those services in a community, and to offer more options to families. Grantors encourage family support programs in search of supplemental funding to join with other agencies and programs. Each agency brings strengths, varying services, and opportunities that, when offered jointly, expand the options for families. Collaborations help to build an integrated network of support in a community.

For example, a parent education program offered through the public schools may focus on providing a parent educator to teach parents positive parenting strategies and support them in their efforts. It may not be the program's mission or within its financial abilities to provide transportation, case management services, or ongoing home visits. Targeting particular populations, typically lower-income families with multiple challenges may not be successful because of the additional needs of families for these critical services. Another community family support agency may be able to offer these services but may not offer formal parent education. Collaborative partnerships provide opportunities for the families to participate in and take advantage of a full range of appropriate services of both agencies.

There are, however, many challenges in collaborations. Each collaborating partner has particular mandates and regulations that govern the funding, eligibility, mission, and scope of services. Problems can occur in collaborative relationships when regulations or mandates don't align. Direct service staff, as well as administrators, may differ on philosophy and approach for serving families. Local, state, or federal requirements may add stress to the partnering relationship as staff members attempt to adhere to standards and expectations. For example, school-sponsored programs may have strict boundaries that keep services focused on education. Parent educators may not be allowed to transport families or provide case management, because other agencies take on this role. Head Start teachers may be allowed to provide rides for families to receive services that adhere to program performance standards addressing a social service component. These issues can cause tension in a team relationship when boundaries are set in different places for staff working with the same families. Differences in salaries and status of positions between professionals from partnering agencies can also cause blurred boundaries and tension among team members. Finally, as in any system, a variety of problems can occur that result from poor communication, lack of time for team members to meet, debrief, and plan with each other, misconceptions about or differences in philosophies, and ownership issues.

One common issue that frequently occurs in collaborative programs happens when families work with multiple agencies and professionals, receiving a variety of services. Occasionally, these parents will criticize one agency or specific professional either during group time or individually with the parent educator.

From our experience ... In our work with a universal access program in Minnesota for over 35 years, the primary focus has been on serving all parents. The program focused on building parents' capacity to be protective factors in their children's lives through information on child development and guidance that led to developing skills, creating social support networks and connections to community resources. This has led, in many cases, to partnerships with other community agencies, in order to serve parents with greater needs, and providing parent education services to targeted groups, as outlined in Chapter 10. In recent years, we have embarked on projects that focus on early childhood and infant mental health in our community. Through this initiative, we have worked closely with community mental health professionals, county social services, non-profit agencies, the local Head Start, and other entities to create a coordinated network to serve families with young children. This has involved a number of professional development opportunities that have addressed early brain development, trauma, attachment, and specific parent support approaches. Because of these initiatives, parent educators have been working with a greater number of parents with multiple challenges in collaboration with other agencies, which requires the development of new skills. Collaborative work has helped all members have greater clarity about family needs, available services, and referral processes for families needing mental health services.

This puts the group leader in a difficult position, as they try to support parents and yet remain neutral. The following recommendations provide guidelines when handling these awkward moments in groups of parents.

1. Listen carefully for cues that the discussion is beginning to move into more personal complaints. Anticipate your response to refocus the group.

2. Remain neutral. Be aware of the words you use in response, as well as facial expressions that can convey agreement versus openness to listen.

3. Limit the discussion. "I understand that you have concerns, but I'd like to move us back to our topic."

4. Use phrases that show understanding for the parent's feelings without supporting. "I can see this is a big concern for you."

5. Use comments that show you are not "siding" with one party or the other. "It's difficult when parents and those they are working with have different perspectives."

6. State your discomfort with the discussion. "This puts me in an awkward position. Let's move back to our topic."

7. Encourage the parent to speak with the proper person.

8. Learn enough about your collaborative partners to feel comfortable giving positive comments.

9. Move the discussion to a private conversation with the parents, so the entire group is not drawn into the discussion.

10. Stay professional, keep an open mind, and imagine that the person of concern is able to hear your response.

While collaborative partnerships require professionals from different disciplines and agencies to work together, a major goal is to function cooperatively and show genuine respect for each other. However, sometimes a parent brings a serious complaint regarding a collaborating partner. This can result in an ethical dilemma for the parent educator who feels a genuine responsibility to ensure that the complaint is brought forward and addressed. Generally, in cases such as this, the parent educator may guide the parent through a complaint process, giving them information and guidance on how to make their concerns known to the appropriate person. If the concern is serious enough to constitute a breach of ethics or critical boundary violation, it will be necessary for the parent educator to become involved by reaching out to their supervisor for guidance.

It is clear that collaborations require a commitment from all partners. It is not enough for the decision makers or administrators to be committed to working together. Without a commitment from all staff involved, collaboration will not succeed. Ongoing support and opportunities for team meetings for direct service staff, including parent educators, are crucial. Regular staff meetings that focus on debriefing and updating information on families' needs and progress and on learning about each agency will assist staff in functioning as a real team. Release of information procedures need to be followed that document parents' understanding of, and permission for, professionals from different organizations to share information regarding the families they have in common.

For programs to succeed, supervisors need to choose staff who are open to working collaboratively and who are flexible in their approach. Parent educators and others who can approach a new challenge in a positive manner and are able to put the needs of the families first are good candidates for collaboration. Those who think that their methods are the only ones that work and that their agency is the most important will not be good team members. Careful attention to staff selection for collaborative projects is a key factor in designing a partnership.

Collaboration typically requires emotional energy and time demands on parent educators. However, the benefits of working together for families outweigh the challenges. Approaching parent education with recognition of the importance of varying the delivery of services to meet the diverse needs of families should result in quality programs and appropriate options for all families.

Within collaborative programs, parent educators may expand the teaming relationship with professionals from other agencies. In some programs, parent education groups may be co-facilitated. This type of group leadership requires a different perspective of the group process. The relationship between the co-facilitators is critical to the success of the group. The parent educator may focus primarily on parenting issues, whereas the other facilitator, perhaps a mental health professional, may take on leadership when personal or more intense issues arise. A public health nurse may co-facilitate groups and bring a medical perspective to parenting topics, while a social worker will bring a wealth of information about community resources.

Co-facilitation requires both facilitators to work in tandem with each other and agree upon roles and expectations for leadership. Will one person take on more leadership than the other? Are both willing to share responsibility and ownership? Who will plan the sessions? Are both facilitators accepting of the other moving the discussion along, adding immediacy to a situation, changing the flow of the group, or interjecting another point of discussion not on the agenda? Co-facilitators who work well together will need to openly discuss their expectations and perspectives about group leadership.

Although co-facilitation of parent education groups is not the primary model of most programs, in collaborative programs, it may be more practical and likely to occur. There are advantages for groups that are facilitated by two group leaders (Corey, 2000). Participants can benefit from the insights of two perspectives, rather than one. Co-facilitators can also complement each other's strengths and expertise, as well as consult, debrief, and plan together. When facilitators respect each other and approach co-facilitation in a positive manner, group members can benefit from this experience.

SUMMARY

Group parent education for parents with complex needs provides many challenges for group facilitators. Collaborative relationships with other helping professionals, a deeper understanding of behavior and family dynamics, and advanced intervention skills are all necessary in this role. Although not every group parent education setting needs this level of intervention, parent educators should be prepared with the knowledge and skills to respond appropriately.

DISCUSSION QUESTIONS

1. Of the common parenting issues described by Kristensen, which do you identify with most from your own family of origin? Which do you feel would be most difficult to deal with from a parent in a group? Why?

2. How might behaviors and attitudes influenced by culture and ethnicity be misinterpreted by a parent educator? How can parent educators minimize this possibility?

3. Reflect on the roles of parent and family educators in a trauma-informed system and steps that you might take to take on these roles and become more effective in working with families with multiple challenges.

CLASS ACTIVITY

Research the various organizations and agencies in your community that work with parents, children, and families. What services and resources might each of them bring to a collaborative parent education program? What would some advantages and challenges be to working collaboratively with these providers?

REFERENCES

Blume, E.S. (1989). *Secret survivors: Uncovering incest and its aftereffects in women.* New York, NY: Ballantine.

Bowman, T. (1982). Daring to confront ... with care. *Vocational Parent and Family Newsletter, 13,* 2.

Corey, G. (2000). *Theory and practice of counseling and psychotherapy.* Pacific Grove, CA: Brooks/Cole.

Cormier, W., & Cormier, S. (1998). *Interviewing strategies for helpers.* Monterey, CA: Brooks/Cole.

Doherty, W.J. (1995). Boundaries between parent and family education and family therapy. *Family Relations,* 44, 353–358.

Ellison, J. (2015). Using a Different Lens. Slide from a presentation on Infant Mental Health and Trauma.

Forward, S. (1989). *Toxic parents.* New York, NY: Bantam.

Goldenberg, I., & Goldenberg, H. (2000). *Family therapy: An overview.* Pacific Grove, CA: Brooks/Cole.

Harden, B.J. (2015). Services for Families of Infants and Toddlers Experiencing Trauma: A Research-to-Practice Brief. Brief prepared for the Office of Planning, Research and Evaluation, Administration for Children and Families. U.S. Department of Health and Human Services.

Kristensen, N. (1990). Parenting in the dark. in Comeau, J.K. (ed.) *Family Information Services Professional Resource Materials,* Minneapolis, MN: Family Information Services.

Kristensen, N. (1991). A sampling of parenting issues that affect adult children of dysfunctional families. Unpublished paper.

National Academies of Sciences, Engineering, and Medicine (2016). *Parenting matters: Supporting parents of children 0–8.* Washington, DC: The National Academies Press. Doi: 10.17226/21868.

Olson, D.H., & DeFrain, J. (2000). *Marriage and the family.* Mountain View, CA: Mayfield.

SAMHSA (Substance Abuse and Mental Health Services Administration) (2017). Trauma-Informed Approach and Truama-Specific Interventions. Retrieved from https://www.samhsa.gov/trauma.

St. Pierre, R. G., Swartz, J. P., Gamse, B., Murray, S., Deck, D., & Nickel, P. (1995). *National evaluation of Even Start Family Literacy Program: Final Report.* Cambridge, MA: Abt Associates.

Wheeler, C.D., & D'Andrea, L.M. (2004). Teaching Counseling Students to Understand Use Immediacy (Abstract*). Journal of Humanistic Counseling.*

University of Minnesota Extension (2014). Historical trauma and cultural healing: Articles list-historical trauma. Retrieved from http://www.extension.umn.edu/family/cyfc/our-programs/historical-trauma-and-cultural-healing/docs/ht-articles.pdf.

12

WORKING INDIVIDUALLY WITH
PARENTS: *Individual Consultation and*
Home Visits

[handwritten margin note: Betty Cook VIP = home visiting program (early days) extra $ came via Judiciary! saw value in a preventive step mental health special needs

can build towards joining group social capital connections very important!]

There are many advantages in working with parents in groups. Group work is typically more efficient; it offers more resources, perspectives, and ideas; and it promotes a sense of commonality and belonging for members (Jacobs et al., 2016).

While the focus of this text is primarily on group parent education, it is important to note that there are occasions when one-to-one parent education and support are warranted. The Continuum of Parent/Family Services Model presented in Chapter 3 shows a progression of types of programs, based on the needs of parents. As the programs become more involved, the likelihood of working individually, either as a supplement to the group experience or as the primary intervention, increases. Therefore, the expectation of parent educators working in these programs is to have group skills as well as the necessary skills to work individually with parents. However, individual work with parents can be a component of many different types of parent education programs.

In each of the following examples, a group experience may need to be replaced by, or supplemented with, individual consultation with a parent educator. A mother of a two year old attends a group regularly yet asks to meet with the parent educator of her toddler group to discuss some difficulties she is experiencing with her child. A recent immigrant family is enrolled in a family literacy program, and as a part of the program, there are monthly home visits to provide a more intimate and individualized experience. A social worker meets with a new 17-year-old mother and asks if she and her partner would like to enroll in a home visiting program with a parent educator. A parent educator meets individually with a noncustodial parent as part of ongoing supervised visitations with his child. In each of these examples, whether initiated by the parent, the educator, or an agency, a more personalized parent education experience may be beneficial.

For the purposes of this text, we will define "individual consultation" as individual meetings with a parent, or co-parents, and a parent educator. These personalized consultations are in contrast to individual therapy, parent coaching, or skill-based training sessions. However, they may include elements of each. For example, individual consultation with a parent educator may be therapeutic without being therapy. That is, the parent may benefit in similar ways as he or she might from therapy, as related to their functioning as a parent and their experience in family life. They may feel more confident, have greater insight, and have a better sense of wellbeing in their role. The focus of these consultations remains on parenting issues that can best be addressed on a one-to-one basis, rather than in a group setting. This chapter will assist the parent educator in providing individual consultation that is unique from the work of the parent education group leader.

DETERMINING THE NEED FOR WORKING INDIVIDUALLY WITH PARENTS

Many early childhood programs, such as Early Head Start, Family Literacy, Early Childhood Special Education, Infant Mental Health, and Nurse Home Visiting, incorporate home visits and individual consultation with parents as a regular and ongoing component (National Academies of Sciences, Engineering, Medicine, 2016). Other programs reserve this option for those with the most challenging parenting issues. Some programs include individual work with parents with the primary focus on the child's developmental or behavioral challenges, special needs, school readiness, or health care. For the purposes of this text, it is assumed that individual work with a parent is warranted due to complex parenting issues or concerns about the parent-child relationship that would not be addressed as effectively in a group setting. These issues may revolve around the parent's struggles with setting limits, responding in non-punitive ways, or developing a nurturing relationship with the child.

These issues can be complicated, and it is important that staff who work individually with parents have the necessary skills and knowledge about parents and parent-child relationships. It is, therefore, critical that parent educators who work separately with parents have adequate training and appropriate ongoing supervision in their work. Regular dialogue with supervisors or consultants about relationships with parents, personal biases, and professional challenges will help parent educators keep appropriate and healthy boundaries in their work. Additional information on supervision and reflective practice is addressed in Chapter 14.

While the majority of parents will benefit from participation in parent education group experiences, there are those who may be better served through individual consultation with a parent educator. The following are examples of factors that may help parent educators identify parents who are contraindicated for participation in a group setting:

individual settings when

- Poor social skills that alienate them from other group members
- Intense parenting challenges that require one-on-one intervention
- Complex family problems that are outside the realm of common parenting issues and where a referral would be appropriate
- Mental health issues or cognitive limitations that interfere with group participation
- Practical challenges with attendance (lack of transportation, childcare, work schedules, etc.)

Depending on how the parent enrolls in a program, a decision will need to be made about the appropriateness of participating in a group. For example, if a parent is either self-referred or referred from another agency, a process of screening or intake can indicate that a one-on-one experience may be the most appropriate parent education service. The parent or referring agency may describe one of the above challenges that clearly would not be best served in a parent group setting.

Often a parent's challenging behaviors or complex needs will not be obvious until they begin participating in the group. Parent educators should ask themselves the following questions. Is this an appropriate experience for this particular parent? Are their needs being met? Are the needs of this parent interfering with the experience for others? It is at this point that the parent educator will need to make a decision about a referral for an individual experience that will be beneficial both for the parent and the other group members. With a caring approach, this should not feel like a dismissal or failure on the part of the parent, but rather a way to best meet their needs.

Examples

A. *Clairice is a full-time parent who is not employed outside of the home. She is lacking in social skills, which causes her to dominate the group discussion. Clairice is seeking adult companionship through the group experience and brings up her many parenting challenges that are often beyond what others* *are experiencing. She interrupts other parents when they speak and frequently shares personal and family issues that make others visibly uncomfortable. Several other parents have stopped coming to the group, confiding in the parent educator that Clairice's behavior is negatively affecting their experience.*

Terrance, the parent educator, has tried a variety of different group facilitation strategies for working with a monopolizing group member, but Clairice's behavior issues have persisted. He decides to speak privately with her about how important it is for her to allow others in the group to speak, to not interrupt, and to limit her sharing to related parenting issues. Terrance feels comfortable with his relationship with Clairice and brings up his observations and concerns in a gentle and respectful manner. She admits that she doesn't always give others an opportunity to talk. Terrance suggests that perhaps her needs are bigger than what the group typically addresses and asks if she is interested in having some individual sessions with a home visitor, a service that is offered through the program. With a few clear guidelines and expectations for group behavior, Clairice is welcomed to remain in the group while she meets with a home visitor to address her more involved and complex challenges with parenting. The addition of regular home visits is used as a supplemental experience so that Clairice can remain in the group and yet get her individual needs met.

B. *Thomas is a single father who regularly attends a parent group each week. He has suffered a traumatic brain injury from a car accident several years ago and struggles to keep up with the discussion. He often asks basic questions, requests that the facilitator repeat what has been said, and becomes frustrated with his inability to understand and follow the discussion.*

Eleanor, the parent educator, notices that, at first, the other parents were understanding and patient, but as time has passed, there has been a noticeable growing level of frustration from other group members, as much of the group time is devoted to Thomas and his needs. Eleanor approaches Thomas individually after the group one evening and asks how things are going for him in the group. Thomas readily admits he is often at a loss to keep up with the discussion and attributes it to his disability. Eleanor gently suggests that perhaps it would be helpful for him to have a parent educator meet with him individually, either in his home or at the center, to cover some of the same material, allowing for more time for his questions and individual needs.

Thomas asks about whether he should drop out of the group, and Eleanor suggests "stopping out" for a short time to see how things go with the individual consultation with plans to return to the group in the future if he chooses. Eleanor makes arrangements for the individual session with another parent educator at the center and plans to bridge the first meeting by attending, as well.

From our experience ... Home visiting is one of the most challenging assignments for many parent educators. We believe that this work requires the highest level of skills due to the complex issues that arise when working individually with parents. While peer-led home visits can provide support and information to participating families who generally function well, parents with more intense challenges will benefit most from highly trained professionals who are skilled at addressing complex needs.

INITIAL INDIVIDUAL MEETING WITH PARENT

Before the initial meeting with the parent, the parent educator may have limited information about the parent. Some basic information would have been shared if the parent has been referred, but the initial meeting is an opportunity to meet the parent, discuss their parenting goals, determine the roles of the parent and the educator, and agree on next steps. This initial meeting sets the stage for what will follow with the individual consultation process.

Goals of the initial individual session with a parent include:

1. Developing a relationship of trust and caring

2. Explaining the purpose and expectations of the sessions

    a. What will happen during the sessions?

    b. What does the parent want to gain from the experience?

    c. What practical information regarding scheduling, guidelines, etc. need to be shared?

3. Determining the concerns of the parent

THE INITIAL INTERVIEW FORMAT

The format of the initial interview will vary depending on the specific target audience, program goals, and funding sources. There may be a program requirement to collect specific family background information using standardized intake forms. In order to determine eligibility and collect data, this is often done through a series of forced-choice questions about the family and family members. For example, programs such as Even Start Family Literacy may require a multiple-page form to be completed during the initial interview for research and tracking purposes. There are ways to introduce this task that can help to build rapport and trust, instead of it being an impersonal interview process. It is challenging to be a careful listener and at the same time read off questions and record the required information. If a standard form is required, it would be helpful for the parent educator to spend some time at the beginning of the interview building rapport and trust. The interview could begin with introductions, information about the parent educator's role in the program, and explaining what kinds of questions will be asked and how the program will use this information.

An interview protocol could also be designed that would be useful in learning about the parent and family in a more informal, open-ended way. One of the authors has had the opportunity to adapt an open-ended set of questions about fatherhood to be used as an individual interview for a parenting program for incarcerated fathers. Table 11.1 lists some of the key questions that have been formulated to build rapport and understanding to help make the mutual decision about whether the class is a good match for the parent. The interview begins with asking about the current family situation, beginning with the names and ages of the children. This question personalizes the family members so that they are not impersonal numbers or family structure descriptors and opens the door for other sharing of information about the family. Providing an opening for a parent to share their story conveys genuine interest and gives the interviewer more contextual and meaningful information. The question about the birth story and holding the baby for the first time invites sharing of an emotional experience. The sequence of the questions and how they fit together are important in constructing initial interview questions. This example of interview questions illustrates how the questions can lead to a discussion about the individual options, what the parent would like to address, and finally, how open they are to this experience.

There is also a time for any additional questions and a discussion about match of the program to the parent's expressed need and interests. In this particular context, it also serves as a screening process to determine if the parent is a good candidate for the parenting program.

Table 12.1 Initial Interview Example

INITIAL INDIVIDUAL INTERVIEW: PARENTING PROGRAM
I. Introduction (After introducing self to the parent)
"I like to meet with dads to find out about your family situation, your thinking about fatherhood and how it is working for you, and about your current needs and interests related to the parenting class. Then we can decide if this is a good match from your perspective and my perspective."
"Tell me about your current family situation, how many children, their names, and ages."
"How would you describe your current relationship with your child(ren)'s mother(s)?"
"How old were you when you had your first child? Were you at the birth? What was it like holding your child for the first time?"
"When was the last time you spent time with your child?"
II. Fatherhood Role Models
"What makes a good father?"
"Who are your role models for being a father? What have you learned from them?"
"Are you trying to be different from your own father? How and why?"
III. Relationship with Your Child
"How would you describe your current relationship with your child(ren)?"
"What do you do to communicate and keep close to your child(ren)? "
IV. Effects of Fatherhood
"What role has fatherhood played in your life up to this point? How has it changed you as a person?"
V. Parenting Class Needs and Interests
"What would you like to take away from a parenting class?"
"What would you like to talk about in a parenting class? Look at the schedule and pick out two or three topics that are most meaningful for you."
"What ways do you learn best? For example, discussion, exercises, videos, listening?"
"What is your level of commitment to the class right now? Is it a good time? Are you feeling open to learning about yourself as a father? Why?"
VI. Summary Statement
"Do you have any other thoughts about fatherhood? Any areas that we haven't talked about that you feel are important for me to understand?"

During the initial session, it is critical to set the tone of this experience and to address expectations of both the parent and the parent educator. If the setting is in the home, there may be uncertainty or even confusion about roles, particularly from the perspective of the parent. Visitors in the home are typically friends, and the parent may interpret this experience as similar to those they have within personal relationships. It will be important, therefore, for the educator to maintain a friendly, caring approach without developing the perception or expectation of a personal friendship.

Generally, the initial session is an opportunity to begin a relationship of trust and genuine concern. It is a time to develop rapport with the parent by engaging in a conversation to learn more about this family and to offer their services as a resource and a support for the parent. This is an opportunity to affirm what the parent is doing well, to help them identify their strengths and needs, and to build the trust that will be necessary to continue with the experience.

During this first meeting, the educator may talk briefly about what he or she can provide in terms of information and linkages to other resources in the community and answer any questions. The parent educator will pay close attention to both the verbal and nonverbal responses from the parent. Is this person open to continued visits? Is the parent resistant or hesitant about this arrangement? It is important for the parent to understand that he or she is always free to make the decision whether or not to continue.

Closing the initial session will include a brief summary of the visit and a commitment from the parent to continue. The parent educator and parent will identify agreed upon goals and set another time to meet.

Following the initial meeting, the parent educator should be able to answer the questions below in order to form a better understanding of the parent and the work they will do together. These questions could be reviewed with a supervisor, a consultant, or team member.

- What is the purpose of the individual consultation?
- Does this experience replace or support participation in a parent group?
- What are the cultural values and beliefs of this parent, and what is important to know?
- What is the cognitive level of this parent?
- What are their strengths?
- What does the parent identify as the most pressing need?
- Would a referral for more intensive intervention (e.g., parent mental health services) be appropriate?
- Would the presenting concern be better served if both parents participate?
- Is this a "one-time" consultation, or would ongoing sessions be helpful?

- Do I feel safe working in this setting (particularly relevant for home visiting)?
- How can I keep the relationship professional and yet caring and helpful?
- What other support services are being utilized?
- What level of informal support is available?

CONTRASTS WITH GROUP WORK

When leading groups, there are multiple "clients." The parent group leader must be aware of the needs of the group as a whole, as well as those of each individual group member. It is necessary to pay close attention to both the verbal and nonverbal behaviors of each person to gauge their understanding and involvement. At the beginning of a new group, it is likely that a parent educator may have a limited amount of background information on parents. However, it is most helpful to learn as much as possible about each group member's past and present situation, cognitive abilities, reasons for participating, and family dynamics, which will help the facilitator make the experience positive for everyone. This can be a daunting task, particularly for beginning group leaders.

Working individually with a parent allows the parent educator to focus solely on one parent, one family, or occasionally, the parenting partner. While this may appear to be less complicated, focusing so intensely on one individual requires a different set of skills. It will require the ability to ask probing questions without prying into the life of an individual. The parent educator will also need to be keenly aware of tailoring suggestions and information to the unique needs of this parent, rather than providing generic solutions for their challenges. It will also require the educator to use great caution to maintain a professional relationship with this parent and avoid the appearance of a friendship. Additionally, the parent educator needs to recognize mental health and other complex needs that will require a referral to more intensive services. This remains a challenge for parent educators who are not well trained (Marchand, 2014).

The role of privacy in individual consultation is different from that in group settings, as well. In a typical group, the parent educator is aware of the choice each member makes to either conceal or reveal information as they choose. In parent education groups, it would be inappropriate for the group leader to delve deeply into the personal issues and individual needs of members. However, when working individually with a parent, the expectation of confidentiality only involves two people, the parent and the parent educator. It is natural, because of the more intimate connection during individual consultations, that the level of sharing on the part of the parent will have more depth than in most group settings. However, it is critical that the parent educator stays within the realm of their role and avoids allowing the interaction to move into areas that would be better dealt with in therapy.

PLANNING, CUSTOMIZING, GOAL SETTING

Planning for individual sessions is, in many ways, similar to planning for working with groups. However, the individual parent will typically take a more active role in the direction of the work. The parent educator's role is to join together with the parent to help determine what specific issues of parenting will be addressed. What information would be helpful? What challenges are they experiencing? What strengths do they have? What would they wish their parent-child relationship to be like?

This can be overwhelming for some parents who find themselves overcome with multiple, and often immediate, challenges, such as health issues, housing needs, or problems in their relationship with a partner. The parent educator will listen carefully and guide the parent in identifying which parenting challenge the parent would most like to address. It is important that parenting issues remain the primary focus and that the parent educator not act in the role of a case manager for the parent and family if it is outside their responsibility. Typically, this is more appropriately the job of a social worker, unless the parent educator has a dual role.

Home Visit Example

Terisha is a young single parent, living in a small apartment with her three children, ages 1, 3, and 4 years. She has no relationship with the father of the children who is living in another state. Her mother resides in another apartment building nearby and helps Terisha with the children. Terisha explains that some of her mother's parenting suggestions are fairly punitive and make her uncomfortable. The public health nurse who is concerned about the children's behaviors and Terisha's lack of discipline skills has referred her for parenting home visits. The children have little structure in their lives, exhibit poor social skills, and seem to control the household with their demands and unruly behavior. They have been threatened with eviction from the landlord who has noticed damages to the apartment and has received complaints from other residents about noise.

Rosa, the parent educator, makes an initial visit along with the public health nurse to meet Terisha and her family. It is clear that the family's life is chaotic, and the parent has little control over the children. There are multiple temper tantrums during the visits, and Terisha's responses are to give in to each of the children's demands. Rosa agrees that Terisha would benefit from one-on-one intervention regarding her parenting.

The public health nurse engages with the children, while Rosa joins Terisha at the kitchen table. They talk about how Terisha feels things are going with her family and she admits that she is clearly overwhelmed with many issues. She is struggling financially and is grateful to her mother, yet feels she often meddles and gives bad advice. Generally, she is at a loss for how to respond to her children without yelling and hitting them.

Rosa offers to continue the home visits and explains how she could help and what resources she would be able to share. They agree that, in order for any progress to be made, a paraprofessional will need to accompany Rosa to be with the children, so the adults can focus on their discussion. A schedule is set up for the next visit.

Over the next few months, Rosa visits Terisha's home once each week. She helps her identify and prioritize her concerns, as well as her strengths. Terisha identifies the children's temper tantrums and unwillingness to listen as her biggest areas of concern. Rosa helps Terisha understand that her own responses are an area they can work on that will change the children's behaviors. Rosa shares simple strategies that would be helpful, demonstrates them with the children, and asks Terisha to try them out. They set goals for each week, post reminders on the refrigerator door, and discuss the progress at each of the following visits. Since the grandmother is also playing an active role in parenting the children, Terisha agrees to include her mother in some of the visits. Grandma readily agrees and joins them when invited.

Rosa can see real progress in Terisha's parenting, as well as the children's behavior, over the course of time. She refers her to other community resources to help with her finances and suggests a grandparenting class for her mother. Rosa also helps Terisha arrange for the oldest child to enroll in a preschool program near her home. After several months of visits, Terisha decides to attend an ongoing parent education group in the local community center where Rosa works, and she feels more confident and successful as a parent.

PARENTING ASSESSMENTS/ ASSESSING PROGRESS

Each program will have unique requirements for documentation of individual sessions or home visits. It is important for parent educators to complete these forms after each session, noting what was accomplished and what goals were set for the coming week. These notes should also include any information that is needed for the next visit and any tasks to be completed beforehand. Since parent educators often work with many different families each week, it is important to document what occurred and what follow-up will be necessary. The documentation notes will also need to be written in non-judgmental, objective language that describes what happened and include observations of progress and goals.

Assessment can be done on an ongoing basis through the use of a home visiting log. The templates that follow are examples of 1) documentation from the initial home visit and 2) log of ongoing visits. These samples include information about the date and time, those present, the major focus of the visit, the parent's response to the session, and if there are any notes to prepare for the next session. This could include additional information or resource materials and any specific adaptations for changing family needs.

Table 12.2 Initial Home Visit Form

Initial Home Visit

Date_____ Teacher/Visitor _____Referred by_____

Child's Name _____DOB_____

Parent/Guardian Name_____

Home Address_____Phone_____

Present at home visit _____
  (Include ages of any other children present)

General information about family:

Family strengths:

Concerns:

What information is the parent interested in receiving?

Activities for child:

Materials left at home:

Next appointment date and time_____

Information to bring to next visit:

Table 12.3 Ongoing Home Visit Log

Home Visit Log (Ongoing)

Date_____ Teacher/Visitor _____HV #_____

Child's Name_____

Parent/Guardian Name _____

Present at home visit_____
(Include ages of any other children present)

Parent-child activity:

Parent education information shared:

Updates from parent:

Materials left at home:

Goals:

Next appointment date and time_____

Information to bring to next visit:

Ongoing assessment through logs can also be complemented by a set of questions on a periodic basis (e.g., half way through a 10-week program). This form of assessment gives parents an opportunity to talk about how the program is working for them. It can provide some specific feedback about what is working well and what are some possible changes to better meet the parent's needs. An example of some of the specific questions that could be asked include:

- When have you felt most engaged with a topic or activity?
- When have you felt least interested in a topic or activity?
- What is the most important lesson you have taken from the sessions? How have you used this lesson?
- Are there any topics that you want to make sure that we talk about in future visits?

A simple check-in process on a regular basis will help determine how a parent is experiencing the program. This can be affirming that the parent educator is on the right track and help determine if any changes need to be made.

Parent education can be individualized through home visits

SETTINGS

With the proliferation of home visiting programs for the purpose of parent education, most individual consultations with parents will most likely occur in the parent's home (Hall, Kulkarni, & Seneca, 2008). Some parents may, however, feel uncomfortable inviting a professional into their home. This can be due to embarrassment of the condition of the home or neighborhood, uncertainty about the purpose of the visit, the presence of others living in the household, or a variety of other reasons. In these cases, an alternative setting may be more appropriate. Other options can be offered, such as a conference room in the center where classes are taught, a private room in a public library, or another public setting that provides privacy, safety, and comfort.

A home visitor who encounters a family of a different culture from their own may be met with new rules and expectations. Whether it is a family of a different ethnicity or socio-economic level, a home visitor may experience uncertainty or confusion within the home. Being open to these differences will assist the parent educator in avoiding barriers to developing a trusting relationship with the parent.

Home Visiting Example

Sarah is a new parent educator who has work primarily with leading parent groups. She has shown confidence in her work, relates well to the parents, and has received positive feedback on her evaluations. Her supervisor encourages her to try working individually with parents though the home visiting program.

Sarah's supervisor has received a referral from the county social service agency for parent education to be provided for a family in a rural area. Social service has received calls from concerned neighbors about lack of supervision of the children. Public health nurses are also working with the family on general hygiene issues and health care of the children. The parents are quite young, live in a home with extended family, and are fairly isolated from others in the community.

The referring social worker suggests that Sarah accompany her on the initial visit. When they arrive at the home, they are met by two large dogs that run to the car and bark. Sarah has always been afraid of dogs and hadn't thought to ask the referring social worker about animals. The social worker explains that this always happens when she arrives. They wait patiently in her car until an adult comes out of the house and secures the dogs.

The social worker and Sarah are invited into the house and find a number of people present, including the children, parents, grandparents, and a couple of teenage siblings. It is difficult to hear each other, since the television is on at a high volume, and the children are running through the house. Several of the adults are smokers, and the room is filled with smoke. There are three cats in the living room that jump up on the furniture and keep startling Sarah. She notices how unconcerned and comfortable the social worker appears.

The condition of the house is very disorganized and unclean. Sarah has not been exposed to a setting like this before. She tries to connect with the parents and children and hopes to get through a couple of forms she has brought along but is distracted by the chaos. This is not what she expected to encounter in her new role as a home visitor.

Sarah's reaction to the family will be critical in developing a relationship. Her ability to be accepting and nonjudgmental is key to being able to work with this family. Her inability to do this may create a distance between herself and the family and impede the development of a positive relationship. She will need to recognize that she is entering into their space, which is in contrast to her past experience with parents attending the groups at the center.

Sarah will benefit from working closely with the social worker until she is more comfortable with this setting and can develop a trusting relationship with this family. By accepting the family's lifestyle with a nonjudgmental attitude, she can move toward helping the parents be more successful in their parenting roles.

Frequently, families who participate in home visits with a parent educator are also receiving services from, or are involved with, other family support agencies. Examples include public health, social services, public school early intervention, and/or corrections. Since professionals from multiple agencies are involved with a family, it is helpful for some communication between programs to occur with the permission of the parent. This type of collaboration makes the work of the parent educator more efficient and reduces the possibility of duplication of services or conflicting goals.

Because children and other family members are often present when an individual session is held in the home, there can be distractions for both the parent and the parent educator. Programs can assign a second staff member to accompany the educator to supervise the children. This person can share age-appropriate activities, engaging them during the visit, and allowing for a more intentional and productive interaction between the adults. Having children present can also provide an opportunity for learning. The parent educator can model desired behaviors with the child and encourage the parent to "try out" a particular strategy. Some time during the visit can be reserved for this type of interaction. Research reviews indicate that opportunities for practicing new strategies are critical for the success of parent education (Mbwana et al., 2009).

Safety is always a primary concern for staff conducting home visits with families. In many programs, the families who participate in home visits present with multiple and complex risks, including domestic violence, substance abuse, poverty, and neighborhood crime (Harden & Lythcott, 2005). Parent educators and support staff should never stay in a home setting where they have reservations or concerns about their safety. The following suggestions are taken from a variety of sources to help staff maintain safety:

- If possible, schedule home visits early in the day.
- Keep in contact with the program regarding schedule, addresses, etc.
- Stay alert to surroundings.
- Never enter a home if you suspect unsafe conditions.
- Travel in pairs, as much as possible.
- Carry a cell phone for emergencies.
- Leave your purse at office; carry only essentials on your person or in an assembled home visiting kit.

- If you feel unsafe in any way, end the visit and leave.
- Make a mental note of all entrances and exits as you arrive.
- Trust your instincts.
- Respect that this is the parent's space.

RELATIONSHIP ISSUES UNIQUE TO INDIVIDUAL WORK

The relationship between the parent and the parent educator in individual consultation models is more vulnerable to confusion of roles. Parents with complex needs may be challenged in understanding the professional-to-parent role and may mistake the relationship for one similar to a friendship. This is especially true for parents who struggle with relationships, have complex family needs, and participate in individual work with other professionals. Cultural differences and expectations may also contribute to uncertainty regarding the nature of this relationship.

The parent educator should be alert to changing dynamics in the relationship. Requests for favors, questions about the parent educator's family or personal life, giving of gifts, invitations to events, and conversations that stray from the topic of parenting are all examples of warning signs that the relationship is moving to another more personal level. If the parent educator anticipates the possibility of these kinds of changes to the relationship, it will be easier to stop them before they become boundary crossings or boundary violations. (See Chapter 7 for more information about professional boundaries.)

REFERRALS

During the course of individual consultation with parents, it may become necessary for the parent educator to conduct a referral either for the parent, the child, or both. The challenges the parent faces may be beyond the realm of parent education, and a referral to individual therapy or parent-child therapy may be appropriate. After spending individual time with the parent and child, the parent educator may become aware of developmental or behavioral concerns with the child and feel that a referral for special education or other services would be warranted. Common services addressed through referrals are mental health, public health, human services, special education, domestic violence shelters, and financial assistance programs. Referrals are always done privately, one-on-one with a parent. A detailed description of steps in making a referral is addressed in Chapter 8.

BRINGING CLOSURE TO THE INDIVIDUAL PARENT EDUCATION EXPERIENCE

Bringing closure to individual work with parents can be challenging both for the parent educator and the parent. Some programs are structured for a particular number of visits and may follow a prescribed curriculum that covers various topics. However, other programs design curriculum according to the individually expressed needs of the parent, bringing pertinent information and providing support on an ongoing basis. It is important, therefore, for the parent and educator to communicate frequently with the parent about their impressions of whether goals are being met and if progress is being made.

It is also possible that either or both the educator and/or the parent can become comfortable in the relationship and may extend the experience beyond what is really necessary. This can cause a dependency issue for the parent and a shift in the relationship away from being professional to becoming closer to a friendship. The educator should be able to avoid this by keeping the parent on track, assessing progress, and ending the experience with appropriate evaluation, which can include "next steps" for the parent.

EVALUATION

One of the final aspects of individual consultation or home visiting services is an evaluation of the experience for the parent. This may be very informal for a one-time or short series of sessions. It is an opportunity to find out from the parent what they are taking away from this experience. Did it meet the goals that both the educator and the parent had for this type of service? One example of a more formal evaluation form for a 10-visit home visiting program follows in Table 12.4. This form asks parents to rate program goals and provide some feedback about the overall experience.

This can also be accomplished with a more open-ended set of questions that address both the program goals and the specific activities that were part of the visit. For example, what did the parent think about the handout that you left each time? Was the videotaping process helpful for gaining new insights? Did

Table 12.4 First Step Series Evaluation

Number of Sessions Completed _____
Age of Child_____

Goals of the Program: Rate your level of agreement with meeting each goal

1. I felt supported in my relationship with my infant/toddler:
    Strongly Agree   Agree   Disagree   Strongly Disagree

2. Because of the sessions and books provided, I read more often to
    my infant/toddler:
    Strongly Agree   Agree   Disagree   Strongly Disagree

3. I received valuable information about parenting my child:
    Strongly Agree   Agree   Disagree   Strongly Disagree

4. The song sheets have encouraged me to sing more often with my
    infant/toddler:
    Strongly Agree   Agree   Disagree   Strongly Disagree

5. Because of the sessions, I have a better understanding of the needs
    of my child at this age:
    Strongly Agree   Agree   Disagree   Strongly Disagree

6. The First Steps sessions have helped reduce parenting stress:
    Strongly Agree   Agree   Disagree   Strongly Disagree

Please rate your overall impression of the First Step sessions:

Poor   Excellent

    1   2   3   4   5   6   7   8   9   10

Other Comments about the sessions:

they use the set of songs and books that the parent educator left at their home? Literacy levels of the parents will also determine how the evaluation is given.

It is helpful to find out from the parent about their experience at the end to know how to improve the program and to reflect on ways to improve the parent educator's own skills in working individually with parents.

SUMMARY

While this text deals primarily with working with parents in groups, there are instances when parents will benefit most from individual interactions with a parent educator. This work can be done in a variety of settings, either as a replacement for the group experience or as a supplemental offering. Individual consultation can be provided in the parent's home, in a private room offered by the sponsoring program, or in a conveniently located public space. Working with parents individually requires the ability to focus on the unique needs of a particular parent and family within the realm of a caring and professional relationship.

DISCUSSION QUESTIONS

1. What are your feelings about working individually with a parent? What boundary challenges can you imagine might arise and how might you address them?

2. What distractions might you encounter working individually with a family in the home setting? Which ones would you feel a need to address? How would you maintain an attitude of respect for the parent's lifestyle, culture, and living arrangements?

3. What are your reactions to the example of Sarah and her initial home visit with the family described in this chapter? How would you respond?

CLASS ACTIVITY

In groups of three, assign the roles of 1) parent educator, 2) parent, and 3) observer/note taker. Design an example of when a parent educator may need to speak individually with a parent about whether the group experience is appropriate and/or helpful for the parent. Use the skills covered in the examples and text within this chapter to approach the parent and work out a plan for either continued participation or suggestions for another level of service. The observer will take notes and share observations after the role play.

Questions for the observer:

1. What skills do you notice the parent educator using to approach this parent?

2. As the parent, how would you feel if the parent educator brought up this conversation with you?

3. What constructive suggestions do you have for the parent educator?

REFERENCES

Hall, N., Kulkarni, C., & Seneca, S. (2008). *Your guide to nurturing parent-child relationships: positive parenting activities for home visitors.* Baltimore, MD: Paul H. Brooks Publishing.

Harden, B.J., & Lythcott , M. (2005). Kitchen therapy and beyond—Mental health services for young children. In K.M. Finello (Ed.) *The Handbook of Training and Practice in Infant and Preschool Mental Health* (pp. 256–286). San Francisco, CA: Jossey Bass.

Jacobs, E.E., Masson, R.L., Harvill, R.W., Schimmel, C.J. (2016). *Group counseling: strategies and skills.* Boston, MA: Cengage Learning.

Marchand, V. (2014). *Making a difference for families and young children: the intersection of home visiting and mental health.* Washington, DC: Center for the Study of Social Policy.

Mbwana, T.K., Terzian, M. & Moore, K., (2009) *What Works for Parent Involvement for Children: Lessons from Experimental Evaluations of Social Interventions.* Washington, DC: Family & Youth Services Bureau, National Clearinghouse on Families and Youth, Child Trends. Publication no. 2009–47.

National Academies of Sciences, Engineering, and Medicine (2016). *Parenting Matters: Supporting Parents of Children Ages 0–8.* Washington, DC: The National Academies Press. Doi: 10.17226/21868.

13

PARENT-CHILD INTERACTION TIME: *Opportunity for Connection and Practice*

Parent-child interaction time has become an essential part of many parent education programs over the past three decades. Kristensen (1984) referred to parent-child interaction time as the heart of Early Childhood Family Education (ECFE) programs in Minnesota's program for parents with young children. Family Literacy programs in Kentucky have designed Parent and Child Time (PACT) as a key component of their family literacy model (Darling and Hayes, 1989). During parent-child interaction time, parents and children come together in schools and other settings to participate in group and individual early childhood activities. There are also some classes that focus on parenting skills (e.g., Brock, 1989) where parents are able to practice the skills that they learn in parenting sessions. Recent research has identified practice as an important factor for effective parent education program design (Center for Disease Control and Prevention, 2009; Grindal et al., 2016). Parents Are Teachers (District 742 Parent-Child Program, 1993) uses parent-child time as a time for parents to observe their young child and follow the child's lead in exploring the learning environment. There are also some prison programs (e.g., Moore & Clement, 1998) that incorporate parent-child visitation time as part of a parent education program. Parent-child interaction time is an opportunity for both parent learning and a quality experience for parents and children (Palm, 1992: Campbell & Palm, 2004). The focus on parent-child interaction time in this chapter will be on how to design and integrate these experiences into group parent education classes.

This chapter will explore the different goals of parent-child interaction time with an emphasis on young children ages 0–5 years old, although programs could extend activities through age 8, as some Even Start Family Literacy programs do (St. Pierre, Layzer, & Barnes 1995). Parent-child time has many potential benefits for both parents and children. Parent roles vary according to program philosophy, beliefs about children, and specific program goals. Designing parent-child interaction time is often a team effort between a parent educator and an early childhood educator. In this chapter, some basic design principles will be outlined along with ideas for parent-child activities for various age groups. The integration of parent-child interaction time with parent education will also be discussed, giving examples of parent-child interaction as an opportunity for parent observation and for linking parent-child interaction time to parent discussion. Finally, this chapter will examine some typical difficult moments in parent-child interaction time and possible responses that can turn potential problems into opportunities for parent learning.

EXAMPLES OF PARENT-CHILD FORMATS

PARENT-INFANT SESSION

Seven mothers and one father of infants ages 4–8 months sit around the edge of a large rectangular area with gym mats covered with sheets and sprinkled with infant toys, rattles, brightly colored balls, and teethers. At the beginning of the session, most parents put their babies down on the mat in front of them. Some of the infants are sitting up and others are on their stomachs exploring the environment. The parent educator greets each parent and baby as they enter the room and asks how they are doing today. After everyone arrives and has had a few minutes to settle in, the parent educator begins a circle time routine of short songs and finger plays. The group has been together for 5 weeks, and when the songs begin, the babies become quiet and attentive, watching as the parent educator and parents sing twinkle, twinkle, little star with hand movements. When the songs are over, the parent educator goes around the group to check-in with each parent about any new changes in their babies or any new issues that they are dealing with since the last time they met. The babies continue to explore the toys, other babies, and adults. Some infants stick close to their parents, while the two oldest venture out into the middle of the circle and explore the environment. Parents occasionally redirect an infant who may be too rambunctious and invades another baby's space or takes away a toy. The parent educator talks about emerging social skills with a few posters on the wall that outline these skills and how parents can support these emerging skills. The interaction of the infants provides concrete examples to weave into the discussion on social skills.

Parents' strengths can be observed during parent-child interaction time

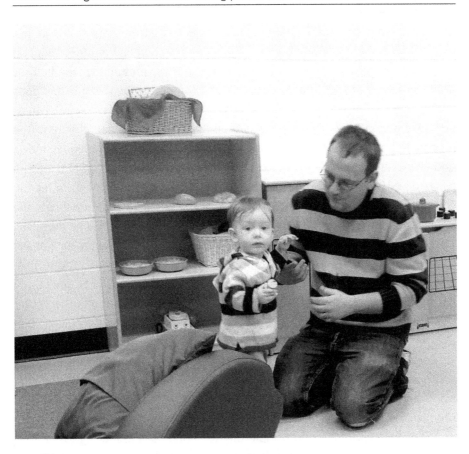

SUPER SATURDAYS—FATHER AND CHILD PROGRAM

Another example of a parent child interaction time comes from a Saturday morning program for dads and their young children aged 2–5. This group meets twice a month, and many fathers come to this program to spend quality time with their young children. The parent-child interaction time takes up 1.25 hours of the 2-hour-long session and is the main attraction of the program for both fathers and their children. As one father stated, "My daughter looks forward to this time that she has together with me without the distractions we have at home."

Some of the members of this group have been coming to the Super Saturday class for 2–3 years. The children walk in with a smile and work on making a name tag while their dads sign in. The parent educator greets the dads and kids and tells them about the activities for the day, giving them a sheet that describes the special activities for the day. Today, the activity is cooking with kids, and there are seven different food projects that are spread out in two classrooms and the hallway. Some of the children run ahead of their dads and go down to the gym to play floor hockey or ride a tricycle down the long hallway at the other end of the building. After about 15 minutes, the children and dads gather together in one of the classrooms for circle time. There are 13 dads and 18 children today. The dads introduce themselves and their children. One 4-year-old boy decides to change his name to Sam during introductions today, and everyone laughs. The early childhood teacher plays his guitar and sings a song about Herman the worm and what he will be eating. Children volunteer an odd assortment of worm food as they join along. After a couple of songs, the parent educator and the early childhood teacher take turns describing the seven different food projects. Today, the menu includes a banana yogurt milk shake in a blender and trail mix with dried fruit, peanuts, cereal, M&M's, and raisins. Out in the hall, children are rolling out tortillas from round balls of dough into flat, thin pancakes. They will fry them in an electric frying pan and then cover them with cheese to make quesadillas. At another station, dads and kids chop up apples and place them in a blender to make applesauce. Finally, a small group of dads and their children are making chocolate pudding by shaking milk and pudding mix in a small jar. The dads with younger children do most of the work, but find ways to engage their children, such as putting the apples into the blender and pushing the button. The children and dads sit at small tables in one of the classrooms and sample their creations before moving to the next activity or taking a break by going to play in the gym. Most dads are attentive to their children's interests and follow their lead in selecting the next activity. As the activity level winds down, the dads take their children to the first classroom where the early childhood teacher and two assistants have set up activities for the children, while the dads join the parent educator in a room down the hall for parent discussion time.

Large motor activities provide special experiences for parents and children

GOALS FOR PARENT-CHILD INTERACTION TIME

The various goals of parent-child interaction time reflect the program philosophy, target group of parents, and the age of the children. The focus of this chapter is on the parent and what the parent can learn from parent-child interaction time. There are three general goals for parents with a number of important direct and indirect benefits for both parents and children.

The first goal is **to create a quality time and space for both parent and child**. Parent-child interaction time provides a special time for parents and children to be together in a supportive environment created for children with limited distractions. Parents appreciate this time together where they can enjoy being with their children in a child-oriented environment without the stresses and distractions that creep into time at home.

A second goal is **to provide time and a comfortable environment to practice parenting skills.** For example, parents practice observation skills and become more aware of their child's social interactions and sensitive to their child's cues. Parents observe which activities are most engaging for their child. They also may observe how their child slowly moves into new activities and they gain new insights into their child's temperament. Parents may get a chance to guide their children through an art activity of making hand prints and have to set limits about using the paper, not the table or the wall, for their project. There are many opportunities to practice a variety of parenting skills during parent-child interaction time. The parent educator can model ways of talking to children about their art work or redirecting a child to a more constructive activity.

The third goal of parent-child time is **to provide parents with ideas for developmentally appropriate learning activities that can be extended into the home.** This is done by creating a child-centered environment with a variety of fun, stimulating activities where children learn by doing. For example, this can be accomplished by setting up a post office dramatic play area where children can "write" letters or postcards and sort mail into different categories. Simple art projects can be prepared for children to experiment with cutting and pasting different materials. Cooking with kids provides parents with new ideas for healthy snacks to make at home.

BENEFITS FOR PARENTS AND EDUCATORS

Parent-child interaction time provides direct opportunities for parent learning, as well as some indirect benefits to parents. Parents are able to observe their children in a social context with other children. In the process, they learn about the range of typical behaviors, as well as different temperaments and approaches to learning. Parents also learn more about a child's perspective by being in a child-oriented environment and observing how the staff organizes the environment. The variety of different parenting styles and strategies, as well as the modeling of program staff, exposes parents to new parenting ideas and approaches in a real-life setting. This experience provides a range of choices for parenting behavior and the message that there are many different "right" ways to parent. Parents are encouraged to select the strategies that reflect their family values and goals for their child. They observe that a child's temperament may be an important factor in selecting effective parenting strategies. These indirect messages can be explored during parent discussion time to take advantage of the multiple examples of interactions between parents, children, and educators during parent-child time.

BENEFITS FOR STAFF

The parent educator also learns from participating in and observing parent-child interaction time. This is an opportune time to observe parents in a variety of interactions with their children. They may observe the parent encouraging the child in the gym in a game of catch. They watch parents structure a task that is too difficult by breaking it into simple steps, thus making it easier for their child to succeed. Two parents work with their children as they build a set of train tracks in a corner of the room. These observations lead to a greater understanding of parent strengths. Watching a mother who is really patient with her son who is moving non-stop from one activity to another raises the educator's awareness and appreciation of the parent's strengths. Parent educators may observe parent-child tensions as a mom attempts to persuade her 2-year-old daughter to share the painting easel. The parent educator also has the opportunity to observe children and their style of interacting with other children and adults and how they approach new activities. Parent-child time provides numerous teachable moments where parent educators can model respectful but firm limit setting with children. Sometimes, a parent needs a subtle suggestion to make a project work better, like adding food coloring to the water before mixing up the play dough recipe. Other times, parents need an empathic or reflective response. "Jeremy looks like he is having a hard time connecting with the other children after being gone for 2 weeks." Parent-child time can be an appropriate opportunity for parent educators to videotape parents and children in interaction (Erickson & Kurz-Reimer, 1999). These videotapes can be used to point out parent strengths and unique child characteristics. Parent educators who can directly observe and interact with parents and children together have a deeper understanding of the unique strengths and specific issues that challenge parents.

DESIGNING EFFECTIVE PARENT-CHILD INTERACTION TIME

SELECTING AND ADAPTING PARENT-CHILD ACTIVITIES

There are a number of important considerations for creating parent-child activities that work for both children and parents. The environment should be sensitive to child development with appropriate and engaging activities for different age groups. The Boxes that follow (Boxes 13.1–13.3) list some examples of favorite activities for different age groups.

Box 13.1 Activities with Parents and Infants (Birth–12 months)

1. Mats with boxes of different sizes for babies to crawl into and through.

2. Mirror Play—Set up different sizes of mirrors around the room for babies to explore.

3. Crawling on different textures that are taped to the ground for babies to explore with their hands as they crawl.

4. Peek-a-Boo game with colorful silky scarves.

5. What Makes Baby Laugh—Try out different activities written on cards, such as blowing on baby's stomach for infants 4 to 12 months to see which ones make them laugh.

6. Sensory table with small soft toys inside for babies who are beginning to stand and walk.

Box 13.2 Activities for Parents and Toddlers (12–30 months)

1. **Sensory Table**—Fill table with rice and containers, cups, and funnels for pouring.

2. **Art Collage**—Toddlers can rip tissue paper and stick onto contact paper.

3. **Shaving Cream**—Parents can squirt shaving cream on a clean surface for children to explore. They can also add food coloring to make different colors.

4. **Dramatic Play**—Set up the water table with some soapy water and use washable dolls with towels for the children to bathe and dry off.

5. **Trains**—Children like to set up train tracks with small wooden trains to move around the track. Parents can offer guidance and support in setting up the tracks.

6. **Pounding**—Set up a pounding area with golf tees and a small wooden hammer to pound into styrofoam.

Box 13.3 Activities for Parents and Preschoolers (3–5 years)

1. **Cooking**—Children can paint a piece of bread with a small paintbrush and a mixture of food coloring and milk. Toast and eat.

2. **Art Mural**—Put a large piece of paper on a wall and use a variety of media (chalk, markers, crayons) to make a mural.

3. **Magic Wand**—Begin with a small dowel rod about 18 inches long. Make a notch in the top of the dowel rod about 1/3 inch deep. Cut small colorful ribbons about three or four different colors about 12 inches long and place in the top slot with glue. Parents can also trace a small star out of card stock and cover with glitter to place in the same slot with the ribbons.

4. **Dramatic Play**—Set up a camping area with two or three tents and a pretend campfire with props (sleeping bags, cooking pots and pans, flashlights, etc.). Turn down the lights and play a nature tape as background noise.

5. **Cooking**—Mix 1/2 cup of grape juice, 1/2 cup of milk, and three to four ice cubes in a blender to make a purple cow. Blend until smooth.

6. **Science Parachutes**—The parachutes can be made from colorful pieces of nylon fabric cut into large squares (12–18 inches). Tie a piece of string to each corner of the fabric. Then, attach all four strings to a wooden clothespin. The clothespin can be decorated with markers to make a person. Fold up and throw into the air.

It is helpful to balance projects that are sensitive to both parent and child interests. While the child's abilities and interests have to be the primary focus, it is also important to observe parents and select activities that will be appealing and engaging for both the parent and the child. It is helpful to give parents specific instructions about their role in doing an activity with their child. More challenging activities that are just beyond a child's ability in a specific age group can be completed only with a parent's assistance. This creates a role for parents to guide and work with their child in completing an activity. Parents are thus challenged to practice scaffolding or modifying an activity to match a child's ability.

Offering a variety of activities is usually a good idea to meet the needs and interests of different parents and children. This may include balancing active with quiet activities and open-ended or process-oriented with product-oriented activities.

It is most important to design activities that will be fun and enjoyable for both children and parents. Activities that are simple, provide some challenge, and promote feelings of competence help both children and parents enjoy themselves. Parents enjoy the feeling of doing something with their child in which the child has fun and feels successful.

PREPARING THE ENVIRONMENT

Parent educators who team with early childhood educators can work together to select activities to engage both parent and child. Once activities have been chosen, the next step is to prepare the environment. Activities must be arranged to indicate space boundaries while also considering activity and noise levels. Parent-child activities should also be presented in an appealing or attractive manner. This can be done by arranging materials in new ways, adding a new twist to a favorite activity, and carefully organizing materials into classroom spaces. For example, in one program, making name tags for parents and children is often part of a "registration routine." While masking tape and markers had been used, recently, the staff decided to use colored shapes of animals, apples, etc. as nametags. The children are more excited about making name tags from specific shapes and colors. The aesthetics and detail of preparing an attractive environment for parents and children convey messages of "we care," "welcome," and "have fun."

INTRODUCING AND MODELING ACTIVITIES

The parent educator can be involved in explaining the specific parent-child activities so that parents have an understanding of how to do an activity, as well as the purpose of the activity for supporting child learning. This could be done verbally before beginning parent-child time. It could also be written on small cards or signs posted near an activity area for parents to read, or parent and early childhood educators could circulate and assist parents as necessary, explaining the purpose of each activity.

SETTING A POSITIVE TONE

The parent educator can set a positive, light, and playful tone for this time by their own attitude about parent-child time and by helping parents understand the expected roles and appropriate behavior. Since parents are in the program's or educators' environment, they need clear descriptions and explanations about the purpose of parent-child time and expectations for parent and child behavior. Parent educators can model respectful interactions with children and describe how parents can help their children with an activity. For example, what are the expectations during circle time? Should all children come to the circle and participate, or can they just watch? Do children need to try all of the activities, or can they spend the whole time with one activity? When parents know the rules and expectations, they can relax, have fun, and not worry about making "mistakes" and being judged.

CLARIFYING PARENT ROLES

Programs may have varying philosophies about parent roles during parent-child interaction time. Some programs want parents to be relatively passive observers. Parent-child time is a time to observe children interacting with the social and physical environment. This role allows parents to observe their child's behavior in a different social context with peers and provides parents with opportunities for new insights into their children. In other programs, parents are expected to be cooperative playmates who follow their children's lead. Parents in this role may be encouraged to practice reflective listening, encouragement, and expansion of a child's dramatic play.

Another role that parents may play is the teacher/guide who demonstrates to children how to complete a task and encourages their efforts. In this role, parents are expected to teach through modeling or scaffolding tasks, such as putting together a puzzle or working on a collage of different fabric pieces.

Parent educators sometimes express impatience about parents not exhibiting appropriate role behavior during parent-child interaction time. A parent may spend more time talking to other adults than following their child with attention and encouraging statements. It helps when the program is clear and explicit about the roles they want parents to play during parent-child time. This can be conveyed in a number of ways. One way is through an initial orientation to the program and the purpose of parent-child interaction. The role expectations can also be addressed in a handbook. The parent educator must also model the roles that they would like parents to play during the parent-child time.

This information and demonstration of appropriate role behavior will help the parents feel more comfortable and be aware of the program goals and role expectations for parents.

Activities during parent-child time can provide topics for parent discussion time

CIRCLE TIME: CREATING A GROUP FEELING

Circle time can be an important component of parent-child activity time. It provides a time for the group to come together and connect around a shared activity. It can provide a routine for both younger and older children. It should be engaging and fun for both parent and child. The length of circle time will vary with the age of the child. The pace and variety of activities, from songs to finger plays to stories, will change with the age of the child.

Circle time often begins with recognizing each child by name through a song or chant. Some children like to hear their name and are pleased to be recognized and acknowledged in the group. Other children hide their faces when their turn comes. Not all children like to be the center of attention, and educators should be sensitive to inviting children to participate but still give them a choice not to be part of a name song. The parent educator has the task of engaging both children and parents in the circle time activities by creating both a feeling of safety and sense of fun. Circle time itself should become a comfortable routine for both parents and children. Box 13.4 presents some favorite ideas for circle times for parents and young children together.

Box 13.4 Circle Time Favorites for Young Children & Parents

1. **Name Songs**—To greet and welcome children and parents,

   - Chant "_____ is here today, _____ is here today, ..."
   - Sing "Oh I see _____ over there sitting ..."

2. **Action songs**—To engage parents and children in actions and interactions, while singing,

   - Raffi's "Bumping Up and Down" (child sits on parent's lap and gets a ride)
   - Ella Jenkins' "Stop and Go" (different actions can be incorporated, such as clapping, jumping, dancing)
   - "Row, Row, Row Your Boat" (parent and child row facing each other and holding hands)
   - "Skip to My Lou" (a circle song with holding hands and various actions)
   - "Head, Shoulders, Knees, and Toes"

3. **Animal Sound Songs**—Ask children to name animals and make the different sounds that each animal makes.

   - "Old Mac Donald's Farm"
   - "When Cows Get Up in the Morning, They Always Say Good Day"
   - Raffi's "Down on Grandpa's Farm"

4. **Parachute Games**—with small parachute,

   - Popcorn with balls—place small plastic balls on the parachute and make them "pop" like popcorn as they group moves the parachute up and down.
   - Dome house—parents can hold on to the edges and lift the parachute up to create a dome house for the children to go under.

SELECTIVE INTERVENTION DURING PARENT-CHILD TIME

Parent educators can intervene in a number of different ways during parent-child time. It is important not to disrupt parents and children who are engaged in an activity. Parent educators can watch to see if parents need help with a project or need materials to complete the project. Although unintentional, it is easy to disrupt the parent-child connection during this time. While it is important to connect with parents and children, it helps to keep a respectful distance from parents and children who are engaged and having fun with an activity. Sometimes, the educator feels awkward or left out to only be observing parent-child activities. Other times, one is concerned about being too intrusive or wondering if parents feel as if they are being monitored. This time can be an opportunity to mentally note parent strengths to acknowledge at a later time, or child behaviors that can be discussed with parents during parent discussion time.

Sometimes, parents and children may be struggling with their own interaction, and parent educators can intervene by making a simple comment to a parent to support their efforts or redirect both the parent and child. The final section of this chapter will address a number of common difficult moments between parents and children that occur during parent-child interaction time. These interventions can be seen as opportunities for learning and can be resolved with a variety of effective strategies.

GUIDED OBSERVATION OF CHILDREN

Parent education programs offered in settings that include children provide a unique opportunity for parents to learn from observing their children in an environment with other children and adults. Just as teachers of young children learn observation skills, parents can learn to observe in new ways that provide insight into their children's behavior, development, temperament, and skills. In these programs, typically offered for families with younger children, parent educators not only facilitate group discussion, but also structure and guide a process of observation for parents (District 742 Parent-Child Program, 1993). This section will address methods of designing, guiding, and debriefing observations to enhance the experience of parent education.

SETTINGS FOR GUIDED OBSERVATION

Guided observation is designed for parent education settings that include children. Programs where parents and children attend together include parent-child activities, as well as a separate time for parent education that provides a rich opportunity to learn through a combination of observation and discussion.

Children's environments that include a separate viewing area with one-way windows and sound systems are most effective for guided observation. However, many parent-child programs include guided observation without these features. Parents can separate within the same room as the children by gathering in a corner to watch with the parent educator. Classes with very young infants and toddlers may struggle with separation issues and find that even with separate viewing areas, parents and children are most comfortable and secure within the same room. Either way, a structured time for parents to pull back from their children and observe with guidance from the parent educator can provide another way of learning about their child.

Settings such as these typically include the children's teacher, who can work together with the parent educator to facilitate a positive observation experience for parents. The children's teacher will need to know what the parents are observing in order to structure an environment that supports the observation focus. For example, if the focus is on language development, the children's teacher may demonstrate particular communication strategies that encourage young children's speech. Teaming between the parent educator and the children's teacher is critical for a successful observation experience.

VALUE OF OBSERVATION AS PART OF PARENT EDUCATION

Including guided observation as part of the parent education experience allows an immediate and individualized opportunity for parents to learn about their children by watching them. It provides a practical reinforcement of concepts and ideas covered in the discussion group as parents learn about development through observation of their children. There are a number of benefits of guided observation for parents. They include:

- Learning about child development through demonstration
- Seeing their children within a social context with peers
- Gaining insight about learning styles, conflict resolution skills, and temperament

- Gaining observation skills that provide a new appreciation of child learning and development
- Experiencing a more objective perspective and understanding of their children
- Gaining new insights into their child's behavior from the parent educator who interprets behavior
- Understanding their child's perspective or view of the world

From our experience ... One of the groups I facilitated for parents of children ages 18–24 months had, as can be expected of this age group, many behavioral challenges. During the observation time, parents pulled aside in the room as I guided the observation, commenting on what was occuring and pointing out developmental and behavioral issues. The children's teacher was a wonderful model of when and how to intervene, and the parents were supportive of her choices. It was helpful, though, to talk about what to expect during observation time, how to trust in the children's teacher, and to know that it would be common for children to have some typical toddler behaviors. At first, parents were very concerned and embarrassed when their child "acted out." However, after a few times, the group decided that every child took a turn, and they began to support and reassure the parent whose child was challenging that week that "it was just their turn." It was important to make them understand that this was typical behavior and that they were not being judged.

PARENTS' AND CHILDREN'S REACTIONS TO OBSERVATION

The concept of observation may be very foreign to parents in educational settings. Parent educators may hear comments, such as "I spend all day with him. Why would I want to observe?" Observing may seem like a waste of time or something that can put parents in an uncomfortable or embarrassing situation if their child misbehaves. These reactions are not uncommon, and the parent educator can acknowledge parent feelings and support parents when introducing the observation time.

Without careful guidance during observation time, parents may lose interest and begin interacting with each other or become distracted. Some parents may begin visiting about unrelated events and disrupt this quiet time for others. It is the responsibility of the parent educator to keep parents focused and involved in the observation process. Commenting on what is happening, moving between parents, and encouraging parents to put themselves in their children's shoes will help to keep parents' attention on their children.

The role of the parent educator during observation is to guide and interpret what is happening in the play environment. The parent educator can softly comment to keep everyone engaged with the observation. The following statements help to sustain their interest:

- Notice what is happening in the book area.
- It's interesting to watch some of the children as they are content to play alone.
- Listen to the words the early childhood educator uses to calm the children.
- Let's make sure we talk about this during our discussion time.
- Watch how the children interact with each other.
- Think about the choices your child is making during this time.
- I wonder what William is thinking right now.
- This is a very common reaction for children this age.
- Sometimes it's hard not to intervene, but watch when the teacher decides to respond.

Notice that none of these statements encourage immediate discussion or responses during the observation, which has been designated a quiet time. Yet, they ask parents to notice particular situations that will provide a rich discussion when parents gather for their group time.

Children sometimes have reactions to observation time that can cause challenges. Issues of separation may be disruptive as children move from the classroom environment to their parents during this time. They may realize they are being observed, especially during the early stages of this activity, and "act out" for attention. Children may embarrass their parents by misbehaving or being aggressive or emotional during observation. Teamwork between the children's teacher and the parent educator is important during these times. The children's teacher can demonstrate appropriate responses to the children, and the parent educator can identify these strategies while affirming and universalizing the situation for the parent. For example, a child may hit or bite another child while parents are observing. The children's teacher can use this as a "teachable moment" by modeling appropriate limit setting, guiding, and comforting responses to both children. At the same time, the parent educator may point out what is happening, provide insight into developmental behaviors, and reassure parents. Overall, these issues may present challenges for the parent educator but also provide an opportunity for learning for the parents.

Parents learn about their child's development, abilities, and interests during interaction time

STRUCTURING AND GUIDING OBSERVATION

Structuring a guided observation includes thought and care from the parent educator. Selecting the right focus, designing and maintaining "ground rules" for observation, and guiding the actual observation are necessary skills. With careful consideration, observation can become an important part of the learning process for parents.

Steps for effective observation include the following:

1. Select a focus for observation that matches the topic of group discussion. For example, if the session's topic is social development, the focus may be to observe signs of social skills with other children and adults. An observation for the topic of self-esteem could be for parents to watch the ways their children demonstrate confidence and how the children's teacher fosters self-esteem.

2. Post the focus where parents can read it. The language used in the focus should be simple, easy to read, and without jargon or questions. Questions may intimidate parents who feel they are being tested or instructed to find the right answer. Statements such as "Notice how your child gets his/her needs met" and "Watch for new skills your child has acquired" are good examples of observation focuses that encourage parents to look for specific behaviors or skills. Occasionally, the parent educator may have a particular focus in mind that just doesn't happen. Parents are watching for social skills while children are playing alone. A confident guide of observation will focus on what is happening at the time and use it as a spontaneous learning opportunity.

3. Keep parents focused during the observation. Parent educators need to give guiding comments regarding what is happening with the children, as well as statements that challenge parents to put themselves in their child's place. Parents can be given the option of taking notes during the observation that can be used later during a debriefing time. The parent educator might provide clipboards to facilitate note taking. Attention and sensitivity should be given, however, to parents with low literacy levels, as well as to varying learning styles. A creative alternative method of note taking might be to provide a general floor plan of the room. Ask parents to move the pencil across the paper to "track" where their child moves during the observation time. This activity could be linked to the discussion of motor development or activity levels in children.

4. Design and maintain ground rules of observation. They may include the following:

- Observation time is quiet time.
- Put yourself in your child's place to understand them.
- Watch the children and listen to their words.
- Avoid judgment about your child and others.
- Note your own feelings as you observe.
- Respect all of the children as you observe.

5. Focus primarily on what is happening, not why. Although this is often difficult for parents, it keeps the observation objective and helps to avoid judgment. During the debriefing time, the parent educator's tentative interpretation may be helpful for the group.

DEBRIEFING THE OBSERVATION

Generally, after the observation, parents will gather to begin their discussion group. A good strategy for bridging the observation with the topic is to begin with a short debriefing of observation. During the watching time, parents are encouraged to observe, not talk. Debriefing offers an opportunity to discuss what they saw, how they felt, and what they learned about their children.

During the debriefing time, the parent educator should try to include everyone by checking in with each parent and commenting on something they observed about each child. These comments can be as simple as noting what a particular child played with or an interesting social interaction between two children.

Debriefing time can also offer an opportunity to address a difficult situation that may have occurred during observation. An affirming or universalizing comment regarding a child's behavior can assure a parent that everyone understands and that this behavior is not uncommon.

During the guided observation, the focus typically remains on what is happening. By including a debriefing time within a discussion with parents, the facilitator can offer tentative interpretations of particular behaviors that occurred. Parents may wonder, for example, why their child responded in a particular manner. The parent educator can draw on both experience and knowledge of development and behavior to offer possible explanations. This insight offers parents an opportunity to learn about their children from another perspective.

The end of the debriefing time should flow directly into the topic of the session. By carefully designing an observation focus that matches the session's topic, the parent educator can move the group directly from observation to discussion. Reversing the order of discussion and observation is also an option. The parent educator may lead a discussion on a particular topic and end by offering parents an opportunity to observe their children as a way to demonstrate a particular concept or idea.

Including observation in groups where parents and children attend together has many benefits for parent learning. Observation can strengthen the group discussion as parents and educator share their perspective of each individual child. Designing, guiding, and debriefing observation requires different skills than those involved in the group process. A competent parent educator will combine both observation and discussion to enhance the parent learning experience.

LINKING PARENT-CHILD TIME TO PARENT DISCUSSION

Another advantage of parent-child activities in parent education programs is the potential impact on parent group discussion time. Parent-child time can be used by the parent educator as an opportunity to build relationships with parents and children. It can provide a means to initiate deeper involvement with parents with greater needs through referrals or more intensive services. Parent educators can link parent-child time to discussion by debriefing the experience and connecting it to the discussion topic. This section will explore the role of the parent educator during parent-child activity time and address the positive outcomes that are possible by linking this experience with group parent education.

THE ROLE OF THE PARENT EDUCATOR DURING PARENT-CHILD ACTIVITY TIME

RELATIONSHIP BUILDING

While parent-child time is typically planned and facilitated by the children's teacher, the parent educator also plays an important role. Parents and children spend time together actively engaged in a variety of learning opportunities. It is a special time for parent and child to enjoy the company of each other, in addition to engaging in developmentally appropriate activities. While it is important for the parent educator not to intrude into this special interaction time, an opportunity exists to connect with each family and strengthen the educator-parent relationship.

The parent educator moves through the classroom setting, checking in, cautiously joining in the play, affirming, and commenting on the interaction that is occurring. A few minutes with each family strengthens the relationship, which will enhance participation in the parent group. A parent who has not connected with the educator before separating into the parent discussion time may be less likely to openly share and participate in the group experience. This brief but important connection by the parent educator with each parent builds trust and rapport that follows the parent into the parent group setting. Comments that support the parent and encourage the child help to build a positive relationship. This preliminary connection impacts the quality of interaction during parent discussion. Parents who feel close to the parent educator, who feel affirmed, supported, and comfortable, are more likely to engage in open discussion later in the session.

Example

Mary is a parent educator in a group of parents with preschoolers. The parents and children have arrived to find a variety of activities set out for them to explore during the first part of the class. The room is comfortable and inviting with soft background music playing as parents and children move between activities. Mary greets each family as they arrive. When everyone is settled in with activities, she slowly moves through the room, sitting near each dyad, yet being careful not to intrude. She joins Amy and her daughter Aisha as they play together at the sand table. Mary makes affirming comments about what they are making, how soft and smooth the sand feels, and how much they are enjoying playing together. She is careful not to intrude in the play between parent and child, but may linger nearby, observing the interaction. The focus of Mary's involvement is primarily on the play that is taking place. Amy begins to draw Mary into a conversation about a parenting issue. Mary assesses the situation and decides that Aisha is content pouring sand from one container to the other, and Amy seems to need this time for one-on-one parent education. Mary keeps in mind that she wants to avoid talking about Aisha in front of her, and since Amy's concerns are general, she responds to her questions. After a few minutes Aisha clearly wants her mother's attention for another activity, and Mary says, "It looks like Aisha is needing you right now. We'll talk more later." She moves on to another parent-child dyad to connect before parent discussion time begins. These informal few minutes together have connected the parent and educator and will help them begin the group experience on a closer level.

MODELING BEHAVIORS

The parent educator can also use parent-child interaction time as an opportunity for modeling positive relationship building skills. While it is important not to interfere in the play between parent and child, it may be appropriate to provide a model for a parent who is uninvolved with their child or for one who is clearly struggling with a behavior issue.

Example 1

Max is a parent educator with a group of young fathers. Some of the dads bring their children to the group each week and are actively involved in their lives. Others attend sporadically and have limited involvement. Brad attends today with his daughter Brittany. She is an active 3-year-old who loves art activities. As Brittany approaches the art table covered with a variety of materials, Brad settles back in his chair. Brittany wants to paint but needs an apron. She begins to pull some of the art supplies toward her but clearly needs assistance. Brad seems distracted and unaware that she needs his help. Max moves closer to the table. He senses that Brad doesn't realize what is happening. "Brittany," he says, "You can ask Dad for help rolling up your sleeves and putting on the apron." Brad looks up and moves closer, taking the verbal cue from Max who mentions Brittany's interest in painting and use of bright colors. This interaction helps Brad become engaged in the painting activity.

Example 2

Judy is a parent educator in a group of parents and children who are between 2–5 years old. Kia and her 2-year-old son Matt have just joined the group, and this is their first day. Matt is a very active 2-year-old and occasionally is aggressive with other children. Today, Matt is playing next to Timmy, who is also 2 years old. Timmy is playing with a little truck that Matt wants. Matt eyes the truck, hits Timmy, and grabs it from him. Timmy begins to cry. Kia looks embarrassed by her son's behavior but doesn't respond. Judy is nearby and moves in a little closer. She gently pats the backs of both boys and says, "Timmy is upset. We can't hit people. That hurts." She continues to talk gently to both of them, comforting Timmy, who begins to calm down. Matt moves in closer with the truck. He holds on to the truck, but keeps watching Timmy's reaction. Judy says, "Let's look for another truck for Timmy. Matt, can you help us?" Kia watches in amazement and Judy comments that they can talk about this later during parent group.

In this example, the parent educator sensed the parent's uncertainty of how to respond to a difficult situation. She was clearly embarrassed and unsure of what to do, especially in a group setting with other parents watching. The parent educator provided a positive model for intervention. She comforted both children and helped them work out a solution in finding another similar toy. She modeled respect and elicited a gentle response from the child. The mother had the opportunity to see a different way of responding. Parent education can sometimes occur through modeling, sometimes in one-to-one interactions, and sometimes in groups. During the parent group, the educator can later use this example in a universal way to talk about realistic expectations of children, common 2-year-old aggression, and the importance of intervening calmly and gently.

UNDERSTANDING PARENTS' NEEDS

Parent-child time also provides an opportunity for the parent educator to observe the relationship between parents and children and the strategies employed by parents to nurture, guide behavior, and gain cooperation. Knowing what challenges exist for individual parents will help the parent educator plan topics. For example, observing attachment behaviors between parent and child offers valuable insight into their relationship and assists the parent educator in assessing the needs of group members. It is important for the parent educator to observe informally and unobtrusively during parent-child interaction. This will lessen parent feelings of being observed and judged. This type of observation can also offer the parent educator opportunities to share affirming comments with individual parents.

Example
Lydia is a parent educator in a group of parents and infants. She notices that one of the parents, Maria, does not seem emotionally connected to her infant son, Juan. Maria does not always respond to his cues, often holds him at a distance,

and seldom strokes or cuddles him in nurturing ways. Lydia observes informally during interaction time and throughout the session. She had planned several topics on infant attachment and nurturing behavior, but because of Maria's behaviors, she adjusts her plans to include more basic information. She also brings in a videotape for the parents about the importance of touch. During play time, Lydia holds Juan for short periods of time. She models good eye contact and positive connections and then comments on how well he engages and enjoys this type of interaction. Maria seems more interested in what is happening and Lydia notices that she is soon trying some of the behaviors Lydia has modeled. When a strong trust level has been established, Lydia approaches Maria after class one day and tells her about a series of home visits that are available to parents and their infants. Maria explains that these visits include some play time, as well as an opportunity for the parent and teacher to talk one-on-one about parenting issues. She will also bring a video camera along each time to tape Juan and Maria together. At the end of the series, Maria can keep the video as a keepsake. Maria is interested and agrees to the visits. Lydia feels encouraged that she will be able to work closely with this parent and child and is hopeful that she will continue to see changes in interaction patterns and nurturing behaviors.

Parent educators guide observation to help parents learn more about their child's development

DEBRIEFING PARENT-CHILD INTERACTION

Occasionally, parents have difficulty seeing the value of parent-child interaction time. "We play at home all the time." "I thought we would do more here than just play together." Parent-child interaction can be validated when the parents gather for discussion by debriefing what occurred. Each session might begin with a short check-in as an opportunity for parents to share their impressions and gain insight into this part of the session. If debriefing is to be meaningful, therefore, the parent educator needs to have played an active role and be aware of what happened. The following are sample questions for debriefing parent-child interaction time:

- "What was it like for you playing with your child today?"
- "What did you notice about your child's choices?"
- "How have things changed from earlier in the year to this time?"
- "How is it different playing here with your child than it is at home?"
- "What surprised you as you played together?"

Finally, linking parent-child interaction time with discussion allows the parent educator to use professional judgment in tailoring topics and sessions to meet the needs of a particular group. If there appear to be power struggles during interaction time, the discussion group can focus on appropriate strategies. If the educator observes parents whose expectations are unrealistic about what their children should be able to do in the classroom, a time of focusing on child development is appropriate. In the absence of strong trust and rapport, it is difficult for the parent educator to focus individually on the challenges of a particular parent. Bringing the information into the parent discussion group in a more universal way allows everyone to learn without targeting or over-emphasizing the needs of a particular person.

The time spent by the parent educator during parent-child interaction is a solid investment in the quality of the parent discussion group. Building a relationship before the group, learning as much as possible about each parent and child, and sharing insight about this experience all have a positive impact on the parent group. Parent-child interaction provides an opportunity for the parent educator to know the parents in a way that would not be possible within a typical discussion group. Seeing the parent-child relationship in action provides a more accurate understanding than relying on information gathered through parent reports. Parent-child interaction is not only an enjoyable component of many parent education programs, it is a valuable method for the parent educator to connect with and understand parents and their children.

DIFFICULT MOMENTS AS TEACHABLE MOMENTS

Parent-child interaction time is not always fun or easy for parents and children. Like any parenting of young children in public, there are trying and embarrassing moments. The educator can see these times as opportunities to intervene with support and empathy. Other times, modeling ways to guide or redirect a child or set limits can be appropriate. Difficult moments between parent and child during the early years are typical and to be expected. While some preventative measures can be taken to limit the number of difficult moments, they are inevitable, and the parent educator's skill in intervening is crucial. These tend to be times where parents are emotionally invested and real learning can occur or, conversely, parents can leave a class feeling incompetent, embarrassed, and not wanting to come back. A couple of typical problem scenarios will be described below. There are a number of possible strategies for successful intervention that can be used in different combinations. It helps to consider options that may fit different parent personalities and different parent educator-parent relationship levels.

SITUATION 1: SEPARATION BLUES

Parents in a 3-year-old group are getting ready to go to the parent discussion in another room. Jamal protests when his mother Tenisha starts to leave, grabs her leg, and begins to cry. Tenisha looks embarrassed and uncertain about what to do. She enjoys parent discussion time and could use a break, but she feels guilty leaving Jamal.

This is a typical situation for young children and likely to occur when a new class is beginning. A number of suggestions for addressing this situation follow.

1. Reassure the parent that Jamal will be okay and that, if he doesn't calm down in a couple of minutes, the staff will come to the parent discussion room to get her.

2. Give mom the option to stay if she feels this is best for Jamal. Leave the decision to the mother and let her know that Jamal's behavior is a typical reaction for some children at his age. Children will get more comfortable as they come to understand the program routine and develop a trusting relationship with the early childhood teacher. Sometimes, it helps for a parent to stay for a while until the child calms down. It can be easier to say good-bye when the child is engaged in an activity. Child teachers can help by working with the parent to help the child find something to do and by being with the child when the parent is ready to leave.

3. Spend some time with Tenisha after the session to share information from the parent discussion. The parent educator could also spend time with Tenisha planning a strategy for her to help Jamal to feel comfortable so that she can begin to join the other parents. These might include showing Jamal where mom will be, leaving her jacket or other personal item in the room so that he remembers she has not left, or suggesting that she stay in the room as an observer without playing with him to encourage him to explore and enjoy play opportunities with the early childhood teacher and other children.

SITUATION 2: CIRCLE TIME WANDERER

Parents and children ages 2–3 are singing songs and doing finger plays during circle time. Traci tries to get 2-year-old Josh to join in. Josh says no and runs off to a corner of the room to play with the train set. Mom yells at him to come back to the circle and sing with the rest of the children. He ignores her, and Traci is both angry and embarrassed. The positive energy in the circle begins to fade.

1. **Assure mom that it is okay for Josh to be on his own if he is safe**. He will come to join the group when he is ready.

2. **Change the activity level in the circle time to a more active song** that might be inviting for Josh and keeps the other children and parents focused on circle time.

3. **Talk to Traci privately about circle time**. Discuss the purpose of circle time and expectations for children who are Josh's age. Josh's behavior can be described as typical for some 2-year-olds. This helps to normalize the behavior and helps Traci feel assured that Josh is not a bad child, nor is she a bad parent, because her child is not participating in circle time. The parent educator can address the issue of circle time in the group setting and discuss the purpose, expectations for children this age, ways to help children with the transition to circle time, and what to do if a child doesn't want to participate.

SITUATION 3: INATTENTIVE PARENTS

Five-year-old Amanda is working on making playdough cookies. She keeps trying to show them to her dad. Dad is talking to another parent whose daughter Felicia is clinging to her leg and whining to go play at the water table. Both parents seem oblivious to their children's demand for attention and continue talking about the upcoming school bond issue.

1. **Model a positive response to the child.** The parent educator can come over to Amanda and tell her, "Your cookies look delicious." This may get the parent to also pay attention.

2. **Redirect the parent's attention to the child's activity with a comment.** The parent educator can ask the parent to "check-out" the cookies Amanda has

made. Gently guide the parents to refocus on their children without making them feel they are being corrected.

3. Affirm the importance of the parents' concerns. The parent educator may join the two parents and ask them if they would like to talk more about the bond issue during the parent group time. The parent educator can affirm that it is an important issue and also note that the children both look ready to play right now.

The goal in this situation is to help the parent and child reconnect and interact around an activity. This means that parent educator has to redirect a parent's attention and still give time for the adults to connect in other ways. Sometimes, parents don't have the skills to interact with their children in a child-oriented environment, and educators need to model interactions. Other times, parents are bored with child activities and find it more interesting to talk to other adults. They may feel that they spend enough time paying attention to their child at home. If this is the situation, the parent educator must help the parent understand the purpose of parent-child interaction time and what children gain from getting this focused attention from their parents. Programs may also try to create a space during parent time for informal sharing that promotes connection between parents.

SITUATION 4: THE BORED CHILD

Seven-year-old Ramón is looking bored while his mother Carlita finishes a book-making project. He refuses to help her and wants to go play outside with his friends.

1. Redirect Ramón to help his mother finish the book so that he can go join his friends outside. Make a suggestion about a specific task that Ramón could do to help his mother finish the book.

2. Engage Ramón in a conversation. Find out what activities Ramón likes to do, and look for opportunities to create parent-child activities that would be more engaging for Ramón in the future.

Designing parent-child activities for older children can be more challenging. If activities are too much like "school projects," they may not be appealing to some children. A child may also not feel successful at certain activities and avoid them. It can help to provide a range of activities so that children can have some choices that are more appealing and more likely to match with children's interests. The goal in parent-child interaction is to support parents and children in having a good time doing activities together. It helps to have projects that are both novel and challenging for children and parents. Parents may also need some modeling about how to engage children in an activity and work with the child to finish the activity.

SITUATION 5: REFUSING TO SHARE

Sharon, the mother of 2-year-old Angela, asks her daughter to stop painting and let another child who has been waiting have a turn. Sharon begins to take the brush out of Angela's hand and Angela tries to hit mom with a messy paintbrush and gets paint on her mom's shirt. Mom gets mad and smacks Angela on her bottom. Angela begins to cry.

1. Assist the parent and child in calming down. Move closer to the parent and child and talk in a calm voice. You might offer to help mom get the paint off her shirt or to stay with Angela while mom goes to clean the paint from her shirt. Some distance between parent and child may help both cool off at this point.

2. Help the mother to understand the child's behavior. Describe how sharing is difficult for most 2-year-olds and talk about the process of learning to share. Assist Sharon in thinking about how to encourage Angela to share, focusing on supportive strategies and realistic expectations.

3. Set clear limits for the parent about physical punishment in the program. Parents need to know program rules about spanking children in "school." Sharon can be reminded privately about this rule when she calms down. Parents in a situation like this can be angry and frustrated and feel the program is not allowing them to discipline their own child. Sharon may also be embarrassed if she lost her temper and didn't really want to hit her daughter. It helps to know how the parent is thinking and feeling to decide what to do next.

In a situation with an angry parent and child, the most important goal for the parent educator is to remain calm. The parent in this situation may not be able to hear about appropriate child development, alternative strategies for teaching sharing, or program rules about hitting. The parent educator can move in and help to deescalate the parent-child conflict by helping the child to calm down, as well as spending some time with the parent just listening to her version of what happened and why she got upset. Once the mom has calmed down, you can address other issues knowing which areas are most important to emphasize with this mom. If a trusting relationship has already been established, the parent educator can help mom to understand her daughter's behavior and other ways to handle this situation. This should be done in a tone of caring and concern. Mom may be stressed out and need support for her own issues. She may also be defensive about her actions. Remaining calm and respectful will help create a space to talk about this situation and make it easier to talk about program rules and support alternative discipline strategies.

SITUATION 6: THE LITTLE PERFORMER

Paul wants to show the parent educator Joanne how his 5-month-old daughter Alicia has learned to crawl. He puts Alicia down on the floor and takes a rattle away from her. Alicia tries to get the rattle but only manages to go backwards. Paul continues to prod Alicia who gets frustrated and begins to cry. Paul says one more time, "You know how to crawl."

1. Redirect the parent to try another activity. "It's okay, she may not be up to crawling today, but it looks like she really wants her rattle." The parent educator can move the rattle into baby's reach and let her calm herself.

2. Use reflective language with the baby to model how to get a child to calm down. "You're feeling frustrated that you can't get your rattle. Let's try a new position." The parent educator can move the baby to a different position.

3. Help the parent understand the process of how a child learns to crawl. The parent educator can explain that some children end up going backwards until they are a little older and have the coordination to get all parts of their body moving in the same direction. The parent educator can focus on other new abilities that Alicia has acquired. In this situation, the parent wants his baby to perform and is not being sensitive to the baby's cues. He may need some help to appreciate what his baby can do and how to read his baby's cues when she is frustrated. Clear information about development of motor skills can also help Paul understand the sequence and range of developing skills.

PARENT-CHILD INTERACTION AND OBSERVATION WITH INDIVIDUAL PARENTS

Parent-child interaction and observation and can also be important components of home visits or individual consultations with parents. Children are typically present during these times, and the parent educator usually includes parent-child activities. The parent educator brings activities that can easily be replicated in the home and offers an opportunity for the parent and child to enjoy this special time together. Additionally, the parent is provided an experience to learn more about their child, and the parent educator can model and affirm the dyad as he or she gains new insight into their relationship. The one-to-one relationship in a more intimate setting allows for a focused learning opportunity for the parent, child, and educator.

Observation can be incorporated when working individually with a parent., as well. As the child plays with a toy or engages in an activity, the parent educator and parent can pull back and observe. "Watch how your child is figuring out how this toy works." "What might he be thinking right now?" "Notice what choices she is making." These questions, quietly posed to the parent, guide the observation to make it meaningful. Parent educators can give parents, either in groups or individually, simple "assignments" for the week that ask them to take a few minutes and observe as their child is playing alone. They might take a few notes on what they observed, along with their own feelings and reactions to observing, and then share those reflections at the next group meeting or home visit. With some encouragement to set aside short periods of time to truly observe, this can become a treasured part of the parent-child relationship.

SUMMARY

The following tips summarize important ideas from this chapter for creating effective parent-child interaction components for parent education programs:

1.   Parent-child interaction time can address a variety of goals in a parent education program. Parent educators should consider both parent and child needs and clearly articulate the program goals for both parents and children.

2.   The expectations for parents and children should be explained to parents. Parents will appreciate knowing what roles the program wants them to play and what rules or limits the program has for their children.

3.   Parent-child interaction should be designed to bring parent and child together with activities that require active participation for both parent and child.

4.   Parent-child interaction time can be threatening to some parents who are concerned about being judged. Sensitivity to parent feelings of embarrassment when children misbehave can support parents through difficult moments.

5.   The tone and energy in parent child time should be light and fun. Careful design of activities that incorporate parent and child interests can increase the likelihood that both parents and children will have fun and enjoy their time together.

DISCUSSION QUESTIONS

1. What can a parent educator learn about a child during parent-child interaction time?

2. What roles can the parent educator play during observation time? What are the benefits of each of these roles?

3. Give examples of observation questions that fit with with specific discussion topics?

4. Discuss how parent-child activities might be adapted for children ages 6–12 and 13–18.

CLASS ACTIVITIES

1. Observe a program that uses parent-child interaction time, and interview staff about their goals and philosophy around including this component in their program.

2. Plan a set of five different parent-child activities for parents of infants, toddlers, and preshoolers. Discuss the different goals for parents and children for each age level.

3. Role play some of the difficult moments, and discuss various approaches and how parents and parent educators feel with different approaches.

REFERENCES

Brock, G. (1989). Parenting program with parent-child interaction. Paper presented at the National Council on Family Relations Annual Conference in New Orleans.

Campbell, D., & Palm, G.F. (2004). *Group parent education: Promoting parent learning and support.* Thousand Oaks, CA: Sage Publications.

Centers for Disease Control and Prevention (2009). *Parent training programs: Insight for practitioners.* Atlanta, GA: Centers for Disease Control. Retrieved from https://www.cdc.gov/violenceprevention/pdf/parent_training_brief-a.pdf.

Darling, S., and Hayes, (1989). Breaking the Cycle of Illiteracy: The Kenan Family Literacy Program. Louisville, KY: William Kenan, Jr., Charitable Trust Family Literacy Project.

District 742 Parent-Child Program (1993). PAT Educator's Manual. St. Cloud, MN: Parent-Child Program District 742 Community Education Early Childhood Family Education.

Erickson, M.F., and Kurz-Reimer, K. (1999). *Infants, toddlers, and families: A framework for support and intervention.* New York, NY: Guilford.

Grindal, T, Bowne, J.B., Yoshikawa, H., Schindler, H.S., Duncan, G.J., Magnuson, K., & Shonkoff, J.P. (2016). The added impact of parenting education in early childhood education programs: A meta-analysis. *Children and Youth Services Review, 70,* 238–249.

Kristensen, N. (1984). A Guide for developing early childhood and family education programs. White Bear Lake, MN: Minnesota Curriculum Services Center.

Moore, A.R. and Clement, M.J. (1998). Effects of parenting training for incarcerated mothers. *Journal of Offender Rehabilitation, 27*(1/2), 57–72.

Palm, G. (1992). Building intimacy and parenting skills through father-child activity time. In L. Johnson & G. Palm (Eds.), *Working with fathers: methods and perspectives* (pp.79–100). Stillwater, MN: nu ink unlimited.

St. Pierre, R., Layzer, J. & Barnes, H. (1995). Two generation programs: Design, cost and short term effectiveness. *The Future of Children: Long-Term Outcomes of Early childhood Programs, 5*(3), 76–93.

14

PROFESSIONAL GROWTH AND DEVELOPMENT OF PARENT EDUCATORS

"This [parent education] is a lot more complicated than I thought. There is so much to learn and keep track of."

"It looked so easy from my perspective as a parent. I thought it would be fun and easy to facilitate a parent group. I never realized what goes on beneath the surface."

These quotes represent common responses from parents who have entered the parent education licensure program during the last 25 years in Minnesota. The skillful parent educator can make parent group facilitation look easy. As parents enter our program at St. Cloud State University as students of parent education, they realize that the role of parent educator is both complex and demanding. However, research on parent education effectiveness has focused on curriculum, ignoring the complex role of the parent educator in providing high-quality programming. Studies in the past often included a small sample of parents and measured parenting knowledge and skills using a pre- and post-test design (e.g., Todres & Bunston, 1993). In more rigorous studies, a control group and random assignment to a group are used. This type of program research examines connections between a parent education curriculum and parent acquisition of new knowledge, attitudes, or skills. The competence of the parent educator who implements or teaches a curriculum is a salient variable that has been ignored in this type of parent education research. Educator competence is a highly complex variable to assess and study. However, it is, perhaps, the most important variable of all. Kumpfer and Alvarado (1998), after reviewing many parent education programs for program efficacy, estimated that 50% to 80% of the quality of a program is related to the parent educator. Evidence-based parenting programs or curriculum packages (National Center for Parent, Family, and Community Engagement, 2015) are important tools for parent education, but focused professional preparation and ongoing professional development are also needed to improve the quality and effectiveness of parent education.

We believe that competent parent educators are the heart of an effective parent and family education program. Curriculum materials are important tools that can add to program effectiveness, but they are *not* the program. Parent education curricula don't function like a software program that can be loaded onto multiple computers (i.e., parent educators) and operate in the same way. Curricula are most effective when they are implemented by a competent, caring parent educator who has developed the knowledge, technical skills, and artistry necessary for effective parent education programs. A skilled professional parent educator has the ability to individualize and structure a curriculum to meet the needs of a particular group; to respond to unexpected questions and concerns of parents; and to support parents by directly addressing and processing emotions in the group setting. He or she facilitates a group process that is fluid and responsive to the unique makeup of each parent group. The skills involved in this role are highly sophisticated and differ from the beginning skill levels expected to present a packaged curriculum on specific parenting topics.

The focus of this book thus far has been on the knowledge, dispositions, and facilitation skills that individuals need to be competent and effective parent educators in group parent education contexts. This final chapter will examine the topic of professional growth and development in parent educators. This growth process will be described from a developmental perspective that outlines different stages of professional development for parent educators from beginners/novices to master teachers. The key to supporting professional development in parent educators is the application of reflective practice principles, strong supervision and mentoring, and ongoing reflective supervision. Reflective practice in parent education includes a thoughtful exploration of practice with general goals of improving the effectiveness of practice and promoting ethical practice.

Assessment in parent education is one practical aspect of reflective practice that will also be explored in this chapter. Support for professional development in parent education has been limited by the embeddedness of the parent educator role in other primary roles described in Chapter 2. Professionals in related fields tend to view parent education as only a part of their larger role and may find limited opportunities for professional development around specific parent education competencies. Because of the embeddedness of parent education, there has been a tendency to discount the role of parent educator, and the lack of research on characteristics and preparation of parent educators has limited the understanding of the professional development of master parent educators. In this final chapter, we borrow insights about reflective practice and reflective supervision from education and related fields. We also draw upon our own clinical experiences as teacher educators, supervisors of parent educators, and program evaluators to outline a model of professional growth and development for parent education.

DEVELOPMENTAL STAGES OF PARENT EDUCATORS

The development of professionals often follows some specific pathways toward greater competency, comfort, and effectiveness. There has been no specific research focused on parent educators and their professional development over time. Both authors have had the unique opportunity to observe the development of parent educators in the Early Childhood Family Education (ECFE) programs in Minnesota, which started in the mid-1970s (Kurz-Riemer, 2001). Our own professional development as parent educators and our roles as teacher educators and supervisors have given us a unique vantage point to observe typical patterns of growth and development in parent educators. Professional development opportunities for ECFE teachers have been provided through state-wide inservice workshops twice a year, as well as conferences and workshops offered by related professional organizations. All licensed parent educators in Minnesota have to complete 125 hours of approved continuing education every 5 years to maintain their licensure. This environment has nurtured professional growth in licensed parent educators who often teach multiple groups per week.

Table 14.1 outlines three general stages of growth and development for parent educators in five different areas of development: content knowledge, facilitation skills, teaching skills, self-awareness, and understanding diversity. The potential knowledge bases for parent educators to incorporate into practice are extensive, including interdisciplinary knowledge of child development, child-rearing strategies, family system dynamics and development, and awareness of community resources for parents, families, and children.

The novice is often overwhelmed by the breadth of child development and family dynamics content. Beginning parent educators often feel anxious or

Table 14.1 Levels of Professional Development for Parent Educators

NOVICE LEVEL	INTERMEDIATE LEVEL	MASTER TEACHING LEVEL
KNOWLEDGE		
Aware of basic child development and parenting information. Some apprehension about being able to answer parents' questions.	Possesses broader knowledge base. Aware of a variety of resources on development and parenting issues.	Confident about being able to answer questions and to find resources. Committed to ongoing learning.
Aware of basic stages and theories of family dynamics and development.	Able to identify individual families' circumstances in reference to stages and characteristics.	Uses holistic perspective to understand each family's journey. Able to link current challenges and successes to stages and cycles of development. Understands and provides insight into impact of family of origin as well as current family dynamics.
Beginning to understand community resources. Some uncertainty about what is available and how to refer parents to other services.	Aware of basic community services and some comfort with access. Understands referral process in own program.	Able to access information and services easily. Comfortable approaching parents with referrals. Uses a holistic perspective and a collaborative approach with parents.
GROUP FACILITATION SKILLS		
Understands group process but feels challenged with the complexity of skills needed for group leadership.	Enjoys group leadership. Focuses primarily on content and plans for sessions.	Confident as a group leader. Able to blend support and possible intervention with content. Understands group behavior and can utilize skills to respond.
Understands dynamics of conflict and behaviors. Uncomfortable dealing with difficult group/individual dynamics.	Has some skills to address challenging behaviors, mostly to defuse them and refocus group.	Is comfortable with addressing challenging or difficult group dynamics. Recognizes and uses "teachable moments." Takes responsibility for healthy group process and development.

TEACHING SKILLS		
Understands adult learning styles.	Plans and executes sessions with a variety of teaching methods but uses discussion as a primary method.	Able to assess parents' needs and styles and match methods accordingly. Shows insight in planning and leading to meet diverse needs of group and parents.
Able to develop and implement an appropriate parent education lesson plan.	Able to tailor a plan to an individual group. Able to assess ongoing needs of group and modify plan as needed.	Uses creative and varied methods for group education. Has clear goals and objectives, and is flexible in adjusting plans.
PROFESSIONAL IDENTITY AND BOUNDARIES		
Shows basic self-awareness, but has limited understanding of impact on relationship with group and role as facilitator.	Has insight into self and family-of-origin experiences and their impact on the role as a parent educator.	Has maturity and life experiences that reflect deeper understanding and self-awareness. Aware of values and emotions and their impact on practice.
Uncertain about skills and abilities as a parent educator.	Growing confidence from positive experiences with parents that affirm abilities as a parent educator.	Has quiet confidence in own abilities. Leadership role within the parent group as well as within the profession as a mentor and a guide for other professionals.
UNDERSTANDING DIVERSITY		
Shows basic awareness of and sensitivity to importance of diversity issues. Not sure how to integrate into practice.	Growing awareness of family and cultural diversity and its impact on family and parenting issues.	Values family structure and cultural diversity in programs. Willing to learn from parents. Respectfully addresses and facilitates discussion about differences.

inadequate when a parent asks a question that is beyond their current knowledge base. For example, a beginning parent educator has designed a parenting session on nutrition for toddlers and has prepared a lesson plan based on what types of food to eat and how much food is necessary for the typical toddler. A parent then asks how long she should expect her toddler to sit down with the family for dinner. Although this is a common concern of parents, it is new to the parent educator and outside the topic information that she has prepared. Parent educators who are able to use resources to find information to address specific parent questions begin to expand their knowledge base around common parenting issues. A parent educator at the master teacher level has learned to listen carefully to parent questions and has built a solid knowledge base around this set of typical parent concerns. He or she is also able to understand individual parent and family needs and match information and resources to these needs on the basis of a more complex and sophisticated understanding of both children and families, as well as firsthand knowledge of relevant community resources.

The growth in facilitation skills over time and a growing confidence in those skills prepares parent educators to address difficult situations more directly and effectively. The parent group leader at the master teacher level has the ability to blend support with content and intervention for group members. Teaching skills also evolve from a basic understanding of adult learning and session design to the ability to informally assess parent needs and styles of learning and match appropriate teaching methods to these needs. The master teacher level includes parent educators who use creative and varied strategies to engage parents and facilitate their learning. At times, experienced parent educators use a very limited repertoire of methods that feel safe and comfortable to them. They design sessions in the same way for every topic. They begin with a short brainstorm of issues, go on to a mini-lecture with content material, and finally introduce a small group discussion of three to four important points. The master teacher continues to ask, "How do I improve my session on self-esteem?" and explores new ideas and strategies for teaching parents. He or she also continues to create and evaluate different theoretical models for teaching parents.

The professional identity and self-awareness of parent educators also change over time in some predictable ways. New parent educators have limited understanding of their impact on parents and are often uncertain about their own skills as parent educators. However as their professional identities develop, they begin to understand their own values and biases. They are able to set clear boundaries for their practice. They also begin to mentor other professionals and articulate important insights and share effective practices. They are more confident about their skills and more aware of their limitations.

The final area of growth and development that is described in Table 14.1 concerns understanding diversity. Diversity issues within parent and family education are essential for parent educators to understand. Novice parent educators start with a basic awareness and sensitivity about diversity. They often don't know how to integrate this understanding into their practice with families. As they work with families, their experience with and understanding of family diversity expands. Parent educators at the master teacher level embrace cultural and family diversity as a rich and powerful asset to a parent group. They are able to address family differences respectfully and directly and draw upon these differences to create a richer learning environment. When they meet a parent in their group whose culture or family system is different from that of other group members, they know how to use this as an opportunity to explore different ideas and practices in a respectful manner that can benefit the whole group. Small and Kupsik, 2015) describe the "Art of Practice" that is similar to the master level where the parent/family practitioner is able to deal with unpredictable and challenging situations in groups.

The growth process outlined in Table 14.1 begins to capture some of the depth and breadth of knowledge and skills that parent educators can develop over time if they are given support and resources to continue to grow and learn. The embeddedness of parent educators within other roles can slow down the pace and direction of the growth that is described here. For example, a social worker who facilitates parent education groups may develop some of the facilitation skills but may not develop a better understanding of teaching methods or may be limited in understanding child development. A clear and direct focus on parent education as a primary professional identity can support professional growth in a more balanced manner. The professional identity also creates opportunities to develop and articulate artistry in the role of parent educator.

SUPERVISION OF PARENT EDUCATORS

The role of the supervisor is critical in any program offering parent education. High-quality, well-trained, supported, and committed parent educators are the core of a successful program. Ongoing support and continuing education of staff are the responsibility of the supervisor. This section will address the role of the supervisor and the types of support and continuing education that will enhance and maintain high-quality programs.

The formal process and requirements of supervision will be dictated primarily by the sponsoring agency employing the parent educator. In school settings, there are procedures and policies that require formal observations by administrators, feedback, staff development plans, goal setting, and evaluation. Other settings will have similar, as well as their own unique, requirements for supervisors of parent educators. Ideally, the supervisor will be able to fulfill the requirements of the organization, and at the same time, make the experience meaningful for the parent educator.

In many ways, the identity and affiliation of the parent educator can be complex. Parent educators may work in a school system and yet have a role that differs greatly from traditional teachers and their students. For example, they could be assigned to hospitals but are not part of the medical staff. Or they may work in public health, human services, or prisons where their roles and responsibilities are different from other employees, and their needs for professional development are also different.

A good example of this challenge is in school settings where many parent educators are employed. Since parent education is a very specific professional role, and the "students" in groups are typically not graded or tested, the requirements that administrators must follow when supervising teachers may not always fit the professional development needs of the parent educator. For instance, teachers in a school system may be evaluated based on their students' achievements in various subject areas. Traditional teachers whose students do not make adequate progress might receive lower ratings from their supervisors. Goals are set based on particular outcomes. Evaluation tools are designed for traditional classroom teachers. In a parent education program that often focuses on prevention, the concepts of adequate progress, testing, and grading for parents as "students" do not apply. The system in which the parent educator works may not offer a comparable objective way to measure progress and meet accountability expectations.

Providing high-quality and appropriate supervision to any helping professional is integral to the fidelity of a program. In the educational realm, Glickman et al. (2001) write that effective supervision is the glue that holds together individual teachers' needs and school goals. Glickman also noted, "Glue, if functioning properly, cannot be seen" (p. 9). In response to this analogy, Fritz and Miller (2003) state, "Likewise, when supervision functions properly, it also goes unnoticed; but when glue quits sticking, as in the case of inadequate supervision, the object (the school system) will collapse" (p. 15). High-quality, meaningful supervision is integral to the professional growth of all teachers, including those in the field of parent education. The question is how to provide ongoing supervision that promotes professional development in a relevant and meaningful way for parent educators. As with other conceptual frameworks, theories, and models, it is helpful to examine related professional approaches to supervision.

Bashirinia (2013) distinguishes two models of supervision for social workers, which closely relates to parent education. In procedure supervision, the goals focus on updating on individual clients, addressing family progress, reviewing procedural issues and expectations, and other more measurable objectives of the social worker's role. Process supervision, on the other hand, addresses feelings that arise in working with parents, developing self-awareness, and examining how individual values influence the work of the social worker. These two models from the field of social work also apply to the supervision from which parent educators would benefit. While the organizational requirements are met through procedural supervision, the parent educator should also have the opportunity to experience process supervision as a way to reflect on the more emotional aspects of the work.

In another helping profession, the field of counseling and therapy, new therapists are typically required to participate in supervision with a more experienced therapist who has been trained to provide this service. A variety of models are utilized that often mirror the therapeutic approach used by the therapist and the supervisor. Psychotherapy-based models reflect the approach of therapy itself, which includes strategies such as affective reactions, defense mechanisms, and transference (Smith, 2009). For example, cognitive behavioral supervision addresses the observable behaviors and reactions of the supervisee. Person-centered supervision provides an approach from the supervisor that he or she is not an expert, but more of a collaborator with the newer therapist who is seen to have their own resources for successful professional development. In parent education, a similar parallel process often develops between supervisor and supervisee that mirrors the relationship between the educator and the parents with whom they work. An in-depth discussion of reflective practice and consultation approaches that are also being used in parent education settings are included later in this chapter.

Supervision of parent educators can incorporate and blend useful strategies and approaches from other helping professions. Adhering to the requirements of sponsoring agencies is necessary and will bond parent educators to the system in which they work. Utilizing adaptations and appropriate approaches from other professions will make supervision experiences meaningful and beneficial to a parent educator's professional growth and development.

One of the tasks within the role of the supervisor is to provide experiences that promote ongoing professional growth of parent educators. This can be done through a variety of methods that expose teachers to current ideas and strategies, as well as experiences, that support them in their work. Attendance at trainings, workshops, and conferences is helpful to keep parent educators energized and up to date on current research, theory, and practice materials. Yet, it is important that this information be shared and reflected upon after returning to the program. Staff and peer meetings provide an opportunity for parent educators to share new information they have learned, process it with colleagues, and determine how it might be useful in the parent education setting.

Since parent educators are expanding their roles through collaborative efforts with other community professionals, cross training offers ways to be better partners when working with parents and families. Chapter 3 presents a continuum model that identifies examples of collaborative partnerships where this type of training would be beneficial. If parent educators are to move outside the isolation of leading parent groups, having contact with the larger professional community, cross training is important. Attending trainings together, serving on advisory councils, inviting representatives of collaborative partnerships to staff and team meetings, and providing informative sessions about each other's programs all enhance the knowledge of parent educators while providing a means of developing positive relationships within those partnerships.

Additionally, mentoring programs can be an excellent way for parent educators to learn from others in similar roles. Within the profession, seasoned parent educators have an obligation to nurture new staff who are beginning their professional lives. These experienced staff can observe and be observed by entry-level parent educators, provide valuable feedback and suggestions, and offer ongoing support. In addition to one-on-one mentoring, group mentoring is another model that can maximize the support given to beginning parent educators, as well as to those who are more experienced. Peer group meetings where parent educators can bring up challenges in their groups, discuss possible strategies, and identify feelings about their work benefit all staff.

From our experience ... Mentoring and peer support can be powerful experiences that enhance the professional growth of parent educators. In the program I directed, peer group meetings, observations and feedback sessions by mentors and peers, and videotaping were all ways parent educators could learn from others. One challenge was that, occasionally, a mentee or a parent educator who received feedback from another peer felt they were being evaluated by that person. It was important for all staff to understand that this feedback was not the same as an evaluation, which was my responsibility as the supervisor. Additionally, the feedback from peers was confidential and was not included in the evaluation process. Most staff valued the opportunity to hear from peers they trusted and also to share their ideas and impressions with others.

Supervisors who develop formal mentoring programs assigning experienced staff to entry-level teachers look for particular qualities of mentors that promote professional growth and healthy colleague relationships. Longevity in the field is not the only consideration. Rowley (1999) suggests these qualities in effective mentors:

- Shows a commitment to the role of mentoring
- Promotes an acceptance of, and respect for, the beginning teacher
- Demonstrates skill at providing instructional support
- Exemplifies effective interpersonal skills in different contexts
- Models the role of continuous learner
- Encourages hope and optimism

Successful mentors soon realize that they also benefit from the experience of mentoring and supporting less experienced parent educators. In addition to sharing their expertise, they are often challenged to consider their own choices in discussions with their mentees. They also gain new ideas and perspectives from the incoming parent educator and develop a new relationship with an emerging professional.

Supervisors can view staff and peer meetings in different ways. Some see them as a means of disseminating information, while others view them as opportunities for reflection, problem solving, and sharing experiences. In this digital age, procedural and informational sharing can be done quickly and efficiently through emails and other means. Much of this type of sharing, when done in staff meetings, takes valuable time away from staff. Parent educators typically express appreciation for staff and peer meetings that include time to discuss and share ideas and challenges, help each other with problem solving, and offer support to one another.

From our experience ... I have learned how important it is for parent educators to have allotted time within their schedules for teaming, debriefing, and supporting each other. Peer meetings that offer opportunities to bring challenges to the group and share experiences and suggestions are a wise investment in maintaining a quality program. Parent educators who lead groups and who work with parents individually can feel isolated without the opportunity to connect with others who understand their challenges. While it is helpful for supervisors to provide this type of support to those they lead, it is also important for parent educators to spend time either one-on-one with mentors or in peer groups to learn from and support each other.

Supervision of parent educators is an important aspect of an administrative role. While the supervisor has some expertise, knowledge, and access to resources, his or her role can be enhanced and expanded by enlisting the help of those within the program as mentors along with experienced experts from the community to provide options that are relevant and meaningful to parent education professionals.

REFLECTIVE PRACTICE IN PARENT EDUCATION

The Alert Novices, the more reflective interns in this study, had a tendency to ask "why" questions—questions directed at the roots of problems and at the meanings of ideas and action.

—V. La Boskey, Development of Reflective Practice:
A Study of Preservice Teachers

Reflective practice has been a general term used to describe the attitudes and behaviors of practitioners in a variety of fields who continue to improve their own knowledge and skills and seek to understand how effective practice works (Dewey, 1933; Kirby & Paradise, 1992; LaBoskey, 1994; Palm, 1998; Schon, 1983). Reflective practice will be explored as a paradigm that supports professional growth and development in parent education. This section will introduce different strategies and processes related to reflective practice that have emerged during recent years. Reflective practice has become a central paradigm in education and currently has a strong influence on pre-service and in-service programs for early education, educational administration, and elementary and secondary education (LaBoskey, 1994). Reflective practice in parent education has been less visible and has not been discussed in professional literature on parent education (Palm, 1998). Auerbach (1968) described the complexity of group parent education and the need for balance of many competing factors and goals, such as facts and feelings, individual and group focus, and general and specific information. Her insights into the complexity of parent education demonstrate an understanding of reflective practice and the complexity of the skills and knowledge base necessary for effective parent group facilitation.

The next section will examine the multiple meanings of reflective practice (LaBoskey, 1994). The history of reflective practice from Dewey (1933) to contemporary ideas (Dokecki, 1996; Schon, 1983, 1987) will be traced to describe the evolution of thinking about reflective practice. A definition of reflective practice for parent education will be outlined, and specific ideas for application to group parent education will be presented. Reflective practice is presented as a practical model to support professional development in parent education. The complexity of parent-child relations within diverse family systems makes the field of parent education a good match for applying a reflective practice paradigm.

MULTIPLE MEANINGS OF REFLECTIVE PRACTICE

Reflective practice is a concept with many different dimensions that has been applied in various professional settings (Schon, 1987). The recent applications in the field of education are the most relevant to understanding how it can be applied to parent education. Confusion about reflective practice often stems from the integrative nature of the paradigm. This integration includes knowledge, values, attitudes, skills, and emotions (LaBoskey, 1994). The appeal of reflective practice is that it attempts to include so many different elements in trying to understand and improve practice. It also presents many different interpretations of how it can be implemented. The three elements of teacher competencies all come into play: dispositions/attitudes, knowledge/content, and skills/techniques. A subtle emphasis on one of these areas can change the tone and focus of reflective practice. On another level, LaBoskey (1994) identified three other dimensions of reflective practice: practical/technical, social/political, and moral/ethical. Although there may be wide agreement about the importance of these dimensions and different types of competencies, the application and focus of reflective practice are likely to end up on one area of competency and one dimension of content. For example, the focus on specific teaching skills and best practices as the content area is one combination that appeals to many practitioners. It helps to understand these broad parameters of reflective practice as a starting point for applying this paradigm to parent education.

Reflective practice is often traced back to Dewey (1933), who described it in a general way as a mode of thought that includes skepticism, perplexity, and mental difficulty. Reflective practice is an attempt to reduce the uncertainty and understand ambiguity by conducting a careful inquiry and searching for new understanding that can improve practice. Dewey understood the complexity of educational practice and the necessity of careful and reflective inquiry to address the complexity and manage the accompanying uncertainty. He had faith in the power of logic and the utility of thoughtful inquiry as the path to greater understanding and improved practice. He also described the basic dispositions that have become essential character traits for reflective practice. Dewey presents three basic attitudes that undergird reflective practice: open-mindedness, responsibility, and wholeheartedness.

Open-mindedness is the desire to know why and keep asking questions and looking at different perspectives to gain a deeper understanding. In parent education, this translates to listening to parents, researchers, and peers to gain a more complete understanding about the complexity of parenting and parent education practice. Responsibility is a sense of social commitment to improving the field, family life, and society by understanding the long-term impacts of practice. The final disposition is wholeheartedness, which represents a passion that allows educators to take risks and follow their ideals and ethics in the face of criticism and tradition. Dewey's ideas about reflective practice represent his ideals about education and reflect some of the basic principles of progressive education. They continue to have meaning and relevance to education and can be applied to parent education in a fresh and meaningful way.

The reemergence of reflective practice in the 1980s (Schon, 1983, 1987) was in response to the increasing awareness of complexity and uncertainty in society and in professional practice. Schon questioned scientific research as the only way to inform practice and solve real-world problems and made a strong case for increased understanding of and appreciation for the artistry of practitioners in a variety of professional fields. The gap between research, theory, and practice has been traced back to professionalization in the beginning of the 20th century. Schon (1987) described the real world of the late 20th century as a "swampland" with messy and confusing problems that were a poor match with the traditional approaches of academic research and theory, which tended to outline clear-cut rational-technical solutions. In addressing problems in real society and real families, practitioners face complexity, change, uncertainty, and value conflicts. Family life in the late 20th and early 21st centuries reflects the characteristics of Schon's swampland: increasing diversity, complexity, and fragility. Schon's focus on trying to understand the artistry of the practitioner who faces the "swampland" problems and makes progress is also relevant to the field of parent education. Our increasing research knowledge base of child development and family dynamics has not always informed the practice of parent education or interfaced with the real problems that parent educators face in working with parents in complex and fragile family systems. At the same time that Schon (1987) acknowledged the artistry and intuitive understanding of practitioners, he supported the reconnection of academic research and practice in a spirit of mutual respect and collaboration (Palm, 1998).

Dokecki (1996) explored reflective practice within human service professions and added some important ideas to our understanding. He introduced the term *ethical reflective generative practice.* In his model, all practice in human services is grounded in the ethical principle of promoting the common good. Dokecki also connected his idea of reflective practice to generative theory, "where the practitioner is an inquirer who pursues the development of theory to improve the human condition according to rationally chosen values" (Palm, 1998, p. 9). Dokecki's contribution to reflective practice includes (a) the clear focus on the ethical nature of practice; (b) the connection to generative developmental theory with a focus on long-term outcomes; and (c) the emphasis on practitioner-client relationship as a collaborative partnership in solving problems. This model also can be applied to parent education practice and provides both clarity and specific direction for reflective practice.

Palm (1998) applied a number of important ideas from reflective practice to parenting programs for fathers. These ideas can be applied to the broader field of parent education. The specific characteristics can be adapted for all parent educators.

1. The reflective practitioner recognizes the ethical nature of working with parents and families.

2. The reflective practitioner maintains a clear focus on the goal of enhancing human growth and development in both parents and children.

3. The reflective practitioner takes responsibility for establishing collaborative relationships with parents and researchers in order to improve practice.

4. The reflective practitioner takes responsibility for continuing to develop technical expertise based on theory, research, and practice.

5. The reflective practitioner understands the critical role of artistry/intuition in parent education practice and works to articulate and enhance this artistry. (Palm, 1998)

This description serves as both an operational definition and as a model for reflective practice in parent education. The next step is to describe what reflective practice looks like in action in parent education.

Parent educators engage in reflective practice as they discuss challenges of group facilitation

REFLECTIVE PRACTICE IN ACTION

Reflective practice provides many opportunities to enhance professional growth and development in parent education. A basic theme or thread that runs through the descriptions of reflective practice is assessment, which includes self-assessment, group process assessment, and outcome assessment. Assessment, as a theme, includes creative/intuitive thinking, technical skills, and ethical dimensions of practice and professional development in parent education.

SELF-ASSESSMENT

Self-assessment is a starting place, especially for the beginning parent educator. Self-assessment can help the beginning parent educator focus on his or her own knowledge, dispositions, and skills. The checklist introduced in Appendix A as an example of a self-assessment tool can be used to identify technical skills and help a parent educator identify specific group facilitation skills to practice and refine. Reflective practice for beginning parent educators includes a number of possible methods to assist with self-assessment. A parent session can be videotaped to provide a detailed record of group facilitation skills for critical analysis. This analysis should be guided by focusing on a limited number of specific technical skills. For example, the parent educator may want to focus on listening and attending skills. The videotape of the session can capture both verbal and nonverbal behaviors that demonstrate different listening and attending skills. A video analysis is one assignment that student teachers in parent education classes complete that includes a written report focusing on specific skills and how they were demonstrated in a parent education session.

Self-assessment can also include peer or supervisory observations. These can address technical skills around teaching and group facilitation, as well as ethical issues. A careful observation by another parent educator can help to affirm skills and offer insights and another perspective of parent-parent educator interactions within a specific session. Peer observation and feedback can also focus on more advanced skill sets, as parent educators move beyond the beginning levels of competence and start to integrate more advanced skills. It is most helpful to focus on specific skills or issues when an observation by a peer or supervisor is planned. This focus provides more direct and specific feedback. It also requires the parent educator to carefully define and focus on his or her own skills and areas of concern.

Another form of self-assessment can include parent group feedback on the class. The more specific and focused the questions are that are posed to the parents, the more useful their responses will be. Student teachers working in parent education often create a short questionnaire to give to a group of parents at the end of their student teaching experience. This helps the students get direct feedback from the parents about their developing skills. It provides affirmation of their strengths and possible areas to focus on for further development.

Keeping a journal is another common form of self-assessment. Student teachers are often asked to keep a journal of their experiences and observations. Journal writing should be focused not only on descriptions but also on analysis of difficult moments. Journals are an effective form of self-reflection and can provide some insight into our own feelings and reactions, in addition to stimulating new ideas to try as we address some specific concerns. A journal can be used by the experienced parent educator to focus on a specific group that may be more challenging. It allows the parent educator to reflect on the group dynamics more carefully and systematically. This may help the parent educator carefully assess different strategies and how parents respond.

Self-assessment is important for both beginning and master-level parent educators. There are several ways to assess practice skills. Most parent educators tend to work alone with parent groups or individual parents. Parent satisfaction surveys that include specific questions about practice skills can provide useful feedback. For example, a question like "How did the parent educator show sensitivity to your needs?" can elicit the parents' perceptions about parent educator sensitivity as a specific skill area. Parent educators also benefit from supervisor and/or peer observation and debriefing of a parenting session. The motivation for self-assessment comes from a strong desire to understand and improve practice through fine-tuning or developing advanced group facilitation skills.

ASSESSMENT OF GROUP DYNAMICS AND PARENT LEARNING STYLES

A second area of assessment focuses on the parent group and on examining group dynamics in systematic ways. One simple measure of group dynamics is an observation of frequency of participation by different group members. This type of assessment can be completed by asking a supervisor or peer to observe the class and record the number of times each person in the group talks. Parent educators usually know which parents are most and least involved in discussion, but they may gain a more objective perspective on how a group is functioning through this simple type of group assessment. Another level of sophistication is the observation of specific task and maintenance functions that each group member fulfills during a specific session. This may be done by audio or video recording a session and analyzing the interactions by reviewing the tape. It also can be done by a peer or supervisor who comes to observe the class. This can provide more information about specific parents and point out some of the group's strengths and some potential problems. The assessment of parent learning styles through a parent group activity is described in Chapter 6. The awareness of different learning styles through an informal assessment process with parents provides a topic to increase parent awareness of different styles, as well as greater self-understanding. The benefit for the parent educator is having a clearer picture of learning styles in a group and specific ideas for methods to use to engage the different learners in the group.

A final assessment of group process can come from a midterm evaluation of the class with some specific questions that focus on group dynamics and individual parents' perceptions of their own engagement in the group process. Ongoing observation of group dynamics is an essential part of facilitating parent groups. The assessment ideas outlined here can provide additional information for monitoring and intervening, as necessary, in group process.

ACTION RESEARCH: ASSESSMENT OF PROGRAM OUTCOMES

Action research, in this context, refers to parent educators defining important questions about practice that they want to address more systematically. For example, Van Nostrand (1993) raised some interesting issues about gender and group interaction patterns. In the context of parent education groups, do men tend to display patterns of either dominance or withdrawing from and discounting the group? Most parent groups are predominantly mothers, but as more fathers participate, different patterns of group dynamics will occur. Will men and women in the context of group parent education display more collaborative relationships, or will more stereotypic gendered group dynamics characterize parent groups? A research project could evolve from these questions that leads a group of parent educators to decide to observe a number of classes and record patterns of interaction that they see occurring in mixed-gender groups versus father-only or mother-only groups. They could then work with a researcher to develop a coding system for recording group interactions. Such action research may help illuminate group dynamics and the role of gender to improve practice.

Collaborative action research may also focus on parent and child outcomes. Parent educators have been uncertain about how to approach the assessment of changes in parenting skills and attitudes. Measuring parent education program efficacy is neither simple nor easy. Our concerns with diverse values and beliefs about parenting practices create a complex situation for both researchers and parent education practitioners. The pressure from funding sources to provide empirical evidence of success or change is moving parent educators to look more carefully at outcome questions. This is an ideal opportunity for researchers and practitioners to cooperate in defining realistic goals and indicators of progress. One of the authors has been involved in developing a staff observation measure of adult growth and development in family literacy programs. The measure was developed by asking experienced staff to describe growth trajectories that they have observed in parents who have been in their programs for extended periods of time (some up to 3 years). The measure examines a general set of parenting skills that includes nurturing, guidance strategies, and parent-child play interactions. In each of these areas, staff described four to five developmental steps that they had observed in parents who started with low parenting skills and improved these skills as they moved through the program. This measure has been adopted by a number of programs to be used as an observation tool for staff to assess progress they have observed in parents as they interacted with them in different settings.

Box 14.1 Parent Education and Reflective Practice

1. Self-Reflection

   a. Keeping a journal about a specific class

   b. Analysis of video of a session

   c. Curriculum writing as a way to share ideas

   d. Self-assessment of knowledge, skills, and dispositions

2. Parent Perspectives

   a. End-of-the-year evaluations: parent satisfaction with program components

   b. Parent self-assessments of learning

   c. Parent responses to parenting situations/critical incidents

   d. Parent journals: experiences with application of new ideas

3. Peer Perspectives

   a. Professional Learning Communities

      i. Critical conversations with peers about group process issues

      ii. Peer observations: focus on specific issue or skill to observe

   b. Guided discussions about ethical issues (See Box 14.2)

   c. Observations of other programs and parent groups

4. Research Perspectives

   a. Teachers as researchers: identify projects that address important practice issues

   b. Evaluation research: participate in defining and assessing parent and child outcomes

c. Review research on curricula for a specific group

d. Review research on a specific topic to integrate recent findings in an area.

5. Reflective Supervision/Consultation (Box 14.3)

Box 14.1 summarizes a variety of ways for parent educators to be engaged in reflective practice. The different perspectives allow parent educators to collaborate with peers, parents, and researchers in a variety of activities to both examine and improve practice. These different ideas provide opportunities for both individual professional growth and development and advancement of the field of parent education. This is not meant as an exhaustive list but one that is suggestive of the wide variety of activities that can be included in reflective practice. Parent educators can reflect on practice individually through self-assessment and also collaboratively with peers, parents, and researchers, as indicated in Box 14.1.

REFLECTIVE PRACTICE AND ETHICAL ISSUES

Another area of reflective practice is the development of ethical thinking and practice in parent education. Dokecki (1996) included ethical awareness as part of reflective practice. An increase in family diversity and greater sensitivity to cultural diversity create a social context where parent educators are more likely than ever to face ethical dilemmas in their day-to-day practice. The following situations are examples of these dilemmas:

- A mother in a parent group of middle-class mothers shares her new discipline tip of using liquid soap in her 4-year-old's mouth as a way to punish her for using bad words. The other parents respond positively.
- A group of Mexican American fathers have recently moved from a state with different laws about corporal punishment of children. They are attending a family literacy program and begin to complain about the child abuse laws as unfair, because they feel that these laws restrict their right to use physical punishment with their school-aged children when the children are misbehaving and really need to have strict discipline.
- A parent educator conducts a home visit with a family with a 9-month-old child who has been identified as a child with special needs based on delayed

physical development. The parents are both Deaf and want to raise this child as part of the Deaf culture even though the child is not deaf. They are requesting that early intervention teachers and therapists limit their verbal interaction with the child so that she can be socialized into the Deaf culture.

These situations provide examples of possible ethical dilemmas that parent educators may face on a regular basis. A true ethical dilemma is a situation where there is conflict between two or more important principles or values that the profession embraces. For example, in the case of the Deaf parent family, parent educators believe in the principles of respecting cultural beliefs and values, respecting parents' rights to choose parenting practices and do no harm to children. This situation clearly points out the conflict between parent values and child wellbeing. There is no easy answer to this situation if the practitioner wants to equally honor all of their principles.

Parent educators in Minnesota have developed a practical approach to ethical issues through the work of the Ethics Committee of the Minnesota Council on Family Relations (MNCFR). This group has designed an approach to ethics that integrates three different ethical frameworks: (a) a principles approach that articulates important principles to guide interaction with parents and other groups; (b) a relational ethics approach that incorporates the understanding of relationships as the context for making ethical decisions; and (c) virtues ethics, which focuses on the moral character of the parent educator. These three approaches form the basis of a case study process for exploring difficult ethical situations in a group setting. MNCFR (2016) has published a booklet that explains this approach and the group process with examples of case studies. The process is outlined in Box 14.2.

Box 14.2 Ethics Case Study Process

This process is one way to examine a difficult ethical situation to help identify potential ethical dilemmas and to generate possible ethical actions. See the MNCFR website (www.mn.mcfr.org) for the list of principles.

1. *Identify Important Relationships*: Identify important relationships in the situation, using the family practitioner as the primary focus.

    A.   What is the relational field? What are the important relationships to consider in this case?

    B.   What are the primary relationships the practitioner should address?

    C.   What do we know about these relationships— length, strength, etc.?

2.   *Identify Relevant Principles*: Look over the list of principles that apply to the relationship. Decide which principles may be relevant to guiding practitioner behavior in this situation.

    A.   Which are the three or four most relevant principles?

3.   *Identify Contradictions between Principles*:

    A.   What are the contradictions among the relevant principles?

4.   *Identify Possible Solutions*: Brainstorm possible action by parent and family educator, keeping in mind the relationship, the relevant principles, and the virtues.

5.   *Select Action(s and Implement)*: Select an action or combination of actions and keep in mind that all principles are important to honor through your actions.

COMPASSION FATIGUE AND BURNOUT

Anyone involved in one of the many helping professions can be vulnerable to compassion fatigue and, ultimately, burnout. Nurses, social workers, therapists, counselors, teachers, and other caregivers are often noted in the literature concerning the potential of experiencing this phenomenon. However, little has been written specifically about parent educators who are susceptible to compassion fatigue and burnout. This is particularly true for those who work with parents with complex needs, multiple challenges, and trauma in their lives. This section will describe and define compassion fatigue and burnout, in addition to providing ideas for prevention and supportive intervention.

An initial reference to compassion fatigue focused on the nursing profession, defining it as a form of burnout that affects people in caregiving professions (Joinson, 1992). By 1998, Figley updated an earlier definition to read, "Compassion fatigue is defined as a state of exhaustion and dysfunction—biologically, psychologically, and socially—as a result of prolonged exposure to compassion stress and all that it evokes" (p. 23). Compassion fatigue continues to be an issue in various professional fields. Pace (2014) refers to the phenomenon as it affects social workers and defines it as a combination of physical, emotional, and spiritual depletion associated with caring for clients in distress.

The concept of compassion fatigue is also referred to in a variety of terms. It is sometimes called secondary traumatic stress disorder (Figley, 1995), burnout syndrome (Freudenberger, 1974), vicarious trauma (Jenkins & Baird, 2002), burnout (Maslach, 1982), vicarious traumatization (McCann & Pearlman, 1990), and empathy fatigue (Stebnicki, 2000). Whatever the term used, some commonalities of symptoms and causes exist. Professionals experiencing compassion fatigue typically begin to have a reduced capacity for, or interest in, being empathic toward those for whom they are caring (Abendroth, 2011). They may become more impatient, feel overwhelmed in their role, and approach their work without focus (Pace, 2014). Additionally, there is often a more cynical attitude, along with loss of hope. These changes often occur quite suddenly.

Why do some professionals develop compassion fatigue and others do not? The prevalence of trauma and ongoing crisis in the lives of families can take a devastating toll on any professional. Parent educators assigned to work intensively with families in crisis often begin their work with a high level of altruism and hope for themselves to make a difference in the lives of the families. Listening to their challenges, trying to assist them in making positive changes, becoming involved (often over-involved) all begin to weigh on the parent educator and promote a sense of being overwhelmed and hopeless. This emotional exhaustion can result in compassion fatigue.

A distinction is sometimes made between compassion fatigue and burnout. Abendroth, (2011) indicates that compassion fatigue typically has a more sudden and acute onset, while burnout gradually wears down caregivers who are overwhelmed and unable to make a positive change. Compassion fatigue results from witnessing another's trauma, while burnout evolves over time from dissatisfaction with a person's working conditions.

Unrecognized and untreated compassion fatigue can cause people to leave their profession (Panos, 2013). Early recognition is important, and yet, most professionals enter their field with little information about this phenomenon. Strategies for self-care in order to prevent compassion fatigue and burnout include:

- Being aware of possible symptoms and changes in attitudes
- Using peer and supervisory support to discuss your feelings and challenges
- Fostering good relationships with coworkers and utilizing their support
- Keeping a healthy balance between personal and professional lives
- Journaling after a group or at the end of the day
- Using "off-time" for yourself, rather than filling it with work tasks
- Accepting your limitations
- Adhering to professional boundaries

Example

Martina is a mother of two school-age children. She is a former elementary teacher who has decided to re-enter the workforce after several years of full-time parenting. After attending parent-child classes with her own children and enjoying the parent education component, she decides to pursue a career as a parent educator. Martina completes her training with courses in child development, adult learners, group process, and family systems. She is soon hired within a local school district to lead parent groups.

Martina's begins her new role with enthusiasm, and she is rewarded with good reviews from her supervisor, successful relationships with the parents and children, and a connection to a peer group of other parent educators who are supportive, knowledgeable, and willing to share their expertise and resources.

Martina's supervisor recognizes her potential, and after 2 years of assigning her to lead parent groups at the school, she suggests adding home visiting and working within a family literacy program. The families with whom she will work have many complex issues and Martina is looking forward to the challenge. The parents include those struggling with mental health and chemical dependency issues, homelessness, and domestic abuse. She feels great empathy for the families, after overcoming a difficult childhood herself and begins her new assignment believing she can make a difference in their lives.

One of Martina's challenges is balancing her personal life with her professional role. While she has the ability to feel empathy for the parents, she is easily pulled into their daily challenges and finds it difficult to stay within the boundaries of parent education. Thinking and worrying about the families during her time off, putting in many extra unpaid hours, making phone calls for and to the parents after class, and agonizing over particular parents are beginning to consume her time.

Martina begins to feel the stress of her relationship with the families. Her coworkers and supervisor notice that her attitude about work is beginning to shift. She is more negative in her descriptions of the families, less likely to participate in peer meetings, and generally less motivated. Instead of her earlier displays of empathy for the parents, Martina is quicker to judge and more impatient when dealing with them. It seems that Martina is heading for "burnout" from what was not too long ago a very rewarding position.

The program director recognizes the changes in Martina and decides to intervene. In a private conversation, she gently describes the changes she has observed in Martina's behavior and attitude. She supports Martina with comments that universalize the difficulties of working with challenging families. She affirms her skills and potential, yet challenges her to recognize how her attitudes are changing. Together, they develop a plan that encourages her to take care of herself and to make sure she is participating fully in the consultation and peer support groups that are part of the program. Since all parent educators can benefit from reminders about self-care, the director arranges for several presentations on this topic led by a local therapist. After the sessions, staff time is spent identifying ways that the parent educators can maintain a healthy balance in their professional and personal lives. Discussion on updates and challenges with these issues become part of their regular peer meetings.

Box 14.3 Reflective Supervision/Consultation

Reflective Supervision (RS) is a process to promote professional growth and development in practitioners who work with families. It is linked to clinical supervision in mental health and has evolved in the field of Infant Mental Health (IMH). IMH includes parent educators as one of the groups of family practitioners who could benefit from RS.

Shahmoon-Shanok (2009) defines RS as a "collaborative relationship for professional growth that improves program quality and practice by cherishing strengths and partnering around vulnerabilities to generate growth" (p. 8).

RS is a powerful reflective practice strategy that allows the family professional to explore the emotional experiences that are triggered in practice in a safe environment (Tomlin & Heller, 2016). The core components of RS are reflection on practice, a collaborative relationship with a supervisor/consultant, and regular participation. The reflective supervisor can be someone who is also a program supervisor or a consultant from an outside agency. The heart of RS is the focus on relationships and shared exploration and reflection on practice by the supervisor and family practitioner (Ellison, 2009). RS relates to both professional and personal development of the practitioners by attending to the emotional content of the work. This allows a supervisee to discover insights, concepts, and solutions while the supervisor listens as a trusted partner. The process of RS allows for the integration of emotion and reason in developing self-awareness that leads to professional growth and improved practice. This is a process that can benefit parent and family educators as a way to reflect on relationships and emotional content in their work with parents. This focus on relationships is a critical aspect of effective parent education practice (See Chapter 5). The field of IMH is a valuable source of information on RS as a process.

(See Heller and Gilkerson, 2009 as a resource, as well as the Zero to Three website (*https://www.zerotothree.org/*), for additional information and resources on reflective supervision.)

In summary, compassion fatigue and burnout are linked to a wide variety of helping professions that share commonalities with parent education. Box 14.3 describes the process of reflective supervision that is one way to address and limit these problems. Those educators who work closely with families who have complex needs and challenges are more likely to experience these occurrences. Being aware of the possibility, the symptoms, and the strategies to prevent and respond to compassion fatigue and burnout will assist parent educators in maintaining their roles within a rewarding and meaningful profession.

ARTISTRY AND INTUITION IN PARENT EDUCATION

We want to end the book with a model of the parent educator as artist. The notion of artistry seems to best capture the spirit and capability of master teachers in parent education. The parent educator as artist is involved in the creative process of combining group facilitation and educational skills in different parent groups. He or she relies on both the development of excellent technical skills and the use of creative intuition to guide parent groups in learning from and with each other. The parent educator as artist is able to flow with the group while managing the progress and direction of the group. Skilled practitioners in parent education make this work look easy. Parents are aware of the power of the group and also experience the wisdom of the parent educator, who models respect, care, humility, humor, and curiosity. We believe that reflective practice, as described in this final chapter, can help support artistry in parent education. Reflective practice strategies should be used to explore artistry in parent education to better describe and map out the dimensions of excellence in practice. We are only beginning to understand and appreciate the value of intuitive genius in parent education.

SUMMARY

The basic knowledge, skills, and dispositions of the beginning parent group leader are essential as a starting place for understanding professional development. We have seen many licensed parent educators move successfully through predictable stages of growth and development. The professional development of parent educators, as described in this chapter, has three distinct stages. These stages begin to articulate specific areas of growth that have been observed in long-term parent educators.

Reflective practice, a pathway to individual professional growth and development in a variety of fields, can be usefully applied to parent education. Several activities described in this chapter can be used by parent educators as reflective strategies. Reflective practice can assist the parent educator in improving technical skills, developing a better understanding of complex parent group dynamics, creating more engaging instructional strategies and addressing ethical dilemmas in a more thoughtful manner.

The model of "parent educator as artist" offers a new way of thinking about and valuing the individual parent educator. Artistry describes and honors the complex work of parent educators and the value of intuitive thinking, in addition to a broad knowledge base and technical skills.

The field of parent education has grown and developed over the past 100 years, as described in this text. We believe that it has evolved into a unique profession that requires specific training and a specific knowledge base that draws from a variety of disciplines (NPEN, 2017). As representatives from the field, we believe that parent education needs to continue its evolution and be recognized for the complex and technical profession that it has become.

Under ideal circumstances, it would not be acceptable to continue adding parent education to the job descriptions of other professionals. Although nurses, mental health professionals, social workers, teachers, and others bring valuable information and skills to the field, their primary focus is on the physical or mental health of adults, education of children, or assistance for families in accessing resources. Parent educators should be trained specifically with an interdisciplinary understanding of child development, parenting strategies, family systems, adult education, and group facilitation.

In reality, parent education is practiced by a variety of professionals in diverse settings. Many of these professionals have training and backgrounds of enough depth to successfully facilitate parent education and support groups. The contributions of these professionals to the field of parent education should not be minimized. However, to move the profession beyond a focus on either support or education, we need to promote programs that provide extensive training and pre-service learning opportunities that blend the skills and expertise of both approaches. Professionally trained parent educators need to learn about working with parents in groups that are both educational and supportive. Teaching skills, as well as helping skills, should be combined so that parent educators can move from presenting information to meeting the diverse needs of groups of parents. It is no longer sufficient to offer parents learning opportunities that provide primarily support or education. It is no longer acceptable to present parent education experiences that do not adhere to the high standards demanded by other professions.

We believe the information in this text will be valuable to any professional who works with parents in groups. Additionally, it will provide insight and strategies for those without specific training in group parent education. It is our hope that, for anyone who works with parents in groups, the information will substantiate our view that parent education is a viable profession of worth and merit. We hope that this perspective will challenge other helping professionals, as well as those with limited training, to continue to explore the field and grow in their professional development and practice of parent and family education.

DISCUSSION QUESTIONS

1. Use Table 14.1 to assess your current level of expertise in parent education. What are areas of strength, and what are some areas that are still under development?

2. Describe the advantages of applying reflective practice to the field of parent education.

3. What responsibility do experienced parent educators have to mentor those new to the field? As a novice parent educator, what would be most helpful to you?

4. What does the concept of artistry mean in the field of parent education?

CLASS ACTIVITIES

1. Think/Pair/Share. Individually, THINK of someone who has had a positive impact on your personal or professional life. Would you identify them as a mentor? Why? What qualities did they have? Why were they helpful? PAIR with another classmate. SHARE your experiences.

2. In small groups, outline a possible research question that would be an important action research project for group parent education. How would you go about addressing this question?

REFERENCES

Abendroth, M. (Jan 31, 2011). Overview and Summary: Compassion Fatigue: Caregivers at Risk. *OJIN: The Online Journal of Issues in Nursing, 16*(1). Retrieved January 3, 2017.

Auerbach, A. (1968). *Parents learn through discussion: Principles and practices of parent group education.* New York, NY: John Wiley.

Bashirinia, S. (2013). Social Work Supervision: Process or Procedure? Retrieved December 30, 2016, from https://www.theguardian.com/social-care-network/2013/nov/01/social-work-supervision-process-procedure.

Dewey, J. (1933). *How we think.* New York, NY: D.C. Heath.

Dokecki, P. (1996). *The tragic-comic professional: Basic considerations for ethical reflective-generative practice.* Pittsburgh, PA: Duquesne University Press.

Ellison, J. (2009). Reflective practice: Definitions. Unpublished document.

Figley, C.R. (1995). Chapter 1/Compassion fatigue as secondary traumatic stress disorder: an overview. In C.R. Figley (Ed.*), Compassion fatigue: coping with secondary traumatic stress disorder in those who treat the traumatized.* New York, NY: Brunner-Routledge.

Figley, C.R., (1998). Chapter 1/Burnout as a systemic traumatic stress: a model for helping traumatized family members. In C.R. Figley (Ed), *Burnout in families: the systemic costs of caring.* New York, NY: CRC Press.

Freudenberger, H.J. (1974). The staff burnout syndrome in alternative institutions. *Psychotherapy: Theory, Research, and Practice, 12*, 73–82.

Fritz, C., & Miller, C. (2003). Supervisory options for instructional leaders in education. *Journal of Leadership education, 2*(2), Winter, pp. 13–27.

Glickman, D.D., Gordon, S.P., & Ross-Gordon, J.M., (2001) *SuperVision and Instructional Leadership.* Needham Heights, MA: Allyn & Bacon.

Heller, S.S., and Gilkerson, L. (2009). A practical guide to reflective supervision. Washington, DC: Zero to Three.

Jenkins, S.R. and Baird, S. (2002). Secondary traumatic stress and vicarious trauma: a validation study. *Journal of Traumatic Stress, 15*, 423–432.

Joinson, C. (1992). Coping with compassion fatigue. *Nursing, 22*(4), 116–122.

Kirby, P., & Paradise, L. (1992). Reflective practice and effectiveness of teachers. *Psychological Reports, 70,* 1057–1058.

Kumpfer, K., & Alvarado, R. (1998, November). Effective family strengthening interventions. *Juvenile Justice Bulletin,* (pp.1–15).

Kurz-Riemer, K. (2001). *A guide for implementing Early Childhood Family Education programs.* St. Paul, MN: Department of Children, Families, and Learning.

LaBoskey, V. (1994). *Development of reflective practice: A study of preservice teachers.* New York, NY: Teachers College Press.

Maslach, C. (1982). *Burnout–the cost of caring: how to recognize, prevent, and cure the burnout syndrome for nurses, teachers, counselors, doctors, therapists, police, social workers, and anyone else who cares about people.* New York, NY: Prentice Hall.

McCann, L., and Pearlman, L.A. (1990). Vicarious traumatization: a framework for understanding the psychological effects of working with victims. *The Journal of Traumatic Stress, 3*(1), 131–149.

Minnesota Council on Family Relations. (2016). *Ethical thinking and practice for parent and family educators.* St. Paul, MN: Author.

National Center on Parent, Family and Community Engagement. (2011). *The head start parent, family, and community framework: Promoting family engagement and school readiness from prenatal to age 8.* Washington, DC: National Center on Parent, Family, and Community Engagement, Office of Head Start, U.S. Department of Health and Human Services.

NPEN (National Parenting Education Network) (2017). Professional standards. Retreived from http://npen.org/professional-development/professional-standards/.

Pace, P.R. (2014) Compassion fatigue: a growing concern. *NASW News, 59*(1).

Palm, G. (1998). *Developing a model of reflective practice for improving fathering programs.* Philadelphia, PA: National Center for Fathers and Families.

Panos, A. (2013). Understanding and Preventing Compassion Fatigue–A Handout for Professionals. Retrieved January 3, 2017, from http://www.giftfromwithin.org/htm/prvtcf.html

Rowley, J.G. (1999), The good mentor. *Educational Leadership, 56*(8), 20–22.

Schon, D. (1983). *The reflective practitioner: How professionals think in action.* New York, NY: Basic Books.

Schon, D. (1987). *Educating the reflective practitioner.* San Francisco: Jossey-BassTodres, R., & Bunston, T. (1993). Parent education program evaluation: A review of the literature. *Canadian Journal of Community Mental Health, 12*(1), 225–257.

Shahmoon-Shanok, R. (2009). What is reflective supervision. In S.Heller & L. Gilkerson (Eds.). *A practical guide to reflective supervision.* (pp.7–24) Washington, DC: Zero to Three.

Smith, K.L. (2009, September). *A Brief Summary of Supervision Models.* Unpublished Paper.

Stebnicki, M.A. (2000.) Stress and grief reactions among rehabilitation professionals: dealing effectively with empathy fatigue. *The Journal of Rehabilitation, 66*(1); 23–29.

Tomlin, A., & Heller, S.S. (2016). Measurement development in reflective supervision: History, methods and next steps. *Zero to Three, 37*(2), 3–11.

Van Nostrand, K. (1993). *Gender-responsible leadership.* Newbury Park, CA: Sage.

CONCLUSION

This final section of the book is a reflection on important issues that have emerged as we have revised the 2004 text *Group Parent Education*. It focuses on summarizing practice issues and questions raised by current research and literature. There have been significant advances in our understanding of young children and their development, including research on early brain development, adverse childhood experiences, and trauma. This research has affirmed the importance of parenting and has identified salient parenting practices (National Academies of Sciences, Engineering, and Medicine, 2016). The refinement of the role of parent educator comes from a number of different groups identifying competencies needed for parent education (NPEN, 2016). The influx of information and communication technologies into family life and education has created new opportunities and challenges for parent educators. Recent reviews of early childhood systems have revealed the complexity, mixed results, and quality of parent education programs (Center for the Developing Child, 2016). Research on program practice has revealed important factors related to positive outcomes and approaches to improving practices (e.g., Grindal et al., 2015).

PROFESSIONAL PREPARATION AND CREDENTIALS

One of the advances in the field is the articulation of competencies for parent educators. The National Parenting Education Network (NPEN) has reported that there are currently 250,000 people who deliver parenting education in the United States, including a range of professionals from different disciplines, paraprofessionals, and volunteers. NPEN has established a Professional Preparation and Recognition Committee that is in the process of creating a resource document of parent educator competencies and has posted a number of articles related to the preparation and recognition of parent educators as an emerging profession. There are a number of state initiatives that have developed a credentialing system for parent educators (NPEN, n.d.). The National Academies of Sciences, Engineering and Medicine report *Parenting Matters* (2016) also supports the need for in-depth preparation for parent educators beyond the specific curricula training provided for evidence-based programs. The National Council on Family Relations Certified Family Life Educator (CFLE) credential is one example of setting clear standards for competencies through preparation at the bachelor's degree level. This has established a professional identity for individuals delivering parent and family education services. The numbers of staff delivering parent education services that would benefit from this type of preparation is significant. It will be important to continue to define the necessary competencies and then design delivery systems that would match the varied needs of individuals from different disciplinary backgrounds for additional education. The training on specific evidence-based curricula has an important role to play, but it does not provide a consistent foundation for individuals who need to have knowledge about child and parent development, group facilitation skills, educational methods, family systems and dynamics, and skills for working with diverse cultures and family systems. NPEN has provided a solid foundation for clarifying roles and identifying core competencies.

INFORMATION AND COMMUNICATION TECHNOLOGY

The dramatic increase in the availability and use of information and communication technologies (ICT) (i.e., smart phones, tablets, laptop computers, and smart watches) and the connection to instant information through the Internet has changed our thinking and approaches to family education (Walker, 2015).

Information on child development and parenting is now available to parents through multiple websites, apps, texts and social media. This introduces a new array of delivery systems that give parents the ability to access parenting information and support at their convenience. These changes also create new opportunities for parent and family educators to design new services. Research on online programs (Nieuwboer, Fukkink, and Hermanns, 2013) and computer-mediated parenting education has been positive and has shown promise for reaching more parents. The opportunities from ICT create a need for new knowledge and skill sets for parent educators. How will the group skills that are presented in this text fit with new technologies? One of our insights into how parent education groups in Minnesota have had long-term impacts on parents is the social support function of face-to-face groups meeting on a regular basis. We believe that there will still be a need and a place for these types of parent groups and that the benefit of building a sense of community is important. At the same time, there will be opportunities to use the new technologies and networks to create hybrid systems and even enhance a feeling of community in new ways. Some of the competencies we have addressed in the text and those NPEN has identified will still be important for parent educators, but adapting them for the new delivery systems will be a critical challenge. Research on new delivery systems has to look carefully into both the possible positive and negative impacts of ICT on parenting education and parenting. What will be the cost-benefit of providing parent education services through different delivery systems? How will this impact workforce numbers and the preparation of parent educators?

BUILDING COORDINATED SYSTEMS OF PARENT EDUCATION AND SUPPORT

The discussion in Chapter 3, exploring models of a continuum of services in parent education, helps to envision what kinds of systems might best serve parents. There is a clear consensus that universal parenting programs are desirable and that there is also a need for more programs for targeted populations, based on our understanding of different risk factors and more intensive intervention for families who face persistent adversities (National Academies of Sciences, Engineering, and Medicine, 2016). Different systems are currently involved in delivering parent education, and building upon the systems that have contact with parents is a way to increase access. It will be critical to find new ways to collaborate at the community level to be both more effective and efficient. Two-generation programs will be able to work more intensively and on different types of support for parents with multiple challenges (Mosle & Patel, 2012). The creation of parent and family services along a continuum model holds promise for reaching all parents and families with the services that match their needs.

RESEARCH THAT IMPROVES PRACTICE

Research on parent education practice holds promise for not just proving that programs work, but more importantly, improving programs. Research on parent education has advanced during the past decade, and we have identified a number of evidence-based programs. There have been several meta-analyses that have been conducted that begin to delineate some common practices in effective programs (e.g., Grindal et al., 2016). The Center for the Developing Child (2016) describes a new paradigm for thinking about program development research to help identify which programs work best for which parents. This will help in tailoring programs to specific parents and parent needs. This can help lead to programs that have more focused and powerful impacts. We would like to see more research focused on the role, characteristics, and skills of the practitioner as a major influence on parent education program outcomes. A deeper understanding and appreciation for the role of artistry in parent education should also be explored through qualitative research to inform preparation programs and improve practice. Local evaluation research approaches and tools should be developed to help programs focus on continuous improvement.

Parent education will continue to be an important service for supporting the healthy development of children and parents. The paradigm of parent education as a public health practice that provides both information and support for all parents and can be tailored to family context and needs creates a framework for future development. ICT has the potential to improve access but also has the risk of limiting relationships and social support that are an important outcome of group parent education. This trade-off should be carefully monitored as technology is integrated into parent education services. Parent education as a profession and service should continue to play an important role in creating a network of support services for families at the community level.

We are hopeful and optimistic about the future of parent education. We have had the privilege of being part of the growth and refinement of programs that truly serve a cross section of the population, both through groups and individual consultation with parents. It is our hope that a new generation of parent educators will continue the important work of teaching and supporting parents in their most important role.

REFERENCES

Center on the Developing Child at Harvard University (2016). From best practice to breakthrough impacts: A science-based approach to building a more promising future for young children and families. Retrieved from http://www.developingchild.harvard.edu

Grindal, T, Bowne, J.B., Yoshikawa, H., Schindler, H.S., Duncan, G.J., Magnuson, K., & Shonkoff, J.P. (2016). The added impact of parenting education in early childhood education programs: A meta-analysis. *Children and Youth Services Review, 70*, 238–249.

Mosle, A., & Patel, N. (2012). *Two generations, one future: Moving parents and children beyond poverty together.* Retrieved from http://b.3cdn.net/ascend/f52f62b126af-c10fd6_2rnm60p51.pdf

National Academies of Sciences, Engineering, and Medicine. (2016). *Parenting matters: Supporting parents of children 0–8.* Washington, DC: The National Academies Press. Doi: 10.17226/21868.

National Center on Parent, Family and Community Engagement. (2015). *Compendium of parenting interventions.* Washington, DC: National Center on Parent, Family and Community Engagement, Office of Head Start, U.S. Department of Health and Human Services.

Nieuwboer, C.C., Fukkink, R.G. & Hermanns, J.M.A. (2013). Online programs as tools to improve parenting: A meta-analytic review. *Children and Youth Services Review, 35*, 1823–1829.

National Parenting Education Network (n.d.) Framework for understanding parenting educator professional preparation and recognition (Draft). Retrieved from http://npen.org/profdev/forum/standards/framework.pdf.

Walker, S.K. (2015). Family life and technology: Implications for the practice of family life education. In M.J. Walcheski & J. Reinke. (Eds.), *Family life education: The practice of family science*, pp. 117–130. Minneapolis, MN: National Council on Family Relations.

PARENT GROUP LEADER COMPETENCIES: A SELF-ASSESSMENT CHECKLIST

Instructions: review each item in each of the three major areas and rate yourself from 1 (Not developed) to 5 (Exemplary).

Knowledge: This area outlines knowledge that is specifically related to understanding group dynamics and facilitating parent learning in a group context.

_____ 1. Understanding the developmental stages of group process as applied to parent groups.

_____ 2. Understanding different theories of group dynamics and their applications to parent groups.

_____ 3. Understanding the roles and boundaries of the parent group leader.

_____ 4. Understanding the emotional aspects of parenting issues and how these influence learning in parent groups.

_____ 5. Understanding different leadership styles and their effects on parent group behavior.

_____ 6. Understanding multiple ways to assess parent and family strengths and challenges in the context of parent groups.

_____ 7. Understanding the importance of using a variety of active learning methods to assist parents in solving problems and making decisions.

_____ 8. Understanding and being aware of various community resources for parents, children, and families and how to connect parents to these resources.

_____ 9. Understanding family and community diversity and how diverse values and beliefs inform parenting behavior, as well as parent group dynamics.

_____ 10. Understanding of how adverse childhood experiences can affect adult behavior, both in parenting and in participation in group education.

_____ 11. Understanding of the impact of gender composition on group process.

Dispositions: This category of competencies refers to character traits and emotional attitudes that have been identified as important for parent educators (Auerbach, 1968; Braun et al., 1984; Clarke, 1984). These are different from general personality traits or types, like introvert and extrovert. Each individual will have his or her own unique blend of these dispositions.

_____ 1. _Maturity_: Parent group leader is clear about his or her own identity and able to clearly focus on the needs and issues of parents in the group.

_____ 2. _Caring_: Parent group leader is able to focus on the needs of parents and demonstrate understanding, compassion, and support for parents.

_____ 3. _Nonjudgmentalness_: Parent group leader appreciates the complexities of parenting and accepts parents without blaming them for their problems or mistakes. The focus is on helping parents and understanding that there are no easy answers.

_____ 4. *Sensitivity*: Parent group leader is able to perceive and respond to individual parents' needs and feelings.

_____ 5. *Organization*: Parent group leader is able to express goals clearly and provide direction toward parent learning.

_____ 6. *Flexibility*: Parent group leader is able to change direction as needed and balance between individual and group needs of parents.

_____ 7. *Creativity*: Parent group leader is able to design interesting and engaging parent sessions.

_____ 8. *Enthusiasm/Optimism*: Parent group leader has a positive attitude about people and the subject matter and is able to excite parents about learning.

_____ 9. *Honesty*: Parent group leader is clear about his or her own knowledge and limitations.

_____ 10. *Genuineness*: Parent group leader is honest and open in his or her relationships and interactions with parents.

_____ 11. *Humor*: Parent group leader is able to appreciate and express what is humorous without ridiculing people or their problems.

Skills: These are presented in general areas followed by very specific behavioral indicators of each general skill area.

1. **Creates a warm and welcoming environment.**

    _____ a. Greets each parent or family member in a welcoming manner.

    _____ b. Demonstrates a genuine interest in parent and child well-being.

    _____ c. Uses effective openings for a session—involves parents in an engaging and nonthreatening manner.

2. **Creates a safe environment for parents to share ideas and feelings.**

    _____ a. Helps group establish and implement ground rules that indicate respect for all group members.

_____ b. Elicits a variety of opinions, values, and philosophies from parents.

_____ c. Affirms parents in a genuine and supportive manner.

3. **Guides a discussion, giving it form and structure.**

_____ a. Informs parents of agenda and goals for the session.

_____ b. Helps parents identify needs and concerns.

_____ c. Keeps parents focused on the group goals and the topic of discussion.

_____ d. Asks clarifying questions to better understand parent issues.

_____ e. Restates and clarifies parent ideas/issues.

_____ f. Summarizes important ideas/issues.

4. **Models acceptance of each individual as someone to be listened to and respected.**

_____ a. Listens carefully to parents.

_____ b. Gives nonverbal messages of acceptance.

_____ c. Accepts and acknowledges negative feelings and distress.

_____ d. Restates and/or acknowledges parent contributions to the discussion.

_____ e. Addresses diversity and facilitates discussion around differences in values, culture, and family structure.

_____ f. Includes opportunities for parents to make decisions about topics/content in the group.

5. **Takes responsibility for establishing a positive and supportive learning environment.**

_____ a. Helps parents identify and set their own goals.

_____ b. Invites parent participation using a variety of methods.

_____ c. Challenges parents to evaluate and reconsider their ideas.

_____ d. Uses concrete examples to bring abstract concepts to life.

_____ e. Adapts information to meet different parent capabilities.

_____ f. Recognizes limitations of self and conducts referrals for parents with concerns beyond the scope of parent education.

6. **Fosters relationships and interaction among group members.**

_____ a. Encourages participation of all group members.

_____ b. Connects parent comments and experiences to point out common themes.

_____ c. Engages the group in problem solving for individual group members.

_____ d. Addresses conflict directly and respectfully.

NATIONAL ORGANIZATIONS AND WEBSITES THAT SUPPORT PARENT EDUCATION

The following is a list of national organizations and their websites that support the field of parent education through information and advocacy. Although there are many websites currently available for parents, we selected these as well-established organizations and associations that have succeeded in their mission to support parents and families. This is not intended to be a comprehensive and complete list of resources; rather, it is provided as a starting point for students and professionals to access available information. These websites are also networked to other important internet resources for parent educators.

American Academy of Pediatrics is composed primarily of medical professionals dedicated to the attainment of optimal physical, mental, and social health and wellbeing for all infants, children, adolescents, and young adults.

Website: http://www.aap.org

Child and Family WebGuide is designed by faculty at the Eliot-Pearson Department of Child Development at Tufts University for students, practitioners, and parents. It describes and evaluates websites that contain research-based information about child development.

Website: http://www.cfw.tufts.edu

Educational Resource Information Center (ERIC) is an online library of education research and information sponsored by the Institute of Education Sciences of the United States Department of Education.

Website: https://eric.ed.gov

The Future of Children is sponsored by the David and Lucile Packard Foundation. It provides research and analysis to promote effective policies and programs for children and families.

Website: http://www.futureofchildren.org

Head Start is an office of the Administration for Children and Families, Early Childhood Learning and Knowledge Center. Information on Head Start programs and the National Center on Parent, Family, and Community Engagement, which offers information on evidence-based parent education programs and implementing parenting programs.

Website: https://eclkc.ohs.acf.hhs.gov/hslc/tta-system/family

National Association for the Education of Young Children is dedicated to improving the quality of programs for children from birth through third grade. Brochures for parents and professionals are available; information about policy and legislation, research reports, and critical issues are also addressed.

Website: http://www.naeyc.org

National Center for Family Learning, formerly the National Center for Family Literacy, advances literacy and education by developing, implementing, and documenting innovative and promising intergenerational strategies.

Website: http://www.familieslearning.org

National Council on Family Relations provides a forum for family researchers, educators, and practitioners to share in the development and dissemination of knowledge about families and family relationships, establishes professional standards, and works to promote family wellbeing.

Website: http://www.ncfr.org

National Parenting Education Network (NPEN) is committed to advancing the field of parent education by facilitating linkages among practitioners, knowledge development in the field, and professional growth and leadership.

Website: http://www.npen.org

Zero to Three supports parents and professionals in a multidisciplinary focus on infant and family professionals, medicine, mental health, research, science, child development, and education related to the first few years of life.

Website: http://www.zerotothree.org

INDEX

CPSIA information can be obtained
at www.ICGtesting.com
Printed in the USA
LVHW102252260819
629044LV00013B/868/P